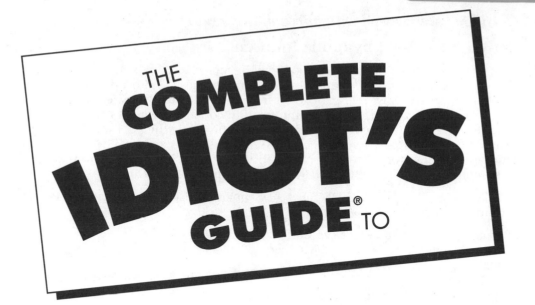

THE COMPLETE IDIOT'S GUIDE TO

Hinduism

by Linda Johnsen

ALPHA

A Pearson Education Company

To Hindus everywhere, with affection and respect.

Copyright © 2002 by Linda Johnsen

THE COMPLETE IDIOT'S GUIDE TO and Design are registered trademarks of Pearson Education, Inc.

International Standard Book Number: 0-02-864227-9
Library of Congress Catalog Card Number: 2001094733

04 03 02   8 7 6 5 4 3 2 1

Interpretation of the printing code: The rightmost number of the first series of numbers is the year of the book's printing; the rightmost number of the second series of numbers is the number of the book's printing. For example, a printing code of 02-1 shows that the first printing occurred in 2002.

Printed in the United States of America

Publisher
Marie Butler-Knight

Product Manager
Phil Kitchel

Managing Editor
Jennifer Chisholm

Acquisitions Editor
Mike Sanders

Development Editor
Michael Thomas

Production Editor
Katherin Bidwell

Copy Editor
Cari Luna

Illustrator
Jody Schaeffer

Cover Designers
Mike Freeland
Kevin Spear

Book Designers
Scott Cook and Amy Adams of DesignLab

Indexer
Angie Bess

Contents at a Glance

Contents

Part 5: God's House Has Many Doors   257

20   The Path of Action   259

21   Straight from the Heart   271

22   The Razor in the Mind   283

Foreword

The Hindu religion is an ocean of spiritual teachings about all aspects of life and consciousness. It's the world's oldest religion, going back to the very dawn of history. It sees its origin in the cosmic mind itself. Yet Hinduism is also perhaps the world's youngest religion because it emphasizes the authority of living teachers and allows for correction and evolution over time.

Hinduism is the most diverse religious tradition in the world. It could be said that there are probably more religions inside of Hinduism than outside of it. It has numerous saints, sages, and yogis, both male and female, from ancient to modern times, and today still has what is probably the largest number of monks and renunciates (including a number of Westerners). The recent Hindu religious gathering, the Kumbha Mela of January 2001, had tens of millions of people in attendance. It was the largest gathering of any type and the largest religious gathering in the history of the world.

Hinduism is the world's largest non-biblical tradition, with nearly a billion followers worldwide. It could be called the world's largest non-organized religion as it emphasizes individual spiritual experience, the realization of the higher Self over any religious institution, book, dogma, or savior. It's also the world's largest native or pagan tradition, reflecting the ancient spiritual traditions that once existed all over the world. Like native traditions everywhere, it honors God or the sacred throughout all of nature. It has many insights in harmony with the ecological age, as it affords reverence to the Earth as a conscious and loving presence and asks us to respect our environment.

Hinduism contains the world's oldest and largest tradition of Goddess worship—worshipping the Divine not only as father but also as mother. It recognizes all the diverse forms of the Goddess and her powers of wisdom, beauty, strength, love, and compassion.

Perhaps most notably, Hinduism is the world's largest pluralistic tradition, recognizing One Truth—an eternal reality of Being-Consciousness Bliss in all beings—but also many paths to realize it. Hinduism recognizes theism (the belief in One Creator) but only as one portion of the human religious experience that includes polytheism, pantheism, monism, and even atheism. As the most inclusive of the world's great religions, Hinduism has room for all these views and yet guides us through these to Self-realization that transcends them all.

Hinduism has probably the world's oldest and largest literature of spirituality, mysticism, and yoga. It provides a complete spiritual culture including art, dance, sculpture, medicine, and science, with all these subjects explained according to a science of consciousness.

Hinduism has a view of the universe in time and space that is compatible with modern science. Aspects of the Hindu tradition such as Yoga, Vedanta, Ayurveda, and Vedic astrology are already popular in the West. Hindu terms such as guru, mantra, shakti, prana, kundalini, and chakra have entered into the English language. Great gurus from the Hindu tradition such as Ramana Maharshi, Yogananda, Ramakrishna, Shivananda, Aurobindo, and Mahatma Gandhi have extensive followings and much respect in the West today.

There are now nearly two million Hindus of Indian origin in the United States, as well as significant numbers in Canada, the United Kingdom, and the Caribbean, with Hindu temples in most of the main cities of the United States. This Hindu group is one of the wealthiest and best educated in the West and contains many successful scientists, computer engineers, and doctors. India itself, the home of most Hindus, is the second largest country in the world and is expected to be a major superpower in the coming century.

The New Age Movement in the West honors Hindu gurus and teachings. Most New Age followers believe in a higher Self, God as both Father and Mother, karma and rebirth, and spiritual practices such as Yoga, much like the Hindu religion.

Clearly examining Hinduism will geometrically expand your ideas of religion and spirituality. *The Complete Idiot's Guide to Hinduism* is the best place to begin such an adventure in consciousness. Linda Johnsen—herself a practitioner in the tradition—does a superb job of making this very different religion relevant, understandable, and appealing to the modern mind. Her book is remarkably refreshing and dynamic, showing the living beauty and profundity of this great spiritual tradition. It makes an excellent, engaging textbook for teaching Hinduism.

As one who has traveled throughout the world, including all over India, teaching aspects of the Hindu tradition to both Hindus and Westerners, I can attest that Johnsen's book is probably the best introduction and overview of the Hindu religion available in English today. The book is written with humor, love, consciousness, and inspiration. It shows the Hindu religion alive and expressive today, so that we can easily access it in our own life-experience. I doubt that a single serious reader will come away without finding their view of Hinduism challenged, expanded, and transformed—and along with it their view of the entire universe, humanity, and all of history.

—Dr. David Frawley (Pandit Vamadeva Shastri)

Author, *Yoga and Ayurveda, Hinduism, the Eternal Tradition*,
Director, American Institute of Vedic Studies

Introduction

Many of us in the West think of India as a poor and backward country. We forget that for at least four thousand years the Hindus were recognized (and envied) as some of the richest, best-educated, most scientifically advanced, and most profoundly religious people on the planet. History shows that Hinduism has provided the spiritual foundation for one of the most successful and enduring cultures in the world.

The Sumerians dominated the Middle East in the third millennium B.C.E. At one time, they were believed to be the founders of civilization. Today we know they imported goods by the ton from equally civilized trading partners in India. They even adopted the system of weights and measures used by the Hindus. The Sumerians' most famous myth is the amazing tale of a flood that wiped out almost all life on earth. This same story is found in India's earliest scriptures and may date as far back as 4000 B.C.E.

Manetho, the Egyptian priest who wrote a history of his country in the third century B.C.E., counts the immigration of a colony of Hindus to Egypt around 1400 B.C.E. as one of the most significant events in Egyptian history. Apollonius of Tyana, a traveler from Turkey who visited both India and Egypt during the time of Christ, noted the amazing similarities between the Egyptian desert ascetics and the Hindu mystics. He was convinced the Egyptians had been trained by Hindu immigrants centuries earlier.

Alexander the Great, during his brief military foray into India, was fascinated by the Hindu holy men. His troops brought home incredible stories about the wisdom and incorruptibility of these Indian sages.

A major problem in the Roman Empire from the time of Caesar Augustus through Emperor Hadrian was Rome's massive trade imbalance with India. It brought Rome to the verge of an economic meltdown! Hindu philosophers were teaching in Rome by the third century C.E. at the latest. Some scholars believe they profoundly influenced Neoplatonic thinkers like Plotinus (who tried to get to India) and, through them, the Western and Kabbalistic mystical systems.

In medieval times, the Arabs praised the Hindus as the world's leading astronomers, mathematicians, and philosophers.

In the fifteenth century, Christopher Columbus risked his neck (and the lives of the rest of the sailors on the *Nina*, the *Pinta*, and the *Santa Maria*) trying to reach India. He mistakenly thought he'd gotten there, too, which is the reason many people call Native Ameri-cans "Indians" to this day. The monarchies of northern Europe were the backwater states of the time and desperately needed trade with the prosperous Hindus to jumpstart their sputtering economies.

And when the British conquered India in the seventeenth century, they hailed the vast wealth of the subcontinent as "the jewel in the crown" of the British Empire. The English made off with much of India's riches, leaving India bankrupt when they finally granted it independence in 1947. For the most part, though, they missed its greatest treasure. This was the spiritual knowledge hoarded by brahmin priests in their carefully guarded scriptures and secretly practiced by yogis and yoginis in the caves and forests of Hindustan.

Today, there's a resurgence of interest in "the wisdom of the East." Many of us in the West flounder spiritually, confused by the inability of our religions to square with scientific reality and craving actual spiritual experience of which our lives seem so devoid. We're impressed by the ability of Eastern religions like Hinduism to meet science head on, agreeing in many respects about important topics, such as the age and size of the universe. Hindu yogis have gone into the laboratory and proved that at least some of their alleged superhuman powers—like the ability to control their brainwaves and heartbeat and stop breathing for extended periods—are for real.

Hinduism is the one world religion that reaches out to embrace other faiths with respect, a welcome change from groups who expend enormous amounts of energy condemning the sincere beliefs of others. There is no eternal damnation in Hinduism because Hindus believe absolutely no one is excluded from divine grace.

The Hindu tradition has held the culture of greater India together for thousands of years, through fair times and foul. Increasingly, we in the West are looking to Hinduism with the respect and appreciation it deserves, realizing we modern people have a great deal to learn from the oldest religion on Earth.

What We'll Be Looking At

The Complete Idiot's Guide to Hinduism is divided into six parts so we can come at the many facets of Hinduism from several different directions.

Part 1, "The Eternal Religion," explains how Hindus look at time and space. Westerners who've been to India sometimes admit that it was like visiting another planet, the world-view there is so radically different from our own. The Hindus' cyclical view of time leads to a unique understanding of human history and of our role in the divine plan.

We'll look at the beginnings of a religion its adherents themselves believe is beginningless, pausing to explore how nineteenth-century European scholars actually created a history for India out of thin air—because the true story struck them as unbelievable!

In its multimillennial development, Hinduism has collected so many scriptures that no one person can become familiar with even a fraction of them in the course of a lifetime. We'll examine some of the most important ones, the ones Hindus admit were composed by human authors and the ones they say came from the heart of the universe itself!

Part 2, "What Hindus Believe," introduces you to the Hindus' amazingly liberal ideas about God and the value of other faiths.

It also takes you into the realm of karma and reincarnation, ideas that seem very New Age to us but are age-old to Hindus. For those who find that incarnating again and again gets tiresome after a while, there is a way out. You'll see what enlightenment really means, and what it takes to be "liberated."

There are six major schools of thought about the divine reality in Hinduism. We'll look at how each of the major schools of Hindu theology contributes their piece of the puzzle to the complete picture. You'll also read about India's sacred sciences, essential adjuncts to religious life.

Part 3, "Who Hindus Worship," will, I hope, clear the air about some mistaken ideas Westerners often have about Hindu polytheism and "idol worship." You'll get to know some of India's more popular deities, the gods and goddesses who still inhabit the inner world of the Hindu people. You'll also see what an "avatar" actually is, another concept that's gotten somewhat garbled in its translation into Western New Age thought!

I'll introduce the main Hindu denominations as well as a few especially important break-away sects.

Part 4, "How Hindus Live," details the caste system and the stages of life orthodox Hindus go through. We'll examine Indian ethics, take a look at some of the Hindus's many sacraments and holy days, and visit some of the temples and sacred sites of the tradition.

Part 5, "God's House Has Many Doors," examines the paths to God in Hinduism: the paths of action, of love, of the intellect, and of meditation. We'll also discuss Tantra, perhaps the single most misunderstood aspect of Hinduism.

Part 6, "A Timeless Tradition," offers a look at Hinduism's many saints and sages, the spiritual masters whose wisdom and blessing power keep the tradition so vibrant. And finally we'll consider the issues Hindus face today as they endeavor to reconcile a very ancient religion with a rapidly changing world.

I've also included four appendixes to help you get a handle on Hinduism. Appendix A is a glossary of commonly used Sanskrit terms. Appendix B is a list of some of the most important figures in Hindu religious history. If you're interested in learning more about this ancient tradition, Appendix C offers a list of outstanding books for further reading, and Appendix D refers you to some organizations and Web sites you'll find useful in future explorations.

India is poised to surpass China as the most populated country on earth. As it continues to pull itself up by the bootstraps economically, what Hindus believe and practice is becoming increasingly important for others to understand. Hopefully this book will help you gain a clearer concept of what Hinduism, "the eternal religion," is all about.

A Few Extra Points

Scattered throughout this book, you'll find a number of special messages to help speed you on your way.

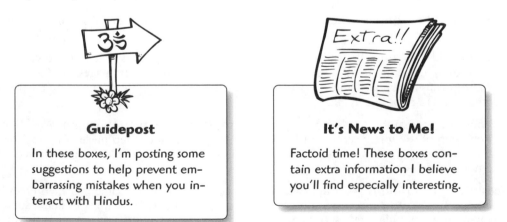

Guidepost

In these boxes, I'm posting some suggestions to help prevent embarrassing mistakes when you interact with Hindus.

It's News to Me!

Factoid time! These boxes contain extra information I believe you'll find especially interesting.

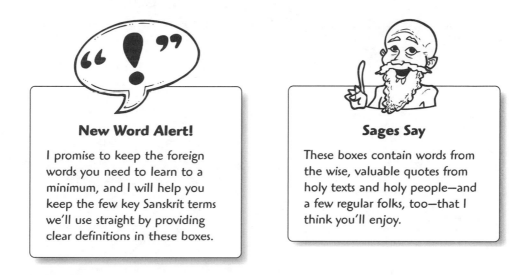

New Word Alert!

I promise to keep the foreign words you need to learn to a minimum, and I will help you keep the few key Sanskrit terms we'll use straight by providing clear definitions in these boxes.

Sages Say

These boxes contain words from the wise, valuable quotes from holy texts and holy people—and a few regular folks, too—that I think you'll enjoy.

In each chapter, you'll also find a "Quick Quiz" to ensure that you remember some key points in the discussion. I'm hoping you'll find these quizzes more fun than the ones you took in school!

Acknowledgments

I'd like to thank the editors and staff at Alpha Books and Pearson Education, Inc., who helped materialize this book, especially Mike Sanders, Michael Thomas, and Katherin Bidwell. Thanks also to Jessica Faust at BookEnds, who made the connections that made the book happen.

I want to acknowledge all my friends and teachers in the Hindu community who invited me into their profoundly wise tradition, but the list is way too long! My *pranams* to you all!

Thanks also to my husband, Johnathan Brown, who held my hand on all my journeys through India.

Trademarks

All terms mentioned in this book that are known to be or are suspected of being trademarks or service marks have been appropriately capitalized. Alpha Books and Pearson Education, Inc., cannot attest to the accuracy of this information. Use of a term in this book should not be regarded as affecting the validity of any trademark or service mark.

Part 1

The Eternal Religion

Hinduism is so ancient its origins are lost in the mist of prehistory. Many sages are associated with it, but none claims to be its first prophet. Hindus believe their religion has existed forever, even before the universe came into being. They say the truths of their faith are inherent in the nature of reality itself—and that all men and women peering into the depths of their inner nature will rediscover these same truths for themselves.

The image too many outsiders have of the Hindu tradition is of primitive, superstitious villagers worshipping idols. As we get to know the Hindus better, we'll see that their understanding of who and what God is is incredibly sophisticated. In fact, their view of the world and our place in it is so stunningly cosmic in scope that our Western minds practically start to boggle!

Let's enter the universe of Hinduism, an amazing world where inner and outer realities reflect each other like images in a mirror, and the loving presence of the divine is as close as the stillness behind your own thoughts.

Chapter 1

Time for God

I've spent the past twenty-five years shuttling back and forth between two universes: India and the West. My friends from India live on the same planet I do, yet in some respects we're from completely different worlds.

Here in the West we see things as either true or false, black or white, animate or inanimate—you're either logged on or you're logged off. But when I ask one of my Hindu companions a straightforward question, and she shakes her head in that characteristic way that means both yes and no, my Western mind shrugs in defeat. For Hindus, life is multidimensional, and to nail things down to yea or nay is to miss the bigger picture.

For us in the West, the universe is a material entity, made up of atoms starting with hydrogen and helium. We are physical beings in a material cosmos that evolved out of random combinations of nuclear particles. For the Hindu, though, the universe is rooted not in matter but in consciousness. Nothing is random—there is life everywhere and meaning in everything. Divine consciousness is quite literally present in all things. The universe is held together by God's constant, loving attention.

The Hindu Universe

Here are a few ways the universe of a traditional Hindu differs from the world of an average educated Westerner:

➤ Hindus believe all things, from trees and the wind to inanimate objects like mountains and buildings, are in some sense living entities.

➤ Hindus stay in close touch with their relatives, including those who have died. Spirits of the departed are believed to still take an active interest in family affairs and are even still fed during special ceremonies!

➤ The reality of psychic phenomena, like telepathy and precognition, poo-pooed by scientists here in the West, is taken for granted in Hindu culture. These experiences are accepted as evidence that everyone in the universe is interconnected in a vast inner network of consciousness called *Mahat,* "the Great One."

Sages Say

"You must realize that it is Pure Consciousness which projects this universe like images in a mirror of its own unlimited awareness. Merge in that Supreme Consciousness and you will experience unlimited bliss."

—*Tripura Rahasya* 2:13.91

Hindus believe the mind is the sixth sense, that it is able to perceive entities, objects, and fields of energy the other five senses can't register. So for them the living spirits in the fire and flowers and ocean froth, as well as the souls of the dearly departed, are just as real as hammers and nails. We can sense their presence even if we don't actually see them.

The laws of physics behave as if they're different for Hindus, whose world includes subtle dimensions we in the West can barely imagine. Unlike us, they haven't learned that miracles can't really happen. To them, the laws of consciousness, understood by saints and yogis, make miracles happen routinely.

I'll tell you more about all this later, since understanding the subtler dimensions of life is an important part of Hindu spirituality. But first we need to define some terms and learn a little more about the conceptual cosmos Hindus inhabit.

Who's a Hindu?

One out of every six people on Earth is a Hindu. A Hindu is basically any person born into the indigenous religion of Greater India. By Greater India I mean the region where Hindu culture was in force till the advent of Buddhism and Islam. This includes the country we call India now, as well as Afghanistan, Pakistan, Bangladesh, Nepal, Bhutan, Ladakh, Sri Lanka, and even parts of Tibet. Indonesia and Malaysia became predominantly Hindu around 1400 C.E.

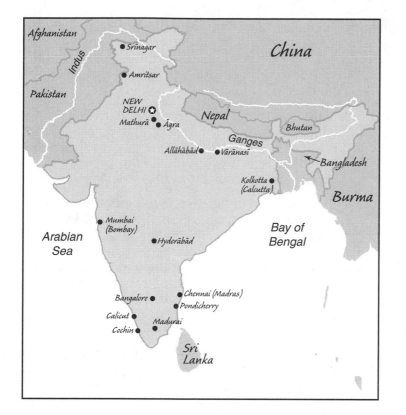

Mother India.

Today, Hinduism is still practiced by over 80 percent of the population of India. Nepal and Bali also both remain largely Hindu—in fact, Hinduism is the state religion of Nepal. Malaysia has over a million Hindus. More than 11 million live in Bangladesh.

In the past few decades, the population explosion in India has motivated millions of Hindus to emigrate to other countries, like Great Britain, the United States, Canada, Reunion Island, Mauritius, and some parts of Africa. There are well over a million Hindus in South Africa, the country where Mahatma Gandhi first started his campaign for social justice.

Today, there are more than 60 million Hindus living outside India. Over a million of them live in North America. Very rapidly, Hinduism is becoming less an exotic Eastern religion and more a familiar global presence.

It's News to Me!

India's population of some one billion souls is made up of about 82 percent Hindus—that's over 800 million people! There are around 80 million Muslims in India, 14 million Sikhs, and 14 million Christians. Small pockets of Parsis (Zoroastrians), Jews, Jains, and Tibetan Buddhists also make their home in the Indian subcontinent.

Generally speaking, Hindus are born, not made. For the most part, Hindus are not interested in converting anyone else to their religion. "If all roads lead to Rome," one of my Hindu teachers told me, "all religions lead to God. Why should I insult your beliefs by saying God can't use your religion to call you to Him? Not everyone is lucky enough to be born a Hindu. God will still find a way to illuminate your life."

New Word Alert!

In India, **guru** means "teacher." It also specifically means your spiritual master, the man or woman guiding you to enlightenment.

A **swami** is an ordained Hindu monk.

New Word Alert!

The Hindus' own term for their religion is **Sanatana Dharma,** which means "the eternal religion."

The **Veda** is Hinduism's most ancient and most sacred scripture, its Holy Bible.

Mahat is the cosmic mind, the network of intelligence through which all living beings are interlinked.

Basically, a Hindu is any person born into a Hindu family who accepts the *Veda* (the Hindu Bible) as the source of their tradition and who participates in the Hindu sacraments which I'll describe later (see Chapter 18, "Sacraments and Holy Days").

In the last half of the twentieth century, as Western fascination with India increased, some outsiders have asked to be initiated into the Hindu faith. Several of my friends, born Christians or Jews, have formally entered the fold of Hinduism. This ancient religion is gradually expanding its self-definition to accommodate foreigners. Today Hinduism includes some well-known *swamis* and *gurus,* such as Krishna Prem and Sivaya Subramuniyaswami, who were not born Hindu.

The word Hindu actually came from Persians mispronouncing Sindhu (Persians thought of Hindus as the people living to the east of the Sindhu River). Europeans picked up the term when they began setting up shop in India in the eighteenth century. Most Hindus are now so used to being called Hindu that they've finally started calling themselves that. The more traditional term for the native Indian spiritual tradition is *Sanatana Dharma,* "the eternal religion."

Beginningless Truth

You might think it takes a lot of chutzpah (if I may borrow a Jewish term) to claim your religion is eternal. What Hindus mean when they say this is their tradition doesn't come from any one founding father or mother, from any single prophet towering over the bastion of hoary antiquity. In fact, the first few verses of the Veda—an incredibly old book, parts of which were composed some 6,000 years ago—acknowledge the sages who were already ancient to its composers living in 4,000 B.C.E.!

Very old Hindu texts speak of a time when it became almost impossible to survive on Earth because of ice and snow. This could be a reference to the last Ice Age, some Hindu scholars believe. Archeologists have unearthed small statues of goddesses from 10,000 years ago (that's about the time the Ice Age was ending) like those still being worshipped in Indian villages today. So even if we're not willing to grant that Hinduism is eternal, we still have to admit it got the jump on the other major religions.

But even more fundamental than the question of how Hinduism first got rolling (a very complicated and surprisingly interesting issue we'll explore in Chapter 2, "Hindus in History") is the fact that Hindus consider their tradition eternal because it's not based on the words of any one inspired man or woman. It's based on the eternal laws of nature.

Scientists of the Spirit

The Hindu sages were scientists of the spirit. In olden times before people had better things to do, like watch wrestling on television, these men and women conducted investigations into the nature of reality. They looked to nature itself as their teacher and guide. If there were spiritual laws we ought to be following, they should be apparent in the cycles of the stars, the flow of mountain streams, and in the way the mind itself operates.

Natural law is called *Rita* in Sanskrit. There were a number of basic laws these early scientists observed:

➤ Everything that's born dies.

➤ Everything that dies is re-created in another form.

➤ Everything in the universe is directly or indirectly related to everything else.

➤ Everything anyone says, does, or even thinks has an effect that reflects the original word, action, or thought.

➤ Everything in the external world is constantly changing.

➤ The only lasting peace people experience happens when they rest their awareness in the lucid stillness hidden behind their own thoughts.

Sages Say

"Hindu religious philosophy is based on experience, on personal discovery and testing of things. It does not say, 'Believe as others do or suffer.' Rather, it says, 'Know thy Self, inquire and be free.'"

—Sivaya Subramuniyaswami, Publisher, *Hinduism Today*

Guidepost

Don't automatically assume that any person you meet from India is a Hindu. Most Indians are, but a substantial minority are Muslims, some of whom take offense at being considered Hindu.

Observations like these became the basis of Hindu beliefs about karma and reincarnation, ritual practice and meditation.

Hindus believe that any truth worth setting up as the foundation of your religion has to be *akriti*—that is, it has to ultimately come from beyond space and time. It has to be true forever. In other words, billions of years from now, after this solar system has disintegrated and a whole new universe has begun to take shape, the things that were ultimately true in our world must be equally true in the cosmos to come.

Hindus believe that the messages of the sages preserved in the Veda are eternally true in just this manner. That's why they call Hinduism Sanatana Dharma, "the eternal religion." A trillion years from now in some other world system, inquiring minds will look to nature and rediscover the same truths Hindus believe today.

A Recyclable Universe

From the Hindu perspective, universes come and go.

Hindus experience time as cyclical, not progressing forward toward a final point as folks do in Judaism, Christianity, and Islam. This concept is important because it leads to a completely different understanding of human history and of our role in the divine plan.

Hindus have been around for a long time, so it's not surprising that a cyclical model makes more sense to them. They have watched other civilizations, their erstwhile trading partners, rise and fall. Sumer was a great civilization in its heyday, but it's gone now. Ancient Egypt rivaled India in the depth of its spiritual knowledge, but all that remains are some dusty old monuments. The Greeks and Romans strutted around like peacocks once, but their empires crumbled, too. Not very long ago the British controlled much of the world; today their empire is a fading memory. In India itself, great cities like Harrapa and Mohenjo Daro saw the light of day almost 5,000 years ago. Then they, too, disappeared into the darkness beneath the earth.

Western scholars sometimes assume Hindus believe time is circular because they're attuned to seasonal and agricultural cycles as well as to the cycles of the planets and stars. But there's more to it than that. Medieval Hindu scriptures mention also the cycles of mountains, which they describe as growing incrementally over the millennia and then sinking back into the ground. (In fact, the Himalayas are getting higher and the Vindhya mountain range in central India is getting shorter. But you'd have to sit watching them carefully for a *very* long time to notice.)

The texts mention the changing course of rivers, and how lush and fertile lands, like the grazing grounds of their ancient homeland, slowly turn to sand, transforming into the Thar Desert in Rajasthan and the Sindh today. They describe cities, like ancient Dvaraka, disappearing into the sea, and whole branches of advanced technology that were lost long, long ago.

Hindus have been kicking around a long time, and they've seen it all.

It's not only empires that eventually bite the dust. Very old Hindu compendiums called the *Puranas* say that in the end (and here modern astrophysicists agree) the very atoms that form the universe will dissolve away. And then slowly, incredibly slowly, the universe will reform.

In Hinduism, everything is recycled. Even the universe itself!

It's News to Me!

For most of the last 2,000 years, the Judeo-Christian-Islamic traditions have taught that our world started quite recently (around 4000 B.C.E.) and will come to a complete end when God stops the flow of time and establishes us in eternity. Hindus don't believe this. In 4000 B.C.E., their culture was already ancient.

Hatching a World

In India, there are many different versions of the re-creation of our universe. This is Hinduism, where when you shake your head you mean both yes and no, so we're not going to ask which of the versions is most authoritative. Instead we're going to assume, as many Hindus do, that all the different stories refract some light of a reality far too vast to be reflected in just one story.

Following is one version. If you want to understand this story, keep in mind that Brahma is the creator of our local world system; today we might call it our solar system. Vishnu is lord of our local universe; today we might say that's our galaxy. The modern name for the milky ocean He sleeps on is the Milky Way. And the Goddess is the one in control of all the universes in all dimensions of being forever, everywhere.

In a beginning (not in *the* beginning because there have been many previous beginnings), Vishnu is lying asleep on an ocean of milk. If you object that no god worth his salt would be caught napping, remember that even the Judeo-Christian God rested on the seventh day.

Vishnu's bed is an enormous cobra called Ananta, whose coils serve as his mattress and whose numerous hoods form a canopy over the slumbering deity. Vishnu's wife, the Goddess, who never sleeps (a woman's work is never done!), sits lovingly massaging his feet.

Sages Say

"Divine Being, like a sea, surges upward in a wave of creation, then subsides again into its own nature. Waves of universes rise incessantly, in infinite numbers, one after another."

—*Yoga Vasishtha* 2:19

It's News to Me!

Think you've got just one body? Hindus believe there's a subtle body made of energy that underlies our physical body. And there's a still subtler body made of consciousness that underlies the energy body. Treatments like homeopathy and acupuncture work on the energies in the subtle body, according to both Hindu and Chinese medical systems.

In the course of Vishnu's dream, a lotus grows out of his navel, and lying there in the petals is a shiny golden egg. This egg will hatch into our solar system if everything proceeds according to plan.

Guiding the egg's development is Brahma. He's the mastermind behind our local universe, the intelligence who put our world together. He wants to shape a Sun and Moon and several planets, which shouldn't be too hard because debris from the last time the solar system formed is still floating around in space.

Getting God Out of Bed

Finding people to inhabit this new world won't be hard either. There are plenty of souls left over from the last incarnation of the solar system who didn't manage to find their way back to God before the world dissolved out from under them. They've been sound asleep in their *subtle bodies* for eons, just like Vishnu. Once a physical planet is in place, Brahma will toss these souls back into physical bodies, so they can complete their unfinished business from previous lives.

There are a number of problems Brahma needs to resolve before he can proceed, but he can't do it all himself. So he tries to wake up Vishnu because some support from an even higher power would be incredibly helpful. But Vishnu is dead asleep.

At this point, Brahma turns to Vishnu's wife, the Goddess, and pleads, "You are the supreme, primeval power, the limitless store of energy that continues to exist even after the material worlds fade away. You remain active even when God, the primordial intelligence, passes into an unconscious state. He sleeps on the snake Ananta, whose name means infinite time, who floats in the milky ocean of primordial matter. Please remove the inertia from the Lord's awareness, so he can wake up!"

Having been asked so nicely, the Goddess lifts the veil of unconsciousness from the cosmic intelligence called Vishnu. Vishnu leaps up, refreshed and invigorated. He and Brahma set about clearing out the negative energies obstructing manifestation. Now Brahma can spend the next few days building our world.

A Day in God's Life

I'd really like to bring home to you the vastness of the time scale Hindus are talking about here. One area where Hinduism and the Judeo-Christian tradition agree is in saying that at the moment we're in the seventh day of creation. But according to the Hindu sages, a day for God is a bit longer than our human day of 24 hours.

The following schema was taught to me by Swami Veda Bharati, a *renunciate* who lives in a tiny *ashram* in Rishikesh in northern India. He's a devotee of the Divine Mother. (The Goddess is a major league player in Hinduism, as you'll soon see.)

New Word Alert!

An **ashram** is a house where a group of Hindus who have completely devoted themselves to spiritual life live together under the guidance of their guru.

A Hindu **renunciate** gives up ordinary worldly pleasures and responsibilities to focus exclusively on the quest to know God or to selflessly serve humanity.

Shiva is one of the main Hindu names for the Supreme Consciousness, the ultimate reality. Shiva is also one of the three main gods of Hinduism, the one who destroys the universe at the end of this cycle of creation.

Swami Bharati's time frame, preserved in the Hindu mystical tradition, starts with a day and a night in the life of our local creator god. Years here mean human years:

➤ One day and night in the life of Brahma is 8,640,000,000 years.

➤ The lifetime of Brahma is 311,040,000,000,000 years.

➤ One day and night in the life of Vishnu equals 37,324,800,000,000,000,000 years.

➤ The life of Vishnu is 671,846,400,000,000,000,000,000 years long.

➤ One day and night in the life of *Shiva* lasts 4,837,294,080,000,000,000,000, 000,000,000 years.

➤ Shiva's lifetime corresponds to 87,071,293,440,000,000,000,000,000,000,000 years.

➤ One glance from the Mother of the Universe equals 87,071,293,440,000,000, 000,000,000,000,000,000,000 years.

It might surprise you that Hinduism speaks of gods dying. Not to worry—they're re-born again later like the rest of us! According to Swami Veda Bharati's tradition, at any one moment there are trillions upon trillions of Brahmas, Vishnus, and Shivas manifesting their universes within the endless expanse of the Divine Mother's aware-ness.

This, folks, is Hinduism's Big Picture.

Quick Quiz

1. India is …
    a. Mostly Hindu.
    b. Half Hindu, half Muslim.
    c. Composed primarily of the lost ten tribes of Israel.

2. The word Hindu comes from …
    a. A mispronunciation of the name of the river Sindhu.
    b. A misspelling of "Indian."
    c. The Sanskrit word for chutney.

3. Sanatana Dharma is the name of …
    a. A famous Hispanic rock star.
    b. A character from a popular American sitcom.
    c. The Hindu religion.

4. For Hindus, time …
    a. Began about 6,000 years ago, when the world was created.
    b. Is without beginning or end.
    c. Starts with a hot cup of coffee.

Answers: 1 (a). 2 (a). 3 (c). 4 (b).

The Boy Who Lived Between Universes

Many of us in the Western world are so proud of what our scientists and technologists have achieved, we're tempted to laugh at the insights of other cultures, particularly if we don't understand them! Let's pause a minute to look a little more closely at one of the fables from Hinduism's supposedly primitive past.

Markandeya was not born in our world. He was actually born (according to this famous myth) in a previous world cycle, the last incarnation of our planet.

One day Markandeya noticed his parents were extremely upset. When he asked what was wrong, his father tearfully admitted that when Markandeya was born, the village astrologer predicted the boy would die on his sixteenth birthday.

Well that very day was his sixteenth birthday. Rather upset, Markandeya ran to the temple and threw his arms around the image of the god Shiva, begging him for protection.

At that very moment the god of death entered the temple, ready to slip his noose around Markandeya's neck and drag him out of his body. But just as Death reached for the young boy, Shiva materialized in front of them, furious that Death would dare approach a devotee while he was worshipping him. Death was so terrified he ran away and never dared approach Markandeya again.

That was fine for the time being, but after a few billion years, it got to be a problem. The Sun eventually flickered out of existence, the Earth passed away, and Markandeya floated around in empty space for eons. Finally the Earth reshaped itself back into existence, and Markandeya was able to walk on terra firma once more. He reported what he'd experienced between worlds to anyone who asked.

What happens when the solar system dies, he explained, is that the Sun slowly turns red and expands to many times its present size. The surface of the earth eventually becomes so hot, no living thing can survive, and the planet becomes as bare as a turtle's back. Then the Sun explodes, emitting a burning wind that blasts the planets to ashes.

Rather startlingly, this extremely old Hindu myth describes the end of the world exactly as our own astrophysicists predict it will in fact occur. Carl Sagan, the well-known twentieth-century scientist from Cornell University, noted that the parallels between Hindu teachings and new scientific findings about the evolution of the universe are "astonishing coincidences." Indeed!

Sages Say

"At the end of the cosmic night, that Great Being who sleeps on the primeval ocean awakens. He finds a vast void where previously there had been a world filled with living beings. Then that most excellent soul begins to recreate the world."

—*Linga Purana* 4:59–60

Inner Vision

I'm not suggesting there really was a boy who survived the death of the last solar system. (Though, just as we have Elvis sightings here in America, Hindus from time to time do report running across Markandeya.) But the thought I'd like to leave with you is that for many millennia the Hindu sages have claimed that if we purify our minds with spiritual practices and open our hearts to learn from her, the Mother of the Universe begins to share her secrets with us.

In the West, we peer into space with powerful telescopes hoping to learn the origin of the universe. The Hindu approach is to couple astute observation of the world outside us with a self-disciplined inner journey. Peering into the depths of consciousness in our own minds, we connect with the consciousness that underlies the entire cosmos. Truths other cultures need radio telescopes to ferret out simply present themselves to our concentrated inward attention.

To India's mystics, Brahma, Vishnu, and Shiva are not just characters invented to make a good story. They represent actual states of divine awareness that are available to devotees, provided only that the devotee is prepared to do the spiritual work to access them.

In fact, in Hinduism the point of doing spiritual practices is to attain *jnana,* living knowledge of Divine Being. It's an ambitious agenda!

Cycles Within Cycles

God's agenda plays out across vast panoramas of space and time. Or at least what seem like eons to us even if they're only an eyeblink to God.

Hindu theologians speak of *yugas,* great expanses of time through which the course of spiritual evolution runs. There are four yugas, which roll by one after another within even larger repeating cycles:

➤ Krita Yuga: 1,728,000 years

➤ Treta Yuga: 1,296,000 years

➤ Dvapara Yuga: 864,000 years

➤ Kali Yuga: 432,000 years

The cycles are named after dice throws. Krita means you win. Treta means you mostly win. Dvapara means you nearly lose. And Kali means you wipe out completely!

In the Krita era, everyone is pure-hearted and people live together in peace. When the Treta period rolls around, folks lose one fourth of their good qualities. By the time the Dvapara Yuga begins, we're down to being half as good as humans originally were. And in the Kali age, people are mostly bad. There's only about a fourth of altruism and spirituality left in us. The rest is selfishness, hatred, and self-delusion.

The bad news is that the Kali Yuga began only about 5,000 years ago. That means we've got a *long* way left to go at our worst behavior. The good news is that there are cycles within cycles within the Kali Yuga, and in some of them things start looking up.

Dr. Rajmani Tigunait, a *pandit* from Allahabad, told me, "Don't be discouraged we're in the Kali Yuga. If you do your spiritual practices and purify your heart, it is as if you are living in the Krita Yuga. Your home and your community will become a center for the Krita Yuga." In other words, you can live in the Garden of Eden if you prefer, but you have to plant it yourself.

The BIG Picture

Why did God create the universe? Hinduism offers several suggestions:

1. He was lonely. He looked around and saw He was by Himself. He desired to become many. And whatever God wants, God gets. The moment that wish entered His mind, an infinite number of souls emerged from His limitless intelligence to keep Him company.

2. She likes to play. The Goddess can't sit still for a moment. She's always got to be doing something. All these worlds are Her game, or "Her sport" as Hindus like to say.

3. The Divine Being is so brimming with bliss, He/She spills over. Shiva/Shakti (God and Goddess who are both two and one in Hinduism) spontaneously generate cosmos after cosmos. Creative energy simply pours out of the Divine. It's the nature of the Supreme One to create, as it's the nature of light to shine.

Sages Say

"He who experiences the whole of creation as his very own Self, who sees everything around him as the limbs of his own body, although he appears like an ordinary man to others, I consider him to be truly blessed. Strive to experience this sense of unity with all things, to feel yourself in the universe and the universe in you. I'm telling you again and again: There is no greater experience than the awareness of oneness."

—*Jnaneshvari* 6:403–409

In the Western religious traditions, God creates us out of nothing. In Hinduism, Divine Being creates us out of itself. This means we are literally one with the divine, one with everything else in the universe, and one with each other.

Hinduism is about finding our place in an immense universe. It shows us how to deal with suffering and where to find joy. It reveals how learning to know our own inner Self is the key to entering the consciousness of God.

In the Western world, until very recently, there's been a tendency to consider Hindus "primitive" and "superstitious" because they believe there is living spirit everywhere. What I hope you remember is that Hindu thought isn't primitive at all. In fact it's fantastically sophisticated. Hindus look at reality through a different lens than Westerners do, but in the context of Hindu culture, their understanding of who God is, how His laws operate, and what our position is in relation to him is just as insightful as the Western viewpoint.

The Least You Need to Know

➤ The Hindu tradition is extremely mystical.

➤ Hindus consider their faith to be "the eternal religion."

➤ Time doesn't end; it spins on in cycles through eternity.

➤ Direct personal experience of God is the purpose of life.

➤ Everything arises out of consciousness.

Chapter 2

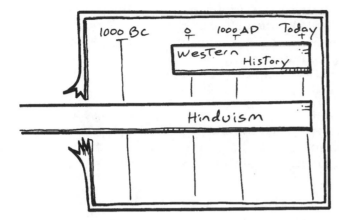

Hindus in History

If you had been around in the third millennium B.C.E. (and if the Hindu theory of reincarnation is correct, you might have been!), India is where you would have wanted to be. The quality of life was higher there than practically anywhere else in the world. In fact, the towns of North India in 2600 B.C.E. were more comfortable and technologically advanced than most European cities till nearly the time of the Renaissance!

Religious life was vibrant in ancient India. Some of the oldest surviving spiritual writings come from this part of the world. They reveal a religion that was both boisterously earthy and transcendently mystical—not unlike Hinduism today.

But somewhere between then and now the history of these deeply religious people was erased. What happened?

The History That Vanished

Since the early 1920s, archeologists have been unearthing an astonishing ancient civilization in northwestern India, now called the Indus-Sarasvati culture. It was enormous, at least seven hundred miles from north to south and eight hundred miles from east to west. If you had dropped the entire Egyptian civilization along with all of Sumer (two high cultures which were flourishing at about the same time) into that same geographical area, you still would have had *lots* of room left over!

Here researchers found the best-planned cities anywhere on the planet. The neatly arranged gridiron pattern of streets and houses revealed organizational and construction skills unparalleled in the ancient world, and not always equaled in the world today. The cities were gargantuan for the time—three miles in diameter, which isn't a bad size for a town even today.

Sages Say

"The dumbest thing in the world is to delude yourself that anything in this impermanent world will last forever."

—The *Tirukural*

The quality of the drainage system in these towns, which included brick-lined sewers complete with manholes, would not be seen again till Roman engineers set up shop two thousand years later.

The people who lived here had many of the trappings of civilization as we know it today (except maybe TV). They had nicely appointed bathrooms where they took bucket showers. They had one of the earliest written languages in the world. They had a sophisticated system of weights and measures that was borrowed by the businessmen of Mesopotamia.

They had seaports, but those excavated docks are eerie to look at these days because the river tributaries they once serviced have gone away. The long-abandoned piers now overlook the bleak Thar Desert.

Messing with the Past

Western archeologists were astounded by these findings but orthodox Hindus weren't surprised at all. Their ancient chronicles—enormous religious anthologies like the *Puranas* and the *Mahabharata,* which you'll learn about in Chapter 5, "The People's Religion"—often mentioned glorious cities of the distant past. They even mentioned legendary architects like Asura Maya who could whip up spectacular buildings with beautiful gardens and lotus-laden pools and mirrored walls.

But Western scholars never believed those ancient chronicles for a minute. The surprising thing is that even as they dug up more and more evidence that the Hindus' own version of their history was more or less correct, Western scholars *still* couldn't believe it!

Here's why. In nineteenth-century European intellectual circles, Oxford University scholar Frederick Max Müller was held in only slightly less esteem than God. One day Müller announced that the Veda, India's most ancient spiritual classic and the very foundation of its faith, had been composed between 1200 to 1000 B.C.E. As far as Western scholars were concerned, God had spoken. This in spite of the fact that some of the positions of the stars and planets mentioned in the Veda could only have occurred sometime between 3500 and 4000 B.C.E.!

Tampering with Time

Where did Müller come up with a date as late as 1000 B.C.E. for a scripture Hindus themselves considered much older? It turns out that unlike the Hindus who believed the universe was billions of years old, as a Christian Müller believed the world had been created in 4004 B.C.E. By adding the ages of the patriarchs listed in the Bible who lived between Adam and Noah, Müller could calculate the number of years that had passed since the creation and the Great Flood. This brought him to 2448 B.C.E.

Now, Müller was no fool. He knew it would take time for Noah's descendants to immigrate to India, repopulate the subcontinent, and create the hundreds of different languages and distinctive cultures flourishing there. This, he figured, must have taken at least 1,200 years, maybe as much as 1,400. Ergo, the earliest Hindu scripture could not have been written earlier than 1200 B.C.E. University textbooks uncritically repeated this date through the mid-1990s!

To give the guy credit, later in life Müller had second thoughts about his guesstimate, admitting, "Whatever may be the date of the Vedic hymns, whether 1500 or 15,000 B.C., they have their own unique place and stand by themselves in the literature of the world." But the damage was done: Everyone believed that when he'd given out the date of 1200 B.C.E. he had known what he was talking about.

Müller's mistake had catastrophic consequences for the study of Indian history. Saints who according to the Hindus had lived before 3000 B.C.E. were

It's News to Me!

The majestic Sarasvati River ran through northwestern India till it dried up 4,000 years ago. To this day, the Indian name for the goddess of learning is Sarasvati. Could this be because the people of this region were once among the best educated in the world?

Guidepost

Scholarship on Indian chronology is currently in a state of uproar. In any book on Hindu history you look at—including this one—dates for events occurring before about 1000 C.E. should be approached with plenty of healthy skepticism.

shifted to 1000 B.C.E. The Buddha, who according to Northern Buddhist schools lived around 1000 B.C.E., got shuffled to somewhere around 500 B.C.E. No less an authority than the sixteenth Dalai Lama has appealed to Western scholars to get together, clear their minds, and straighten out this mess for once and for all!

"There is no more absorbing story than that of the discovery and interpretation of India by Western consciousness," noted the renowned Rumanian professor of religion, Mircea Eliade. You can say that again, Mircea!

Chronological Conundrums

Back to our archeologists. They've discovered a high civilization that flourished in northwestern India between 2700 and 1900 B.C.E. Since the Veda wasn't composed till maybe 1000 B.C.E. (according to Max Müller) and the sages who composed the Veda were the founders of Hinduism (according to Western scholars), then the people who lived in these cities must not have been Hindu. They supposedly lived nearly 2000 years before Hinduism was invented! Who were these people and where did they go?

Enter the Aryan Invasion Theory. It was decided that the original inhabitants of India were the Dravidians. These are the people who fill up much of South India today. They speak a totally different language from most north Indians, and some of them have skin that's a little darker in color. Till 1000 B.C.E., they must have inhabited the whole of India, Müller's twentieth-century disciples decreed. The ancient cities in the north were built by them.

Then, the Western experts concluded, somewhere between 1500 and 1000 B.C.E., the primitive barbarians who composed the Veda invaded northern India, driving the helpless Dravidians into the southern part of the subcontinent where they live today. There were two difficulties with this popular theory:

1. Today's northern Hindus have absolutely no memory of having ever driven the Dravidians out of north India. None of their ancient manuscripts mentions any such thing.

2. Today's Dravidians have absolutely no memory of ever having lived in North India. In fact, their ancient traditions suggest that their forebears came from the south, not from the north.

The Aryan Invaders

Minor problems like these did not discourage the European and American scholars of the time. Thousands of pages of the Hindus's own historical records were simply dismissed as fiction.

These white scholars were sure a virile race of white warriors, much like themselves, had invaded India. The Veda mentioned a people called the *Aryans,* "the noble ones."

They spoke a language related to German, Russian, Italian, and English. They worshipped deities who sounded quite a bit like some of the gods in the old European pagan tradition. Obviously then, they were proto-Europeans. And one of the symbols they frequently used in their religious art was a twisted cross called a swastika. They must have been the invaders who destroyed the ancient cities!

This theory of ancient white-skinned proto-Europeans sweeping across the eastern world establishing a vibrant new culture appealed to many Europeans in the 1930s—Adolph Hitler for example. Hitler borrowed the term "Aryan" from the Veda and adopted the swastika, too, for his own campaign of world domination.

It's News to Me!

The swastika was originally a Hindu symbol representing happiness and good luck. You'll still find swastikas everywhere you travel in India. Hitler, however, flipped the swastika over on its side and adopted it as the symbol of the Nazis. This has given it a very different shade of meaning in the West.

Back to the Beginning

Let's go back to the top and start over again. This time we'll tell the story as it appears in the Aryans' and Dravidians' own records—the Hindu version of Hindu history.

The descendants of the Vedic Aryans, that is, the people who live mostly in northern India today and speak languages related to Sanskrit, believe they have been right where they are today since time immemorial. The Veda, their ancient Bible, describes the landscape of northern India and Pakistan. It never mentions countryside like the area in the Caucasus near the Caspian Sea that Western scholars thought was the Aryans' original home.

In fact, to explain why the Veda describes a lush homeland like India rather than a barren location like the Caucasus, these scholars decided that throughout the Veda the Aryans were imagining what they *wished* their homeland looked like, not describing how it actually appeared!

Over and over the Veda mentions a mighty river called the Sarasvati where Aryan communities flourished and Vedic priests sang the hymns of glorious gods, like Indra, slayer of the terrifying dragon Vritra, and Agni, lord of fire who transports prayers to heaven on flames and smoke. Western scholars speculated that the Sarasvati might have been one of the rivers to the east of the Aral Sea in Soviet Central Asia. Perhaps, some even speculated, it had never been anything more than a figment of the ancient poets' imaginations! Hindus insist the river was real, but disappeared in the course of time. They say it continues to flow underground, where only saints with very pure vision can see it.

The Veda, orthodox Hindus maintain, is immeasurably old. It portrays a temple-free religion where priests officiate at outdoor fire sacrifices. It mentions other religious traditions of nearby people who worshipped images of deities inside temples. The indoor worshippers and the outdoor worshippers sometimes squabbled, but they were all indigenous people, natives of India. The Veda talks about various groups who left India, but never mentions invaders arriving from the outside.

Meanwhile, the Dravidians of South India, who mostly speak languages related to Tamil, have always been extremely proud of their own native traditions. They had gods like Vel, their own warrior deity and loving protector. Their legends also place their distant ancestors where they still are today: smack dab in South India.

The Mountains Bowed Before Him

Enter Agastya. Agastya lived long ago—so long ago, in fact, that by the time the Veda was composed he was already a legendary figure. Agastya decided it was time for his fellow Aryans in the north and those mysterious Dravidians in the south to get it together. So he crossed the Vindhya mountain range in central India to meet the Tamil-speaking neighbors on the other side.

There's a story about this. The Vindhyas were extremely jealous of the Himalayas because the Himalayan mountains were much higher and kept getting even taller century by century. (Centuries seem like an eyeblink to a mountain.) So the Vindhyas started working out, increasing their own size, too. This disturbed the balance of the Earth, and Agastya decided somebody had better do something about it.

So when he arrived at the Vindhyas on his journey south, Agastya said to them, "You're getting so tall these days it will take weeks for a short guy like me to climb across you. Would you mind bowing down so I can make the trip a little faster?"

New Word Alert!

Arya is the Sanskrit word for noble, virtuous, worthy. An Aryan was a particularly noble person, though the word came to mean specifically the ancient people who practiced the rites associated with the holy book called the Veda.

Purusha means a man. We'll see later that it also can mean an individual soul, or even God, the greatest soul of all.

Now, the Vindhyas were very spiritually advanced mountains. They knew how to treat a sage with respect. So they bowed low and Agastya quickly scrambled over. If you visit central India today, you'll see the Vindhyas are not that imposing—they're kind of puny. That's because Agastya never went back north. The Vindhyas are still lying low so Agastya can cross easily when he finally decides to return home.

Agastya established the Vedic religion in South India, teaching the people there the outdoor fire sacrifice and the beautiful hymns of the Aryan people. Over thousands of years, the southerners were profoundly influenced by Aryan religion, while the Aryans were deeply affected by Dravidian religious concepts and practices, too. The two cultures jumbled together—along with the beliefs of a number of other minority races, like the Austro-Asiatic people who also inhabit India—creating the rich and complex religion we call Hinduism today.

Reclaiming the Hindu Heritage

From the Hindu perspective, by the time sophisticated cities like Mohenjo Daro and Harrapa came up in the middle of the third millennium B.C.E., the religion of the Veda was already incredibly ancient in India. In fact, the Veda refers to hundreds of cities existing even way back then.

This makes sense when you think about it. It's hard to believe well-designed towns like those the archeologists dug up in the northwest just shot up out of nowhere. You would think the Indians had had plenty of practice building cities before they created classy towns like Mohenjo Daro. In fact, the ancient Vedic word for "man" is *purusha,* which is probably derived from roots meaning "city dweller."

Remember how I said in Chapter 1, "Time for God," that we're now in the Kali Yuga, the cycle of time where people are the least intelligent and least spiritually inclined of all? The Kali Yuga supposedly began around 3100 B.C.E., with things getting worse by the day since then. It's not hard for Hindus to believe that the more intelligent people of the past built incredible cities or even that they had advanced technologies like those described in the *Mahabharata* and *Ramayana.*

Western scholars had trouble wrapping their minds around the Hindu version of history. That's because folks in the West believe in linear time. Things started from zero at some point (according to fundamentalist Christians and Muslims, around 6,000 years ago). They've been progressing from there, continually improving until we reach the most intelligent, most enlightened creatures who ever lived on Earth: us.

Hindus believe time is cyclical. Yeah, there are some smart, technologically advanced people around today. But it's happened before. History repeats itself. Civilizations arise, work their way toward greatness, then gradually destroy themselves. The clock gets set back and the process begins again. But Western archeologists wanted to believe civilization began in the Middle East because that's where the Bible said the Garden of Eden had been.

It's News to Me!

The ancient Indian epic called the **Mahabharata** describes weapons of mass destruction unlike anything seen on earth again till the twentieth century. So many people were killed in a massively destructive war in North India, says the text, that no one was left alive who knew how to build more of the weapons! The **Ramayana** claims that in ancient times some advanced civilizations even knew how to build flying machines called *vimana.*

That advanced cultures had existed elsewhere long before the Garden of Eden was even planted was not what they wanted to hear.

Return of the Invisible River

In the early 1980s, proponents of the Aryan Invasion Theory got a terrible shock. Satellite imaging was revolutionizing our knowledge of Earth's geography. It allowed scientists to get a look at the planet from low orbit out in space. Satellite photos of the area called the Punjab, in far northwestern India and into Pakistan, revealed the dry bed of an enormous river, so huge it may have been five miles across at one site. While that river was in business, it may have been the largest in the world, bigger even than the Amazon is today.

So there it was, the Sarasvati River the Veda had been talking about—just exactly where the Veda had always said it was. The problem was that geologists quickly established the river had dried up around 1900 B.C.E. The Veda described this river as one of the centers of Aryan culture. Yet according to our friend Max Müller the Veda hadn't been composed till at the very least 700 years after the river disappeared. What was this? Poets pretending they still lived alongside a river that vanished centuries before? Not darn likely.

This was the first nail in the coffin of the Western version of Hindu history. More nails quickly sealed the lid shut. After sixty years of searching, archeologists had not been able to find a shred of evidence that northern India's ancient urban culture had been destroyed by violent foreigners, as the Aryan Invasion Theory demanded. Instead it appeared the culture petered out gradually as geographic and climatic conditions changed.

Furthermore, the bulk of the physical evidence pointed to a continuance of culture, not an abrupt break as one would expect if nomadic warriors had replaced an older city-based culture.

It was starting to look like the people who lived in northern India in 2500 B.C.E. had a lot in common with the people who lived there a thousand years earlier and even with the people who still live there now. Researchers unearthed numerous images of the god Shiva and various household goddesses, all still immensely popular in India today. Then fire pits designed for the performance of Vedic rituals were found just about everywhere archeologists dug, even though according to the Aryan Invasion theory, the priests who performed those rites weren't supposed to immigrate into India for another 1,500 years!

Sages Say

"May Sarasvati, mother of abundance, guide and protect us, inspiring us to noble thoughts! Her unlimited waters rush past us in a constant flood, racing onward with a deafening roar!"

—*Rig Veda* 6:61.4,8

Meanwhile, evidence for a substantial Dravidian presence in the north never materialized. And most impressive of all, recent DNA evidence shows barely any difference
whatever between the north Indians and the tribal Indians of the south. The proof is
stacking up. Max Müller and his colleagues were seriously mistaken. The religion of
the Vedas is thousands of years older than Western scholars originally thought, and
no bloody invasion by merciless Aryan hordes ever occurred.

It turned out the Hindus had the history of their religion right all along.

Quick Quiz

1. The North Indian Aryans were …

   a. Blond-haired, blue-eyed, white-skinned super-racists.

   b. Devotees of Vedic gods like Indra and Agni.

   c. A cricket team from New Delhi.

2. The Dravidians …

   a. Were the original authors of the holy Veda.

   b. Claimed they were run out of North India by marauding blond-haired,
   blue-eyed Aryans.

   c. Were a South Indian culture speaking Tamil or languages related to it.

3. Max Müller was …

   a. The greatest German composer who ever lived.

   b. Owner of the most successful brewery in Munich.

   c. An Oxford professor of immense stature.

4. The Sarasvati River …

   a. Bowed before the Aryan sage Agastya.

   b. Dried up around 1900 B.C.E.

   c. Was a favorite destination for trout fishermen.

Answers: 1 (b). 2 (c). 3 (c). 4 (b).

A Crisis of Self-Identity

In the late twentieth century, news about new findings vindicating old truths sent
shockwaves through the Indian intellectual community. Since the British took over
India in the late eighteenth century, many of India's elite had been educated in
European-style universities where they had been taught to sneer at their own ancient
traditions.

Part 1 ➤ *The Eternal Religion*

The majority of Hindus, taught in the traditional Indian guru system, clung to the old beliefs. But lots of prominent Indians had swallowed the Western retelling of their past hook, line, and sinker. Important Hindus like Jawaharlal Nehru, independent India's first Prime Minister, had undergone painful crises of self-identity, rejecting much of their Hindu heritage and identifying instead with their British conquerors. After all, the Europeans were men of science. India, they had been told, was a backwater of superstition that substituted myth for reality.

Now it turned out it was the European view of Hindu history that was the myth! Disillusioned Hindus quickly began to form influential new academic organizations like the World Association for Vedic Studies, designed to sort out the truth about their Vedic legacy. Their exciting work is reshaping the way educated Hindus think about themselves and their ancient sciences and religion.

Our Hindu Connections

If you're wondering why I've gone on for a whole chapter about the ancient history of the Hindus, there are two important reasons.

The first is because most of the books you'll find on Hinduism written before about 1995 contain badly outdated material. Be advised that early Hindu history is being seriously reevaluated by Western academics at this very moment. A few still cling to the old theories, and some are struggling to adapt them so that they'll somehow stretch to fit the newly uncovered facts. But most researchers knowledgeable about the latest archeological findings have acknowledged the crying need for an overhaul of Western ideas about ancient Hinduism.

The second reason may be even more important, at least for those of us born in the West. The new archeological information, it turns out, has immense implications not just for Hindus, but for the whole history of Western civilization.

"East is East and West is West/The twain shall never meet," wrote Rudyard Kipling, who spent a good chunk of his life in India. He wasn't right either. You've probably noticed the majority of Indian people are Caucasian, like the majority of people with ethnic European backgrounds. They have somewhat darker skin, but their skull shape and facial features are purely Caucasian. This is an important tip-off: Many Indians are actually quite closely racially related to most Europeans.

That's not the only surprising connection Europeans have with Hindus. Most of the languages of North India, like Hindi, Bengali, Gujarati, Marathi, and Punjabi, are related to the majority of European languages, such as English, French, German, Italian, Greek, and Spanish. In fact, when British scholars first started studying Sanskrit in the eighteenth century, they were dumbstruck at how closely it paralleled European languages.

Let's compare a few Sanskrit words and their English equivalents to see why the scholars were bowled over. There's *matri* and mother, *patri* and father (think of Latin

26

pater or Spanish *padre), bratri* and brother, *duhitri* and daughter. There's *dvi* and two (think of duo and duet), *tri* and three. And there's *deva* and deity, *yoga* and yoke, *mrityu* and mortality. Clearly, the North Indians are related to most people of European descent not only racially but linguistically.

Next consider this. Somewhere in the hoary past the ancient Vedic sky god Dyaus Pitar (literally "sky father") seems to have hooked up with the Latins. How else can you explain why the ancient Romans called their sky god Jupiter (they pronounced his name "Dyu-piter")?

The most important god in the Veda is Indra, the thunder god who wields a lightning bolt. He's an invincible warrior who sometimes drinks a little too much. His main job is to kill the serpent Vritra. Since I'm Norwegian, I immediately flash on Thor, the Norse thunder god who wields a lightning bolt, drinks too much, and is to be congratulated for his victorious battle against the terrifying serpent named Midgardsorm.

I'm also struck when I hear one of the oldest names for the gods used in the Veda is *asura*, since I know the old Norse name for the ancient Scandinavian gods is *aesir*. The myths I learned as a child in Norway speak of a great world tree along whose roots and branches the entire cosmos is arranged. So do Vedic myths.

If you're beginning to suspect the North Indians are somehow culturally related to the Europeans, you hit the nail right on the head. Those of us of European descent for the most part junked our old gods when Christianity came to town. The Hindus never got on board with Christianity. They're still worshipping *our* old gods.

The North Indian and European civilizations are definitely related. Their common culture is called Indo-European by academics today. Apparently, most Hindus of North India and most Europeans came from the same root stock. It's not "East is East and West is West." It's "East is West and West is East!"

The clearer we can get on early Hindu history, the nearer we'll be to solving the puzzle of our own past.

It's News to Me!

Sir William Jones's discovery in 1786 of the link between Sanskrit and many European languages led to the founding of the science of comparative linguistics in the West. Linguistics, a fairly new science in the Western world, has been a major preoccupation of Indian pandits like Panini and Patanjali since the second millennium B.C.E.

Sages Say

"Imagine this universe as a tree. Its root reaches far above, its branches spread out below. The branches are these many worlds. The root is the Supreme Being from whom all these worlds receive life, who is their innermost being, who is the everlasting transcendent reality."

—The Yajur Veda

The Hindu Homeland

One of the most baffling mysteries of prehistory is where to find the original homeland of the Indo-European people. Where did our earliest ancestors come from?

Over the last two centuries an incredible number of locations for the Indo-European Garden of Eden have been offered, including the North Pole.

It's News to Me!

B. G. Tilak, a close associate of Mahatma Gandhi, suggested the Indo-Europeans may have originated in the far north. He pointed out that ancient Hindu texts mention a divine land where one day and night is equal to an entire year for the rest of humanity. The only places on Earth where 24 hours literally equal a year are the North and South Poles. Antarctica is uninhabitable, so he concluded the ancient Indo-Europeans might have immigrated southward from latitudes near the North Pole.

Just about everywhere from Germany to Kazakhstan has been considered a viable homeland site, with Turkey being a current favorite. The issue remains highly controversial and evidence for new contenders continues to be brought forward every few years.

Recently a number of authorities have raised an intriguing new possibility. The Veda is the oldest surviving record of the Indo-European people, or at least the only one of any length. So wouldn't it be interesting to see if the Veda has anything to say on the topic, they wondered.

It turns out the Veda has plenty to offer in this connection. According to some Hindu researchers, tribes the Veda calls the Prithus, Parsus, Druhyus, and Alinas may be the Parthians, Persians, Druids, and Hellenes (the Greeks). The Veda says all these groups lived in India at one time. It also explains that many communities migrated out of India. Might northern India be the original homeland of the Indo-Europeans peoples?

It will take years to sort out the complex historical issues involved here. For now, no one knows for sure. Still, it's intriguing to think there's a slim possibility that the fascination some Westerners feel for Hindu religion may be an unconscious attraction toward their own original spiritual homeland.

The Least You Need to Know

➤ A highly advanced culture existed in northwestern India in antiquity.

➤ The Aryans of North India were the authors of the Veda.

➤ Aryan religion spread into South India and was in turn influenced by Dravidian (South Indian) spirituality.

➤ Errors by prominent European scholars have led to massive confusion about early Hindu history.

➤ The North Indians and many European cultures are culturally, racially, and linguistically related.

Chapter 3

The World Discovers Hinduism

In This Chapter

➤ Alexander the Great admits defeat

➤ Apollonius of Tyana and the Hindu "god-men"

➤ A Hindu Goddess protects Rome

➤ Chinese pilgrims in India

➤ A Muslim scholar checks out Hinduism

"India has created a mystique about itself. It is the sacred land for which everyone seeks." So wrote the German philosopher George W. Hegel.

Since time immemorial, India has been synonymous with spiritual knowledge. Merchants from as far west as Egypt traveled to India routinely to benefit from its fabulous wealth, but pilgrims also made the difficult journey to sit at the feet of Hinduism's fabled spiritual masters.

Until recently, most modern Western scholars were reluctant to believe there'd been much contact between India and the ancient West. Recent archeological finds, like the site of a Roman colony at Arikamedu in South India, prove them wrong. We now know that Rome imported so many luxury items from India, it developed a massive trade deficit and nearly went bankrupt!

Heading East

Educated people in the ancient West had at least some basic knowledge of the Hindu tradition. After all, following Alexander the Great's foray into the part of Greater India we call Pakistan today, Greek soldiers who set down roots in India were continually sending news about Hindu culture to relatives back home in Greece.

But reports about India went back further than Alexander. If you look at a world map, you'll see the Middle East is just a hop, skip, and a jump from India. Take a boat down the Persian Gulf, then sail a few hundred miles along the coast of Persia, and you're in the Indus Valley. If you could get to Babylon, India was actually quite accessible.

We read in ancient Greek biographies that a number of important Greek intellectuals, such as Pythagoras, studied in Persia. Even if Pythagoras never visited India himself (as some students of history have speculated), he would have learned some of the doctrines of India's yogis and brahmins in Babylon, where he lived for twelve years.

It's News to Me!

Ancient Hellenistic biographers mention a number of famous Greek philosophers who made the trip to India. One was Pyrrho, who returned to Greece and founded a philosophical tradition emphasizing inner tranquility and self-control, the chief virtues practiced by the Hindu sages.

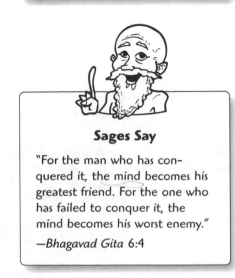

Sages Say

"For the man who has conquered it, the mind becomes his greatest friend. For the one who has failed to conquer it, the mind becomes his worst enemy."

—*Bhagavad Gita* 6:4

Conquering Alexander the Great

Some 2,300 years ago, a fellow by the name of Alexander conquered the world. Or at least just about all the world he and his fellow Greeks had ever heard of. He was planning to conquer northern Europe, too, but died young before he could get to it. He passed away under rather suspicious circumstances incidentally, perhaps poisoned by former friends disgusted with his alcoholism and maniacal ego.

At any rate, Egypt fell to the overachiever from Macedonia, then Persia. India was next on his hit list. Alexander fans will tell you he conquered India, too, but that's a slight exaggeration. In 327 B.C.E., he made a few incursions into what we'd call Pakistan, but the Greco-Indian kingdom he left behind, called Bactria, was really more in Afghanistan than India.

As far as Alexander knew, India was the final frontier, the end of the world. To his shock, India turned out to be a heck of a lot bigger than he had figured. He also learned once he got there that there was yet another country still further east called China. This excited Alexander: Still more worlds to conquer! But his soldiers were fed up and wanted to go home.

Indian Surprises

Alexander made a number of other truly astonishing discoveries.

The first was that there were Greek-speaking communities in India. (Imagine if Columbus had landed in America and found Native Americans speaking Spanish!)

It turns out these were descendants of Greek citizens from Turkey who had been repatriated to India by the Persians. Some of their ancestors had sold out to Persian rulers in the distant past. When Alexander found out about this, being the big-hearted world conqueror he was, he had them all slaughtered to the last man, woman, and child.

Another surprise was that people this far from home were worshipping the familiar Greek gods. Alexander found devotees of Hercules (probably the popular Hindu avatar Krishna) and Dionysus (most likely the Hindu god Shiva). Today we know the reason these deities seemed so familiar to Alexander was that, like his own gods and goddesses, they were part of the ancient Indo-European pantheon.

Alexander Meets His Match

It was in India that Alexander met the only men on earth he couldn't conquer. The yogis. Greek historians traveling with the feisty commander brought back a record of the encounter.

In the woods, lying on a bed of leaves, Greek soldiers stumbled across a brahmin sage named Dandamis. Alexander was intensely curious about the fabled wisdom of the holy men of India. He sent Dandamis a message: "Alexander, Son of God and Lord of the Earth, invites you into his presence. If you come, you will be richly rewarded. If you don't, you will die."

It's News to Me!

In India, Alexander the Great excitedly announced he'd found the source of the Nile River. This says something about the ancient Greeks' grasp of world geography. In fact they'd arrived at the Indus, which some Indians called "the blue river." Blue is pronounced *nila* in the native tongue, which is probably what threw Alexander off.

Sages Say

"The wisdom of the ancients has been taught by the philosophers of Greece, but also by a people in Syria called the Jews, and by the brahmins in India."

—Megasthenes, Greek ambassador to India, writing around 300 B.C.E.

Dandamis was not impressed. "There is only one king," he answered, "the one who created light and life. He's the only king I obey, and He abhors war."

Dandamis continued:

> How can this Alexander be the greatest king on Earth as long as he remains subject to the king of death? And what can he offer me when my mother the Earth already supplies everything I need? I have no possessions I need to protect, so I sleep peacefully at night. Alexander may kill my body, but he can't touch my soul.
>
> Tell your king that at the time of death each one of us will be asked to account for our actions in this life. Ask him how he's going to explain the agony of those he has murdered and oppressed.
>
> Your king can tempt those who crave gold. He can terrify those who fear death. But we brahmins care for neither. Go tell Alexander he has nothing I want and I will not come see him.

When Alexander heard Dandamis's answer, he admitted that he, the conqueror of the world, had been conquered by a naked old man.

It's News to Me!

Ancient Greek medical centers often used sleep therapy. A patient would rest, lying without moving, until a dream revealed the cause and cure of their illness. Psychological counseling, requiring patients to take an honest look at emotional and moral imbalances in their lives, was part of the healing methodology physicians like Apollonius of Tyana made use of.

A Visit from Apollonius

Apollonius of Tyana was a physician living in Turkey in the first century C.E. In those days, doctors worked out of temples dedicated to Greek gods of healing like Asclepias, which served as the medical centers of the time. Apollonius had heard lots of stories about the sages of India and eagerly wanted to go there.

Apollonius was a follower of Pythagoras, a remarkable Greek sage who had lived six centuries earlier. Apollonius knew that many Pythagorean teachings, such as the belief in reincarnation, vegetarianism, and keeping silent for years at a time as a form of spiritual discipline, were part and parcel of the Hindu tradition as well.

We know what happened next from a biography of Apollonius written by one Philostratus, a leading literary light of his era, who carefully researched his subject. The book was commissioned by Julia Domna, the empress of Rome, who was fascinated by Apollonius.

With a small group of devotees, Apollonius set out for India, pausing in Babylon to study with the Magi,

Zoroastrian priests whose scriptures were closely related to the Veda. Then they headed on through Afghanistan, crossing the Khyber Pass into India.

Apollonius in the Ashram

With the help of a local maharaja, Apollonius was ushered into the ashram of a yogi named Iarchas. Before Apollonius could open his mouth, Iarchas greeted him by name, told him his parents' names as well, and mentioned a few salient details from Apollonius's life, including some incidents that had occurred during his long journey to India.

Needless to say, Apollonius was dumbfounded. (Many of us who have had run-ins with the yogis' amazing powers have felt the same way!) "How can you know all these things?" he demanded.

"We begin," Iarchas explained, "by knowing ourselves."

In the ensuing months, Iarchas taught Apollonius to know himself. He put him through intensive yogic training and introduced him to the Vedic method of performing *pujas* (sacred rituals) and other Hindu occult techniques. Apollonius learned to work with *mantras* and how to empower *yantras* (sacred diagrams). For centuries after his death, the yantras empowered by Apollonius were famous throughout the Western world for their alleged miraculous properties.

As he left for home, Apollonius told his guru, "I came to you by land, and you poured over me an ocean of knowledge, knowledge which enables mortal men to rise to heaven. When I return to the West I will tell the entire world of your wisdom. I will honor you till the last breath of my life."

New Word Alert!

A **mantra** is a sacred sound, word, or phrase that leads the mind to a higher state of consciousness.

Puja is a religious ritual, usually involving making offerings to an image of a deity.

A **yantra** is a geometric diagram into which divine energy is either permanently or temporarily infused.

Egypt and India

Apollonius traveled throughout the Roman Empire, from Spain to Rome to Africa, relating his experiences in India. "I have seen men dwelling on the earth but not of the earth. I saw them well defended without fortifications. I saw they owned nothing, yet possessed all things."

Apollonius eventually decided to visit Egypt also, the other ancient civilization famous for its spirituality. There he was bitterly disappointed. Apollonius found the religious institutions of Egypt in decay. The Egyptian priests' knowledge of their inner tradition was in sad decline.

Apollonius made the long pilgrimage up the Nile to see for himself the Ethiopian gymnosophists, the famous desert ascetics. He was stunned at how similar their spiritual beliefs and practices were to those of the ascetics he'd studied with in India. There must be a connection, he concluded.

Guidepost

There are two kinds of wonder-working yogis in India: the genuine article and the flat-out fraud. Frauds use tricks not unlike those of stage magicians to delude you into thinking they can read your mind and know your past and future. The real McCoy may offer words of advice but will never demand money or try to manipulate you.

Inquiring into Egyptian history and legend, Apollonius found evidence that the ancestors of these Ethiopians had emigrated from India in remote antiquity. Modern scholars have confirmed this hypothesis. We now know Manetho, an Egyptian priest who wrote a history of Egypt in the Greek language, specifically mentioned the arrival of immigrants from northern India who settled in Ethiopia somewhere around 1400 B.C.E. (Ancient authors frequently confused India and Ethiopia. This helps explain why.) Manetho considered this one of the major events in Egyptian history.

Apollonius visited many Egyptian temples where he couldn't resist offering helpful suggestions to the staff on how to spiritually enliven their practices. "Who dares teach Egyptian priests their own religion?" one hierophant demanded.

"Anyone," Apollonius answered calmly, "who comes from India."

A Tribute to India's Sages

Apollonius was on the road much of his life, traveling virtually the whole of the civilized Western world as well as Egypt and Persia. Yet he insisted that he never found such great wisdom anywhere else as he had experienced in India. He went so far as to claim that many of the mystery schools of the West had originated in India in the distant past. He called the yogis "god-men" both because of their miraculous powers and because of their profound spirituality and extraordinary compassion.

Apollonius wrote a four-volume book about the teachings of the Hindu spiritual masters, which unfortunately has been lost. But we know that for the first several centuries of the Common Era, Apollonius of Tyana was one of the most celebrated and respected spiritual teachers of the Western world. During his lifetime, the Roman emperors Nerva and Titus counted themselves among his devotees.

Emperor Severus Alexander, who reigned from 222 to 235, considered Apollonius one of the greatest men in world history. And in 271 when Emperor Lucius Aurelian set out with an army to destroy the city of Tyana, Apollonius appeared to him in a vision and commanded him to show mercy.

Aurelian stopped the war.

A Hindu Goddess in Rome

There is another surprising connection between the Hindu tradition and ancient Rome.

When the Romans were fighting the Carthaginian Empire for control of the Mediterranean (and in the beginning, pretty much losing), they appealed for help from an oracle. It advised them to seek the aid of Magna Mater, a ferocious goddess who had been worshipped in Turkey since at least the eighth century B.C.E. So in 204 B.C.E., a Roman delegation was sent to Phrygia in Asia Minor to beg, borrow, or steal a sacred image of the goddess. After a considerable amount of wheeling and dealing, the image was finally brought back to Rome.

Now, Magna Mater knew the Romans didn't really have much confidence in her abilities, so just before the boat carrying her image was about to enter the city, she grounded it in the Tiber River. It was completely stuck—it absolutely wouldn't budge. It wasn't a good omen that the Goddess of Victory refused to enter Rome!

A priestess of the goddess, whose name was Claudia, was summoned to the scene. Tying her belt around the ship's prow, Claudia respectfully requested Magna Mater to enter Rome. The boat lurched forward instantly.

Shortly afterward, the Romans finally got the better of Hannibal and gleefully sacked the city of Carthage. Until Rome's conversion to Christianity, Magna Mater remained the presiding deity of Rome, divine protectress of the cradle of Western civilization.

The Great Mother

But who was Magna Mater? Her religion at one time extended all the way from Turkey to India. Three hundred feet up the north face of Mount Sipylus in Turkey travelers today can still find an ancient thirty-foot-high image of the goddess carved into solid rock. But in India, portraits of this same goddess riding her lion into battle are present everywhere. You'll find Durga posters hanging in people's homes. You'll even see her painted on truck boxes and lunch boxes.

Sages Say

"We take refuge in the Supreme Goddess Who appears through the concentration of mental attention. We bow to the Goddess Durga Who illumines the mind immersed in meditation, Who bestows the results of our actions, Who removes all difficulties. We bow to Her who clears the mind of thought, so that the light of pure spirit can shine through."

—Sri Devyatharvashirsham

Magna Mater, her Latin name, means "Great Mother," which is surprisingly reminiscent of her age-old titles in India: Sri Mata ("Great Mother") and Maha Devi ("Great Goddess"). In ancient Turkey, she was also called Truqas, which some scholars believe is related to her Indian name, Durga.

In ancient Turkey, a small number of her more zealous male devotees would castrate themselves in her honor, a practice which shocked the Romans—who didn't shock easily. Amazingly this unique way of propitiating the Great Mother survived in some areas of India until quite recently. (I'll have more to say about Durga in Chapter 13, "Meet the Hindu Goddesses!")

Hindu Gods Abroad

The worship of Magna Mater in Turkey leads to an important point. For the most part, we think of Hinduism as being confined to Greater India. However, the further we go back in time, the fuzzier the borders of Hindu culture become. That's because the north Indians, as I explained in Chapter 2, "Hindus in History," are related to many of the European peoples. When you understand this, it becomes less surprising that a goddess we unmistakably recognize as Hindu today was being worshipped in Turkey in the first millennium B.C.E.

In fact, a thousand years earlier, the Mitanni people of Turkey are known to have propitiated Indra, Mitra, Varuna, and the Ashvins—gods straight out of the Veda. Mitra, whose worship was already ancient in India in 4000 B.C.E., reincarnated as Mithras, one of the Persians' most important deities, and eventually found work as the patron deity of the Roman army!

Chinese Pilgrims Check It Out

Two other famous pilgrims to India whose accounts of their trips have survived were Chinese Buddhists. Faxian passed through India in the fourth century C.E. (keep in mind Indian dating at this point is speculative). Xuanzang made the 10,000-mile round trip journey three centuries later, following along the Silk Road trade route up through Kashmir and then down into north central India where Buddha had lived and taught.

Faxian marveled at the peace, prosperity, and high culture of the Hindus, though his primary focus was on the Buddhist sites he had come to see. Having grown up in China, war-torn through much of its history, Faxian was deeply impressed by a land whose leaders were more concerned with promoting commerce and religion than with slaughtering substantial portions of the population.

Faxian noted that it was possible to travel from one end of India to other without fear of crime and even without a passport! The culture was safe, stable, and deeply spiritual. By the time Xuanzang showed up, however, the effects of the Kali Yuga were setting in more firmly. (Remember the Kali era from Chapter 1, "Time for God," in which human behavior degenerates to its worst possible point?) He was robbed twice and almost murdered on another occasion!

Xuanzang spent several extended periods studying at Nalanda Buddhist University in Bihar. Buddhism was in serious decline in India by the mid-600s, but Xuanzang was still able to study Sanskrit, grammar, and logic as well as weighty Buddhist philosophical tomes.

About three thousand Buddhist monks and 150 faculty lived at the university, but non-Buddhist students were welcome, too. Hindu fields of study were included in the curriculum. You could learn the Vedas there or study Vedic mathematics and astronomy as well as the Hindu medical arts and Indian literature.

Ironically, the concentration of Buddhist talent at large centers like Nalanda was a major contributing reason to the fall of Buddhism in India. Hindu students usually studied in small groups in the homes of their teachers, while Buddhist students congregated at large centers like Nalanda. Serious Buddhist practices were carried out at the monasteries. Hindus performed their spiritual practices in their homes or in the woods or mountains.

Guidepost

Be careful not to mix up Hinduism and Buddhism! You should be aware that just as Christianity broke away from Judaism to become a completely distinct faith, the Buddhists broke off from the Hindu tradition. Buddhists do not accept the Hindu Veda as divine revelation and claim not to believe in an individual soul—though they do believe in reincarnation.

When the Muslims came to town around 1000 C.E., they simply burned down the Buddhist university-monasteries and killed all the monks. *Poof!*—Buddhism was gone. The only way the Muslims could have wiped out Hinduism was to burn down every Hindu home in the country. Not even the most fanatical Muslim invader was capable of that!

Al Biruni Takes Notes

Al Biruni was born in Khwarizm (today's Khiva in Uzbekistan) in 973 C.E. He was a brilliant astrologer and scholar who published books on optics, mineralogy, chemistry, mechanics, astronomy, mathematics, and the calendars and dating systems of many different cultures.

Khwarizm was raided by the Muslim despot Abu-Said Mahmud in 1017. Al Biruni was taken to India as one of Mahmud's reluctant human prizes, and lived there for 13 years.

Al Biruni despised Mahmud, who he complained wrecked northern India economically as well as killing Hindus "like specks of dust scattered every which way." He found a good use for his time, however, in purchasing all the Sanskrit manuscripts he could find and consulting endlessly with Indian pandits about Hindu science and spirituality.

The result was the *Indika,* Al Biruni's monumental study of Hindu culture and spirituality.

Notes on the Hindu God

Al Biruni was a good Muslim and was by no means always sympathetic to Hindu ideas or culture. He thought the Hindus' claim that the universe was billions of years old was ludicrous, and mocked their tendency to think in terms of incredibly long cosmic cycles. But he made a sincere effort to report Hindu beliefs objectively, so that Muslims interested in India could clearly understand the Hindu perspective.

In the *Indika*, Al Biruni described the Hindu view of God.

> There is one God only Who is without beginning or end. He cannot be reached by thought but is sublime beyond our ability to conceive. He is infinitely vast, but not in the spatial sense since He exists outside of time and space.

> How can we worship this one whom we cannot perceive? He lies beyond the grasp of the physical senses, but the soul feels His presence and the mind understands His divine qualities.

> Meditating on Him one-pointedly is true worship. When meditation is practiced for a long time without interruption, one attains the highest state of blissfulness.

It's News to Me!

In medieval South and Central Asia, being an astrologer was an honorable profession requiring substantial education and mathematical skill. A thousand years ago Al Biruni wrote a manual on Arabic astrology that holds up today as a superb work on both astrology and astronomy. It was written for a young Muslim girl named Rayhanah who wanted to learn about the stars but was not permitted to attend school. (Islamic schools were exclusively for boys in that era.)

Notes on Reincarnation

Al Biruni's description of the Hindu view of reincarnation is particularly interesting:

> Until it reaches the highest state of consciousness, the soul is not able to experience all things at once, as if there were no space or time. Therefore it has to experience the universe piecemeal, one thing at a time, until it has been through all possible experiences. An awfully lot of experiences are possible, so this process takes a very long time.

> So immortal souls range through the universe in mortal bodies, which have good or bad experiences depending on whether their behavior has been virtuous or evil. The purpose of experiencing heavenly states in the time between physical incarnations is so that the soul learns what is truly good, and wants to become as good as possible. The purpose of experiencing hellish states in the time between lives is so that the soul learns what evil is, and determines to avoid it all together.

The process of reincarnation begins at very low levels of consciousness, like minerals, plants or animals, and slowly winds its way upward toward very elevated states of awareness.

The process ends when the soul no longer desires to explore new worlds, but gains insight into the sublime nature of its own being, and rests content in itself. At that point the soul turns away from matter, and its links with physical existence are broken. It returns to its true home, carrying with it the knowledge it has gained during its many journeys.

Having closely studied all their systems, Al Biruni noted that the Greek, Indian, and Sufi mystics taught essentially the same doctrine.

Quick Quiz

1. Alexander the Great ...

    a. Was deeply impressed by the sages of India.

    b. Conquered the entire Indian subcontinent.

    c. Shaved his head, converted to Hinduism, and spent the last years of his life chanting "Hare Krishna."

2. Apollonius of Tyana ...

    a. Was the god of Sun in ancient Greece.

    b. Moved to New Delhi where he made a living franchising Tandori fast food outlets.

    c. Concluded that the Indian and Egyptian mystical traditions were related.

3. Faxian and Xuanzang ...

    a. Were legendary Taoist martial arts masters.

    b. Were two Chinese Buddhist pilgrims who visited India.

    c. Were star-crossed lovers torn apart by their feuding families.

4. Al Biruni ...

    a. Was a brilliant Muslim scholar living in India around the year 1000.

    b. Is a type of Arabic board game related to chess.

    c. Are the first two letters in the Arabic alphabet.

Answers: 1 (a). 2 (c). 3 (b). 4 (a).

Transcendentalists Groove on the Gita

As European powers gained more control of India in the late eighteenth century, Westerners had a similar response to Hinduism that Muslims had had. Hindus do not believe in forcing their beliefs on others, but both Muslims and Christians were determined to convert all India to their respective faiths. In the minds of sincere Christian missionaries, replacing Hinduism with the Judeo-Christian tradition was the greatest possible blessing they could bestow on India's heathen.

But some open-minded and sensitive Western artists and intellectuals had a very different response.

Emerson Meets the Bhagavad Gita

Ralph Waldo Emerson, a nineteenth-century Unitarian minister who lectured on theology at Harvard University, was becoming increasingly disillusioned with aspects of Christian teaching that just didn't make sense to his active and inquiring intelligence. When he first began reading newly translated Indian scriptures like the *Bhagavad Gita,* the Hindu tradition hit him with the force of revelation. He wrote:

> I owed a magnificent day to the *Bhagavad Gita.* It was the first of books, it was as if an empire spake to us, nothing small or unworthy, but large, serene, consistent, the voice of an old intelligence which in another age and climate had pondered and thus disposed of the same questions that exercise us.

In part due to the mind-expanding influence of mystical Hinduism, Emerson went on to found the Transcendentalist movement in America. The Transcendentalists turned from unquestioning faith in the religious doctrines of their own culture to a more open and honest inquiry into direct spiritual experience.

Thoreau Joins the Club

Emerson excitedly introduced other Americans to Hinduism, perhaps most notably his young protégé, Henry David Thoreau. Thoreau was not busy earning a living or raising a family like Emerson. Instead he was living in the woods outside Concord, composing some of the greatest classics of American literature, such as *Walden.* And reading the *Bhagavad Gita.*

"What extracts from the Veda I have read fall on me like the light of a higher and purer luminary, which describes a loftier course through a purer stratum," Thoreau wrote enthusiastically.

Sages Say

"Standing on the bare ground,— my head bathed by the blithe air, and uplifted into infinite space,—all mean egotism vanishes. I become a transparent eyeball; I am nothing; I see all; the currents of the Universal Being circulate through me; I am part or particle of God."

—Ralph Waldo Emerson

In the morning I bathe my intellect in the stupendous and cosmogonal philosophy of the Bhagavad Gita, since whose composition, years of the gods have elapsed and in comparison with which our modern world and its literature seem puny and trivial.

If Hinduism influenced Thoreau, he certainly returned the favor! Thoreau's great essay, "On Civil Disobedience," had a profound effect on a Hindu born a century later. Mahatma Gandhi acknowledged Thoreau as a major inspiration for the movement he founded calling for nonviolent resistance to British rule in India.

The Least You Need to Know

➤ Alexander the Great's encounter with a yogi became legendary.

➤ Apollonius of Tyana brought back from India fabulous stories of the Hindu sages' wisdom and supernatural abilities.

➤ Chinese pilgrims visited India to observe Buddhism and Hinduism there first-hand.

➤ The Muslim scholar Al Biruni wrote extensively on Hindu beliefs.

➤ The American Transcendentalists were greatly inspired by Hindu scripture.

Chapter 4

Matrix of the Hindu Tradition

In This Chapter

➤ Hinduism's Holy Bible

➤ The enlightened sages of India

➤ A ritual text for fire sacrifices

➤ Gods as interlinking divine forces

➤ The quintessence of Hindu thought

Hinduism is a living lineage of enlightenment. It is very much an oral tradition, passed on from the spiritual teacher to the disciple, from the mother to the child. The Veda, the Bible of Hinduism, was transmitted by word of mouth for thousands of years before finally being committed to writing.

But once the Hindus did start writing down their holy scriptures, well, they just never stopped. All the sacred texts of the other great world religions put together would be scarcely a drop in the bucket of the immensity of Hindu sacred literature.

Veda: The Hindu Bible

The Veda is the massive holy book of Hinduism. It has existed from before the beginning of time. It was carefully preserved by Brahma, the creator god, during the dissolution of the last universe, and then given to humanity once again when the world was recreated.

Hindus do not believe the Veda was written by a group of authors. Rather, the great sages of antiquity "heard" the verses of the Veda in deep states of meditation (today we might say they "channeled" them) and passed them along to other brahmins, the priests who have been the custodians of the Veda from time immemorial.

Other authorities, such as the great yogi Patanjali, had a slightly different perspective. Patanjali said it was not the words of the Veda that were eternal but the wisdom contained in them.

Either way, because the Veda was so holy, it was imperative that it be preserved exactly as it was first given out by the original sages. Therefore, to this day brahmin priests memorize the Veda backward and forward, then backward and forward again but this time skipping every other word, and then backward and forward in various other combinations.

They also used other memorization techniques, such as chanting the Veda to particular rhythms and moving their hands according to prescribed rules as the rhythm changed. Brahmins from different villages would meet regularly to check each others' mastery of the text. These methods helped to ensure that when we hear the verses being chanted today, they are almost certainly still being pronounced exactly like they were thousands of years ago, with not one word or even one syllable lost due to the passage of time.

It's News to Me!

Vyasa, who compiled the four Vedas into their current format, is also credited with writing the *Mahabharata,* a book four times the length of the Christian Bible, and the 18 Puranas, many of which are over four hundred pages long. Cooler heads believe that although there probably was an original Vyasa involved in collecting the Vedas, his name was later applied to other men and women who authored or edited voluminous sacred texts.

What's in the Veda?

The Veda is actually four different books, which is why you'll often hear it called "the Vedas," plural. They are in a language called Vedic, an archaic form of Sanskrit.

Though the Vedic hymns had been known for a long, long time, they were finally compiled into one large edition by the great sage Vyasa sometime before 1500 B.C.E. He then organized the Veda into the four books.

The most important of these is the *Rig Veda,* a collection of 1,017 hymns to a wide assortment of gods, arranged in ten sections. The *Sama Veda* is mostly a selection of hymns taken straight from the *Rig Veda.* The big difference is that the *Sama Veda* is specially notated with melodies so that rather than just chanting these hymns, you can sing them.

The *Yajur Veda* hymns are used specifically for certain types of sacrifices, not just for singing or chanting.

The *Atharva Veda* is in some ways the most practical of all the Vedas. It contains hymns for a variety of useful purposes including attracting lovers, subduing enemies, regulating the weather, and curing diseases, such as urinary tract infections!

Vedic Appendices

There are three very special compendiums of texts that are considered part of the Veda but consist of discussions and explanatory material rather than hymns.

The *Brahmanas* are a huge mass of writings that explain how to perform various Vedic rituals. They throw in a few good myths for added color. The *Aranyakas* and *Upanishads* are philosophy texts that discuss the inner significance of the Vedic rites. (The *Upanishads* are so important I've dealt with them in a separate section, "*Upanishads:* Liberating Literature," later in this chapter.)

Who Were the Vedic Sages?

The sages who composed the Vedas, capturing eternal truths and shaping them into beautiful hymns, are called *rishis,* which means "seers." A rishi is someone who sees the divine reality for himself or herself. These sages are not content to rely on the testimony of others but have gained direct personal experience of divinity.

Hinduism acknowledges that seers come in different flavors. There are advanced seers who see everything. There are beginning level seers, too—great souls for sure, but they have only just begun to glimpse the full majesty of the Supreme Reality. Here is how V. Madhusudan Reddy, a disciple of the twentieth-century sage Sri Aurobindo, outlines them, based on ancient traditions.

1. *Deva rishis* means god-like seers. These sages' level of consciousness is beyond human imagination. Their awareness extends to all worlds and throughout the past and the future. These great beings live in a much higher plane of reality than ours, but when they will to do so, they can enter our world. To us they're practically like gods. The sage Narada is an example. During various crises in India's history he would materialize to advise just the right people at just the right place in order to tweak the course of events back toward the underlying divine plan.

2. *Brahma rishis* means god-realized seers. These are fully enlightened men and women who exist here on earth in physical bodies. They could move into higher worlds if they wanted

New Word Alert!

Rishi means seer. The Vedic seers were saints and sages of the highest caliber.

to but remain here to serve humanity. Babaji, the eighteenth-century Kriya Yoga master who initiated the famous Hindu saint Lahiri Mahasaya, belonged in this category. So did Bengali Baba, the twentieth-century adept who was known for transferring his consciousness from one body to another.

3. *Raja rishis* are "royal seers"—those who have gained mastery in both the physical and the spiritual worlds. The legendary King Janaka, who successfully governed the prosperous and cultured kingdom of Videha while remaining in a continuous state of divine awareness, is a famous example.

4. *Maha rishis* are "great seers" who may not be fully enlightened like the Brahma rishis, but they have a deep and authentic understanding of the divine, and work tirelessly to help raise humanity to higher levels of consciousness. Mahatma Gandhi belonged to this group.

5. *Parama rishis* are "advanced adepts" who are well along the road to enlightenment but have not yet completely purified their minds. The seer Daksha is a case in point. He was such a great saint that the Divine Mother agreed to be born as his daughter. But while he sincerely honored the god of his own tradition, he held the god of another tradition in contempt. This wound up completely undermining his spiritual life.

6. *Shruta rishis* means "learned seers"—those souls who have grasped the truths at the core of their spiritual tradition, and are now working hard to translate that knowledge into living experience.

7. *Kanda rishis* are "striving seers"—the beginners on the path who don't have much technical knowledge about spirituality, yet feel a complete commitment to spiritual life and a burning desire for spiritual truth. They make their best effort to live ethically, discipline themselves, and raise their level of awareness.

The men and women who "channeled" the wisdom inherent in the Vedic hymns thousands of years ago were only able to do so because of their advanced stage of spiritual development. Hindus universally hail them as Brahma rishis, seers of the highest order possible for mortal beings.

Who Reads the Veda?

Not everyone benefited from the Veda. Because the priests considered these hymns so holy, they were very careful about who was allowed access to them. Only members of the three top classes of Indian society were permitted to hear the four Vedas and participate in Vedic sacrifices. Over the centuries, women's access to the Vedas, even if they were high class, became increasingly limited. This is rather ironic since numbers of the Vedic hymns were composed by women!

Today the four Vedas have been translated into many different languages and just about anyone who wants to read them can. However, reading them and understanding them are two different projects. Vedic knowledge remains an oral, initiatory tradition. Without a guru to lead you through the complex symbolism and hidden mystical underpinnings, frankly quite a few of the hymns don't make a lot of sense.

Still, the Vedas are so important in the Hindu tradition, even after 6,000+ years, that the word Vedic is often used as a synonym for anything Hindu, as in "Vedic literature" or "Vedic science."

How Is the Veda Used?

If you qualified for their help by being a member of an upper class and you had a problem or wanted to express your gratitude to a particular deity, you could go to a Vedic priest who would perform a fire ritual for you, chanting the appropriate sacred hymns.

In olden times, the fire rituals often involved blood sacrifices. Animals like goats were commonly sacrificed; on rarer occasions other creatures, such as a horse, might be offered.

Most Hindus abandoned animal sacrifice many centuries ago. Today priests offer objects such as flowers, grains, clarified butter, fragrant-smelling wood, and herbs into the sacred fire. The Vedic fire rituals are no longer practiced as widely as they used to be, but at certain major life events, like marriage, brahmin priests are called in, the ritual fire is lit, and once again the ancient mantras are chanted exactly as they have been at Hindu weddings for at least six thousand years.

Incidentally, I've attended numerous Vedic rituals and seen their effects for myself. It's not unusual following one of these ceremonies for fantastically unlikely events to occur. The individual asking for financial help immediately receives a lucrative job offer right out of the blue. Cancerous tumors go into remission. Business suddenly starts to boom after a several-year slump. We in the West are trained to call these events coincidences. I have to admit I've seen some of the best-timed coincidences in the world right after a traditional Vedic fire offering is performed!

For the Western scientific mind, consciousness is rooted in matter. For the brahmin priest performing the fire ceremony, though, matter is rooted in consciousness. Therefore, according to the Hindu

Guidepost

Today many of us are shocked and disgusted to hear people in ancient cultures used to sacrifice animals. We forget that the animals were killed humanely, their spirits blessed with holy mantras, and their flesh eaten as a source of protein. Was this worse than what goes on in our modern-day slaughterhouses? These days, however, animal sacrifice has been largely abandoned in India, and many Hindus are vegetarian.

laws of physics, if the brahmin sends out a message into the cosmic mind, "Kumar Sharma needs work!" it's not surprising to him when a job offer immediately materializes. It's par for the course.

Who Are the Vedic Gods?

Very few Hindus worship the gods mentioned in the Veda anymore. These deities go back to an era so incredibly long ago, they've gradually been replaced by other more popular gods who've shown up over the years. Still, reading the hymns to these gods provides important insights into the spirituality of the ancient Indo-Europeans, the ancestors of many of us Western peoples.

These are some of the most important gods and goddesses of the Veda:

➤ Indra, heroic slayer of the demon Vritra

➤ Agni, the sacred fire, messenger between humans and gods

➤ Varuna, the ocean of heaven, the night sky

➤ Mitra, the all-seeing sun, the daytime sky

➤ Savitar, the sun, source of life

➤ Ashvins, twin gods of healing

➤ Ushas, goddess of the dawn

➤ Sarasvati, a river goddess and the source of intelligence

➤ Aditi, cosmic space and Mother Earth

➤ Rudra, a fearsome deity who brings destruction and misfortune

Sages Say

"O Indra, if a hundred skies and a hundred earths gave forth their light—no, even if a thousand suns should shine, they couldn't match your stunning radiance, lord of thunder!"

—*Rig Veda* 8:59.5

About one fourth of the hymns in the *Rig Veda* go to Indra, with Agni running a close second in terms of popularity.

You'd be mistaken to think of these gods as a pantheon like the hierarchy of deities we're familiar with from Greek and Roman mythology. In the Vedas, the gods are surprisingly indistinct, blending easily into one another. Indra and Agni even become Indragni, two gods in one! Savitar is hailed as the sun god, but so is Mitra, and so is Agni and Vishnu and Surya and Bhaga and Pushan, and so on.

What's going on? Here it's important to remember again that Hindus live in a different conceptual universe than Westerners. These gods aren't colorful personalities running around having affairs like the Greco-Roman deities. They're personifications of natural forces, which are considered actual fields of intelligence in Hindu cosmology. They work in a unified manner, integrating their functions, and dissolving their identities in each other just as clouds lose themselves in rain and rain loses itself in the earth and sea.

Many Westerners and most Muslims are raised with the firm understanding that there is one God (theirs) and every other deity is a false god. Hindu belief is exactly the opposite. The Veda consistently portrays all the different gods as ultimately just different faces of the one Supreme Being. They are the various ways Its will acts in nature. As the late sage Sri Aurobindo put it, it is the "one central idea of the Vedic religion, the idea of the One Being with the [gods] expressing in numerous names and forms the many-sidedness of His unity."

This is why Al Biruni, living in India at the beginning of the second millennium and surrounded by temples to dozens of different Hindu deities, could honestly report to his fellow Muslims that the Hindus believe in only one God.

Guidepost

The modern democratic nation-state of India was born at midnight on the morning of August 15, 1947. When writers—including yours truly—refer to India before 1947, we're talking about the entire area in and around the Indian subcontinent that was dominated by Hindu culture. This is a much wider geographic area than India's present borders.

Sampling the Veda

Let's take a tiny taste of this enormous literature, sampling portions of some of the Vedic hymns. Here are several verses from a typical hymn to Indra the dragon slayer:

> I will tell you the brave deeds of Indra, lord of thunder!
> He killed the dragon, He made the waters flow,
> He broke open the mountain.
> Indra is the lord of all things living and inanimate,
> of all creatures wild and tame.
> He commands the thunderbolt.
> Indra is the supreme ruler!
> He contains all beings like spokes in a felly.
> —*Rig Veda* 1:32.1,15

The sophisticated understanding of the rishis is evident in many of the hymns, such as the following:

> He to whom the priests sacrifice, what do they know of Him?
> Though set burning in many different fire pits,
> Agni, lord of fire, is only one.

Though His light extends in every direction, Surya, the sun, is only one.
That one Being has become all this. All this is only one.
—*Rig Veda* 8:10.1-2

They call Him Indra, Mitra, Varuna, Agni.
They call Him Garutman.
They call Him Yama and Matarishvan.
There is one God; He is known by many names.
—*Rig Veda* 1:164.46

Many portions of the Veda are extremely mystical. The following hymn was related by the seer Ambrini. In it she celebrates the goddess Vach, Queen of the Universe, with whom she mystically identifies. This is one of the most ancient surviving accounts of the experience of cosmic consciousness.

It's News to Me!

A story about the Vedic god Indra appears in the Bible in disguise! Ancient Indo-Europeans (such as the early Hindus) and ancient Semitic peoples shared many myths. Just as Indra was called on to kill the monster of the cosmic sea, in Assyrian and Babylonian mythology, Marduk had to slay Tiamat. The job eventually passed to Yahweh (see Isaiah 27:1) when the Jews incorporated some of the older Semitic myths into their tradition. If the new dating scholars have suggested for the *Rig Veda* (4000–3500 B.C.E.) holds up, the oldest known version of the story is Hindu.

I move with the winds and the destructive powers,
with the sectors of the sky and with all the gods I travel.

I hold up the day sky and the night sky,
the Sun, the constellations, the planets.

I love and hold high the Moon and the Sun in their many courses.

I shower wealth on those who honor the gods with holy rites.

I am the Queen, dispenser of treasure, the source of thought,
most worthy of those who deserve to be worshipped!

I am established everywhere, I abide in many places.

Your breath, your speech, all your actions are performed
through My power alone. I am the force of movement and will.

I celebrate Myself, the splendor of My power!

I make those who love Me great, I give them divine knowledge.

Destruction I bestow on the ungrateful.

I pervade heaven and earth! From the
    summit of the world
I gave birth to the Creator!

I dwell in the sea, My forehead grazes the sky.

I breathe in all living beings—
My breath is the life of the worlds!

Beyond the earth, beyond the sky, My
    majesty is infinite!

—*Rig Veda* 10:125

It's News to Me!

The word *veda* literally means
"knowledge." It is related to the
English words wisdom, wit, and
even witch! (Witch didn't use to
mean a scary lady. It used to
mean a wise woman.)

The Inner Veda

Beginning with Sri Aurobindo, the twentieth-century "sage of Pondicherry," there has
been an effort by Hindu researchers to reconnect with the original mystical significance of the Veda. Many of the Western scholars who initially looked into the Veda
had dismissed it as primitive nature worship. Aurobindo looked a little deeper and in
Indra, for example, found not a mere weather deity but a king of heaven who "symbolizes the Power of Mind and especially the divine or self-luminous Mind in the
human being."

Aurobindo was probably on the right track. From remote antiquity, the first singers of
the Veda were known as Brahma rishis, the highest human type of meditation adepts.
That advanced meditation masters just sat around making up chants about how
pretty the dawn is and how refreshing the rain feels seems quite unlikely.

Over and over the Veda retells the story of how Indra smashed the mountain with his
thunderbolt, loosening the waters. Yogis often note that the Sanskrit word for the
senses is *indriya*. To them, Indra is therefore "the lord of the senses," a master of the
body and mind. The thunderbolt he controls is the *kundalini*, psycho-physical energy
which yogis learn to draw up the spine into the brain, sparking a genuine mystical
experience.

In Hindu mysticism to this day, a mountain represents the spine because meditators
are supposed to sit as quietly and solidly as a mountain. In heightened states of consciousness, yogis experience the *dharma megha*, the rain cloud of divine knowledge,
which when it begins to pour, fills the mind with wisdom and bliss. Indra is therefore
a yogi who has mastered the kundalini and contacted the life-giving waters of living
spiritual awareness in deep states of meditation.

A Road Map to Higher Consciousness

With this understanding, the Veda becomes not just a collection of nature hymns but a map to higher consciousness. A yogi from Dehra Dun told me, "If you don't understand a Vedic myth on at least seven different levels, you don't understand the myth." Remember, everything in Indian spirituality is multidimensional.

Those who are privy to the jealously guarded oral tradition learn about many levels of meaning compacted into the Veda much like data compression in computer technology, where a small number of variables are configured so that they can contain a massive amount of information. There is the ritual significance of the Vedic verses, and there's another level of meaning corresponding to the intelligent energies inherent in nature. There's an astronomical level keying different deities to various planets and constellations. There's the psychological level of interpretation: Indra fighting the dragon is each one of us grappling with our own inner monsters. Then there's the yogic interpretation having to do with vectors of awareness moving through the subtle body.

Recently, several Hindu scholars have made some fascinating suggestions about yet more information encoded in the Veda. It seemed like overkill to these researchers that the Vedic rishis made such a point of ensuring that the hymns would be reproduced exactly correctly for millennia to come. It now appears that certain mathematical, geometric, and astronomical information essential to the ancient Hindus' concept of sacred space was encoded in the very rhythm, meter, and pronunciation of the verses! The evidence for this hypothesis is surprisingly strong.

If this seems unlikely to you, remember that much of the Indian population has been illiterate for most of India's history, and using mnemonic devices, such as rhythmic chants, which are easy to remember, would be an excellent way to preserve technical information in the absence of writing.

Upanishads: Liberating Literature

The German philosopher Arthur Schopenhauer once said, "The study of the *Upanishads* has been the solace of my life. It will be the solace of my death."

The *Upanishads* are the philosophical portion of the Veda, written as prose rather than in the form of hymns. While many authorities count 108 of them, eleven are most important. These are the *Aitareya, Mandukya, Brihadaranyaka, Mundaka, Chhandogya, Prashna, Isha, Shvetashvatara, Katha, Taittiriya,* and *Kena Upanishads.*

Quick Quiz

1. The Veda is ...

   a. The holiest book of the Hindus.

   b. A line of expensive hair care products.

   c. The bad guy in the *Star Wars* trilogy.

2. The Vedic god Indra is ...

   a. The god India is named after.

   b. Famous for destroying a serpent demon.

   c. Originally from Sunnyvale, California.

3. Today the offerings usually made at Vedic fire sacrifices include ...

   a. Flowers, grain, clarified butter, herbs and fragrant woods.

   b. Horses and goats.

   c. Screaming virgins.

Answers: 1 (a). 2 (b). 3 (a).

The Something in Nothing

Here is a story from the *Chhandogya Upanishad.*

After years away at school, Shvetaketu returned home to his father, Uddalaka. Uddalaka could tell from Shvetaketu's boasting about how much he'd learned that he hadn't learned anything at all. Or at least nothing really worth knowing.

"Did your teacher teach you how to hear that which can't be heard or know what can't be known?" Uddalaka asked.

"Oh-oh. That wasn't in the curriculum."

"Go outside and get me a fruit from the banyan tree." Shvetaketu ran outside for the fruit.

"Now cut it in half," his father instructed. "What do you see?"

"I see the seeds, dad."

"Cut one of those in half." This wasn't easy—banyan seeds are extremely small. Finally Shvetaketu managed to slice one evenly. "What do you see?" Uddalaka asked.

The boy was baffled. "What do you mean, dad? There's nothing there."

Uddalaka looked his son in the eye. "From that 'nothing' an enormous tree arises. When you understand what that 'nothing' is, you will understand yourself. The nothing you can't see is the very essence of the reality of the tree. The unperceivable essence of being is also what you are. You are that, Shvetaketu."

"Pour some salt into this bucket of water," Uddalaka continued. Shvetaketu obeyed. "Now give me the salt back."

"I can't do that!" Shvetaketu objected. "It's gone!"

"Take a sip of the water. You taste the salt, don't you? You couldn't see it, yet it was there all along. Just as the salt pervades the water, so the subtle essence of reality pervades your body. That subtle essence is true being. You are that, Shvetaketu."

Uddalaka is talking about the intelligence inherent in nature—innate in us, too—an all-pervading living presence underlying everything. This story is typical of the way the *Upanishads* teach.

Lighting the Way

If the Vedic hymns represent the heart's response to the divine, the *Upanishads* represent the intellect's attempt to plumb the depths of the spirit. These texts are not naive about the mind's ability to encompass the infinite. "Into a blind darkness enter those devoted to ignorance, but into an even greater darkness enter those devoted to knowledge," admits the *Isha Upanishad*. Too often intellectuals are like the blind leading the blind, caught in the web of words and mental constructs.

The purpose of the *Upanishads* is not to give you enlightenment. Words can't do that. Their purpose is to light your way, helping you discriminate between experiences that have only passing value and the living knowledge of divine being which is the supreme and everlasting value.

Sages Say

"The wise man sees himself in all beings and all beings in himself. Therefore he never feels hostility toward anyone."

—*Isha Upanishad*

It's News to Me!

The word *Upanishad* means "sitting near." It conjures up the image of a disciple sitting near the guru, listening intently.

Vedic rituals have two purposes: to help us obtain the things we need and want in life, and to propel us toward heavenly states after death. The Upanishadic seers noted that worldly success and enjoyment never last very long. Also, no matter how exalted the soul's condition might be in heaven, eventually the cosmic wheel will turn again, the soul's good karma which carried it to heaven will run out, and the soul will find itself back in the physical world, starting from scratch.

There had to be a way off the wheel, a way to happiness that never ends, ever. The *Upanishads* taught a way of wisdom that steers away from the seeming truths presented to us by our senses, toward the unchanging, self-luminous world of consciousness itself.

We'll return to the *Upanishads* in Chapter 22, "The Razor in the Mind," when we explore how the Hindu tradition employs the intellect to get the job of spiritual illumination done pronto. We'll see how we can actually experience the Upanishadic truth, "You are that."

The Least You Need to Know

➤ For millennia, Hinduism's sacred knowledge was preserved in its oral tradition.

➤ The Vedic hymns were composed by enlightened seers.

➤ The primary use of the Vedic hymns is to sanctify religious rituals.

➤ The Vedic gods were not discrete entities but names for different facets of the one God.

➤ The *Upanishads* preserve the highest philosophical thought of the ancient Hindu sages.

The People's Religion

The Veda is India's most sacred book, but almost no one reads it anymore. It was reserved for the exclusive use of certain classes of society, so many people never had access to it anyway.

Besides, the Veda is very, very long. Most people shy away from reading such a thick book, just as most Christians believe in the Bible but hesitate to sit down and actually try reading a book that's way over 1,000 pages. Plus, the style of Sanskrit in which the Veda is written is now so extremely ancient that even people who're top authorities on Hinduism have trouble understanding all of it!

User-Friendly Scriptures

Fortunately, Hinduism has many other fully authorized scriptures which are open to the public and easy and fun to read. Like the Veda they were originally passed on through the generations by word of mouth. There were people whose job it was to memorize these huge texts and then travel around reciting them. When they showed up in a village, everyone would come running. Work was called off and folks would sit for days listening to the expert chant the scripture. It was like going to the movies, except you imagined the scenes on the screen of your mind.

Epics: The Hindu Homer

Move over Homer! Homer's *Iliad* and *Odyssey* are often considered the greatest epics in the Western world. Homer has serious competition in India, however, where the great Hindu epics, the *Mahabharata* and *Ramayana,* have stirred hearts and exalted the spirit for thousands of years.

Does size matter? The *Ramayana* is as big as the Bible. The *Mahabharata* is four times the size of the Bible and eight times as long as the *Iliad* and the *Odyssey* put together!

The *Mahabharata* contains so much material its author couldn't resist a little bragging. "If it's anywhere else, it's here too," he said. "And if it ain't here, it ain't nowhere else neither!"

No, size doesn't really matter; it's the content that counts. If you're wondering about the quality of the content, consider this. When television producers ran a series of hour-long episodes dramatizing these two epics on Indian TV in the 1980s, the entire country shut down! For the hour the program was being broadcast you couldn't get a taxi, you couldn't get a meal in a restaurant, you couldn't find an open shop, your airline pilot wouldn't even take off. Every Hindu in the country had somehow, somewhere, found a TV and was sitting transfixed, watching the great sagas of Hinduism gamely portrayed on the small screen.

Both epics have been around since least 700 B.C.E. but not in their present form. The original texts were undoubtedly much shorter, but they were so popular that succeeding generations kept tacking on more and more of their own contributions. Like a snowball rolling down a snowy hill, by the time the two epics had careened down the hill of history, they'd grown to glacier size. You practically need a shopping cart to carry around all the volumes of the *Mahabharata,* much less the *Ramayana*!

Sages Say

"Ancient India, like ancient Greece, boasts of two great Epics. One of them, the *Mahabharata,* relates to a great war in which all the warlike races of Northern India took a share, and may therefore be compared to the *Iliad.* The other, the *Ramayana,* relates mainly to the adventures of its hero, banished from his country and wandering for long years in the wilderness of Southern India, and may therefore be compared to the *Odyssey.*"

—Romesh C. Dutta

Ramayana: **The Great Rescue**

Valmiki was a thief who plied his trade in northern India many a century ago. After a string of unsuccessful robberies, he was getting so desperate that he actually tried robbing a *sadhu,* a Hindu holy man. Now sadhus own absolutely nothing but the cloth they have wrapped around their private parts. "I don't have anything to give you," the holy man said.

"Give me something or I'll kill you!" Valmiki cried in desperation.

"Okay, okay, how about this? I'll give you a mantra that will make you the richest man in the world. But it will only work if you repeat it constantly, day in and day out."

Valmiki knew that sadhus don't lie. Because they've devoted their lives to God, they would rather die than tell an untruth. So he trusted the sadhu completely. "What's the mantra?"

"Mara," the holy man answered.

An Evil Mantra

This set well with Valmiki. Mara is the Sanskrit word for evil, and it fit his disposition. So, crazed with desire for wealth, Valmiki sat down and started chanting the mantra over and over, day and night. "Mara, Mara, Mara."

As he sat there, Valmiki's heart began to feel lighter. Tremendous peace filled his mind, and he experienced real joy for the first time in many, many years. Then he realized with a shock that the sadhu, in having him chant "Mara, Mara," had tricked him into chanting "Rama, Rama" as the syllables ran together. Rama, of course, is the name of God. While Valmiki had been sitting there lusting for gold, the divine vibrations of God's name had been purifying his mind.

Valmiki had become the wealthiest man in the world. He now had the most valuable thing a person could possibly possess: the living presence of God in his heart.

Guidepost

The chanting of mantras is an excellent way to cleanse and focus the mind. Since mantras can have dramatic effects both subtle and profound, it's not necessarily a good idea to just pick one out of a book and try practicing it. It's better to be initiated in a mantra by an authorized teacher of a spiritual lineage, who is well versed in a mantra's effects.

Sages Say

"Keep the name of Rama always in your mind, remembering it with love. It will feed you when you're hungry, be your friend when you're alone, bless you when you feel cursed, and protect you when you're abandoned. To the crippled it's another limb. To the blind it's another eye. To the orphaned it's a loving parent. Whenever I remember Rama's name, the desert of my heart blooms lush and green."

—Tulsi Das

Valmiki gave up his evil ways and went on to become India's most famous poet. He composed the *Ramayana,* the story of how Rama, Hinduism's perfect son, husband, and king, rescued his wife, Sita, from the evil king of Lanka.

The Perfect Son

Long, long ago, the *Ramayana* goes, the king of Ayodhya had a very special son named Rama. He was intelligent, courageous, compassionate, and virtuous. The people of Ayodhya adored the prince and his lovely wife, Sita. More than once Rama demonstrated both his wisdom in guiding them and his valor in protecting them.

Finally the happy day arrived when the old king decided to retire and hand over the reins of the kingdom to his beloved oldest son. But something's always got to go wrong or there's no story, right? The youngest of the king's three wives decided she wanted *her* son to rule instead.

The youngest wife was able to pull off a coup because many years earlier the king had promised her any two wishes she desired. Now she went to the king and demanded that her son, not Rama, receive the coronation. Rama must be banished into the forest for fourteen years. She knew she couldn't get away with killing Rama, but she figured if he was gone long enough the people would forget him. Life in the forest in those days was extremely dangerous, what with the lions and tigers and bears. Perhaps she was hoping Rama would get eaten by some large, furry, carnivorous animal.

When Rama heard the news, he immediately prepared to leave for the forest, without complaining or losing his composure. He was not just being a goody-goody. Rama understood that people look to their leaders for examples of how to live. Long ago, his father had made a promise to his youngest wife, and if he broke it now, it would signal to the people that keeping your word was not important. Kings must keep their promises even if it causes them grief.

It's News to Me!

In the sixteenth century, the beloved Hindu poet Tulsi Das composed a new, Hindi version of the *Ramayana* called the *Rama Charita Manasa.* An updated version was necessary because most people could no longer understand Sanskrit, the language of the original poem. Mahatma Gandhi considered the *Rama Charita Manasa* the single greatest book in the world.

The Perfect Husband

Sita insisted on accompanying her husband into the forest. They roamed through the woods for many happy years, together with Rama's devoted half-brother, Lakshman. Their numerous adventures, some harrowing, others hysterically funny, are lovingly described in the *Ramayana.*

Rama is very protective of Sita, whom he adores, and Sita is completely devoted to Rama. To this day, Rama and Sita are held up as the best possible example of a loving Hindu marriage.

But something's always got to go wrong. Tragedy strikes again. Rama and Lakshman are lured away from their campsite and when they return, Sita has vanished into thin air!

The bulk of the *Ramayana* is about Rama's desperate search for his missing wife, and the amazingly daring rescue when he finally finds her. It turns out that she was kidnapped by the tyrannical king of Lanka (that's today's Sri Lanka). I'll tell you more about how Rama gets Sita back in Chapter 14, "Avatars: Gods in Human Form."

The Perfect King

After fourteen years, Rama, Sita, and Lakshman return in triumph to Ayodhya, and to the people's infinite delight, Rama assumes his rightful role as king. To this very day, the expression "the reign of Rama" is used to mean an ideal government. During "the reign of Rama" the king ruled with complete integrity and absolute commitment to the welfare of his beloved subjects. It was a time of peace, prosperity, justice, and joy. This is something of a contrast with government in India today, which may be why Indians speak of "the reign of Rama" with such nostalgia!

Mahabharata: The Great War

The *Mahabharata* is attributed to the sage Vyasa, who also appears as a character in the story. (This is the same Vyasa we met in Chapter 4, "Matrix of the Hindu Tradition," who compiled the hymns of the ancient seers, shaping the Veda into its present format.) The *Mahabharata* is based on a war that probably really happened, perhaps around 1500 B.C.E. It was fought at a battlefield called Kurukshetra, which isn't too far from present-day New Delhi.

If the account given in the *Mahabharata* is literally accurate—okay, that's a big if—it wouldn't be much of an exaggeration to call this the real First World War. The story goes that the Indian warriors involved called in help from all their allies, all the

New Word Alert!

A **sadhu** is a man who has renounced the material world and wanders from place to place without any possessions, immersed in meditation and spiritual practice. (Sadhvi is the term for a woman renunciate.)

Mara means evil.

It's News to Me!

When did the *Mahabharata* war actually happen? Favorite guesses among Indian pandits are around 3200 B.C.E. or around 1500 B.C.E. Given that according to the *Mahabharata*, shortly after the war there was some kind of cataclysm and the city of Dvaraka sank into the sea, and given that a few years ago undersea divers located the sunken city off the coast of present day Dvaraka, and that items carbon dated from the lost city appear to be from 1500 B.C.E., the second of the two dates seems to have been vindicated.

way from Turkey in the west to Java in the east. That's pretty outrageous, but not as outrageous as it seems at first.

Remember that India was a major world trade center going back to Sumerian times at the least, and the area around Delhi would have been an important trade capital for international merchants. So there may well have been plenty of foreign leaders with a vested interest in who won the war.

So is this a holy text or a war story? The *Mahabharata* is considered a scripture because it illustrates in dramatic form how good Hindus should live. The characters are constantly facing tough moral issues and having to make difficult choices. This gives their spiritual mentors an opportunity to advise them about Hindu ethics and spirituality, sometimes for a hundred pages at a stretch! Then we learn from the wise or foolish decisions of the main characters and the consequences of their actions, what happens when people choose to follow *dharma* (righteousness) or *adharma* (unrighteousness).

New Word Alert!

Dharma is the best possible course, righteousness, the fulfillment of one's true purpose, virtue.

Adharma means behaving unethically, unrighteous action.

Feuding Cousins

The *Mahabharata* is brimming with entertaining and enlightening tales about many different sets of characters. But the main storyline is about two sets of brothers, who are each others's cousins. The five Pandavas—these are the good guys. And the 100 Kauravas—these are the bad guys.

The Pandavas are raised in the forest, where they learn virtue and respect. Their cousins the Kauravas are raised at court where they become cynical and corrupt. If you're wondering how there could be a hundred Kaurava brothers it's because, according to the *Mahabharata,* the Hindus had developed cloning by 1500 B.C.E.! According to the story, when the Kauravas' mother miscarried, a yogi placed the fetus in a pot filled with nutrients. Later he separated it into a hundred healthy baby boys!

The eldest of the good Pandava brothers, Yudhisthira, is supposed to become the next king when he comes of age. But the acting king's eldest son, the oldest of the bad 100 Kauravas, feels *he* ought to be the next king because his dad has been the de facto ruler since the legal king—Yudhisthira's dad—died years ago.

So when Yudhisthira comes of age, his scheming cousin, whose name is Duryodhana, refuses to relinquish the throne. In fact, he experiments with various schemes to get rid of Yudhisthira and his four brothers once and for all. For example, he builds a super-flammable house, invites them to move into it, and then sets it on fire with them inside. Fortunately, his nefarious plans fail. (If you think this plot line is complicated, believe me, you don't know the half of it!)

After numerous attempts to resolve the dispute peacefully, Yudhisthira regretfully realizes the only way he can assume his rightful role as king is to go to war with Duryodhana. This is an extremely painful choice because it means having to fight, and maybe kill, many people he sincerely loves, like former teachers and some of his own relatives. But at this point, it's becoming clearer how truly evil Duryodhana is and that somebody's got to stop him.

Picking Sides

The Pandavas and Kauravas prepare for battle. After both sides call in their allies, the evil Kauravas, who've actually been in power for all these many years, easily amass a much larger army. Yudhisthira sends his younger brother Arjuna to ask their friend Krishna if he'll help them.

Arjuna is one of the greatest warriors of his time and also a really good guy. Take note: He's the main hero of the *Mahabharata*. When he shows up at Krishna's palace, he finds that the evil Duryodhana has shown up, too, also hoping to enlist Krishna's large army and gold-laden treasury.

Now there's something very special about this fellow Krishna. The long and short of it is, he's God. Hindus believe in divine incarnations (more on this in Chapter 14), and Krishna is God in human form, though Duryodhana's vision is too clouded with hatred and greed to see this.

Krishna tells the two cousins, "You're both my relatives. I can't choose sides. What I will do is this. I'll give one of you all my soldiers, my horses and elephants, my artillery and my gold. The other, well I'll come along with you as an advisor, but I won't fight. Whichever of you shows up first tomorrow morning, I'll let him choose which of the two options he prefers."

Choosing God

Duryodhana came rushing in the next morning before the break of dawn and sat anxiously at the head of Krishna's bed, waiting for him to wake up. Arjuna got up at his usual time, took his morning bath and sat for worship and meditation. Then he headed over to Krishna's house, where he stood humbly by the foot of Krishna's bed.

Krishna finally woke up. Even though Duryodhana got there first, Arjuna was the first one Krishna

Sages Say

"The *Mahabharata* has moulded the character and civilisation of one of the most numerous of the world's people. How? By its gospel of dharma, which like a golden thread runs through all the complex movements in the epic; by its lesson that hatred breeds hatred, that covetousness and violence lead inevitably to ruin, that the only real conquest is in the battle against one's lower nature."

—C. Rajagopalachari

laid eyes on because he was standing respectfully at the end of the bed, not sitting behind Krishna's head like Duryodhana. So Krishna gave Arjuna the choice. "My army or Me?"

"I choose You, Lord," was Arjuna's very, very famous reply.

Duryodhana walked away a happy man, with all the military power at Krishna's command. But guess who won the war?

Arjuna had a much smaller army, but with Krishna's advice he was able to outwit the Kauravas and win back the kingdom for his brother, Yudhisthira. The point, which I don't think anyone who's ever heard the story has missed, is that when we choose God over all the strengths and all the temptations of the world, we have made the right decision.

Bhagavad Gita: *The Song of God*

The war between the Pandavas and the Kauravas was about to begin. Arjuna asked his friend Krishna to drive him to the center of the battlefield so he could get his bearings. But sitting in his chariot between the two enormous armies, the full enormity of what was about to happen hit Arjuna like a ton of bricks. Tens of thousands of good men on both sides, including many of Arjuna's friends and relatives, were about to die. Innocent women would lose their husbands and sons. A whole generation would grow up without fathers. It would take decades for the kingdom to recover from the staggering losses about to ensue.

Was it really worth it? So many deaths for control of a piece of land? Arjuna sank to the floor of the chariot in a state of emotional paralysis. He couldn't do it. He couldn't fight these people.

Then Krishna turned to him, and the two of them had a little chat.

A Conversation with God

The *Bhagavad Gita* (which means "Song of God") is the conversation between Krishna, who is God in human form come to guide and protect the righteous, and Arjuna, who is the rest of us in human form, confused about what the right course of action in life is and sickened by the horror we see in the world around us.

New Word Alert!

Bhagavan means God. In the *Rig Veda*, Bhaga is the deity who nourishes and protects His devotees.

Gita is a song or chant. There are many thousands of religious gitas in Hinduism, like the *Avadhuta Gita* or the *Ribhu Gita*, but when Hindus say simply "the *Gita*," they mean the *Bhagavad Gita*, "The Song of God," the most famous song of them all.

Purana means "ancient chronicle" or "book of the ancient times."

The *Gita,* as most Hindus call it, actually consists of eighteen short chapters lifted right out of the *Mahabharata.* It is the most loved holy book in Hinduism. Many Hindus can recite the entire *Gita* from memory. Most have memorized at least a few lines.

Krishna has already explained that in the battle against evil, when all peaceful options are exhausted, men of good conscience must get up and fight. Control of the world cannot be handed over to evil men by good people too weak-willed to stand against them.

Now, in the face of death and catastrophe, Krishna urges Arjuna to look at the Big Picture. Everyone dies: From the perspective of eternity, these men are dead already. Since death is inevitable, why not die nobly, fighting for justice?

During the day, we change clothes several times. Death, Krishna says, is when the soul changes its clothes. It takes off a body that's worn out or damaged and puts on a new one. But the inner Self never dies. It is wrong to identify ourselves with our perishable body. We need to realize that we are immortal spirits, ultimately unaffected by death.

Arjuna may win the battle, or he may lose. He may live, or he may die. The outcome of the events ahead is in the hands of God. Krishna advises his friend to not be concerned with how things will turn out. He should focus instead on fighting for truth and justice simply because, under the present tragic circumstances, it's the right thing to do.

The Vision of God

Arjuna is persuaded by Krishna, but asks for a favor. He's not content with the Big Picture—now he wants to see the *Really* Big Picture. He knows Krishna is God in disguise and wants to see what God really looks like.

Krishna shows him.

Arjuna sees universes without end, galaxies spinning in and out of existence. He sees trillions and trillions and trillions of souls trapped in the cycle of birth and death, being born, suffering, dying.

For a mind that has not yet been completely purified by spiritual practice, the vision is too much to bear. Arjuna screams for Krishna to stop, and the Lord resumes his human form.

"I have taught you the secret of secrets," Krishna concludes. "Now surrender to Me, worship Me in

Sages Say

"When doubts haunt me, when disappointments stare me in the face, and I see not one ray of hope on the horizon, I turn to *Bhagavad Gita* and find a verse to comfort me; and I immediately begin to smile in the midst of overwhelming sorrow. Those who meditate on the *Gita* will derive fresh joy and new meanings from it every day."

—Mahatma Gandhi

all your words and thoughts, and offer your actions to Me as a sacrifice of love. You cannot even begin to conceive how much I care for you. I am your eternal refuge. Don't be afraid! I promise, I will save you."

For 2,500 years, Hindus have clung with unshakable faith to Krishna's loving promise.

Very often, Westerners, when they're first exposed to the *Gita*, complain that it condones war. At one level, there's some truth to this. At another, it misses the point completely. Mahatma Gandhi, the quintessential man of peace, kept a copy of the *Bhagavad Gita* with him at all times. Hindus understand that the battlefield Kurukshetra, where Arjuna and Duryodhana are facing off, is not really near Delhi. It's really in the human heart. All of us are at war with the Duryodhanas inside ourselves: greed, hatred, ignorance. In the *Gita,* God Himself shows us the way to victory.

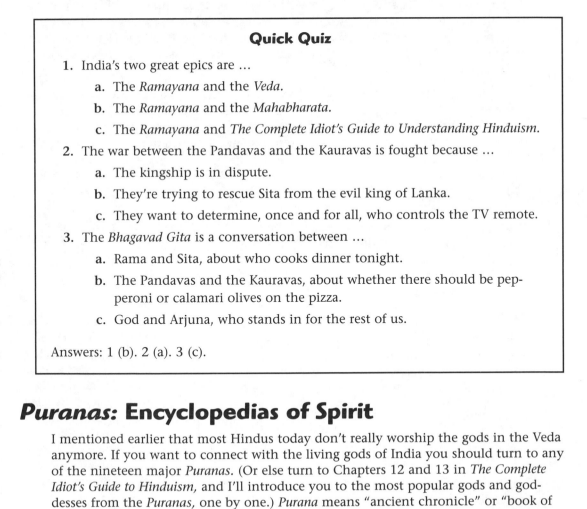

Quick Quiz

1. India's two great epics are …

    a. The *Ramayana* and the *Veda.*

    b. The *Ramayana* and the *Mahabharata.*

    c. The *Ramayana* and *The Complete Idiot's Guide to Understanding Hinduism.*

2. The war between the Pandavas and the Kauravas is fought because …

    a. The kingship is in dispute.

    b. They're trying to rescue Sita from the evil king of Lanka.

    c. They want to determine, once and for all, who controls the TV remote.

3. The *Bhagavad Gita* is a conversation between …

    a. Rama and Sita, about who cooks dinner tonight.

    b. The Pandavas and the Kauravas, about whether there should be pepperoni or calamari olives on the pizza.

    c. God and Arjuna, who stands in for the rest of us.

Answers: 1 (b). 2 (a). 3 (c).

Puranas: Encyclopedias of Spirit

I mentioned earlier that most Hindus today don't really worship the gods in the Veda anymore. If you want to connect with the living gods of India you should turn to any of the nineteen major *Puranas.* (Or else turn to Chapters 12 and 13 in *The Complete Idiot's Guide to Hinduism,* and I'll introduce you to the most popular gods and goddesses from the *Puranas,* one by one.) *Purana* means "ancient chronicle" or "book of the ancient times."

The *Puranas* are often called "the fifth Veda." While the first four Vedas are reserved for particular classes of people, the *Puranas* are for everyone. They're the average person's Veda.

How to Become a Purana

There's certain ground a book has to cover if it wants people to think of it as a *Purana*. It has to include …

➤ An explanation of how the Supreme Being projected the universe out of its limitless awareness. Not just our world, but all planes of existence must be accounted for.

➤ Details of how the multibillion year cycles of the manifestation and dissolution of the universe actually work.

➤ Cycles of the different types of humanity that have appeared and disappeared on our planet since it originally formed.

➤ Historical information about the original lineages of our present humanity.

➤ Genealogies of important early Hindu rulers.

Optional elements you may also find in a *Purana* include …

➤ Information about especially spiritually supercharged pilgrimage sites.

➤ Broad outlines of powerful spiritual practices your guru will explain to you in more detail.

➤ Reports of God's and the Goddess's activities when they visit Earth.

➤ Stunningly beautiful hymns in praise of the divinity.

➤ News about the saints' and sages' efforts to get to know the Supreme Being better.

A Continuing Tradition

Dating the *Puranas,* for all practical purposes, is impossible. Some of the material in the *Puranas* is certainly older than the Veda itself. But unlike the Veda, which priests were entrusted to pass to their children without one syllable being altered, succeeding generations felt free to reshape the *Puranas* according to present needs. So in all the *Puranas,* you'll find something incredibly old and something incredibly new.

More *Puranas* are continually being written. In fact, the swami at my local Kali temple just wrote a new one a few years ago. But they're always based on the same ancient principles, and none of the new ones have quite the same impact as the nineteen VIPs (Very Important *Puranas).*

It's News to Me!

Manu *is* the forefather of the present race of humankind, according to the *Puranas*. He survived the great flood that wiped out the last humanity and began repopulating the world. The name Manu is related to the Sanskrit word *manas,* which means "the thinking mind." Etymologically related English words are *humanity, man,* and *woman.* These are the descendants of *Manu!* We are the animals who have *manas,* who think!

An Expanding Library

As a living tradition, Hinduism is continually generating more spiritual classics. Unlike Christianity and Islam, where the Bible or Koran represent God's word once and for all, in Hinduism God speaks afresh to every generation. Hindu saints and sages constantly create new scriptures, keeping the Vedic vision dynamic and directly relevant to people's present concerns.

During the European Middle Ages, Hindus produced such timeless spiritual masterpieces as the *Yoga Vasishtha* and the *Tripura Rahasya.* Closer to our own time, classics of such exceptional merit as *The Gospe of Sri Ramakrishna* by Mohendranath Gupta and *Adoration of the Divine Mother* by Vasistha Ganapati Muni have taken on the stature of holy scripture in some circles.

Nevertheless, because Hindus believe that men and women of eras long past were actually more illumined than most of us are today, the spiritual authority of Hinduism's earliest scriptures, the Veda, *Puranas,* and *Upanishads,* remains unsurpassed.

The Least You Need to Know

➤ Ordinary Hindus rarely read the Veda—they turn to easier-to-digest, popular texts for inspiration.

➤ The *Ramayana* is the story of the perfect Hindu man and woman.

➤ The *Mahabharata* is the tale of the battle between light and darkness.

➤ The *Bhagavad Gita* is the most popular scripture in Hinduism.

➤ The *Puranas* are the layperson's Veda.

➤ Hinduism continually spawns more scriptures.

Part 2
What Hindus Believe

Hinduism is in some ways the most open-minded of the world's great religions. Maybe this is because India is composed of so many different people and cultures and languages. Respect, or at least tolerance, for other traditions grew gradually over the centuries. People borrowed each other's gods and goddesses, each other's spiritual practices, even each other's saints. In the end, India merged into one more or less unified Hindu culture.

In this part, we'll look at the defining beliefs most Hindus share in common. Reincarnation. Karma. An immortal soul. An infinite ocean of divine energy that underlies the universe we perceive with our senses. And an inner universe of consciousness through which we connect with the whole.

Chapter 6

One God with Many Names

In This Chapter

➤ Where Hinduism differs from Western religions

➤ The roots of Hindu tolerance

➤ Hindu Gods worship each other

➤ Keeping tolerance alive

➤ A visit from Jesus

"God is one. Men call Him by various names," is the eternal truth voiced by the Veda. It doesn't matter what address you send your prayer to. Whether you mail it to Indra or Agni, God or Goddess, Allah or Buddha, Mary or Jehovah, your letter ends up in the same mailbox. The one God always gets your message. No matter who you are, no matter what religion you belong to.

To use another metaphor: Christians say that to access the hard drive, you have to click on the Jesus icon. No other icon will let you access the hard drive.

Muslims say it's a spiritual crime to use any icons at all. Never confuse the hard drive with any of the silly icons on the desktop. Access the drive directly, with the code Mohammed provided.

Hindus say, hey, click on any icon. Every icon on the screen will connect you with the hard drive. Don't see any icon you like? Make up a new one—it will work just as well.

My God's Not Better Than Yours

According to the Veda, it's a serious mistake to confuse your name for God with the Supreme Being Himself. The Big Guy is bigger than you think. In fact, He's not necessarily even a guy at all. It's just as valid to call Him Her or It. If words like "God" or "Goddess" or "Supreme Reality" point you in the right direction, use them by all means.

But the point is not to choose a name for God and then claim that anyone who calls God by a different name is wrong. For Hindus the point is to enter into a living relationship with the Supreme till you feel Its breath in your breath. Till you feel enveloped in the all-encompassing embrace of the infinite wisdom out of which this universe emerged.

There are no false gods according to Hinduism. At least not if your prayer to that god is sincere. Whatever form of the divine you worship, even if it's a man with an elephant's head, the one all-pervading Being who loves you more than you can possibly imagine will use that form to guide you to Her.

Sages Say

"This universe is the outpouring of the majesty of God, the auspicious one, radiant love. Every face you see belongs to Him. He is present in everyone without exception."

—Yajur Veda

It's News to Me!

Jews and Muslims believe God is completely transcendent and has never appeared on Earth in human form. Christians believe God took a human birth once, as Jesus Christ. Hindus believe that whenever humanity calls out to God and the Goddess for help, He and She appear here in physical form to guide and protect us.

Begging to Differ

There is no minimizing the fact that Hindu belief differs dramatically from the Judeo-Christian-Islamic tradition. Before I begin explaining in detail what Hindus do believe, let me clarify what they do *not* believe.

Jews believe that they have a very special relationship with God. God has selected them for His special loving attention and created laws for them that mark them apart from the rest of humanity. Hindus do not accept the concept of a chosen people. For Hindus, God's relationship with every soul is equally special.

A metaphor repeated by Hindu saints is that God is like the sun. The sun shines equally on everyone, no matter what social class you belong to, no matter whether you're male or female, a good person or a not-so-good person. And certainly no matter what religion you subscribe to.

The Jewish idea of what it means to be a prophet and the Hindu idea of what it means to be a seer are also radically different. In Judaism, Yahweh speaks to His prophets, and they deliver God's message to the Jewish people. In Hinduism, the consciousness of the seer merges into the consciousness of God. For Jews, the Creator and His creation—us—are radically distinct. But in Hinduism, the Divine Being emanated us out of Its own all-pervading awareness; it makes sense that our awareness can merge back into its source, like a wave subsiding back into the sea.

Christian Beliefs

Orthodox Christians believe Jesus took on the sins of the entire world. (Hindus also believe saints can take on the karma of their disciples.) To access the saving grace of Jesus, it's absolutely essential to have faith in him.

A Hindu would find this idea perplexing. Many Hindu saints devoted every breath of their lives to the love of God and service of humanity. Why would someone be sent to hell for eternity because they hadn't heard of Jesus?

In Hinduism, two great principles are at work in the universe: *karma* and *kripa,* justice and grace. Despite huge campaigns and the outlay of hundreds of millions of dollars, Christian missionaries have made little headway in converting Hindus. This is largely because Hindus see little justice *or* grace in a God who would damn all their ancestors for no fault of their own.

Hindus believe very literally that "As you sow, so shall you reap." But in Hinduism there is no eternal damnation. No being can have sown enough bad karma that in the vast stretches of eternity, God can't find a way to bring that lost soul back into the light.

The Image of God

There are probably no two religions as radically opposed in their fundamental beliefs as Hinduism and Islam. The meeting of Muslim and Hindu cultures led to catastrophic historical consequences still playing out in South Asia today.

New Word Alert!

Karma is the law of action and reaction at work in the moral universe. Every thought, word, and action produces an effect that rebounds on the person who generated it.

Kripa is divine grace.

New Word Alert!

The **Kabbalah** is a system of Jewish mysticism explaining how the universe emanated from the one transcendental reality.

Sufism is a form of Islamic mysticism which teaches yoga-like techniques leading to higher states of awareness.

Gnosticism was a system of highly mystical beliefs embraced by many early Christians (perhaps—some scholars believe—even by St. Paul, author of portions of the New Testament).

Muslims feel it is a spiritual crime to make an image of God. Hindus feel that, used with proper understanding, images of God, such as the statues of various deities found in Hindu temples, are an excellent way to focus the mind on the divine. Some Muslims feel they are called upon by their faith to destroy any images of God they come across. During the first few centuries of the Muslim occupation of North India, many thousands of Hindu temples were destroyed. The destruction was so complete that today you must travel to South India, where the Muslims didn't penetrate, to find a truly ancient Hindu temple.

Using an image as a focus for worship is a defining characteristic of Hinduism. You'll learn more about it in Chapter 11, "Can You Show Me God?"

Inner Religion

One of the great ironies of religious history is that, although the religions that came out of the Near East—Judaism, Islam, Christianity—adamantly reject most of Hinduism's fundamental teachings, their mystical traditions—the *Kabbalah, Sufism,* and Christian *Gnosticism*—reflect Hindu insights in almost every detail. Numerous students of comparative religion, from Muslim scholar Al Biruni in 1000 c.e. to the world famous writer Aldous Huxley nearer our own time, have expressed their amazement at the parallels between the major mystical traditions of the world and Hinduism.

It's News to Me!

The emperor Chandra Gupta Maurya created a vast Hindu empire, bringing much of the subcontinent under his control perhaps sometime around 300 B.C.E. (Bear in mind that dates in Indian history before 1000 C.E. are being reconsidered.) This was the first time a large part of India was united as one country. Chandra Gupta's grandson Ashoka expanded the empire to its greatest extent in a series of brutal military campaigns. Then he renounced violence and converted to Buddhism!

The Tolerant Religion

Christianity and Islam are aggressive missionary religions. In Hinduism, missionary efforts have traditionally been the exception rather than the rule. For the most part, the Hindu attitude toward other faiths is "Live and let live."

This does not mean Hindus always look at what goes on in other traditions, or even within their own tradition, with unblinking acceptance. Even in the Veda, the rishis rolled their eyes at what they felt were the excesses of some of the tribal practices and urged Hindus to live nobly, abiding by the highest ideals and practicing some rudiments of self-control. How did Hinduism develop this tolerant spirit?

One Culture, Many Traditions

Westerners today tend to think of India in monolithic terms: one country, one culture. In reality, at very few times and for very brief periods in its history has most of the Indian subcontinent been unified—at least until 1947 when the modern state of *Bharat* (the Indian name for India) was created. Instead, for most of its long history, India has been home to an amazingly large number of distinct subcultures.

There are about 80,000 subcultures in India today. That's not a misprint—the correct figure is 80,000. Over 325 languages are spoken there, not to mention thousands of dialects. There are also 25 commonly used written scripts. And we think of America as a melting pot of different cultures!

Hinduism is by far the most complex religion in world, shading under its enormous umbrella an incredibly diverse array of contrasting beliefs, practices, and denominations. Hinduism is by far the oldest major religion. It has had more than enough time to develop a diversity of opinions and approaches to spirituality unmatched in any other tradition.

A Peaceable People

Generally speaking, the Hindus are a peaceable people. Whether or not different communities liked each other, they made an effort to get along. The *caste system*, considered evil in the West, assured that different subcultures, whether they ranked high or low in the pecking order, survived relatively unmolested within the framework of India's highly structured society.

> **New Word Alert!**
>
> **Bharat** *is the Indian's own name for India.*

> **New Word Alert!**
>
> The **caste system** *is the basis of Hindu social hierarchy. Priests and kings are at the top of the social order, manual laborers at the bottom. Foreigners, renunciates, and nonconformists are outside the system altogether.*

The Hindus are perhaps the most peaceful of the major world cultures. Think about it: For at least the last 2,500 years, the only significant military foray Hindus have made outside India was the South Indian conquest of Indonesia, Malaysia, and the Philippines around 1400 C.E. Hindus may fight with each other but they've had very little interest in conquering anyone else—though many of the world's other cultures have certainly had a crack at conquering India!

A Test of Tolerance

Before the arrival of the Muslims around 1000 C.E., Hindus handily assimilated all the would-be conquerors who came storming over its northern borders. The Kushans (Mongolians), the Parthians (Persians), and the Huns all eventually melted into India's embrace, disappearing into the sea of Hindu culture.

The broad-minded Hindus were able to accommodate just about everybody who came knocking on their door—until the Muslims. For the first time, foreign invaders left wounds so deep they refused to heal. Hindu tolerance was being put to the ultimate test.

In ancient times, however, religious tolerance was the norm throughout much of the world. The ancient Greeks and Romans, for example, were astonishingly tolerant of other religions, at least by today's standards. As the monotheistic religions began to dominate world culture, respect for other cultures' religious beliefs largely disappeared. Today Hindu culture is one of the last remaining enclaves of a universal-minded religion.

Exceptions Prove the Rule

I would love to tell you that Hindus have *always* been shining examples of a people who consistently respect other religious traditions, but I'd be lying if I did. Human nature is human nature, and the tendency to believe that one's own faith is not only the best, but perhaps the only valid one, has raised its head in Indian history, too.

If you have a look at the *Puranas,* you'll find that while some of them are quite universalistic in outlook, others are notably sectarian. Some of the authors of the *Puranas* poke fun at their neighbors' gods in a fairly lighthearted manner. In others the insults get edgier.

At times, friction between different Hindu denominations has gotten out of hand. At some points, the devotees of Vishnu have actively persecuted the devotees of Shiva. At other points, the devotees of Shiva have persecuted the devotees of Vishnu. Non-Hindus living in India, such as Jains, Sikhs, and Buddhists, and more recently Muslims, have occasionally taken some serious hits from fanatical Hindus.

The Vedic Vision

Yet religious tolerance is more the norm. A man may be devoted to Lord Vishnu, but when his wife moves into the household, she may place her image of Lord Shiva on the family altar. Their daughter, however, may be more attracted to the goddess Lakshmi and place *her* image in the family shrine. And no one blinks an eye!

In fact, this open attitude can be traced all the way back to the Veda itself. Still, throughout the centuries,

Sages Say

"Everything in the outside world changes constantly. But the Lord of Love in the inner world never changes. He rules both the inner and the outer realities. Meditate on Him. Merge in Him. Wake up from the dream that you exist apart from Him."

—*Shvetashvatara Upanishad* 1:10

Hindu saints and even India's famous divine incarnations have had to make the point over and over again: "God is one. Men call Him by various names."

In one very well-known story, the deva rishi Narada got so fed up with the devotees of Shiva and Vishnu squabbling with each other about which of their gods was higher that he decided to resolve the question for once and for all.

Who the Gods Worship

At this juncture in history, the god Vishnu was incarnating on Earth in the form of a prince named Rama, who was wandering in the forest with his wife, Sita. This seemed like a good place to catch up with Vishnu, who is otherwise quite busy running the universe.

So Narada teleported to the forest where he wound up having to wait several hours to get Rama's attention. Rama was in the middle of making offerings into the sacred fire, an age-old religious ritual. When he finally finished, he ran over to Narada and apologized. "Sir, I'm so sorry to have kept you waiting! I was performing my daily worship of Lord Shiva."

Narada was delighted! Here was his answer without his even having to ask. Rama, who is the embodiment of Vishnu, considered Shiva a greater god than Vishnu himself!

Narada immediately teleported to heaven to tell Shiva the exciting news. But there he found he also had to wait. Shiva doesn't run the universe (that's Vishnu's job). Shiva is the transcendent reality who sits away from the world, always engaged in meditation. Finally the Lord opened His eyes, and looked up and saw the rishi. "Oh Narada, I'm sorry I kept you waiting!" Shiva apologized. "I just couldn't tear myself away from meditating on the lotus feet of Lord Rama!"

Enough Miracles for Everyone

Again and again Hindu scriptures repeat the same point. Rama, before he rushes off to save his wife from her abductor, worships Durga, the warrior goddess. However the members of different sects may feel about the superiority of their own deity, the Hindu gods themselves worship each other!

In the *Bhagavad Gita*, Krishna—the voice of the Supreme Being Itself—assures us, "To whatever god you direct your prayer, by whatever name you call the Supreme, your prayer immediately comes to Me." Call God Harry if you want. If your prayer is sincere, it goes right to the heart of the universe and God responds. This is why miracles don't only happen in the lives of Roman Catholics or only for Sunni Muslims or only for Hindus. People everywhere experience miracles because God attends to the prayers of all.

The Smartas: Intelligent Faith

One of the most famous Hindu sages of historical times, Shankaracharya, was so disgusted with the petty disputes of the different Hindu sects that he formed his own denomination, the Smartas. The Smartas, he directed, would worship all the major gods of both North and South India! To this day, Smarta swamis honor Hinduism's great gods: Vishnu (the one who keeps the universe in good running order and incarnates on Earth from time to time to deal with special emergencies), Shiva (the one who sits in meditation all the time), Devi (the Mother of the Universe), Ganesha (that's the one with the elephant head), Murugan (the young warrior god of the Tamils), and Surya (the sun god).

Shankaracharya was an advanced yogi who believed that in reality God is beyond all form. Yet he was wise enough to recognize that the tremendous faith simple people had in their beloved deities, like Krishna or the Divine Mother, could be mobilized to their spiritual benefit if it was directed intelligently. Directed away from squabbling about whose god was the greatest of all and toward the actual experience of the unity of all gods and all beings in the one Supreme Being.

Shankaracharya founded four great monasteries at the four corners of India: Puri in the east, Badrinath in the north, Dvaraka in the west, and Sringeri in the south. Down through the centuries the heads of these institutions, called Shankaracharyas after their founder, have emphasized the need for tempering enthusiastic devotion with mature intelligence.

Sages Say

"Realizing who you really are, discovering your spiritual identity, is your true purpose in life. If you fritter away your time stoking the fires of your body's endless cravings, you are committing spiritual suicide. The body is nothing more than the vehicle of the immortal spirit. You are living spirit, not the dying body!"

—Shankaracharya

Ramakrishna Samples Religions

Ramakrishna Paramahansa, one of the greatest saints of the modern era, was born into a brahmin family in the tiny village of Kamarpukur in Bengal in 1836. As he entered young adulthood, he was handed a plum of a job. He would be a priest at the new temple complex in Howrah, on the opposite bank of the Ganges directly across from Calcutta.

Ramakrishna soon distinguished himself as a saint of the highest order. He was able to spontaneously enter high states of consciousness it usually took yogis a lifetime to master. His ecstatic devotion to the goddess Kali enchanted visitors and soon created a community of disciples who loved to be near the Goddess-intoxicated master.

Then a disaster of unimaginable proportions occurred. Ramakrishna converted to Islam! During a conversation with a Sufi who had come to see the temple, Ramakrishna was so impressed by the beautiful teachings at the heart of Islam that he decided, "Islam is also a way to reach God. I must practice this path."

Ramakrishna Paramahansa, champion of religious tolerance.

(© Vedanta Society of Saint Louis)

Trying Out Islam

To the unrestrained horror of his family and friends, Ramakrishna refused to even come near the main temple. He started dressing like a Muslim, performed Islamic prayers while bowing toward Mecca five times a day as Muslims do, and wouldn't even look at the image of a Hindu god.

Ramakrishna insisted he was going to eat like a Muslim, too. This meant eating beef, which to a Hindu is the virtual equivalent of eating human flesh. This was just too much. His disciples hired a Muslim cook who prepared a vegetarian meal cooked in the Muslim style. Ramakrishna, who had no idea what beef tasted like, ate the dish in all good faith.

After three days of total commitment to Islam, Ramakrishna had a vision of Mohammed. He saw the Muslim prophet, shining with spiritual luminosity, dissolve into God and then God dissolve into the Absolute Reality. Ramakrishna went into such ecstasy his disciples were hard pressed to bring him back to this plane of reality.

Guidepost

If you're having Hindus over for a dinner party, please don't serve beef! Cows are beloved animals in India, and no practicing Hindu would consider eating one.

When he did return, the master announced, "Islam is a true path. I experienced the highest reality by practicing it." Then, to his family's immense relief, he went back to being a good Hindu. But more trouble lay ahead.

The Radiant Stranger

One day another visitor to the temple started telling Ramakrishna about Isha, as Hindus call Jesus. Ramakrishna was tremendously inspired by the story of Jesus' life, and felt his commitment to Hinduism slipping away. From now on he would be a Christian! He sat in front of a painting of the Virgin Mary holding the baby Isha in her lap and went into ecstasy.

One day shortly after adopting this new religion, Ramakrishna was astonished to see a foreigner with a face glowing radiantly coming directly toward him. "This is Jesus Christ!" he realized. The radiant man walked right up to him and then merged into his heart, throwing the master once more into unspeakable states of bliss.

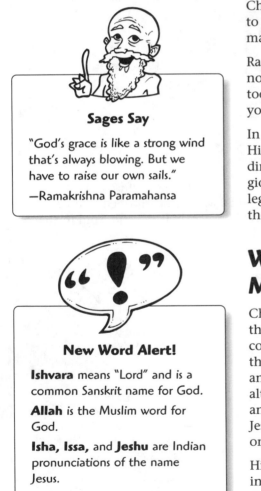

Sages Say

"God's grace is like a strong wind that's always blowing. But we have to raise our own sails."

—Ramakrishna Paramahansa

Ramakrishna resumed his duties as a priest of Kali, but now he also told people, "Christianity is a true faith, too. If you practice Christianity sincerely, it will take you to God."

In his life, Ramakrishna tested three great faiths, Hinduism, Islam, and Christianity. He found, through direct experiential practice, that although each religion differed drastically in doctrine, all of them were legitimate spiritual paths. Any one of them could do the job of bringing us home to God.

What Missionaries Are Missing

Christian missionaries have often complained about the intractability of the Hindus. They're very tough to convert. Hindus may listen with great interest and enthusiasm to the story of Jesus' life and then go home and lovingly place a picture of Jesus on their home altars, right next to the pictures of Shiva and Krishna and the Goddess! They have a hard time grasping that Jesus is supposed to be the *only* God whose picture is on the altar!

New Word Alert!

Ishvara means "Lord" and is a common Sanskrit name for God.

Allah is the Muslim word for God.

Isha, Issa, and **Jeshu** are Indian pronunciations of the name Jesus.

Hindus worship God not only in temple images but in special trees and stones and rivers. For Hindus, God is literally omnipresent and His grace is literally limitless. Divine being never turns away from any soul who turns to It with sincerity, no matter whether they call It Isis or Allah, Rama or Jesus.

And if Jesus really blesses and protects as the missionaries say he does, then by all means, Hindus feel, put his picture on the altar, too!

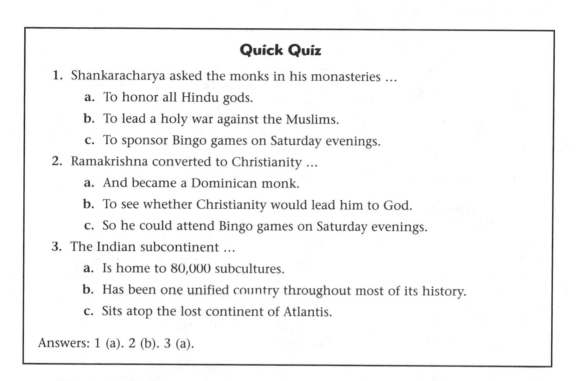

Quick Quiz

1. Shankaracharya asked the monks in his monasteries …

    a. To honor all Hindu gods.

    b. To lead a holy war against the Muslims.

    c. To sponsor Bingo games on Saturday evenings.

2. Ramakrishna converted to Christianity …

    a. And became a Dominican monk.

    b. To see whether Christianity would lead him to God.

    c. So he could attend Bingo games on Saturday evenings.

3. The Indian subcontinent …

    a. Is home to 80,000 subcultures.

    b. Has been one unified country throughout most of its history.

    c. Sits atop the lost continent of Atlantis.

Answers: 1 (a). 2 (b). 3 (a).

Did Jesus Visit India?

Recently, independent investigators have raised the issue of whether Jesus might have studied with the sages of India. Since this question has caught the attention of many New Agers, you and I might as well deal with it here.

We know absolutely nothing about most of Jesus' life. His entire teenage years and young adulthood are missing from the historical record, investigators have pointed out. Could this be because he was absent from Palestine all those years, perhaps on a pilgrimage to the Himalayas?

The question intrigues people because so many of the miracles attributed to Christ—healing the sick, materializing objects like extra food to feed large crowds, controlling the weather, clairvoyance, and mastery over death—are identical to the powers attributed to the greatest of the Hindu masters even today. Could Jesus have learned these techniques from Hindu gurus?

A number of surprising pieces of evidence have been well publicized.

The Tibetan Evidence

In the late 1880s, a Russian explorer named Nicolas Notovitch was cared for by Tibetan monks in a monastery in Ladakh after being thrown from a horse. While he was there, a sympathetic Buddhist monk translated for him a fascinating Tibetan manuscript that described a visit to Kashmir in northern India by a young man from the land of Israel. The man's name was Issa (very close to Isha or Yeshu, the Indian pronunciations of Jesus' name).

It's News to Me!

In 1925, the famous Russian painter Nicolas Roerich arrived in Ladakh and made some inquiries about Norovitch's Jesus manuscript. He was unable to locate it but found that the legend of Saint Issa was well known among the local people.

According to the text, Issa ran away from home at the age of thirteen. He made his way along the well-traveled Silk Road to India, where he spent twelve years studying with both Hindu and Buddhist teachers. By the time he completed the long trek back to Palestine, he was 29 years old. The manuscript gives various fascinating details about Issa's stay in the east.

In 1922, Swami Abhedananda, an Indian monk from the Oriental Seminary in Calcutta, visited Tibet and saw the manuscript. He brought back a translation he worked on with the help of a Tibetan lama.

Before Western scholars heard about the stunning find and could reach the monastery to examine it for themselves, the Chinese army invaded Tibet. During the devastating destruction of Tibetan Buddhist monasteries that followed, this amazing manuscript disappeared.

A Tomb in Kashmir

Other evidence has been brought forward, such as a tomb in Srinagar, the capital city of Kashmir, where legend claims Jesus is buried. Another tomb near Taxila in Afghanistan (Taxila is near the border of Kashmir) has long been recognized by locals as the final resting place of "the Mother Mary."

The Acts of Thomas, an astonishing early Christian text, describes how Jesus commanded his disciple, the famous Doubting Thomas, to sail to India to teach. Then it suggests that Jesus himself visited Thomas in north India.

That Christian missionaries established a church in India not long after Jesus' crucifixion is an uncontested historical fact. But we need to approach the rest of the evidence presented here very cautiously. The resting places of saints have always been big business, and what is now called the tomb of Jesus might just as well have been called the tomb of Mohammed a few centuries ago, depending on what pilgrims were passing through town and how much they were willing to pay to see the tomb.

A Doubting Thomas myself, at the back of my mind is the nagging concern that the famous Tibetan manuscript could be a modern forgery. Or, to put it more generously, a well meaning work of historical fiction. It's extremely unfortunate that the manuscript has vanished, so we'll probably never have an opportunity to examine it more closely.

"Come, Lord"

Since proof that Jesus visited India would have enormous historical implications, I've looked into the issue in far more detail than I have space to outline here. I would love to tell you the evidence is strong. But when I look at it clearheadedly, I can't honestly say that's true. Still, I haven't completely closed my mind to the possibility.

A colleague of mine, the president of the Himalayan Institute, pointed out that the oldest Christian prayer (used by St. Paul in I Corinthians and by John in the Book of Revelation) is *Maranatha*, which in Aramaic means "Come, Lord."

In Sanskrit, *Maranatha* means "Lord of Love."

Oh, and one more thing. The name of the area near Srinagar, Kashmir where Jesus is supposed to have lived is—Amaranatha.

Guidepost

Be advised that the Jewish *Talmud* reports that Jesus spent his missing years in Egypt, not India, studying Egyptian "magic" as Moses had done. Apollonius of Tyana, who visited both India and Egypt in the first century, believed the Egyptian desert ascetics had actually been initiated by Hindu immigrants centuries earlier. If this is true, Jesus may well have learned the secrets of the Hindu masters, but he learned them in Egypt!

The Least You Need to Know

➤ According to the Veda, there's only one God, no matter what you call Him.

➤ Hindus do not believe in eternal damnation.

➤ Hindus accept the worship of images of God as a useful form of devotional practice.

➤ Throughout Indian history, numerous saints have continually reminded Hindus of the value of religious tolerance.

➤ In the nineteenth century, Ramakrishna Paramahansa practiced each major world religion in turn to confirm its validity.

➤ Some Hindus believe that Jesus may have visited India.

Chapter 7

Born Again!

> ## In This Chapter
>
> ➤ The cycle of birth, death, and rebirth
>
> ➤ Memories of previous lives
>
> ➤ Karma drives the cycle of reincarnation
>
> ➤ Washing away bad karma
>
> ➤ After-death states

You've heard about Hindu history. You learned about the holy books that define the Hindu tradition. You read a whole chapter on the fundamental Hindu attitude toward religious life, a view based on tolerance and mutual respect. Now it's time to get down to the nitty-gritty: What Hindus really believe.

The elements of Hindu faith can be summarized in two words: karma and reincarnation. We are *all* born again.

Caught in the Spin Cycle

"The Supreme Being is present in everyone's heart, Arjuna," says Krishna in the *Bhagavad Gita*. "He directs the comings and goings of all living beings. It's as if they're strapped into a spinning machine. That machine is the material universe."

Imagine a gigantic Ferris wheel. Only the top half of it is above ground. It rotates upward from beneath the earth: a child is born. It reaches its zenith: full adulthood is attained. It starts to turn downward: old age kicks in. It disappears beneath the earth: death.

The cycle doesn't stop there. It continues through after-death experiences that those of us still standing on the surface of the earth can't see. Then it swings back up again from beneath the ground: the soul is reborn in another body.

We meet a person we've never laid eyes on before and instantly we feel like we've known her forever. We meet another person and immediately we distrust him. Why?

Some of us are born with exceptional talents. We may be gifted singers, musicians, scientists, business people. We're attracted from early childhood to fields in which we already seem to have notable abilities. How can this be?

The Western scientific answer would be that at some point in our embryonic development the molecule in an unidentified enzyme shifted slightly and shaped our brain chemistry a certain way. Hindus offer an alternative answer that makes at least as much sense as that. They say we're attracted and repelled by new people we meet because we've met them before, and at some level of our awareness, we already know whether they're friend or foe. We have skills in certain areas because we developed them through plain hard work in previous lives.

It's News to Me!

Did Jesus believe in reincarnation? He mentions several times that John the Baptist was the prophet Elijah in a previous life (Matthew 11:2-15, Matthew 17:10-13, and Mark 9:9-13). Many early Christians—including Origen, the most famous Church Father of them all—accepted reincarnation as a fact. In 553, however, Christian theologians at the Fifth Ecumenical Council in Constantinople formally banned the doctrine of reincarnation.

"This Is Not My Real Home!"

Shanti Devi, a young girl growing up in Delhi in the 1930s, spoke very little till she was four years old. When she did start talking, she alarmed everyone in her family. "This is not my real home! I have a husband and son in Mathura! I must return to them!"

This was India, so instead of taking their daughter to a psychiatrist for a dose of Ritalin, her parents told her, "That was then. This is now. Forget your past life. You're with us this time."

But Shanti Devi wouldn't give up. She talked about her former family to anyone who would listen. One of her teachers at school sent a letter to the address Shanti Devi gave as her "real home" in Mathura, inquiring if a woman had died there not too many years ago. To his astonishment, he soon received a reply from Shanti Devi's previous husband, admitting that his young wife Lugdi Devi had passed away some years previously, after giving birth to their son. The details Shanti Devi had given about her old house and members of her previous family were all confirmed.

This launched the most thoroughly researched investigation of a case of reincarnation in modern history. Everyone got in on the act, including Mahatma Gandhi and several prominent members of the Indian government. A team of researchers, working under stringent conditions to ensure that Shanti Devi couldn't possibly be getting her information from any other source, accompanied the little girl to Mathura. On her own, she was able to lead them to her previous home, and correctly described what it had looked like years earlier before its recent refurbishing. She was also able to relate extremely intimate information, such as extramarital affairs of family members, that no one outside the family could possibly have known.

The award-winning Swedish journalist Sture Lönnerstrand spent several weeks with Shanti Devi later in her life, recording her story and verifying information about the famous government investigation. If you have any interest in reincarnation at all, I highly recommend his book, *I Have Lived Before: The True Story of the Reincarnation of Shanti Devi.* In it this remarkable woman describes what it's like to live two lives at once—the one going on now and another that's supposed to be over. She also describes her experiences in the transition period between her death as Lugdi Devi and her rebirth as Shanti Devi.

Guidepost

Young children have vivid imaginations and will often make up the wildest stories. But perhaps not all their wild stories are fiction! In Hindu, Buddhist, and shamanic cultures, when young children describe things that happened to them "before," their parents understand they may be relating real events, but events that occurred in previous lives. Perhaps parents in the West should not be so quick to shrug off similar stories from their own offspring!

Why Don't I Remember?

You don't have to say it. I know you're thinking, "If we lived before, how come we don't remember?" Shanti Devi may have recalled her previous life, but most of us sure don't.

Actually we do, according to the Hindus. The very fact that we're drawn to certain people and certain places is a reflection of the dim memory of previous lives we all possess. The fact that most of us don't remember our last life in detail like Shanti Devi is due to the nature of the soul.

In the West, those of us who believe in a soul at all think of it in a very straightforward way. There's the body. It dies. There's the soul. It lives forever. For Hindus the

New Word Alert!

Vaishnava shakti is the force that stuns the soul at the time of rebirth, so that it loses conscious memory of its past life.

The **karmashaya** is the karmic residue we carry from past lives, our old memories and habits and desires, which are stored in our subtle body.

Guidepost

Don't assume that reincarnation takes place in linear time. Remember, to the Hindu, time and space are multidimensional. According to a Hindu classic called the *Yoga Vasishtha*, your next incarnation, or your last incarnation for that matter, may be happening *right now*. Your next life may actually occur in the past! This is because your innermost spirit exists outside of time and space, and can travel to wherever and to whenever it wants!

topic is not so simple. Hindus believe the universe is multidimensional, and so is the soul. What the soul is and how it operates is a critically important subject for anyone who wants to understand Hinduism. I'll go into it in a lot more detail in Chapter 8, "Turning On Your Inner Light."

Now, to answer your question about why we don't remember our past lives. At the moment of rebirth, Hindus believe, the infant takes its first gulp of air and becomes a breathing being. This jolts the brain and subtle body, causing a force called *vaishnava shakti* to act. In most people, it cuts off detailed memories of the past life.

In fact, it also cuts off detailed memories of *this* life, which is why most people don't remember much of what happened in the first three or four years of their current life either. The soul is still completing its "hook up" to the new physical brain, and not all the data from the previous file is downloaded. It's still there though, preserved in an internal drive called the *karmashaya,* a storage bin of previous thoughts and actions that's a little hard for us to access because it's buried deep in the subtle body, not the physical brain.

Presence of Mind

I'm guessing your next question is, "Well, then how did Shanti Devi remember *her* past life?" This gets interesting.

You may have heard of the *Tibetan Book of the Dead.* Perhaps you've even heard of the *Egyptian Book of the Dead.* Numbers of ancient, spiritually advanced cultures carefully trained people so they would know how to go through the process of death consciously. Often—as in the Egyptian texts and in some Gnostic Christian books, too—this involved memorizing lots of key phrases and detailed imagery.

The point in all these traditions is that if you don't want to lose yourself, if you want to attain the type of immortality that comes from the ability to hang on to your present identity from life to life, then during the process of death you must *keep your presence of mind!*

All those elaborate memorizations and visualizations in the various Books of the Dead are designed to help the newly deceased soul stay focused and conscious.

Lugdi Devi, Shanti Devi's previous self, had been using an old trick recommended by yogis for thousands of years. During her Lugdi life she had kept repeating the name of God constantly, with full devotion, day and night. At the time of her death, her mind stayed with the divine name. It helped her remain calm and alert through a process where most people lose consciousness. As she was being reborn, her awareness remained with the name of God rather than locking into her new physical brain. So she didn't forget her previous identity. Shanti Devi actually describes this procedure in Lönnerstrand's book.

Well, you may believe this story or you may not. But now you know how it's explained in the Hindu tradition.

What's My Karma?

The process of reincarnation is driven by karma. Karma, to borrow from St. Paul in the Bible, means "As you sow, so shall you reap." Where, when, and in what circumstances we next incarnate is due, in large measure, to our thoughts, words, and actions in the past and present.

To be reborn into a human body is a great blessing. Human bodies, far more so than animal and plant bodies, are capable of devoting themselves to spiritual life. Most animals answer primarily to the dictates of nature, but humans have a capacity for self-reflection rarely seen in animals. Vistas of unlimited spiritual growth lie spread before the men and women who turn their attention to inner life.

The capacity to make decisions for ourselves rather than automatically doing what our natural drives tell us to do gives humans our special status: We have free will. With free will comes responsibility, however. You can't blame a tiger if it kills a deer. But if one man kills another out of greed, delusion, or hatred, very serious karmic consequences ensue. Then again, if a person selflessly helps others, superb karmic results will ultimately follow.

We can lose our human status, Hindu sages warn. If we don't take advantage of our human birth but continue living like animals, we may return to an animal body in our next life. (Perhaps some people would be more comfortable in animal bodies anyway. Then they can just eat, sleep, have sex, and never have to fill out tax forms.) Particularly pernicious people, one holy text warns, could even be reborn as "flies, gnats and biting insects"!

Sages Say

"Do not be deceived; God is not mocked, for whatever a man sows, that he will also reap. And let us not grow weary in well-doing, for in due season we shall reap."

—Galatians 6:7,9

Four Kinds of Karma

Four kinds of karma are recognized in Hinduism:

➤ *Sanchita karma:* All the karma we've accrued from all our previous lives.

➤ *Prarabdha karma:* That portion of our total karmic backlog destined to play out in our present lifetime.

➤ *Kriyaman karma:* The fresh karma we're producing in this lifetime.

➤ *Agama karma:* Our plans for the future on which we have yet to act. The karma produced by our thoughts.

Sanchita karma is all the debits and credits in our soul's entire karmic portfolio. Prarabdha karma is the debits and credits we have to deal with in this incarnation. Kriyaman karma is the store of merit and demerit we're adding to or subtracting from our karmic credit account right now.

Agama karma is more subtle. This is produced not by actions we've done but by our intentions to commit an action in the future. If we seriously want to hurt somebody, our karmic account gets docked even if we don't actually do it. Though not as much as if we take action!

Most human souls have an immense amount of karma built up from many previous existences. Due to the constraints of time and space, only a small portion of it can manifest in any one lifetime. In a previous life, we may have intensely desired to live on Mars, for example. But in this life, only our karma to be a soft drink distributor may play out. The space colonizer karma will have to wait till another lifetime. That's the distinction between sanchita and prarabdha karma.

Now, when we're not busy filling vending machines with cans of Pepsi and Sprite, we may spend all our free time studying about outer space and visiting Cape Canaveral to watch Space Shuttle launches. This karma we're creating now is adding to our total account. In a future life, we may be born as a child who desires to travel in space so intensely that she actually grows up to be an astronaut.

Collective Karma

Westerners think karma means that if a person is assaulted, say, or born deformed, they must have deserved it due to something terrible they did in a previous life. This is a terrible oversimplification.

A lot of karma playing through our lives is actually not our personal karma at all. It's group karma. There's no underestimating the impact of the way our personal karmic flow blends with that of the people close to us, with our community, and with our culture as a whole.

Let's compare the collective karma of two prosperous first-world countries. The United States, where I live now, has an incredibly high tolerance for violence.

Violence is glamorized on television and in the movies, and firearms are readily available. In Norway, where I spent part of my childhood, there is zero tolerance for violence and firearms are carefully regulated. The karmic result is that the U.S. has the highest rate of violent crime among first-world countries. Norway has the lowest.

Now suppose it's your karma to have a bad day. In Norway, this might play out as slipping on your skis and breaking your leg. In the U.S., however, due to the power of collective karma, your bad day might involve getting mugged on the way back from a Bingo game. It's not that you personally deserved to be assaulted. It's just that the bad karma of your culture is playing out through your bad day.

In a country where the old gods are no longer honored—the intelligent forces of nature are no longer recognized—companies may feel free to pollute the environment. A child who developed in utero in a particularly toxic neighborhood may be born handicapped due to the high level of poisons the culture tolerates in its landfills and water. It's not necessarily that the child deserved to be born with a deformity. It's that a culture that poisons its environment has karmically invited the birth of genetically damaged children.

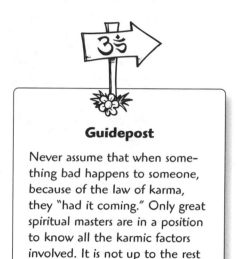

Guidepost

Never assume that when something bad happens to someone, because of the law of karma, they "had it coming." Only great spiritual masters are in a position to know all the karmic factors involved. It is not up to the rest of us to pass judgment.

Fate Is Free Will

Westerners are extremely uncomfortable with the idea of destiny. The Hindus, however, are very conscious that the actions we perform lead to a corresponding karmic result. Sooner or later we get our reward or our comeuppance. The *Mahabharata* says that just as a calf can always find its mother, no matter how large the herd of cows its mother has wandered into, so the karmic results of actions we performed in past lives will eventually and inevitably seek us out.

The Hindus definitely believe in fate. The paradox is that we create our own fate through the use of our free will.

Karma can be strong or weak. If it's strong, a particular karmicly predetermined event will almost certainly occur. If it's weak, you may be able to dodge the bullet. The three levels of karmic magnitude are:

➤ Flexible: We can easily deflect this karma.

➤ Medium: We can change this karmic pattern if we make a substantial effort.

➤ Fixed: There is nothing humanly possible we can do to prevent this karma from playing out. Only God can alter fixed karma.

Maybe you paid $60 for tickets to a World Federation Wrestling match, but on the night of the match you have a cold and don't feel like going. You hate to throw away the $60, but you stay home in bed anyway. The karma you set in motion—to go to a wrestling match—was flexible. It was easy to change.

Suppose you spend twelve years in medical school learning to be a doctor. Then just as you're about to graduate you decide you hate dealing with whining sick people, and you'd rather be an architect. Now you have to lay out lots more money and lots more years going to architectural school. It took a lot of effort to modify the flow of your karma, but you managed it.

Maybe you know of a politician who's repeatedly been accused of graft, who's been in one sex scandal after another, and who never made a promise he didn't break. Yet he keeps getting elected back into office! His fixed karma propelling him into government positions is still in effect in spite of his enemies' efforts to point out his incompetence and corruption. For this lifetime, at least, he continues to enjoy the benefits of positive karma earned in past lives.

Guidepost

Fixed karma is rare. Almost all karma can be altered, at least to some extent, through sincere effort.

Sages Say

"Love God and selflessly serve others. Your past evil karma will become like a canceled check."

—Mata Amritanandamayi

If the karma we've got coming to us is good, everybody's happy. But if we're experiencing a spate of bad karma, we may want to look into some of the traditional Hindu methods for paying off our karmic debts.

Redirecting the Flow of Destiny

If our life doesn't seem to be going in the direction we want it to, we can redirect the flow of our karma. At least so long as the strength of the karmic patterns in our life is flexible or medium—which most karma is.

Here are some of the most popular Hindu methods for clearing out our negative karma:

1. Pilgrimage. Hindus made long and difficult journeys to sacred sites. The journey itself is a form of spiritual practice, strengthening one's faith and reliance on spirit to help see oneself safely through to the journey's end. At Prayag, where the Ganges and Yamuna rivers meet, pilgrims bathe in the holy waters to wash away their sins. I don't know if you can really wash off bad karma with water, but the tremendous faith of the pilgrims I've seen at Prayag must certainly have some effect!

2. Charitable Donations. Since much "bad karma" is the result of debts we've incurred in previous

lives, making generous donations helps us balance our karmic accounts. Hindus struggling with their health may make donations to medical research. Poverty-stricken Hindu families may go out into the woods or meadows near their homes each morning and offer food to wild animals.

3. Rituals. By making offerings to the gods, Hindus hope to restore a positive balance in the karmic forces at work in their lives. They hope to make peace with the forces of nature and request the gods' gracious intervention.

4. Selfless Service. Offering one's time and energy for the benefit of others without any expectation of reward is considered one of the most effective means of defusing bad karma.

5. Self-Discipline. By undertaking vows to perform a certain type of austerity for a certain length of time, Hindus hope to overcome various karmic complexes. An example of a common vow is fasting for a predetermined period or on certain days of the week.

It's News to Me!

One way of dealing with bad karma is to do breathing exercises. You read right—I said breathing exercises. Breathing techniques are used by some Hindus to help manage stress and to promote mental calmness and clarity. When you're in a tranquil state of mind, bad karma just rolls over you—it can't really hit you in the gut.

Washing Out Your Mind

Other methods of making amends for misdeeds of the past are more internal:

1. Meditation. Deep meditation can actually release karmic complexes buried in the subtle body. When an "inner demon" is recognized and released in meditation, it loses its ability to wreak havoc in the meditator's life.

2. Prayer. Many Hindus chant *stotras* or sacred prayers as part of their daily worship. Often these prayers involve listing the many divine qualities of a favorite deity. Regularly contemplating so many good qualities helps elevate your consciousness and transform your personality.

3. Mantras. Chanting the resonant divine sounds prescribed by a meditation master helps purify the field of one's consciousness and neutralizes the effect of bad karmas. Hindus use a rosary of 108 beads and make a promise to repeat a mantra many hundreds of thousands, or even millions, of times. Your mind is not supposed to wander during this practice, which is called *japa*. It's a form of sacrifice. You sacrifice your time and attention to God as well as all the thought energy that would otherwise be expended on romantic fantasies and inner chatter.

4. Self-Inquiry. Self-knowledge is the greatest cure for what ails us. Some Hindus use various techniques of self-analysis to diagnose and correct the problems in their thinking and behavior that are reflected back to them as difficult karma.

5. Devotion. In India, you will often encounter Hindus as devoted to God as many of us are to our closest friends and relatives. Developing a living relationship with the divine takes the sting out of the problems life throws your way and turns life into a love affair with a higher power.

6. Self-Surrender. If all else fails, surrender to the Divine Will may be the last and best prescription for ameliorating bad karma. Sometimes the best we can do is surrender to God and His will for our lives, with gratitude and humility.

New Word Alert!

Deva means a god. A Maha Deva, incidentally, is a "great god" like Brahma, Vishnu, or Shiva, in charge of many minor devas.

A **stotra** is a holy hymn or prayer.

Japa is the continual repetition of God's name or a sacred mantra.

Sages Say

"Reincarnation is a series of dreams within a dream: man's individual dreams within the greater dream of God."

—Paramahansa Yogananda

Life Between Lives

Let's talk about what happens when the Ferris wheel of karma rotates down where we can't see it anymore. What happens after death?

Hindus believe in heaven and hell. But while Christians and Muslims believe heaven and hell are forever, Hindus see these as temporary after-death states.

The Veda talks about the paths most human souls take after death. The first is the path of the misty light to *Pitri Loka,* the world of the ancestors. This is where most of us average folk go, hanging out with friends and relatives who've gone on before.

The second is the path of the bright light into the heaven world called *Deva Loka.* Only very pure souls can enter this realm. It's a high heaven where we experience incredible knowledge and joy. Here we get to dwell with the *devas*, the gods.

The third path, which some texts don't even mention because they assume you've got your act together and aren't heading there, is the path of no light at all. This leads to *Patala,* a very turbulent after-death existence. You want to be a kind person, a decent person, a spiritually oriented person, so you don't wind up in this nasty place.

Designer Heavens

Here is an important twist you need to understand. God doesn't create heaven and hell. We do. Whatever plane of consciousness we find ourselves in after the body drops away is a world of our own making, according to the rishis. If our thoughts have been predominantly cheerful and benevolent, our after-death experience is similar. If our thoughts have been filled with violence and anger, our afterlife will be, too.

The climate in the life after death is the atmosphere of our own minds.

Our karma—the mental vectors we've created by our thoughts and actions—carries us to a high state, a low state, or an okay in-between state like Pitri Loka. We're in control—if we're living life consciously. If we're not directing our lives with awareness, then the unconscious tendencies stored in our karmashaya are in control.

For many Hindus, a long stay in heaven is just what the doctor ordered, and some Hindus devote considerable effort to building up enough karmic velocity to transport them into a higher world after they jettison their bodies.

New Word Alert!

Deva Loka is the heaven world where exceptionally pure souls go after death.

Patala is hell, a transient after-death state of mental terror and anguish.

Pitri Loka is the after-death world of the ancestors where average quality human souls continue to exist.

Surprisingly, however, many of the Hindu scriptures don't consider a long stay in heavenly disembodied states to be a positive thing. Most people in those "between life" states are in a dream-like condition. In our dreams, we're propelled around the images in our subconscious rather involuntarily. We're not in control. Because we're not in control, we're not in a position to expand our awareness or make any substantial spiritual progress. This is why the rishis say it's actually better to be an embodied person on the physical plane, where you're in a state of full waking awareness and can make efforts to know God and yourself better and better.

Eventually, the mental energy propelling you through the disembodied realms peters out. Your stay in that world is up—it's time to return to a physical body. You remember how much you enjoyed sex. You remember how much you enjoyed whipped cream puffs. You remember how much you wanted to go to Mars. You remember that your brother-in-law owes you three thousand dollars.

Your unfulfilled desires draw you back to an appropriate physical body and—*poof!*—here you are again, in another body. You traded the old model in for a new vehicle. Hopefully, thanks to good karma, you've traded up.

Quick Quiz

1. Karma and reincarnation are …

    a. Fundamental beliefs of Hinduism.

    b. Fundamental beliefs of Islam.

    c. Fundamental rights guaranteed in the United States' constitution.

2. According to Hinduism, going on a pilgrimage is a good way to …

    a. Burn off bad karma.

    b. Meet potential romantic partners.

    c. Sample India's varied cuisine.

3. Sanchita karma is …

    a. All the karma in the universe.

    b. All the karma you've accumulated over the course of your lifetimes.

    c. All the karma you can eat.

4. Hindus say you go to heaven …

    a. Forever to be with Jesus.

    b. For a while, if you've been very good.

    c. If you avoid stepping on cracks in the pavement.

Answers: 1 (a). 2 (a). 3 (b). 4 (b).

Breaking the Cycle

A pandit once told me that yogis don't fear death because "They know where they're going." They have, in effect, practiced being dead in deep meditative states where they were completely disengaged from their bodies. They know how to remain fully conscious, alert and awake, in the after-death state, and can direct their out-of-body journey in full awareness.

The great saints and sages aren't driven around in karmic circles by the thoughts and desires stored in their subconscious, as happens to most of the rest of us in life and in death. They're like lucid dreamers, awake while everyone else is asleep. In fact, that's why some enlightened people are called buddhas. Buddha means "somebody who's awake."

You can spend a lot of time cycling through the universe. The cosmos is a long highway—there are plenty of campsites where you can pitch your tent. But when you finally tire of "exploring new worlds and new civilizations" like the heroes in *Star Trek,* there is a way to get off the wheel.

"Stop the universe! I want to get off!" In the next chapter, India's spiritual masters show you how.

The Least You Need to Know

➤ Hindus believe in karma and reincarnation.

➤ Only a portion of our total karma manifests in any one lifetime.

➤ Our present thoughts and actions affect the course of our destiny.

➤ Hindus use methods like meditation and pilgrimage to clean up their bad karma.

➤ Our karma leads us to heavenly or hellish after-death states.

➤ Heaven and hell are temporary; sooner or later we're reborn.

Chapter 8

Turning On Your Inner Light

In This Chapter

➤ The soul's cloaks

➤ Self-knowledge

➤ The guru's job

➤ Getting off the karmic wheel

If karma and reincarnation form the spinning wheel of the cosmic process, the Inner Self is the unmoving axle around which the wheel turns.

"Know Thyself" was the advice chiseled over the portico at the Oracle of Delphi in ancient Greece. No religion has ever taken the quest for self-knowledge as seriously as Hinduism. At its core, Hinduism is not about believing what somebody else tells you about the nature of your soul, or accepting what other people claim about God. Ultimately, Hinduism is about exploring the very depths of your own soul yourself. And about getting to know God personally.

Secrets of the Subtle Body

In the West, a minority of people are interested in weird stuff like astral bodies and out-of-body travel. They're often looked at as harmless New Age flakes or wigged-out occultists. But in Hinduism, coming to grips with the mechanics of what the soul

It's News to Me!

Hindu contributions to science have been exceptional. Very ancient Sanskrit texts called the *Sulva Sutras* demonstrate advanced mastery of mathematics and geometry in ancient times. The Hindus' skill in metallurgy is attested by the Iron Pillar of Delhi, an iron post that hasn't rusted after standing in all weather conditions for centuries. A very old scientific manual called the *Aryabhatiya* demonstrates advanced knowledge of astronomy. The work of Panini, the ancient grammarian, was unmatched in Europe for millennia.

New Word Alert!

Anna means food.

Prana means life energy, vital force, *chi.* It can also refer to the breath.

Homeopathy is a system of medicine widely practiced in Europe and India that uses very minute amounts of medicine to help balance the subtle energies underlying the physical body.

actually is and how it operates are fundamental to understanding karma and reincarnation. If you want to understand how to control your reincarnational cycle, you have to understand this stuff.

Inner realities are legitimate realities to Hindus. They're not cavalierly dismissed as outdated superstitions like they are in the West. We Westerners for the most part only hear about miracles that happened in Palestine 2,000 years ago. In India, however, every generation of Hindu has been exposed to living saints and yogis who demonstrate what seem like superhuman abilities to the uninitiated.

In India, science and religion have always worked hand in hand. There has been no burning at the stake of scientists in India! There the exploration of inner realities is considered just as valid as research into the outer world of nature. While Hinduism produced some of the greatest natural scientists in history, it also excelled in the science of spirit, pioneered by inner researchers called yogis.

Your Five Bodies

According to the yogis, you don't have just one body. You have five. Just as you wear layers of clothes—underwear, a shirt or blouse, a sweater, a coat—so your innermost spirit wears layers of increasingly subtle energies, with which it can operate in increasingly subtle dimensions of the universe.

The *Taittiriya Upanishad* describes five "sheaths" worn by the spirit, like a sword in a scabbard that's in a box that's in a chest that's in a closet that's in a house:

➤ *Anna maya kosha:* the body made of physical matter

➤ *Prana maya kosha:* the body made of vital energy

➤ *Mano maya kosha:* the body of thought energy

➤ *Vijnana maya kosha:* the body of higher intelligence

➤ *Ananda maya kosha:* the body of mystical awareness

The anna maya kosha or physical body is made from *anna,* food. You eat, you grow. The physical matter in food becomes the physical matter of your body.

In a similar manner, the prana maya kosha is made up of life energy. This is the subtle energy medieval physicians in Europe used to call the vital force. In China it's called *chi,* and learning to manipulate it is the basis of acupuncture and the martial arts. In the Western esoteric tradition, the prana maya kosha is sometimes called the etheric body.

Homeopathic medicines do not act directly on the physical body, but are used to balance the pranic fields around which the physical matter of the body takes shape, like iron filings arranging themselves along the lines of force emanating from a magnet.

Sheaths of Living Energy

You're standing in line at the bank waiting to cash a check. Suddenly the man in front of you has a heart attack and falls down dead. How is the dead man so different from you, anyway? You're both made of physical matter and since he just died a few seconds ago, the matter in his body is pretty much as good as the matter in yours.

The major difference between a living person and a dead one, according to the yogis, is the dead one isn't breathing. When the breath stops cranking, the prana maya kosha or life force can no longer animate the body, or keep the mind and body connected. The man's mind may still actually be present, perhaps hovering over his body wondering what the heck is going on. But he can no longer manipulate his fingers or toes because the pranic connection to his body has been severed.

Suppose the man doesn't die. Suppose he just goes into a coma.

This means his pranic body is still operating so his physical body keeps breathing and doesn't start to decompose. But now the mano maya kosha, or mental body, has gone missing. You're shouting, "Sir, sir, can you hear me?" But he can't because his mental body has closed down. He's slipped into an unconscious state, and his ability to think or to connect with his body through his sense organs has shut off.

Let's consider another scenario. A teenager walks into his high school and shoots a dozen of his classmates. How could any human being kill another without the slightest feeling of remorse? In his case, the vijnana maya kosha is not working properly. This very subtle body of living intelligence is responsible for making judgments and decisions. When it operates normally it works as the conscience, the will, and the higher intellectual functions. A sociopath has no conscience. His vijnana maya kosha is barely functioning.

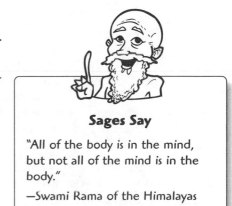

Sages Say

"All of the body is in the mind, but not all of the mind is in the body."

—Swami Rama of the Himalayas

The Body of Bliss

Back to the bank scenario. Let's look at the rest of the people standing around aghast at the poor guy with the heart attack. Most of them are decent, hard-working people. Some are passionately interested in sports. Some love to cook. Others want nothing more than to go home, plop down on the sofa, and watch TV.

Very few of the people here are seriously interested in spiritual life.

This doesn't mean they're bad people—it just means they've got other priorities. Their ananda maya koshas are underdeveloped. They've never tasted the *ananda,* the bliss, of deeper meditative states. The possibility of expanding their awareness to experience higher states of consciousness has probably never occurred to them.

In these people, the body of mystical awareness is not enlivened. If a person doesn't exercise and eat right, her physical body is unlikely to be in good shape. If people don't meditate, or spend some time praying and contemplating a higher reality, then the ananda maya kosha, or subtlest body, atrophies.

I studied the *Taittiriya Upanishad,* the source of this doctrine, many years ago with the yoga master Swami Rama Bharati. I can't emphasize strongly enough that to the adepts of the Hindu tradition, the five separate and distinct yet interlinking bodies are just as real as the circulatory or respiratory systems are to us. The yogis say they use these different bodies as vehicles for traveling through different spatial dimensions.

Life in the Three Worlds

Let's swing around and come back at this stuff from another angle that compacts the five bodies down into three:

➤ *Sthula sharira:* the physical body

➤ *Sukshma sharira:* the astral body

➤ *Karana sharira:* the causal body

The sthula sharira includes both the material body and the body of vital energy. Why? Because at death, when the material body starts to disintegrate, so does the prana maya kosha. According to the yogis, the "wreaths" some people claim to see floating over graves are decaying pranic fields that no longer have a purpose. There no longer is a material body for them to animate, so their energies gradually dissipate.

The astral body is the mental body or mano maya kosha from the previous scheme. It continues to exist after death. Each of us still experiences ourselves as the same entity who used to live in a physical body. Yogic adepts are said to be able to travel outside their physical bodies in this ball of mental energy.

At the time of rebirth, the mental body from the last life now also passes away. Only the causal body reincarnates. The causal body contains all your higher intellectual and spiritual functions (vijnana and ananda maya koshas). Your karmashaya, the habits and attitudes developed in your previous lives, is carried with the causal body like a piece of luggage.

Spiritual masters, because they have aligned their awareness with their causal body, retain full awareness of their previous lives when they are reborn. Most of us identify with our physical or mental bodies, which disintegrate rather than travel with us into the next life, so we don't have detailed past life recall. When the vaishnava shakti I mentioned in Chapter 7, "Born Again!" acts, our connection with our old mental or astral body is broken, and we begin evolving a new mental body or personality which develops along with our new physical body.

If you begin exploring Hindu sacred literature, you will find numerous references to "the three worlds." Western scholars often interpret these as the surface of the earth, the atmosphere, and the upper sky. But to Hindu spiritual practitioners they refer to the physical world accessible to our five senses, the mental world accessible to our mind, and the causal or formless realm beyond the reach of thought. We can travel in the formless world only with the highest intuitive powers inherent in our karana sharira, or causal body.

The mental and physical worlds were originally projected out of the causal or "seed" world, the world of concepts or archetypal patterns, and will eventually dissolve back into it. This is the extra-dimensional world of "ideas" the Greek philosopher Plato spoke of.

New Word Alert!

Ananda *is divine bliss.*

Kosha *means a sheath or covering, such as one of the Inner Self's physical or subtle bodies.*

It's News to Me!

The three bodies or shariras known to the Hindus were familiar to the ancient Greeks as well. The Greeks called the physical, astral, and causal bodies the *soma, psyche,* and *nous.*

"Who Am I?"

If you've got some familiarity with the mystical traditions of the world, bells will be going off in your head like crazy. You'll recognize the breakdown of the soul into the five *koshas* or sheaths as virtually identical to the analysis of the soul found in the ancient Egyptian tradition. And the threefold scheme of the physical, astral, and causal bodies is exactly paralleled in the ancient Greek tradition. Plutarch, a priest from the temple of Apollo at Delphi, described it explicitly in his essays.

When you start to recognize all the amazing links between different mystical traditions, you can understand why, in the first century C.E., Apollonius of Tyana expressed his opinion that India was the motherland of the mystical heart of all the world's religions!

"Okay," you may be wondering. "So I've got all these different bodies. But then—which one of them is *me*?"

Ramana Maharshi Figures It Out

Ramana Maharshi was born in Tiruchuli, Tamil Nadu, in 1879. He impressed no one. He was a mediocre student and something of a bully on the playground. He felt no draw to spiritual life at all.

Ramana Maharshi, sage of Arunachala.

Then, at the age of 17, Ramana Maharshi woke up. "I was sitting alone in a room on the first floor of my uncle's house," Ramana later related. "There was nothing wrong with my health, but a sudden violent fear of death overtook me. I felt, 'I am going to die' and began thinking what to do about it. I felt I had to solve the problem myself, there and then."

Ramana lay down on the floor and acted out the process of death. He stiffened his body as if rigor mortis had set in and held his breath as if his heart and lungs had stopped. "Okay, the body is dead. But am *I* dead?" he inquired.

At that moment, he experienced an overwhelmingly powerful sense of the deathless spirit within himself. "This was not a dull thought but flashed through me vividly as living truth which I perceived directly, almost without thinking. 'I' was something real."

From then on, Ramana was obsessed with his Inner Self. He left home and hid in a small storage cell in the Shiva temple near Mount Arunachala. There he did intense spiritual practice, learning to maintain his focus continually on the deathless reality he felt inside himself. Eventually he experienced the conscious root of his being constantly even while talking or reading. Ramana had become an enlightened sage, living in the unflickering light of spirit.

Sages Say

"The only enquiry leading to Self-realization is seeking the Source of the 'I' with in-turned mind."

—Ramana Maharshi

Remember how I said earlier that Hindus call their tradition "the eternal religion" because anyone who explores the laws of consciousness will rediscover Hinduism's fundamental truths? Ramana was an average 17-year-old boy with no formal religious training whatever. Yet by lying down and focusing intently inward, he had rediscovered the ancient truths of the Upanishadic seers. "That thou art. You are that undying inner awareness."

Ramana had traveled beyond the physical body, beyond the astral body, and through even the causal body. Underlying them all he had discovered the true Self.

The Inner Self

Ramana Maharshi went on to become one of the best known and best loved saints of modern India. Hindus (and later foreigners) would come from thousands of miles away merely to sit in the presence of the master. By remaining fully centered in his Inner Self, he radiated a tranquil luminosity. Those sitting near him reported their minds immediately became still. Some experienced inner peace for the first time in their lives.

Scientists in the West consider consciousness a by-product of the nervous system that ends with death. The sages of India don't buy this. During out-of-body travel they experience their consciousness moving independently of their body. The great masters have also reported remaining conscious and alert after their previous bodies died, and journeying through other inner worlds. To them the physical body is the by-product of consciousness, not the other way around!

The Inner Self is called *Atman* in Sanskrit. The Atman is who you really are—not your physical and subtle bodies, all of which are perishable. The Atman exists beyond space and time. It is the undying reality, your fundamental inner being and truth.

Entering the Inner World

Many people have experienced the Inner Self at some point in their lives. If you haven't—if what I'm talking about here sounds to you like it came from Neptune— let's try a short exercise and maybe you can get a glimpse of Ramana's inner world yourself.

Sages Say

"There is an eternal, all pervading intelligence in which all individual souls are rooted. That Supreme Awareness is the final truth. That is your innermost being. You are that."

—*Chhandogya Upanishad*

Guidepost

Meditation is not for everyone. Mentally and emotionally unstable people should not meditate. Healthy people should undertake a meditation practice under the supervision of an experienced spiritual teacher who can help them handle the tricks their mind may play during the inward journey.

➤ Sit up comfortably with your head, neck, and spine straight.

➤ Close your eyes and relax deeply.

➤ Breathe naturally. Your breath should be even, slow, and continuous. No jerky or shallow breathing!

➤ Don't feel dumb. This is just an experiment.

➤ Bring your full awareness to the point between your eyebrows. Then shift your awareness about three inches behind this point, inside your brain.

➤ If any visual images or mental chatter appear, ignore them.

➤ Rest your attention in the silent darkness in your mind.

➤ Ask yourself, "Who is aware of the silent darkness?" Focus attentively. Be fully aware of your own awareness.

➤ Open your eyes and relax.

Did you experience an intense inner lucidity? A sort of primordial awareness that wasn't thinking or doing anything, just kind of watching?

If you connected, even for a second, with your Atman, you would have felt vividly alive, intensely focused, and very clear-headed. In the Hindu tradition, it's believed that people who visit this state regularly experience dramatic healing, and become much more creative and successful and much less fearful.

Great saints live in this state (and even higher ones I'll describe later). They gain from it the ability to help others with tangible blessing power, as Ramana Maharshi did.

The Inner Sun

Let me state the obvious. Most of our lives we do not walk around experiencing ourselves as a being of pure, radiant consciousness. We experience ourselves as harried housewives, aggressive salesmen, bored students, starving musicians, or whatever.

An athlete or a sick person or a high-fashion model may remain intensely identified with her physical body. Her attention is most often directed at her health or strength or appearance. That is her reality. Hinduism says that no matter how well she cares for her body, one day it will die. But the Inner Self hidden behind her self-image will not.

A scientist or intellectual or computer programmer may be very intensely focused at the level of thought. A lover or a new mother or a neurotic may be very intensely focused on their emotions. But eventually the field of experience with which they're identifying will pass away. Their Higher Self will not.

You may feel who you really are is the mano maya kosha—your work-a-day thoughts and emotions. You may feel your real identity is your good old material body, the sthula sharira. Hinduism says that all our bodies, including the physical one, are nothing more than fields of energy, called *prakriti* in Sanskrit. They reflect the light of spirit and because of this appear to be independent and conscious, just as the Moon appears to shine with its own light but actually just reflects the Sun's.

What you experience as your mind has no more independent reality than your body. When you enter the state of deep sleep, for example, the light of spirit withdraws from your mental body and for all practical purposes your mind ceases to exist!

The *Tripura Rahasya* compares the Inner Self to a splendid gem locked in a chest that's fallen in the sea and become covered with mud. You have to find the chest, clean off the mud, and break open the lock. Then you'll see for yourself the shining gem of incalculable value. All Hindu spiritual practices are designed with the ultimate goal of helping us find the "pearl of great price" that lies buried in our minds and encrusted with the mud of our generally petty, run-of-the-mill thoughts. That gem is the pure, undying awareness that illuminates our lives.

Spiritual Mentoring

"There are some especially pure souls who have attained Self-realization, establishing their awareness permanently in their Inner Self," wrote the Hindu adept Shankaracharya. "They bring blessings to all humanity, like the coming of spring. They have crossed the ocean of birth and death, yet selflessly remain here among us and help others to cross, too. It is the very nature of these great men and women to help others."

In Hinduism, the guru—your spiritual mentor—ranks in stature second only to God. In fact, in some traditions the guru is valued even more than God. After all, it's the guru who introduces you to God in the first place. Without the assistance of this guide, you may never find your way into the divine presence.

The *Upanishads* put it this way. If someone hits you over the head and carries you blindfolded away from your native town, then dumps you off in the middle of nowhere, you have a problem. Many of us may have the sense of being spiritually lost, dropped here in the material world, blundering around without a clue. Now, if someone comes up to you and says, "Oh, you're from Duluth? Duluth is that way!" suddenly you're not so lost. You're headed in the right direction, and with a little effort and resourcefulness on your part, you'll find your way home.

The guru shows you the way home. He or she teaches you the wisdom of the ancients and guides your moral and spiritual development. And most importantly, the guru prescribes the specific spiritual exercises you need to do to grow in self-awareness.

A guru is a very useful resource if you have begun a meditation practice. It's amazing, the crazy content thrown up by your subconscious and the confusion it can lead to. The guru helps you distinguish between the seductive but ultimately not very productive experiences coming out of your subconscious and the genuine insights pouring out of your superconscious. The guru has been through the process and knows how to distinguish what's spiritually legitimate.

New Word Alert!

Atman is the Inner Self, the immortal spirit.

Prakriti is the primeval energy from which the universe is shaped. It's the stuff of which matter is made.

Shaktipat is the transmission of spiritual knowledge and power.

The Guru Hook-Up

Advanced gurus transmit the enlightening energy of their spiritual tradition. They don't generate it—they serve as conduits for the living knowledge to flow. This is the famous process of *shaktipat,* the "descent of spiritual power." You work very, very hard, making every sincere effort to attain higher states of divine awareness. When you can't go any further by yourself, the guru does the hook-up, plugging you into the cosmic circuit box and—*zap!*—you spontaneously rocket into a higher orbit of being.

Swami Rama Bharati told me about his own experience. He was so discouraged with his lack of progress in meditation after years of sincere effort that he actually felt suicidal. His guru, the great master Bengali Baba, called him to his side, touched his forehead, and for the next nine hours, Swami Rama sat motionless in the highest state of bliss he had ever experienced.

My own experiences with Hindu gurus have often been intensely frustrating. This is because I come from the Western academic tradition where teachers exist to give information. You ask a straight question, you get a straight answer. I'll tell you right now that if you want to get a straight answer out of a Hindu guru, you're better off going to dental school and learning to pull teeth.

In the Hindu tradition, gurus don't see their role as imparters of information. Their goal is not to help you become a brilliant authority or a Ph.D. Their goal is to make you a sage. To awaken your intuitive powers so that you can find the answers in the inner world yourself. In Hinduism, it's said that a guru's greatest achievement is to propel a disciple to even greater levels of spirituality than the guru's own.

Into the Pressure Cooker

Gurus do convey information. But more of the training involves character building and purification of the mind. So they throw you into awful situations, like starting a medical center to help the poor and then putting completely incompetent people in charge. Can you maintain your spiritual center and your focus on serving others when your bosses are continually making irrational decisions that irritate the heck out of you? Can you stay calm when your guru, who was always so loving to you before, suddenly starts screaming at you for something you didn't even do?

These are the kinds of tricks of the trade the Hindu guru has traditionally used to help disciples clearly see the play of their egos and to test the strength of their commitment to spiritual life.

Very few, very special people have attained self-realization without the help of a guru. Recent historical examples include Ramana Maharshi, Anandamayi Ma, and Amritanandamayi Ma. Hindus believe exceptional people like these either had spectacularly good karma from the past, when they did work with a guru, or else they are incarnations of great sages of the past or even of deities, who entered our world to serve humanity.

Sages Say

"The spiritual aspirant controls his senses. He controls his life force. He controls his mind. He gains lordship over the faculties of his higher intelligence. Then he becomes one with the Supreme One, Whose body is space, Who is ever tranquil, Who is immortal."

—*Taittiriya Upanishad* 1:6.2

Quick Quiz

1. For Hindus, a human being is made up of …

    a. Physical, astral, and causal bodies.

    b. Flesh, bones, and blood.

    c. Pizza, Pepsi, and potato chips.

2. When he was 17 years old, Ramana Maharshi realized …

    a. He was deeply attracted to girls.

    b. He wanted to be a soft drink distributor.

    c. Within his soul lay a deathless Inner Self.

3. The guru's job is to …

    a. Separate us from the contents of our wallets.

    b. Align us with our real nature.

    c. Teach us how to win friends and influence people.

4. The Inner Self …

    a. Is the deathless awareness hidden behind our thoughts.

    b. Can be experienced with the help of antidepressants.

    c. Is the result of enzymatic action in the brain.

Answers: 1 (a). 2 (c). 3 (b). 4 (a).

Getting On the Innernet

For most Hindus, Self-realization is God-realization. How can this be? "The air closed inside a jar is not at all different from the air outside the jar," said Shankaracharya. "In exactly the same way, your Inner Self is exactly identical with the Self of all. Smash the jar and the air inside it merges seamlessly with the air outside. Smash the illusion that you exist apart from God, and you merge in that divine reality."

The jars we are locked in are the physical, astral, and causal bodies. The physical body is smashed at death. The astral body is smashed at rebirth. But the causal body, the subtlemost vortex of energy in which our Inner Self reincarnates, is smashed only at the moment of final liberation, when the Inner Self merges in the Divine Self.

Think about it. Just as your five fingers are not really separate because they are linked to the same hand, so the Self in you and the Self in me (and the Self in Lassie the dog for that matter) are not really separate because they are linked in the Supreme Self, the consciousness of God.

When you harm someone else, you are literally harming your Self. When you love someone else, you are literally loving your Self.

At the innermost level of our being we are all intimately linked. Apollonius of Tyana was amazed when he arrived in Kashmir and found yogis who knew everything about him. "How can you possibly know me?" he demanded. "We begin by knowing ourselves," was their reply.

The advanced adepts of the Hindu tradition move into a space in consciousness where there is no space between us. They explain that that is how they appear to know their disciples' very thoughts. Hindus assume Jesus was expressing exactly the same concept as their own great spiritual masters when he said, "I am the vine, you are the branches." (John 15:1.) We are linked at the root with God.

Getting Off the Wheel

The goal of every Hindu life is to eventually shift one's awareness to the inner world of divine union. Hindu life is actually structured so that even average lay people can spend the last portion of their lives devoted solely to spiritual practice. (I'll explain how this actually works in Chapter 16, "A Classy Religion.")

As long as you continue to wear a body, whether it's a physical one or a body of subtler energy, you're on the wheel of rebirth. Your identification with a body, your desire to explore a realm of existence whether material or astral, will keep tugging you into the round of birth and death.

In Hinduism, the spiritual master is the one who is no longer tied to any body. From the realm of pure consciousness, this being can choose voluntarily to reenter the worlds and can just as effortlessly exit again when the mission that soul has chosen to complete in the worlds is done. These are the liberated souls of Hinduism, the great enlightened masters. What they've mastered is themselves. Now they live in God-consciousness.

It's News to Me!

Many Christians are puzzled by the words of the Last Supper in which Jesus says, "This is my body, take and eat. This is my blood, take and drink. I am the vine, you are the branches." In fact, these words are adopted directly from the ancient Orphic mysteries in which the god Dionysus uses exactly the same phrases, referring to the mystic identify of his disciples with himself. The Hindu doctrine of our unity with God appears in mystical traditions throughout the world.

The Least You Need to Know

➤ In addition to the physical body, we have increasingly subtle bodies.

➤ The true Self is none of these bodies but the consciousness that operates through them.

➤ The guru helps us connect with our Inner Self.

➤ Self-realization is ultimately God-realization because God is the Self of all.

Chapter 9

Truth Is a Multi-Layer Cake

In This Chapter

➤ A reasonable path to God

➤ Hindu atomic theory

➤ Ritual road to heaven

➤ Counting out reality

➤ Truth and illusion

Warning: You are about to launch into the dizzying world of Hindu theology. If your "Boring!" light is switching on, let me reassure you that the Hindus have some of the most interesting theology on the planet, if I may say so myself.

And I think if you get some of this stuff down, then later when we see how Hindus live their daily lives and what spiritual practices they actually perform, it will seem a lot less like "heathen superstition" and more like something truly beautiful, meaningful, and profound.

Six Views of One Reality

There's a famous story in India about six blind men who try to understand what an elephant looks like by running their hands over its body. One feels its trunk, another its ears, another its leg. A fourth man fingers its tail, a fifth its belly, and the sixth rides around on its back. Not surprisingly, they come to completely different conclusions about what an elephant must look like.

New Word Alert!

Darshana means "seeing." It refers to Hinduism's schools of theology, which are different ways of "seeing" God. It can also mean having the direct vision of the Supreme Being yourself—for example, when you see His or Her image in a temple.

It's News to Me!

People often think scientific materialism is a modern phenomenon. But India's ancient school of Lokayata was wholly materialistic. It taught that there is no reality beyond what we see with our five senses, and that human consciousness ends at death. This school never gained much credibility in India because it failed to explain the extrasensory or "psychic" phenomena so many people experience, and that saints and advanced yogis exhibit all the time.

Hindus believe God is like that. He's so big and so multidimensional and so impossible to grasp with the human mind that everyone who has something to say about His nature may be absolutely correct, but only about the one small part of His nature they are able to understand.

Imagine we're standing together in a dark room. I hold up a sheet of paper. You shine a flashlight on it and see that it's white. Okay, that was a no-brainer.

Now imagine your flashlight has a yellow bulb instead of a white one. This time the paper looks yellow. If your flashlight had a blue bulb, it would look blue. If you turn off your flashlight, you won't see the paper at all. It's merged in the darkness. So what color is the sheet of paper, really?

There are many thousands of different *darshanas,* ways of looking at reality, in Hinduism. But six are most important. They're all looking at the same divine reality, but they see it in different colors.

Please note that in summarizing these complex systems of Indian thought for you, I will be oversimplifying shamelessly.

Nyaya: The Logical Approach

When I was in college, oh, it seems like a century ago, we were taught that the ancient Greeks were the first people in world history to think logically. This always seemed suspect to me. The Egyptians built the pyramids without being able to think logically or scientifically? Humans have lived on this planet for hundreds of thousands of years at least, and Thales of Miletus was the first person ever to have a logical thought? Frankly, my professors thought the Greeks were the only ancient culture capable of logic because the Greeks were the only ancient culture they'd ever studied.

Today, more knowledgeable scholars admit that until very recently, the Nyaya philosophers of India were probably the most skilled logicians in history. These guys had nitpicking down to a science.

Nyaya was founded by a sage named Gotama a long, long time ago. He noted that anyone could run around claiming anything, so how do we decide whom to believe? We have to reason clearly and methodically, Gotama said, so we don't inadvertently delude ourselves and everyone else at the same time.

When we analyze nature critically, we're forced to the conclusion that the objective universe is composed of individual atoms and the subjective universe is composed of individual souls. But how can we souls be sure that our ideas about the world outside ourselves are correct? There are four sources of information we can rely on if we're careful:

1. Data we perceive with our senses.

2. Inferences we make based on this data. ("If there's smoke, there's fire.")

3. Careful comparisons. ("A tiger is something like a big lion with stripes.")

4. Reliable testimony. (Like the statements of the enlightened Vedic seers.)

Nyaya theologians determined that God must exist for a number of logical reasons. Here are two:

1. Atoms can't coordinate themselves into an intelligible universe. Everywhere you look, the cosmos shows evidence of intelligent planning and purpose.

2. Karma doesn't run itself. Some higher intelligence apportions to each soul the karma it deserves.

The Nyayas worked out all their arguments with painstaking attention to detail and logical consistency. They set the standard for clear thinking in Hinduism.

Sages Say

"After a cycle of universal dissolution, the Supreme Being decides to recreate the cosmos so that we souls can experience worlds of shape and solidity. Very subtle atoms begin to combine, eventually generating a cosmic wind that blows heavier and heavier atoms together. Souls, depending on their karma earned in previous world systems, spontaneously draw to themselves atoms that coalesce into an appropriate body."

—*The Prashasta Pada*

Vaisheshika: The Atomic Theory

My professors in college also told me the Greeks were the first people to come up with the atomic theory. That wasn't true either.

The Indian atomic theory was formulated by the Vaisheshikas sometime before the beginning of Buddhism and Jainism, both of which incorporated some ideas about atoms into their own worldviews. This takes Vaisheshika back to, at the very latest, 500 B.C.E. if you accept the Southern Buddhist date for Buddha, or to 1000 B.C.E. at

117

the latest if you believe the Northern Buddhists' date for Buddha. It's attributed to a brilliant founding sage named Kanada.

According to the Vaisheshikas, there are some particular things we can say definitely exist. Atoms do, as do the space and time in which they move. So does God and so do we, in the form of immortal souls who put on bodies to play out our karma during the cycles of universal manifestation.

Here comes an important point. (Prepare not to be confused.) Remember that six blind men can describe an elephant completely differently and still be talking about the same animal.

Remember how I mentioned that Hinduism says we're all one? That our souls all connect in the divine consciousness? Well, the Vaisheshikas don't believe this at all. But that doesn't mean they're not Hindus! Nor does it mean they don't believe in the Veda. It just means they're reading the Veda from a slightly different perspective that makes more sense to them. It's like Christians reading the Bible. Some say the Bible tells us we should follow the pope. Others insist the Bible doesn't breathe a word about the pope.

The Vaisheshikas believe each soul is an eternally separate unit that exists as a whole in itself. When it disengages from involvement with the universe, becoming a liberated soul, it enters a state much like unconsciousness because it doesn't perceive or interact with anything outside itself. It's not happy. It's not sad. It just exists. It's something like the state of your awareness during deep sleep.

Mimamsa: The Way to Heaven

Mimamsa is the darshana favored by many orthodox brahmins whose lives are devoted to performing Vedic rituals.

Mimamsa is attributed to the ancient sage Jaimini. It emphasizes the performance of duty as the structural law which holds families, nations, and the universe itself together. Literally from their first waking moment, Hindus who follow this tradition devote each moment of the day to the conscientious performance of religious duties, from chanting sacred mantras before getting out of bed, chanting other prayers the moment their feet first touch the floor, and so on throughout the day.

The Mimamsas are not deeply interested in defining the nature of God or in spiritual liberation. Their preoccupation is with the performance of sacred ritual in the effort to live righteously here on earth and to obtain a heavenly state after death. They're not interested in getting off the wheel of rebirth, but in living ethically in the here and now.

To the Mimamsas, the universe itself is an unending fire sacrifice. Life is offered back to life as one creature dies to feed another. By aligning ourselves with the self-sacrificial nature of the universe, we live in accord with eternal law.

The Mimamsas have developed elaborate theories built around grammar and sound. That probably sounds like just about the most boring thing in the world, but when I tell you more about their ideas in Chapter 10, "The Sacred Sciences," I suspect you'll agree that Hindu ideas about the "divine word" are a whole lot more interesting than the grammar we learned in grade school!

Sankhya: Spirit and Matter

Here comes my favorite. Sankhya is one of the most ancient, most interesting, and most influential philosophies of all time. Thinkers from other schools would do their best to debunk Sankhya, but in the end, they'd incorporate parts of it into their own systems. If you can grasp the fundamental insights of Sankhya, you'll have a firm handle on the mystical traditions of cultures all over the world.

The yogis and pandits I've studied with claim Sankhya is the oldest known philosophical system in existence. They may be right. The system was founded by the sage Kapila in prehistory. Sankhya terminology already appears in the Veda, particularly the *Upanishads*.

Sankhya literally means "number." Sankhya enumerates the categories that make up physical and mental reality. In prehistory, the great minds of India didn't have particle accelerators to help them analyze different types of atoms. Instead they used astute observation of nature and of their own minds to analyze the components of human experience. These components added up to twenty-five.

Sages Say

"The followers of Sankhya put their trust in the words of the sages. The followers of Yoga put their trust in their own experience. There is no other wisdom equal to Sankhya. There is no other power equal to Yoga."

—*Mahabharata* 12:289

Let's start at ground zero, the most physical of physical matter, and work our way up the ladder of reality:

1. Prithivi: Dense physical matter (like earth).

2. Apas: Fluid physical matter (such as water).

3. Agni: Combustive physical matter (like fire).

4. Vayu: Gaseous matter (like air).

5. Akasha: Extremely attenuated physical matter (like space).

6. Gandha: That which is smelled.

7. Rasa: That which is tasted.

8. Rupa: That which is seen.

9. Sparsha: That which is felt.

10. Shabda: That which is heard.

11. Payu: The ability to excrete.

12. Upastha: The ability to procreate.

13. Pada: The ability to locomote.

14. Pani: The ability to handle objects.

15. Vak: The ability to speak.

16. Ghrana: The sense of smell.

17. Jinva: The sense of taste.

18. Chakshu: The sense of sight.

19. Tvak: The sense of touch.

20. Stotra: The sense of hearing.

21. Manas: Thought processes.

22. Ahankara: Self-identity.

23. Buddhi: The sense of judgment. Intellect and intuition.

24. Prakriti: The material matrix. Root matter.

25. Purusha: The individual spirit.

Guidepost

Is our Western way of categorizing reality the only legitimate way? We say there are the 100-plus elements and four or so basic forms of energy. Other cultures—such as the Hindus and Chinese—described nature in ways that initially appear odd to us. Westerners who have taken the trouble to learn these systems have expressed their amazement at their level of insight and sophistication.

Reality by Number

In other words, Sankhya lists the five physical elements, the five subtle elements, the five organs of action, the five sense organs, the three faculties of mind, then matter and spirit themselves.

Note that the first four elements are often mistranslated "earth, water, fire and air." These four concepts, as they're actually applied in Hindu physics and medicine, are far more complex than these simplistic translations would suggest. Hindus understand them as energy states, as the way matter behaves in its densest forms.

Akasha, the fifth element, is a super fine form of matter that fills space and in a sense actually *is* space. Atomic particles are created from it. Only recently have nuclear physicists begun speculating that such a field of "super matter" must indeed exist to explain the occasional appearance of particles "out of nowhere" during their experiments!

Note that only the first five categories on the list are physical. The second five categories are *not* physical. These subtle elements refer to matter *as you experience it in your mind,* not as it exists outside your body. When you see a fire in a dream, your skull doesn't burn up. According to the Hindu tradition, the substance of your dreams and inner visions is just as real as the substance of the external world. In fact, whole other dimensions exist in this immaterial matter. This is an important point that may help you understand how visualizations and ritual magic—important components of Hindu spiritual practice—actually work.

Hold on to your hat, because the next major point is totally counterintuitive to our Western conditioning. Sankhya holds that the sense organs and organs of action are not physical either. When you read the preceding list, you probably thought it was talking about the hands and nose and feet and eyes. It ain't so.

The Sankhya masters noted that we see and move not only in the physical world but also in our dreams. Yogis and shamans see and move in whole other dimensions all together. So the senses and the ability to interface with the stuff around us must exist in our subtle body. They may express through our physical organs while we're alive and conscious, but in dream states, "astral travel," or after death, they express through our sukshma sharira, our subtle body.

Sages Say

"As milk, without being aware of it, nourishes the calf, so prakriti, matter, unknowingly acts for the benefit of the soul."

—The Sankhya Karika

The Nature of Mind

In other words, it's not the brain that sees and hears. The brain registers sound waves and photons from the physical world, but these are transmitted to a receiving station that's not *in* the brain, though it operates *through* the brain. This receiving station is called manas, the processing port of the mind. It's Sankhya's twenty-first element.

The renegade Western physicist Rupert Sheldrake explains this phenomenon in terms that parallel the Sankhya idea so closely it's positively eerie. He pointed out that a person who doesn't understand how a television set works might believe Andy Griffith and his son Opie really live inside the TV. So if the TV set breaks, Andy and Opie no longer exist. In reality, of course, Andy and Opie filmed the TV show hundreds of miles away and their program is being broadcast to your TV antenna or routed through your cable service, which sends the signals into your TV.

According to Sheldrake, we in the West have a very primitive understanding of the brain. When the brain is switched on, images appear. When the brain switches off, the images vanish. Ergo, scientists assume the images exist only in the brain. But our thought processes may be going on in other dimensions entirely and may only be *routed* through the physical brain if the Hindus, and scientists like Sheldrake, are correct.

In addition to manas, which receives, transmits, and interprets sense data, there's the ahankara, or "me" awareness. In some people, this function shuts down, in whole or in part. You may have heard of people who, due to certain medical conditions, have lost the ability to tell that certain parts of their own body belong to them. The ahankara has flaked out.

Buddhi is the part of the mind in which will kicks in. Manas transmits the immediate presence of Rum Raisin premium ice cream. Ahankara goes, "That's for me! I want it!" Buddhi is the part of the intelligence that then deliberates: "I'm already 25 pounds overweight." And then makes the decision to go ahead and have some ice cream. Animals have manas and ahankara, but buddhi, or the capacity to make wise or foolish judgments based on reason, exists primarily in humans.

The real Self, consciousness, called purusha in this system, exists outside the range of mind and matter all together. The mind is the apparatus through which consciousness interfaces with the inner and outer worlds. But the mind is made of perishable patterns of energy and will dissolve away sooner or later. Unlike the real conscious Self within, which is eternal.

How do the Sankhya masters know this? Because they've been doing yoga!

Sages Say

"Mental states are not conscious in themselves. Mind has a knower. The Self is that knower; it is the real man."

—Swami Satparakashananda

It's News to Me!

The word yoga comes from the Sanskrit root *yuj*. It's related to the English word yoke and signifies union with divine consciousness whether you see it as your own Inner Self or as union with the Supreme Being.

Yoga: Techniques for Higher Awareness

In the West, *yoga* means standing on your head. In Hinduism, it means meditation. Yoga literally means "union." It's about uniting your attention with its source, your everyday awareness with the fountain of consciousness from which it springs.

Hindu thinkers were not into philosophy just to show off how smart they were. Even the driest Hindu thinkers of them all, the Nyaya logicians, had a sacred purpose in mind. That was to use their knowledge as a means to *moksha*, spiritual liberation. To Hindus, philosophy is never just an intellectual exercise as it so often is in the West. It's a door to the living experience of divine reality.

Yoga is the practical branch of Sankhya, the spiritual techniques used to move from talking about higher levels of reality to actually experiencing them.

Sankhya says that everything in the ever-changing universe, including the energy out of which our minds are made, comes from prakriti, energy. Prakriti is the ocean of energy that exists forever in all dimensions of eternity. Its grossest manifestation is the physical matter we see and touch.

Prakriti has three modes called *gunas:*

➤ *Rajas:* Motion. Active, energetic, hot. Kinetic energy.

➤ *Tamas:* Inertia. Heaviness, dullness. Potential energy.

➤ *Sattva:* Harmony. Lightness, clarity. Balanced energy.

When all three gunas balance each other, the universe melts away. It's like the mathematical equation [-1] + 0 + 1 = 0. But when the gunas fall out of equilibrium, a motion rolls through the cosmic ocean of primeval energy, and a new universe begins to form.

Yogis actively work to balance the gunas in their personalities so that they can disengage from matter completely and shift their awareness back fully into pure consciousness itself. When that happens, the karmashaya, the baggage of karma the causal body carries around with it, falls away along with the causal body itself. The yogi is now liberated—free from karma and the cycles of rebirth. She has shifted her awareness totally into the twenty-fifth category of reality, purusha, the Inner Self.

The Sankhya masters say there are an infinite number of purushas floating around the universe, trillions upon trillions of souls. The yoga system adds one more special purusha: God. According to yoga, God is the divine consciousness that never fell into matter when the universe first formed. God has always existed outside time and space, but is so gracious he occasionally lends us a hand in our efforts to escape the eternal treadmill.

New Word Alert!

Moksha means freedom. The liberated man and woman are freed from the wheel of death and rebirth, and from the destiny enforced by their karma.

A **guna** is one of the three modes in which energy operates: active, inert, or balanced.

Purusha and prakriti, spirit and matter, never come into contact with each other in this system. Purusha doesn't "act" in matter. It can't because the power to act, our organs of action, belong to the sphere of prakriti. The purusha is a ball of consciousness that merely observes. Have you been in an accident where your car was spinning out of control? During emergencies, many people report they were thrust into a state of calm clarity where they weren't afraid at all, but were simply observing what was happening. That tranquil inner observer is the purusha.

While purusha never does anything, its mere "proximity" to prakriti causes matter to do everything. It's like a magnet under a sheet of paper covered with iron filings. The magnet never touches the bits of metal, yet they all spontaneously align themselves in accord with the magnet's fields. In the same way, nature, which is not conscious in itself, automatically "serves" purusha, which is consciousness itself. The chaos of primordial energy becomes the ordered cosmos perceived by consciousness.

Guidepost

It's not true that Hindus believe the world is "just an illusion." Shankaracharya, the famous master who is supposed to have taught this, in fact admitted that the world is fully real to those of us living in it. It appears like an illusion only from the point of view of enlightened awareness, because it is constantly changing and finally disappears. The consciousness from which the universe was projected is the *real* reality, Shankaracharya said, not the ever-changing world.

Vedanta: It's All an Illusion!

For many of the educated Westerners who know anything about Hinduism, Hinduism means Vedanta. That's because the first Hindu spiritual leaders to teach widely in the West were Vedantists. If you hear people say, "Hindus believe this world is just an illusion," you're hearing a rather jumbled version of Vedanta.

Vedanta means both "the last portion of the Veda," referring to the *Upanishads,* and "the fulfillment of the Veda," meaning the most enlightening portion of the Veda. For over a thousand years, Vedanta has been the most important theological force in India. This is due largely to the immense impact of Shankaracharya, and to the incredible strength of the reaction against him by other Vedanta masters, such as Ramanuja and Madhva.

One, Not Two!

Shankaracharya was one of those staggering geniuses the world too rarely sees. He was not just a brilliant intellectual but a highly advanced yogi with a living experience of the unity of all reality. He appeared at a time in history when Hinduism was in a slump, having taken some big hits from alternative religions, like Buddhism and Jainism. He traveled all over India, reinvigorating Hinduism through the force of his luminous personality, his impeccable logic, and his yogic power.

Shankara, as he's known, carried the doctrine of Advaita Vedanta throughout the subcontinent. *Advaita* means nondual, or "not two." Shankara disagreed with the Sankhya masters that reality is dual, that spirit and matter exist separately. To Shankara, spirit—by which he means pure consciousness—is the only reality.

Shankara uses the Vedic name for the one reality, Brahman. Atman, our innermost Self, is identical in essence to Brahman, the divine consciousness, just as a drop of water is essentially identical with the ocean. When we achieve moksha, spiritual liberation, we merge back into that ocean of consciousness, as a drop of water merges seamlessly into the sea.

There is no way to describe Brahman. It is far beyond human conception. But if we had to use words to give us a hazy idea of the greatness of that vast reality, Shankara would use the words *sat, chit,* and ananda: being, consciousness, and bliss. To him, the highest state of awareness was not the unconscious state the Vaisheshikas described. It was a luminous and lucid state full of divine knowledge and blissfulness.

If all that exists is pure being, consciousness, and bliss, why do we have to deal with rent payments, incompetent supervisors, and dead car batteries? Shankara would be the first to acknowledge the practical realities we face in day-to-day life. But from the point of view of the deepest states of meditation, where one actually experiences one's own Atman merging in Brahman, the external world is *maya*, the superimposition of our own ideas about the world on an unchanging and ever-perfect underlying reality.

New Word Alert!

Advaita means nondual, one without a second.

Brahman is the Supreme Reality, the one all-pervading consciousness. (Don't confuse Brahman with Brahma the Creator!)

Sat is pure beingness, or pure truth.

Chit means consciousness.

If you see a coiled rope on the road in the dark, you may think it's a snake. Your heart starts pounding, you get sweaty and clammy. For you, at the moment, that's really a poisonous snake. But when you shine a flashlight at it and see it's a rope, your fear disappears instantly and you recognize the fear was groundless from the very beginning. When the flashlight of genuine meditative experience shines in our awareness, we recognize that there is not and never has been anything, anywhere, anytime, but Brahman—pure, perfect divinity.

One, Sort Of

Ramanuja caught hold of a different part of the elephant. Ramanuja, who may have lived somewhere around 1000 C.E., couldn't quite accept that we individual souls are in some sense equal in essence with God. He started his own brand of Vedanta called Vishishta Advaita, which roughly translates as "almost but not quite not two."

For Ramanuja, we souls can experience union, not unity, with Brahman. The world is not an idea superimposed on reality but has a real existence of its own. It is the body of Brahman, and Brahman is the innermost soul of the world. We exist as beings distinct from Brahman, and will forever, though our innermost essence is rooted in that Supreme Reality. We can recognize our unity in Brahman, but we never lose our identity in it.

While Shankara emphasized using the discriminating intellect to contemplate the inner reality, Ramanuja, like the Mimamsas, emphasized the importance of rituals and religious and social duties. While Shankara promoted a mental approach to the truth, Ramanuja felt devotion was a more appropriate way to approach the Supreme Being.

Two, Not One!

Madhva, who lived around 1200 C.E., rejected both points of view. He created a third major school called Dvaita Vedanta, the Vedanta of duality. Some scholars have speculated that his views were influenced by Christianity. He is the only major Hindu thinker distinguished by teaching eternal damnation!

Madhva taught that the world is real, we're real, and God is real, and we're all eternally separate. We're not united or in union or anything to that effect, thank you!

During Madhva's lifetime, the Muslims were creating havoc in India, actively trying to extinguish the Hindu religion. It's possible he felt the need to arouse Hindus from the other-worldliness that the other schools of Vedanta tended to produce and inspire them to deal with real life emergencies in the material world, like homicidal Muslim armies.

The Whole Elephant

Most of my Hindu teachers are not in the least disturbed by the dramatic differences between various Hindu masters like Kapila, Shankara, and Jaimini. To my gurus, these different philosophers were just hanging on to different parts of the elephant. In some respects, their differing doctrines say more about where they were in their meditation practice than about reality itself.

There comes a point in one's meditation where you enter a state much like unconsciousness. There comes a deeper state where you feel yourself to be pure conscious awareness alone, an observer of the material world that seems somehow "outside" you. Continuing the journey inward, there comes a still deeper state where the distinction between you, the world, and God fades away and you experience an expansive state of unity. So these different teachers aren't contradicting each other. They're all correct, based on the level of meditation they attained.

The broad consensus today (with a fair number of contemporary gurus dissenting) is that Shankaracharya grasped more of the elephant than the others. But for practical purposes of advancing in one's spiritual practice, Kapila's Sankhya system is still considered the most useful.

Quick Quiz

1. Hindu theologians are …

   a. Completely incapable of thinking logically.

   b. Among the best logicians in the world.

   c. The world's most devoted rugby fans.

2. Kapila taught that …

   a. There are twenty-five levels of reality.

   b. Brahman is the only reality.

   c. The Beatles are the greatest rock group of all time.

3. Shankaracharya is famous for …

   a. Leading an uprising of the proletariat.

   b. Sitting without blinking for nearly twenty years.

   c. Spreading nondual Vedanta throughout India.

Answers: 1 (b). 2 (a). 3 (c).

The Least You Need to Know

➤ Ancient Hindus mastered logic and the atomic theory.

➤ Sankhya summarized the levels of physical and nonmaterial realities.

➤ Yoga teaches the techniques to actually experience divine reality.

➤ Vedanta has three main schools defining the soul's relation to the Supreme Spirit.

Chapter 10

The Sacred Sciences

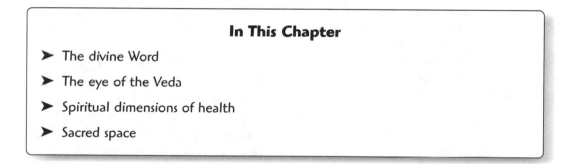

In This Chapter

➤ The divine Word

➤ The eye of the Veda

➤ Spiritual dimensions of health

➤ Sacred space

In Hindu culture science, the arts, medicine, even cooking and lovemaking, have a sacred dimension. Six sciences from ancient times have been considered particularly sacred. The are called *Vedangas,* "limbs of the Veda," because they are especially useful in understanding the Veda, India's most sacred holy book, and in applying its blessing power in practical ways. The Vedangas are Grammar, Phonetics, Meter, Etymology, Ritual, and Astrology.

Four other arts and sciences are considered especially sacred, but are not directly related to study of the Veda. These are called *Upa Vedas.* They include Medicine, Music and Dance, the Martial Arts, and Architecture.

The Word Is God

I would be willing to bet your first reaction to hearing that Hindus consider grammar a sacred science was identical to mine: "You've got to be kidding!"

But consider the opening words of the Gospel of John in the Bible. "In the beginning was the Word, and the Word was with God, and the Word was God." The concept of the sacred word has an extremely ancient pedigree, not only in India but in other ancient cultures as well. The ancient Jews, Egyptians, and Greeks pondered long and hard over the sanctity of the inherent meaningfulness of life and the mystery of meaningful human and divine communication.

Four of the six Vedangas—grammar, phonetics, meter, and etymology—are devoted to the science of language:

➤ Vedic grammar explores in incredible detail the question of how a series of sounds uttered by one person can be understood by another. How complex concepts can be conveyed through the medium of physical sound.

➤ Phonetics looks agonizingly closely at all aspects of pronunciation. This was immensely important to the brahmins whose job it was to ensure that the Veda continued to be pronounced in exactly the same way despite the passage of thousands of years.

➤ Meter means the measured rhythms in which a verse is chanted. This is a big deal in Hinduism because the different meters in which the Veda are chanted are said to have different effects in the human psyche and in the subtle inner worlds.

➤ Etymology looks at where words came from, their present meaning, and their inner significance. As the millennia rolled by, the brahmins continued to pronounce the Veda correctly but they were beginning to forget what some of the words in it meant! Therefore etymology became an increasingly important field of study.

Until only recently—and some would argue even today—no other culture has come remotely close to the Hindus in detailed analysis of language structure or in the exploration of how the human mind actually understands language.

It's News to Me!

The ancient Egyptians believed in the divine origin of sound. To them, the physical world was the material manifestation of sound energy. Their god Thoth, "Lord of Divine Words," measured out and regulated the universe through the power of his divine voice. Magic worked, the Egyptians believed, when humans used carefully selected sounds together with the force of their will to shape reality just as Thoth did in the beginning.

New Word Alert!

Vedanga means a limb of the Veda. This is one of the six sacred sciences used to clarify the meaning and use of the Veda.

An **Upa Veda** is one of the four sacred sciences not directly related to scriptural study.

Recently, American linguists have admitted that, even with the super computers now at their disposal, they would have a very difficult time matching the ancient Hindus in the brilliance of their linguistic analysis.

The Silent Sound

Let's turn from technical linguistics to the practical spiritual significance of the Hindu teaching about the divine Word.

Going back at least to the great Sankhya master Kapila, Hindus have taught that the medium sound travels through is space. This has provided plenty of laughs for modern Western scholars who know that sound waves cannot travel through the vacuum of space. What they don't know is what Hindus actually mean by the word *shabda*, which is translated into English as "sound."

There are four levels of sound in Hindu understanding. You'll need to grasp this point if you want to understand why Hindus say *Shabda Brahman,* "the Word is God":

1. *Vaikari:* Physical sound you hear with your ears.
2. *Madhyama:* Verbal thoughts heard with your inner ear.
3. *Pashyanti:* Abstract concepts perceived in your higher mind.
4. *Para Vak:* Unmanifest meaning inherent in silence. Truth which abides in deep meditative states.

"Okay," you're probably thinking. "Run that by me again."

Pregnant with Meaning

Suppose I see a small white truck driving past outside playing a characteristic jingle. I shout, "Ice cream!" You didn't see the ice cream truck, but when you hear me, you instantly know what I mean. Okay, now you understand the first level of sound, vaikari.

You think to yourself, "Linda Johnsen eats too much ice cream. She really ought to lose some weight." You hear the words distinctly in your mind. Great—now you understand the second level, madhyama.

You don't hear any words in your head, but at the back of your mind you feel a craving, a sense that you'd like to have some, let's say, ice cream. You're

It's News to Me!

In 1300 B.C.E., the Hindu sage Panini composed a Sanskrit grammar called the *Ashtadhyayi.* In 4,000 short verses, it revealed the inner mechanics of Sanskrit—how the language worked and how new words evolved. The word *sanskrit* means "perfect" and suggests that Sanskrit, "the language of the gods," was the "perfect" tongue.

not sounding out words in your mind—"I scream for ice cream!" But the concept of ice cream is present in your awareness. Perfect—that's the third level of sound, pashyanti.

You're dead asleep. You're not speaking of ice cream, thinking of ice cream, or even dreaming of ice cream. Yet if I poke you awake and ask you if you'd like some ice cream, you would understand perfectly well what I mean. Because while you were asleep your memory tapes weren't erased. Even though you weren't thinking about it, the concept of ice cream still existed somewhere within you. That's para vak, the fourth level of sound.

God is para vak. Why? Because even when the universe doesn't exist, when it's hidden in the unfathomable darkness of God's slumber in the Milky Ocean, all of material existence is still inherent in Him. When He "reawakens" and begins to create, he has only to "speak" the word and the dimensions of reality hidden in the profound depths of His silence start to manifest. His meaning, His "thoughts," become our physical reality.

Hearing Without Ears

While shabda is usually translated "sound," a more accurate translation would probably be "meaning." It's meaning, not sound waves, that the sage Kapila meant is transmitted through the medium of akasha, or space.

"What do you mean?" you're probably asking.

Suppose I'm standing near you, and suddenly I fall. I shout, "Help! I'm in trouble!" My message is transmitted to you through the medium of the air in the form of a series of sounds which everyone who speaks English agrees mean, "Linda fell down. Go help her up."

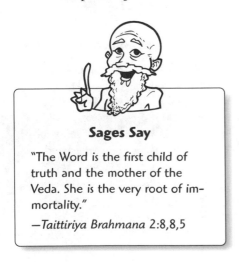

Sages Say

"The Word is the first child of truth and the mother of the Veda. She is the very root of immortality."

—*Taittiriya Brahmana* 2:8,8,5

I'm at work, and you're at home. Suddenly I fall. I cry out, "Help! I'm in trouble!" There's no way you can hear me from miles away, yet you distinctly hear my voice in your inner ear calling, "Help!" This phenomenon, called clairaudience, is said by most Western scientists to be impossible. Hindus, raised on yogic science, know that in the real world this kind of thing happens all the time. The meaning in my mind was transmitted to your mind through a more subtle medium than air. It came through "space," or "ether" as it's sometimes called, a super-fine form of matter.

Let's ratchet the process up a notch. I'm at work and I fall. You don't hear any words in your mind. Yet somehow suddenly you absolutely *know* that I've fallen and hurt myself. This phenomenon is now called telepathy. It involves the third level of sound, called pashyanti, and engages the intuitive powers of your higher mind. How many new mothers just "know" what's happening with their infant even if they're miles apart? How many times have you heard of mothers who "knew" their son was injured the very moment he was shot on the battlefield?

Hindu yogis would say the "information" about your offspring is being "transmitted" through akasha, the material of which "space" is made. Our thoughts are continually "broadcasting" from our minds like radio towers. But most people don't have their "receivers" on and don't hear our thoughts (thank God). Those of us who've spent time with highly trained yogis often have the disconcerting experience that they read our minds like newspapers. Their channel blockers are down, and they're picking up everything that's coming out of our mouths—and out of our minds!

What about para vak, the highest level of sound or meaning? In deep meditation, we contact the "ideas" or archetypal patterns around which the physical and subtle worlds are framed. They exist eternally in Brahman, the Supreme Reality. "In the beginning was the Word, and the Word was with God, and the Word was God." This profound understanding lies at the root of many ancient metaphysical traditions.

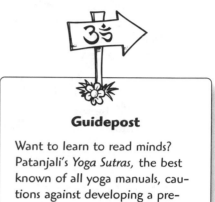

Guidepost

Want to learn to read minds? Patanjali's *Yoga Sutras*, the best known of all yoga manuals, cautions against developing a preoccupation with psychic powers. According to the yoga tradition, saints do not pursue supernatural powers. Rather, supernatural powers pursue the saints!

Ritual: Spiritual Technology

If all this talk about transmitting on mental channels made any sense to you, good. You're now in a much better position to understand kalpa, Vedic ritual science. Or, as it's rather naively called in the West, "ritual magic."

Rituals must be performed with focused attention and exactly correct pronunciation of exactly the correct mantras so that exactly the right waves of mental energy broadcast out into the subtle worlds, reshaping reality to the desired effect. Thought energy is considered extremely powerful (and even potentially dangerous) in the Vedic tradition when it is intensely focused.

Particular rituals were established by enlightened sages and have been performed millions of times over the years by successive generations of priests. This is believed to make them particularly super-charged because a priest who enacts a ritual today is "riding" on waves of energy generated by numberless priests who enacted the rituals in previous centuries.

Rules for ritual science are incredibly elaborate and must be followed to the letter. One slip of the tongue or a part of the ritual performed out of order can sabotage even a multimillion-dollar, 108-day rite. Brahmin priests specialize in different components of ritual science. It's so complex no one person can master the entire field.

Traditional Vedic rituals are performed primarily by brahmin priests. For a few special rites, their wives are required to join in. In the last few decades, as young brahmin men have been abandoning their traditional trade for other professions, there haven't been enough brahmins to keep the old rites going in some communities. Increasingly, women are filling the priestly job openings vacated by brahmin men.

Many communities cannot afford to have a brahmin perform their rituals for them. So members of other castes, who strike their neighbors as especially spiritually gifted, are called upon to perform rituals on their community's behalf. Rites performed by brahmins have more cache, but rituals performed by priests from other castes are effective for most practical purposes.

Astrology: The Mirror in Heaven

Astrology was outlawed in Christianity not because Christian theologians thought it didn't work—obviously the Magi used it to find the infant Jesus. Christians condemned it because they considered knowledge of the future inappropriate for humankind. Hindus have exactly the opposite attitude.

Guidepost

Hindus take astrology seriously. Most Hindu children are given names based on the Moon's position at the moment of their birth. Palmistry and the study of omens are included in astrological analysis. I recommend that rather than reflexively dismissing it, you give Vedic astrology a try. Many of us Westerners who initially approached it with plenty of healthy skepticism found ourselves absolutely astonished at how accurate and insightful Hindu astrology can be.

If you want to go on a long journey into unknown territory, a map is a very useful thing to keep in your glove compartment. Astrology offers a map of the future, showing what part of the terrain will be tough going, and where the roadway is smooth. Hindu scriptures call astrology a gift from God designed to help us find our way.

Vedic astrology is called "the eye of the Veda" because brahmin priests use it to find the exact moment the flow of cosmic energies most strongly support their rituals. Astrology has several specific functions:

➤ Determining the most auspicious time for a particular event.

➤ Gauging the compatibility of two individuals.

➤ Answering specific questions.

➤ Predicting the future.

One of the most important functions of the astrologer is to select the best possible time to start a trip, begin a project, open a business, or get married. The astrologer carefully considers the positions of the Sun, Moon, the five classical planets (Mercury, Venus, Mars, Jupiter, Saturn), and two "shadow" planets called Rahu and Ketu. (These shadow planets are called the Moon's nodes in Western astronomy. They're responsible for solar and lunar eclipses.)

Mapping Your Destiny

In Hindu culture, most marriages are arranged by the parents. The astrologer is responsible for comparing the horoscopes of the prospective couple—who may never actually have met each other—to see whether they'll be compatible.

You can also bring a burning question such as, "If I run for office in the upcoming election, would I win?" The astrologer looks at the position of the planets at the moment you ask the question, and offers appropriate advice.

According to legend, in ancient times the Hindu sages noted that the level of human consciousness had sunk to a point where most people could no longer remember their past lives. They didn't understand why good or bad things were happening to them. They didn't know how to plan for the future because they didn't remember what they'd done in previous lives to cause the karma they were experiencing now. So they went to God and asked for a way to help people understand the flow of their karma and prepare for events coming in the future. God taught the sages astrology, and they passed it on to the rest of us.

The first time I sat down with a Vedic astrologer, who didn't know me from Adam or Eve, he glanced at my horoscope and accurately told me my profession, my interests, when I'd moved into an ashram, when I married, what my husband was like, what I was doing now, and what I'd be doing in the future. I was flabbergasted!

Sages Say

"One who understands the nature of the soul, the nature of karma, and the nature of the nine planets, gains knowledge of the past, present and future. Without the science of astrology, one cannot unlock the mystery of time."

—*Brihat Parashara Hora Shastra*

Talking Stars

How can the stars speak? Vedic astrology is based on the familiar Hindu premise that every part of the universe reflects every other part. The universe folds around itself like sets of adjoining mirrors, reflecting a set number of patterns back and forth across many dimensions of being. The patterns of our lives are written across heaven, in the palms of our hands, and in the flight of birds—in fact everywhere we look—if we have the skill to read the patterns.

For Hindus, the planets and stars, like every other part of the universe, are alive. The Sun is Lord Surya, the Moon is Lord Chandra. The stars along the ecliptic are the glittering wives of the Moon. The Sun, Moon, and planets are the gods responsible for adjusting our karma. They send us the results of our good or bad past deeds at an appropriate moment in their cycles.

Vedic astrologers are Hinduism's physicians of the soul, diagnosing our karma and prescribing spiritual remedies to correct karmic imbalances. These remedies include pilgrimages, charitable donations, the chanting of mantras, and similar methods of clearing our karmic accounts.

Adjunct Sciences

I mentioned that there are four important adjunct arts and sciences—Medicine, Music and Dance, the Martial Arts, and Architecture. These arts help Hindus live more spiritually, attuning themselves to their bodies and their environment.

Medicine: Ayurveda

Medicine is called Ayurveda in India, which means "the science of longevity." This is because poor health can be a major obstacle to success in one's spiritual practice. Early death can be a calamity for a disciple on the spiritual path. Most people want to hang on to their present body for as long as possible because they fear death. For Hindus, a human body is the ideal environment for rapid progress in meditation. You don't want to throw yours away for no good reason if you can help it.

The *Charaka Samhita,* a classic of Hindu medicine, was probably composed near the beginning of the Common Era, though the medical ideas it expressed can be traced back thousands of years earlier. The text opens by explaining that in vast antiquity, the sages noted that humanity was increasingly suffering from ill health. So they held a meditation conference. As they meditated together, they discovered the root causes of disease and how many illnesses can be successfully treated.

Too Much, Too Little

Human actions involving over- or underindulgence are real killers. Problems arise from eating too much or too little or the wrong kinds of foods. Sleeping too much or too little, having too much or not enough sex, exercising too much or not enough, worrying too

Guidepost

Should you see an Ayurvedic practitioner? An increasing number of Westerners are benefiting from consultations with Ayurvedic doctors. Hindu physicians diagnose a client's predominant *dosha* or constitutional type. Is the person fiery in nature, relaxed or even indolent, or nervous and scattered? Cleaning and rejuvenating therapies, herbal remedies and exercises are prescribed on this basis.

much, not going to the bathroom when you need to, sitting in a poor posture—all these and many other factors were identified as contributors to ill health.

But more than any other factor, Ayurveda identified "happiness" as the cause of health and "unhappiness" as the cause of disease. It strongly emphasized the psycho-somatic nature of illness, making Ayurveda a very early form of holistic medicine!

Live Long and Prosper!

Ayurveda is famous for its *rasayana* techniques, methods to promote longevity. According to the *Charaka Samhita,* an exceptionally long, healthy life is not possible unless a person lives a moral life. Ethics are important because they contribute to a clean conscience. Peace of mind is a prerequisite for a really long life, according to Ayurvedic physicians.

Westerners who've heard Hindu legends of immortal spiritual masters often ask if the stories about *kaya kalpa,* the technique for regenerating the physical body and reversing the aging process, are true. Recent masters like Trailinga Swami and Tapasviji Maharaj were credited with extraordinary longevity. Some Hindu holy men are supposed to have lived three or four centuries in the same body.

When I asked the Hindu swamis about this, I was told that the technique really exists and works quite well, but many yogis don't bother mastering it because it's so much trouble! It involves long periods of isolation with intense focus on the physical body. Most saints don't like to take their minds off God for that long.

I was also told that the technique can only be re-applied a limited number of times. Eventually the physical body simply wears out. It just takes too much time and energy to keep rebuilding it.

After several centuries of intense yogic practices, presumably the saint has mastered the technique of transferring his or her consciousness into a fresh body which, they say, is a lot less trouble than kaya kalpa.

Yogis complain that with modern methods of disposing of dead bodies becoming more common in India, it's harder to find a vacated but still usable adult body to transfer one's awareness into.

I was told that the "immortal masters of the Himalayas" like Shankaracharya and Markandeya are not still in their original bodies but take a new physical body every century or so!

New Word Alert!

Your **dosha** is your constitutional type. There are three doshas: fiery, phlegmatic, and nervous.

Kaya kalpa is the technique for regenerating the physical body. It is said to restore youth, turning back the biological clock by decades.

Rasayana is Ayurvedic rejuvenation, Hindu medical techniques for prolonging longevity.

Martial Arts: Draw Your Bow!

Kung Fu devotees are well aware that the Chinese martial arts got rolling in the sixth century C.E. thanks to a Buddhist teacher named Bodhi Dharma. Bodhi Dharma came to China from India, where the martial arts were already an ancient tradition.

I don't recommend you pack your bags and fly to India to study with the Hindu martial arts masters, however. This tradition has been in decline in India for so long it's barely kicking anymore, except for a few locations, such as pockets in Kerala where small groups of enthusiasts fight to keep the old traditions from total extinction.

In ancient times, the most prominent, and most deadly, form of military skill was archery. If ancient accounts are true, Hindu troops used to use arrows like we use missiles today, to carry fatal payloads. The *Mahabharata* describes arrows laden with toxic substances that could stun dozens of troops into unconsciousness.

Hindu martial arts training included mastery of the breath as well as mastery of mantras. Warriors used mantras to "empower" their weapons. By manipulating the breath they could remain centered rather than panicking during an emergency. (Breath control really works, incidentally. I'll show you how in Chapter 23, "The Royal Road.")

The spiritual training underlying the martial arts is of course intended to teach the student self-discipline, courage, and the ability to remain calm even under life-threatening circumstances. These are valuable skills for *anyone* to add to their resume, if you ask me!

Sacred Space: Holy Architecture

The concept of sacred space is critically important in Hinduism. It has to do with aligning human-made structures with the flow of cosmic energies. The Vedic fire pit, for example, was always constructed with painstaking care in a precise geometrical pattern, using carefully selected materials. This maximized its capacity to benefit the sacrificer.

Hindu temples are specially designed by *sutradharas,* master architects, who incorporate spiritual symbolism and cosmic principles into the sacred structure.

The sutradhara has five major areas of expertise:

1. Orientation: How the building aligns with the cardinal directions.
2. Site planning: How the building aligns with its environment.
3. Proportionate measurements: How the building aligns with itself.
4. Building components: How the rooms in a building relate to each other.
5. Aesthetics: The visual effect of the building.

In the past few years, Feng Shui, the Chinese art of building design, has become well known in the West. *Vastu* is the Hindu equivalent. You will often hear Hindus (and even now Vastu clients in the West) report that after modifying their home according to these principles, their health improves. Or after making several structural changes in their place of business following a consultation with a Vastu expert, their client base expands exponentially virtually overnight.

Music: Lord of the Dance

God Himself is Nataraja, "Lord of the Dance." His spinning motions are the orbits of subatomic particles and the rotation of the galaxies.

Watching a skilled sacred dancer from India is an amazing experience. Dancers assume a variety of stylized poses suggestive of different Hindu heroes and deities. Krishna playing his flute. Radha putting on her makeup. Rama carrying his bow. Some dancers are so adept that the audience has the uncanny sensation they're actually seeing the deity itself.

Music is a sacred art in India, and the singing of *bhajans* or hymns is a big part of Hindu spirituality. The Hindus, like most Europeans and Americans, compose melodies using seven musical notes. Our do-re-mi-fa-so-la-ti-do is their sa-re-ga-ma-pa-dha-ni-sa. But while Western music has only two modes

New Word Alert!

A **sutradhara** is a master architect who ensures that buildings are designed according to sacred principles.

Vastu is the Hindu science of sacred space.

A **bhajan** is a spiritual song, often extolling the divine qualities of God or the Goddess.

Ragas are particular styles of classical Indian music.

Sages Say

"Among the Vedas, the most ancient scriptures in the library of man, the *Sama Veda* is devoted to the art of music. How fortunate is he or she who loves to sing or play an instrument!"

—Swami Rama Bharati

to choose from, the major and minor scales, Hindu music uses dozens of different modes. This is why Hindu music often sounds so exotic and complex to the Western ear.

Hindus use different *ragas* or musical styles to create different psychological and spiritual effects. One style is invigorating, another soothing, still another is healing. The power of music and dance to transport both the artist and the audience into higher states of consciousness is fully acknowledged in the Hindu tradition. Musician meditators follow the source of a note back to its source in the original composer, the Goddess herself.

Quick Quiz

1. Hinduism teaches that sound ...

    a. Is a neural affect produced in the ear drum.

    b. Exists at four levels, in the inner and outer worlds.

    c. Can be amplified by shouting loudly.

2. The Hindus think of the planets as ...

    a. Big rocks in the sky.

    b. Divine beings who apportion our karma.

    c. Potential military platforms.

3. Physical immortality ...

    a. Is the goal of Hindu spiritual practice.

    b. Occurs after the resurrection of the dead on Judgment Day.

    c. Is not considered possible in Hinduism.

4. In Hinduism music is ...

    a. Strictly forbidden.

    b. Considered a path to God.

    c. Use to lift large blocks in temple construction.

Answers: 1 (b). 2 (b). 3 (c). 4 (b).

In the West, science, the arts, and religion have become three completely separate domains. In Hindu culture, however, spirituality permeates every department of life. Each activity, from building a house to playing a musical instrument to diagnosing an illness, reflects the sacred and fundamentally interconnected character of all life. Everything in nature is inherently meaningful because it's all the expression of the divine Word. When we live in harmony with this inner truth, our outer lives also gain meaning and spiritual purpose.

The Least You Need to Know

➤ Hindus excelled in linguistic studies and considered the highest level of language to be inherent in God.

➤ Vedic astrology is used to fix auspicious dates for important events and to help Hindus understand their karma.

➤ Hindu holy sites are built according to the principles of sacred space.

➤ Music and dance are sacred arts in Hinduism.

Part 3

Who Hindus Worship

"The one God wears many masks," wrote mythologist Joseph Campbell. In no other religion does the Supreme Being wear so many masks and invite worship in so many different forms as the eternal religion of Hinduism.

Hindus love to worship. Every aspect of life is worship. "Let my walking be circumambulation of You," wrote Shankaracharya. "Let my speech be the recitation of Your holy mantras. When I lie down to sleep, may it be prostrating to You."

The Supreme Being has no form at all and yet is inherent in all forms. In the following chapters, you'll meet the most popular forms in which the Eternal One is honored. Among the thousands of different Hindu sects, you'll also meet the three largest denominations—the devotees of Vishnu, Shiva, and Shakti.

This is the universe of Hinduism, in which any chance encounter can be a meeting with God.

Chapter 11

"Can You Show Me God?"

In This Chapter

➤ A God beyond imagination

➤ What Om means

➤ Hindu "idols"

➤ The root of all evil

➤ Lenses to the infinite

Naren Datta was born in Calcutta in 1863. His parents, hoping for a bright future for their precocious son, arranged for a good British education. His future would be bright indeed. In fact, the future of Hindus everywhere would improve radically thanks to Naren Datta. But not because of his British training.

Naren's European schoolmasters bequeathed to him the same gift they gave almost every Hindu schoolchild entrusted to their care: complete contempt for Hinduism. Naren would roll his eyes when he saw Hindu holy men on the streets. Or the *bhairavis,* the women yogis. How sad that these people lived in complete superstition, never having benefited, as he had, from an enlightened European education!

A Divine Challenge

To express his disdain, Naren would go to Hindu pandits—men who spent a great deal of time talking about God—and ask, "Can you show me God?" Inevitably they would regretfully admit they couldn't.

Then one day a friend took Naren to visit a local priest at the Kali temple in Howrah. "Can you show me God?" Naren haughtily demanded.

"Of course!" Ramakrishna Paramahansa replied.

Naren Datta, a.k.a. Swami Vivekananda.

(© Vedanta Society of Saint Louis)

God Is Mind Blowing!

I don't think there's any schoolchild in the state of Bengal who doesn't know the rest of the story.

Naren was sitting on the floor when he posed his challenge to the temple priest. Ramakrishna lifted his foot and brushed Naren's forehead with his toe. Remember in Chapter 8, "Turning On Your Inner Light," when I told you about shaktipat, the shot of energy some disciples get from their gurus? Well, Naren got a dose of shaktipat. A *massive* dose. He was pitched into cosmic consciousness, his awareness merging into the living universe all around him. It was ecstatic!

Then, Naren suddenly remembered his poor widowed mother, who would starve if he wasn't there to support her. In that moment, his consciousness imploded back into his body. He was Naren Datta again. Or rather, he had just become the man history would remember as Swami Vivekananda, the leading disciple of one of the greatest Hindu masters of recent centuries, Ramakrishna Paramahansa.

Naren—called Swami Vivekananda after he took the vows of a Hindu renunciate—would turn the tables on his schoolmasters. He would be the first swami in modern times to visit Europe and America, teaching the Sanatana Dharma, the eternal religion of Hinduism. He would meet with spectacular success abroad, introducing tens of thousands of eager Western students to yoga and meditation.

But for our purpose here we need to understand exactly what happened in that extraordinary moment when the master touched Naren's forehead. And to do that we need to understand Ramakrishna's own spiritual history.

Sages Say

"Although almost every one of us can speak most wonderfully on spiritual matters, when it comes to action and the living of a spiritual life, we find ourselves awfully deficient. To quicken the spirit, the impulse must come from another soul. The person from whose soul such an impulse comes is called the guru."

—Swami Vivekananda

A Rock in the Eye

Ramakrishna was a priest of the Hindu goddess Kali. It was his responsibility to care for the statue of the goddess in the Dakshineshvar Temple, to bring offerings to her and chant her mantras.

Ramakrishna took his duties very seriously (his brief forays into other religions, which I mentioned in Chapter 6, "One God with Many Names," notwithstanding). He hardly had a life apart from the goddess. He would speak about her, sing about her, meditate on her and worship her in virtually every waking moment. He experienced the statue of Kali as actually alive and would see her leap down from the altar to dance ecstatically around the temple.

A tantric master named Bhairavi Ma noticed Ramakrishna's extraordinary devotion and began calling people's attention to the presence of the great saint among them. As an advanced adept, she could see that his intense devotion was not only giving Ramakrishna divine visions but carrying him into very high meditative states.

Then a master named Tota Puri visited the Kali temple. He was an adept in the Advaita Vedanta tradition. This, to remind you, is the tradition of Adi Shankara-charya which encourages meditators to go beyond every trace of duality (see Chapter 9, "Truth Is a Multi-Layer Cake"). Tota Puri scolded Ramakrishna for his attachment to Kali's form. He explained that if Ramakrishna really wanted to know the goddess's true nature, he must go beyond the image of her he cherished in his mind.

New Word Alert!

A **tantric** uses the techniques of Tantra—an advanced system of yogic practices—to expand his or her mystical awareness.

A **bhairavi** is a female tantric practitioner.

The **ajna chakra** is a center of awareness found several inches behind the point where the eyebrows meet.

It's News to Me!

Hindus will often greet you with the phrase "Namaste!" or "Na-maskar!" Both words mean "I honor you." According to Swami Rama Bharati, the full translation is actually, "I bow to the divinity in you!"

Tota Puri took a sharp rock and pierced Ramakrishna's forehead at the "third eye," the point between his eyebrows. "Next time you go into meditation," the Vedantin instructed, "focus behind this point. If a picture of Kali appears in your mind, take a sword and hack her to pieces."

Ramakrishna was shocked at this advice, but he obeyed. When he next sat for meditation, he brought his full awareness to his *ajna chakra,* the center behind the eyebrows. When he saw his beloved Kali approach, he destroyed the image, moving through the visual image he held of her in his mind into the formless reality beyond.

Embracing Transcendence

This experience transported Ramakrishna into one of the highest meditative states a human being can achieve. He experienced the living reality of Brahman, the all-pervading essence of awareness that exists beyond thought. Ramakrishna became so firmly grounded in this transcendent state that when Naren challenged him to show him God, the master was able to transmit the actual experience of divine being to the unsuspecting young man.

Let me hasten to make a point here, so you don't get the wrong impression. Unlike Naren, precious few of us go to meet a guru and find ourselves thrown into the highest mystical states. Most of us spend quite a few years performing spiritual practices before we get to a point where we can receive the guru's transmission.

Ramakrishna later explained that Naren was in fact a very highly evolved soul who had selflessly entered the physical plane to serve humanity. His European training had temporarily led him away from his innate spirituality. All Ramakrishna had to do to put him back on track was "reawaken" a cosmic state of awareness Naren had already achieved in previous existences!

You will understand Hinduism if you can grasp this concept: There is only one Supreme Reality, called Brahman—but Brahman has two modes, *nirguna* and *saguna*. Nirguna means without qualities. Saguna means with qualities. Nirguna Brahman is the transcendent Supreme Being contacted only in the highest states of meditation. Saguna Brahman is God or Goddess as we know and love Him or Her. This is the deity we can picture in our minds. The one who helps solve our problems and saves us in emergencies. The one whose loving embrace we feel in prayer.

Try understanding it this way. If a physicist was called in to describe you, she would list the fields of matter and energy that constitute your body. It would be a very impersonal description. But if a psychologist was given the same job, he would list your many personality characteristics. Some yogis in very deep meditation experience God as an impersonal absolute. Others, whose awareness is focused at another plane, experience God as a loving, caring personality.

It's that elephant again. One blind man has it by the tail. The other is running his fingers over its flapping ear!

Unthinkable Truth

Nirguna Brahman is "the Godhead behind God" that the Christian mystic Meister Eckhart experienced in deep meditation. It is Absolute Reality itself, pure self-existent being. Any attempt to describe it falls flat. Even the words I just used are a dim reflection of its glory. The Supreme One is totally beyond our imagination. The human mind can't begin to grasp it.

What we *can* do is transcend our own minds, shift back into the pure awareness within ourselves, and

Sages Say

"People of different religions never cease to fight. But think—is religion just another branch of the military? ... The true religion is that in which one becomes aware of one's own Self. That Self is Consciousness, which nothing can surpass. Because it pervades everywhere, Consciousness must accept all; it cannot reject anyone. The religion of Consciousness is God's true religion."

—Swami Muktananda

New Word Alert!

Nirguna means without *(nir)* qualities *(guna)*, without form. **Nirguna Brahman** is the transcendent God beyond the reach of thought.

Saguna means with *(sa)* qualities *(guna)*, with form. **Saguna Brahman** is the personal God.

simply experience the reality. It can be known but it can't be communicated in words—though mystics never tire of trying!

In Hinduism, this transcendent being is symbolized by the sound "Om." Om is produced by running the Sanskrit letters *a, u,* and *m* together. The *Mandukya Upanishad* says that "A" stands for the waking state. "U" signifies the dream state. "M" stands for deep sleep. And the slight pause, the little piece of silence that follows your speaking the sound Om and precedes your repeating it again—that pregnant silence is Nirguna Brahman. It's the "nothing" that contains everything.

Om, the Hindu symbol for the primordial reality.

(© Hinduism Today)

Seeing the Unseen

The seers of the *Upanishads* wrestled with words, trying to show us that which cannot be seen. The *Katha Upanishad* endeavors to explain:

> Beyond the senses is the mind. Beyond the mind is the higher intellect. Beyond the intellect is the Inner Self. Beyond the Inner Self is the vast unmanifest reality, the primal energy from which all things emerge. Beyond the unmanifest is the Supreme Being, who exists everywhere yet cannot be seen. One who realizes the Supreme is liberated. Yes, that one becomes immortal.

> No one can see the Supreme with the eye. The only way to know Him is through deep meditation, after the intellect has been completely purified. Those great souls who know the Supreme One, they are liberated from suffering and delusion. Yes, they become immortal.

Remember that in Hinduism immortality does not mean immortal life in a physical body. It means the Inner Self becomes free from the process of death and rebirth, relaxing into undying divine consciousness.

The somber Swedish filmmaker Ingmar Bergman liked to compare God to a spider. It was meant to be a creepy image, suggesting a malevolent being who captures us in an inescapable web and eats us alive. The *Upanishads* use the image of a spider repeatedly but in a different sense.

To the seers, the Supreme spins the entire universe out of its innate being, just as a spider generates a web from its own mouth. At the end of a world cycle, the Supreme One dissolves the universe back into itself. The nature of that awesome eternal being is far beyond the ability of our intellects to understand. Yet the unseeable one is the very one who is peering out through our eyes. It is the all-pervading awareness in which our awareness abides, our own innermost truth.

We cannot *see* Nirguna Brahman, yet we *are* Nirguna Brahman!

"Idol Worship": Worshipping an Ideal

Let's shift our perspective from the inconceivable reality to the more user-friendly version of God, Saguna Brahman.

"What I am is utterly beyond the capacity of your mind to conceive," the Goddess tells us in the *Tripura Rahasya*. "Therefore, worship Me in whatever form appeals to you. I promise, in that very form I will come to you." As you can see, compared to the Judeo-Christian-Islamic God, the Hindu Goddess has a very liberal policy!

To the Hindu, Kali and Krishna are forms in which the divine appears. Yahweh and Jesus Christ are, too. There's no need to convert anyone because the Supreme One is working through "whatever form appeals to you" to help you grow spiritually.

Sages Say

"There is one Supreme Controller, Who is the Inner Self of all beings. He projects Himself outward, creating infinity from the One. Everlasting joy comes to those wise beings who perceive this great Being within themselves."

—*Katha Upanishad 2:2.12*

Guidepost

That Hindus "worship idols" is probably the single most common misconception about Hinduism. It is very painful for Hindus when Westerners insult their intelligence by suggesting they believe the stone or marble image of a deity in a temple is actually the Divine Being itself. Hindus use images as tools to connect with the Divine. They fully understand that the Divine itself is much greater than the physical image in the temple!

Perhaps the Hindu form of God most poorly understood in the West is the image in the temple, pejoratively called an "idol" by members of monotheistic faiths. From early childhood, my Lutheran Sunday school teachers assured me that the Hindus are primitive and superstitious—and it's our job to "save" them—because they "worship idols."

Let's get this straight right here, right now. *Hindus do not worship idols.* Hindus worship *God.*

Seeing God

There is the God that can't be seen. And there is the God that can. Hindus visit their temples to see God. And be seen by him. Whether it's a statue of the warrior goddess Durga, the ever popular goddess of prosperity, Lakshmi, with her handsome husband, Vishnu, or the powerful South Indian deity Vel, Hindu families come bearing their gifts of coconuts, flowers, rupees, bananas, or whatever is on hand to offer God or Goddess that day.

The priest draws aside the gate that separates the worshipper from the image, and the family members gaze into the eyes of their beloved deity. This is the process of darshan, which means "sight." You see your beloved deity. He or she sees you. A connection is made. A blessing is rendered.

Guidepost

Some people mistakenly believe meditation means emptying the mind. But you can't experience Brahman, the innermost reality, by sitting around in a stupor! Hindus universally accept that an experienced spiritual mentor is necessary to clear away mistaken notions like this one and to guide one through the inner worlds to the highest state of consciousness.

Yet, in spite of what my Sunday school teacher taught me, in all my travels through India from one end of the subcontinent to the other, I have never met a Hindu over the age of seven who actually believes the image in the temple *is* God. In fact, if the "idol" should chip or crack, Hindus will take it out and dump it in the river! That's a pretty unceremonious way to treat God, don't you think?

If you look through a telescope, you can clearly see the planets. Yet no one thinks the telescope is actually Mars. The "idols" in the temples, called *murtis* in India, are telescopes to help us see God and Goddess more clearly. The divine comes into focus, comes closer, comes so near we can reach out and touch the divine feet.

Breathing Statues

Still, the Hindu murtis are not just statues. When an image is installed in a temple, the priest performs a special rite called *prana pratishtha*. Prana is life energy or breath. Pratishtha means "establish." During the ceremony, the living deity is invited to enter the image, to take the statue as one of his or her bodies. The priest breathes onto the image, establishing living energy there, and the statue comes to life.

Once prana pratishtha has been accomplished, the image of the deity is no longer a pretty piece of furniture. From now on, until the life force is formally removed by a priest, the statue is considered as much alive as any other person in the room. Food is brought to the deity throughout the day. The deity is washed and dressed in clean clothes daily, and is fanned and presented with incense and tasty desserts. It's treated as an honored guest. Devotees carefully watch what they say, even what they think, in the deity's presence, so as not to cause offense.

Visiting the deity's form in a temple or—as almost all Hindus do—keeping an image of the deity in their own home is a valuable way to practice the presence of God. But it's not just pretend. When the statue is formally brought to life, a tiny fraction of the total awareness of the real deity actually takes up residence in the statue. A fraction of infinity is still infinity. So through the awakened image the devotee makes contact with the whole of divine being.

Divine Outlets

The "real" God or Goddess is beyond form, existing everywhere at once. It is the "real" deity to whom the devotee offers worship. The "real" source of electricity is the power plant. But you don't go to the power plant to get your electricity. You just stick your plug in an outlet in the wall. Because "living" electricity flows through the outlet, that outlet needs to be treated with respect. You don't just casually stick your fingers into it.

In the Hindu tradition, murtis are outlets for divine grace. The priest hooks up the system and divine energy starts to flow. Since time immemorial, Hindus have energized their spiritual lives using empowered images of divinity.

Speaking from my personal experience, I can report that occasionally a murti is so "juiced up," it's as if a force field surrounds it. You step within several yards of the statue and suddenly feel as if you're walking into a wall of pulsing energy. My guess is that this is an objective rather than purely subjective phenomenon because usually everyone walking toward the murti feels the energy field at the same point.

New Word Alert!

A **murti** is a statue of God or the Goddess. These are sometimes mistakenly called "idols" by non-Hindus.

Prana pratishtha is the process of infusing a murti with life breath, so that the image becomes alive. It now becomes a conduit for divine grace.

Sages Say

"How long do small girls play with their dolls? As long as they are not married and do not live with their husbands. After marriage they put the dolls away in a box. What further need is there of worshipping the image after the vision of God?"

—*Ramakrishna Paramahansa*

Sages Say

"In all the worlds you see, and the worlds you don't see, I am there. In all creatures that move, and in beings that don't move, I am there. In every particle of matter, from the grossest to the subtlemost, I am there. Everything you see or hear, in the external world or in the inner world, My divine awareness pervades it."

—*Sarva Jnana Uttara Agama*

God on Parade

Anyone who's spent some time in India has seen God out parading. On special festival days, Hindus take the murti out of the temple and parade it through town. If the murti is too large or unwieldy to take for a ride, a special substitute image goes instead.

The substitute is just as good as the real thing because during a special ceremony, the priest transfers the living presence of God from the main murti in the temple into the smaller portal one. After all, it's the living presence of God or the Goddess that Hindus worship, not the physical "idol."

The most famous divine parade happens every June or July (the exact date varies from year to year depending on the lunar calendar) in Puri in the state of Orissa. The murtis from the world-famous Jagannath Temple are loaded onto huge carts to be dragged through town. The murtis are of Lord Jagannath (the name means Lord of the World), his brother Balbhadra, and his sister Subhadra. Lord Jagannath's cart is 14 meters high and 10 meters square. It has 16 wheels, each more than two meters in diameter. The carts are so heavy it takes over 4,000 strong men to pull them. Getting them rolling is a real chore. And stopping them once they start moving is, too! The English world "juggernaut" came from British observers who watched this procession.

The three murtis are among the best loved in India. You may be interested to know that every decade or two the murtis are destroyed and new ones fashioned from tree trunks replace them. Let me make my point again: It is not the "idol" itself that is worshipped but the divine presence in it.

The Spirit in the Tree

All of nature is sacred to the Hindu. Some locations seem especially spiritually potent. A river. A uniquely shaped rock. A particularly beautiful tree.

If you travel through the Indian countryside, you will run across many makeshift "people's shrines." Trees in particular are often centers for community worship. You'll find gifts to the tree's sacred spirit left scattered by its roots. Some of these are offerings of thanksgiving for a healing or other blessing the deity associated with the tree has granted.

The cities have their people's shrines, too. It's not unusual to be walking down a street or alley even in the busiest urban area and suddenly stumble across a little shrine, complete with pocket-size murtis and heartfelt offerings.

Show Me the Devil

You may have noticed that in all this talk about divine unity and everything being one, I haven't mentioned a word about the Devil. Where does evil fit in The Big Picture?

First, there is no Satan in Hinduism. At least not in the Christian sense of a malevolent being so powerful he almost rivals God. Hindus do believe in evil spirits and have various methods for exorcising them. But an ultimate evil being like Satan who is capable of giving God a run for his money cannot possibly really exist in the Hindu worldview. The Hindu God has no rivals.

Second, Hindus can't conceive of a hell in the Christian sense either, a place from which God has withdrawn his grace. To Hindus God is literally omnipresent. How could there be any place in any dimension of any world where God isn't present?

Hell worlds do exist in Hindu cosmology, but they are more like the purgatory of the Catholics. They are temporary states in which disembodied souls undergo expiation and purification.

Sages Say

"We have no theory of evil. We call it ignorance."

—Swami Vivekananda

Good and Evil Duke It Out

Christian texts describe a battle between angels and demons that won't end until Judgment Day, when God finally puts the Devil down for once and for all. Hinduism also frequently refers to the continual struggle between the devas (divine beings) and *asuras* (demons) but the significance is very different.

There are stories of devas like Indra behaving badly and the occasional asura like Prahlada who behaves like an angel. Devas and asuras represent different grades of consciousness. Devas are selfless and serviceful—most of the time, anyway. Asuras are selfish and materialistic—though some of them manage to get their act together. The battle between the forces of egotism and selfless love goes on forever, in all world systems where free will—the ability to choose between right and wrong—is a factor. But

New Word Alert!

Asura in very ancient times meant a god. Later the meaning flipped over, becoming synonymous with selfish, aggressive supernatural beings.

Avidya literally means "nonknowledge." It refers to ignorance of our true spiritual nature.

Guidepost

Westerners are sometimes shocked to see Hindus prostrating before their guru. Remember that in India prostration is a sign of respect, not of subservience. Hindus also prostrate to their parents and elder siblings.

Hindus do not believe in evil as something that exists as a living, malevolent force embodied in a Satan.

The Devil in God

In Hinduism, ignorance—not the devil—is the root of evil. Only self-conscious entities can be evil, deliberately choosing to do harm to others or to themselves. When a human being, or some other fully conscious entity, fails to recognize that everything is interconnected, that we are all one, that harming another one is literally harming oneself, then that person is acting out of ignorance of the underlying universal reality.

What Christians call evil is called *avidya* in Sanskrit, which means "lack of knowledge." In mystical states, beginning-level saints first experience the literal unity of all being. They come out of the experience transformed. As Anasuya Devi, the late housewife saint of Jillellamudi, expressed after she became mystically identified with the Mother of the Universe, "I am not anything that you are not. It doesn't appear to me that I am greater than you. The Goddess doesn't exist separately anywhere. You are all the Goddess." Acting from this living realization of primal unity, the saints act for the welfare of all creation. Ignorance has been removed. The choice to commit evil is no longer a viable option in the living light of spirit.

So, in a sense, you could say that God is the ultimate source of evil, because God granted us the free choice between wholesome and unhelpful acts. But God also set the law of karma into place, ensuring that all of us eventually learn our lesson! In Hindu cosmology, the universe is really a university for souls, and overcoming the evil in ourselves, and learning to deal effectively yet compassionately with the evil in others, is a graduate-level course.

Quick Quiz

1. Nirguna Brahman …

    a. Is the transcendental reality.

    b. Is the personal God worshipped by all Hindus.

    c. Is a brand of sports utility vehicle popular in India.

2. Hindus think the images of the deities in their temples …

    a. Dance around the temples at night after the temple is closed.

    b. Are actual gods and goddesses who control the universe.

    c. Are focal points through which we can see the divine.

3. Out of love for her devotees, the Goddess …

    a. Sends non-Hindus to hell for all eternity.

    b. Serves them cookies and ice cream on their birthdays.

    c. Comes to us in any form we choose to worship her in.

4. Hindus believe the Devil …

    a. Will be cast into hell forever on Judgment Day.

    b. Doesn't exist.

    c. Throws great parties.

Answers: 1 (a). 2 (c). 3 (c). 4 (b).

God and the Guru

There is a very special form of God recognized in Hinduism. That is the guru.

Just as a murti is a physical form through which the power and grace of the divine can manifest, a guru is a human form through which divine wisdom and compassion can flow. As my own gurus took pains to clarify, the person isn't really the guru. No more than a tree trunk painted to look like Jagannath is actually the Lord of the World.

During a conference call in which he was simultaneously speaking to many of his disciples at a dozen sites around the world, a swami I studied with explained that considering a person to be the guru is like mistaking the telephone for the person who's calling. In fact there is one divine teacher, called Ishvara or the Supreme Lord, who speaks through innumerable human gurus just as the swami was speaking over multiple phone lines! The real source of truth and spiritual liberation is divinity itself.

157

The Guru Within

Because the human guru represents the divine, he or she is highly honored in Hindu society. The intensity of the devotion many Hindus feel toward their guru is extraordinary. A parent's commitment to a child is for one lifetime. But a guru promises to work with a disciple for as many lifetimes as necessary until the disciple attains God-realization. This is an extraordinary bond.

The guru's job is to introduce you to the guru within. When Ramakrishna touched Naren's forehead, he put him in touch with his own inner guidance. With the guru's grace, Naren Datta (a.k.a. Swami Vivekananda) was able to change the world.

The Least You Need to Know

➤ Hindus recognize the Supreme Being as both transcendent and as a loving, immanent God and Goddess.

➤ God is meant not only to be worshipped but to be experienced.

➤ Images of deities are temporarily brought to life, so the divine can be worshipped in them.

➤ There is no Devil in Hinduism.

➤ Ignorance of one's spiritual nature is the cause of evil.

Chapter 12

Meet the Hindu Gods

In This Chapter

➤ A retired creator

➤ The God in charge

➤ God the yogi

➤ The son of God

➤ The inner Sun

When you travel through India, you'll find the Hindu gods and goddesses everywhere. Their images are tacked to the walls in groceries and sari shops. Small shrines to them are set up in every Hindu home and in most Hindu businesses. Even the big Indian lorries, "goods carriages" as they're called over there, are decorated with smiling divine faces.

Hinduism has hundreds of gods. It's time for you to meet the most popular.

Brahma: The Neglected Creator

Christianity has its Father, Son, and Holy Spirit. Hinduism also has a triune God, called *trimurti,* "God in three forms." These forms are Brahma the Creator, Vishnu the Protector, and Shiva the Destroyer or Liberator.

Hindus believe that if they can visit the main temples of each of these three deities, all their wishes will be fulfilled. Brahma's temple is in Pushkar in eastern Rajasthan. At Vishnu's main temple in Gaya in the state of Bihar, you can actually see his footprint in a black rock. Shiva's main center is the Vishvanath temple in the holy city of Benares.

In the West, God the Father, "maker of heaven and earth," is our principle deity. While we have innumerable houses of worship to him, in all of India there are only four temples to Lord Brahma, the Creator! It wasn't always this way. Judging from the ancient *Puranas,* Brahma was once immensely popular in India. Then he made a mistake he's paying for till this day.

According to legend, Brahma fell in love with his own daughter and tried to make love to her. Incest is a serious crime in India, and Brahma could not be allowed to set such a poor example for humanity. So Shiva the Destroyer cut off one of Brahma's five heads and sent him home to bed without his supper.

Now in Hinduism even the weirdest-sounding myths often turn out to have profound significance. Hindu teachers explain that Brahma was the creative spirit who fell in love with its daughter, matter. When spirit entered matter the whole world process began. But spirit lost part of itself when this happened. It lost its awareness of its true nature. So here we sit, all we children of Brahma, most of us completely unaware of our divine nature.

New Word Alert!

Trimurti means "the three forms of God." It refers to the three main gods of Hinduism: Brahma, Vishnu, and Shiva.

Curiously, in the Jewish and Christian Gnostic traditions, god the creator winds up in the doghouse, much like Brahma. The Gnostics were angry at Yahweh for "trapping" their souls in the material realm. And for pretending to be the only true God when there were other gods far more powerful than he was! Christian Gnostics believed Jesus' beloved Father was not the creator god of the Old Testament, but a God of light from a much higher dimension of reality, more like the Hindu god Vishnu.

Vishnu: The Loving Protector

Vishnu is the most popular god in India. Brahma pretty much retired when he finished creating the world. Shiva is just sitting around in meditation till the day when he's supposed to destroy the universe. So for now, according to his devotees, Vishnu is in charge.

Vishnu maintains law and order in the universe. This sometimes entails getting down and dirty. So from time to time, when things get particularly out of hand down here on planet Earth, Vishnu takes on a human body—or whatever other form works best for him under the circumstances—and sets things straight. Rama and Krishna, the heroes of the *Ramayana* and *Mahabharata* whom you've already met in Chapter 5, "The People's Religion," were human incarnations of Vishnu.

I'll devote most of Chapter 14, "Avatars: Gods in Human Form," to telling you about Vishnu's adventures in his various incarnations. Vishnu preserves the world by ensuring that divine law, including the law of karma, continues to act in the world. He is the great hero, the supreme champion, because you can count on his aid when you are acting for the benefit of the world, as Arjuna counted on Krishna during the war in the *Mahabharata*.

Four Hands for God

You can tell you're looking at Vishnu when you see a *very* handsome blue-skinned Hindu god with four arms. His dark blue color suggests that his nature is as infinite as the sky. Circling one of his fingers is a shining discus that, hurled through the air martial arts style, slices the enemies of goodness and righteousness in two. That discus also represents the spinning universe, which circles his finger like a toy.

In another hand, Vishnu wields a golden baton. He uses this to flatten our egos when we get too big for our britches. A third hand holds a conch, which is a large sea shell Hindus use like a one-note trumpet. This represents Om, the primordial sound from which the universe manifested.

Sages Say

"Vishnu's supreme form is beyond form, though all forms are projected from it. Of it the sages can only say 'It exists.' From the self-existent Lord comes this entire universe. Hold the cosmic being in the mental expanse of your meditation. It will burn away all your sins."

—*Vishnu Purana* 6:7.69–73

Vishnu's last hand holds a lotus, the symbol of purity in Hinduism. A lotus is a beautiful, delicate flower that grows in muddy ponds. Its roots extend down to the mud but the exquisite blossoms float above the water. Just so, our innermost spiritual nature is not polluted by our problems and desires and negative thoughts here in the material world. It floats above in a world of divine illumination.

The World Axis

The *Vishnu Purana* tells the story of *Dhruva*, the son of a Hindu king and one of his courtesans. One day Dhruva ran to sit in his dad's lap, but the king pushed him away. He preferred to pick up his eldest son instead, who was the legitimate heir to the throne.

Dhruva was heartbroken and ran to his mother's arms. She explained that due to good deeds performed in previous lives, Dhruva's half brother had earned the right to sit on the throne with his father. Rather than crying, Dhruva should do his best to earn good karma, too, so he could enjoy similar stature in a future life.

Little Dhruva was still very upset. He ran away into the forest to do penance, so he could earn enough merit to sit on the highest throne in the world. There he met a wandering sage who explained that Vishnu is our real father. He initiated Dhruva in Vishnu's sacred mantra, "Om Vasudevaya Namaha!" (It means "With loving reverence, I bow to Lord Vishnu!")

Dhruva repeated the mantra with such innocent sincerity that Vishnu's heart melted like butter, and he lifted the little boy up into his own lap on the highest throne in the world. You can see Dhruva yourself on a clear night. He is sitting on top of the world axis as the North Star. All the other stars were so moved by his innocent devotion that to this day they circle around Dhruva to express their admiration.

The Supreme Identity

Many of the stories about the Hindu gods are charmingly anthropomorphic, but it's a mistake to take them too literally. The myths point to a higher reality, as the Hindu guru will explain.

The *Vishnu Purana* describes who Vishnu really is. The cosmic waters are Vishnu's body. From this the universe is made, the Earth, the stars, the many dimensions of reality, everything that is and ever will be. He exists in all forms but he is not material. Rather he is intelligence itself. Nothing exists outside him. As the *Vishnu Purana* puts it, "He who knows Vishnu as the unchanging, eternal, universal reality, enters into the Supreme Lord, and becomes one with that preeminent deity."

It's News to Me!

Shiva's primary residence is on the top of Mount Kailas in Tibet. However, his wife Parvati felt the location was too remote. She wanted to live closer to the action in India. So a second residence was established in Kedarnath, Uttar Pradesh. Some Hindus report they've caught glimpses of the god and goddess in the mountains overlooking Kedarnath.

Shiva: Lord of the Yogis

If Vishnu is the most popular god in Hinduism, Shiva runs a close second. You won't be able to miss Shiva if you run into him! He's the naked one sitting on a tiger skin with snakes wrapped around his arms. His body is smeared with ashes.

Shiva is naked because he is the stark reality, pure consciousness itself. He sits in meditation rather than holding down a job because Absolute Being makes no effort at all, yet due to its mere existence, all of time and space unfolds. He is covered with ashes because after the entire universe has blown away into cosmic dust, he alone remains.

The Hindu god Shiva.

(© Hinduism Today)

You will also often see beautiful South Indian statues of Shiva dancing gracefully within a halo of flames. This represents the end of the present cycle of time when Shiva will annihilate the universe, reabsorbing all existence into his pure awareness. (After some eons, of course, Brahma the Creator will reincarnate in the vast expanse of Shiva's consciousness and start the whole cosmic process all over again!)

Drinking the Poison

Many eons ago the gods and demons, who are always at each other's throats, for once decided to cooperate. They had learned that if they worked together they could churn the nectar of immortality out of the Ocean of Milk. Well, everyone wants to be immortal! So they stuck the great mountain *Meru* in the ocean, wrapped the serpent Vasuki around it, and started churning. For thousands of years the gods pulled on one end of Vasuki, and the demons pulled on the other end.

If you're extremely patient, you can actually see the churning going on. In Hindu astronomical

New Word Alert!

Meru is the mountain at the center of the world. Astronomically it represents the north/south axis of the Earth. In yoga, it stands for the spinal column.

Dhruva is the North Star.

texts, the gods are the stars above the celestial equator and the demons are the stars below it. Over thousands of years the stars of the lower hemisphere push some of the stars of the upper hemisphere out of the sky. Then the upper stars push their way back. This apparent motion of the stars is due to the wobble of the Earth's axis. The Veda refers to this cycle many times.

Guidepost

To the Western mind, the linga and yoni, emblems of the god Shiva and his wife, Parvati, immediately suggest, well, sex. Hindus do *not* see the linga and yoni as sex organs and will be horrified if you say you do. Remember the famous quote that ultimately, the male sex organ *is* just another phallic symbol? The linga represents a cosmic principle to Hindus, not a part of the male anatomy.

New Word Alert!

A **linga** is a shapeless stone representing Shiva, divine consciousness beyond form.

A **yoni** is the base in which a linga rests. It represents the Goddess.

Many amazing things congealed out of the churning ocean—magical jewels and horses, that kind of stuff. The nectar of immortality finally came oozing out, but so did a poison so virulent it had the power to destroy the entire world. The gods and demons fought over the nectar but, with Vishnu's help, the pure-hearted gods won the battle and drank the ambrosia of immortality.

But what to do about the searing poison? Only the god Shiva was powerful enough to solve the problem. He swallowed the poison and through his yoga power held it in his throat. This way it couldn't enter the rest of his system and do any damage. That's why you'll see Shiva's throat stained dark in paintings of him.

Hindu holy men and women explain that at one level, this is the story of the yogic process. When you "churn" the prana or life energy up and down Mount Meru, the spine, all kinds of wonderful things appear in your consciousness. The nectar of illumined awareness eventually shows up, but so does all the poison in your subconscious. Some yogis advise that you not even try to deal with all that inner poison because it will tear you to pieces. Instead offer it to the Supreme Consciousness, the great being who is far more capable of dealing with powerful negative energy than you are.

The Mark of Shiva

Many statues of Shiva show him in human form. Some of them show Shiva's right side as male, and the left side as female. This is to make the point visually that God and Goddess are absolutely equivalent, and that male and female are equal. The Supreme Being has both masculine and feminine aspects, whether you see them as pure consciousness and its power, or spirit and matter, or justice and mercy.

Everywhere you travel in India you will also see Shiva worshipped in the form of a *linga*, a conical or egg-shaped stone, resting in a base called a *yoni*. Linga means "the mark of Shiva." While almost all Hindu murtis are shaped into some form, such as a male or female deity, the linga alone remains unsculpted. This is because it stands for God beyond form, pure consciousness itself.

In one famous story from the *Puranas,* Brahma and Vishnu stumbled upon a pillar of blazing light. Brahma flew upward to try to find the top of the light. Vishnu dug downward, looking for its base. Though they traveled for ages, neither could find the beginning or end of the linga of light. The light of pure awareness is infinite, the *Purana* is saying. Hinduism's yogis take the great meditator Shiva as their ideal and devote their lives to merging in His light.

Ganesha: The Elephant-Headed God

At Hindu temples throughout the world, priests regularly bring the images of the gods in their temples something to eat and drink. Usually the deities don't actually touch the food. They just bless it and leave it for us humans to chow down. But on September 21, 1995, Lord Ganesha drank the milk. Within hours, the news was all over India. Hindus rushed to the temples or to their shrine rooms at home to offer their statues of Ganesha a pitcher of milk.

The Hindu god Ganesha.

(© Hinduism Today)

That evening the Milk Miracle was broadcast all over the world on the international news. Camera crews converged on Hindu temples from India to Africa to Canada and filmed the milk actually dematerializing in front of murtis of Ganesha. Thousands of observers, Hindu and non-Hindu alike, who actually watched the milk disappear, described the experience to reporters.

Ganesha has always been known for his delightful sense of humor. On that fall day in 1995 it's possible he gently reminded people everywhere that the ultimate purpose of life lies not in serving themselves but in serving God. And that day he wanted to be served milk!

The God with a Trunk

Ganesha is the portly god with an elephant's head. Elephants are not a rare sight in many parts of India. Hindus appreciate them for their high intelligence, extraordinary strength, and exceptional devotion to each other and to their human peers. Elephants will not abandon a friend in trouble but will risk their lives to save those they care about.

Ganesha is the remover of obstacles. After all, if you are lost in thick jungle, just follow an elephant. Wherever it happens to walk becomes a path you can easily follow. Ganesha has very large ears so that he can hear everyone's prayers. He has a huge belly because he contains the entire universe inside himself. His wisdom, strength, and compassion are indomitable.

You'll often see a small mouse darting around Ganesha's feet. Like cowboys riding their ponies and Californians riding their SUVs, Ganesha goes for a ride on his mouse. Gurus explain that the mouse is the human mind, always scurrying here and there, nibbling at this and that. The mouse doesn't realize that riding on its back there's an elephant with unimaginable strength, wisdom and power. Just so, the mind is often oblivious to the limitless light and power of spirit that "rides around" within its inner recesses.

Throughout history, many Hindus have been illiterate. Their gurus used memorable images like an elephant-headed god astride a mouse to teach unforgettable lessons about the nature of the Supreme Being.

Sages Say

"Miracles like Ganesha drinking the milk come as a healthy blow to the human intellect. Such incidents stir us out of our deep sleep, at least for a time. It serves as a shock treatment, a wake-up call. An unknown power, beyond the reach of the intellect, constantly maintains a balance in the universe. Those who have experienced it say this power is all-pervading, all-knowing and all-powerful. If God is omnipotent, is there anything He cannot do? If He chooses to drink milk through the statue of Lord Ganesha, it is all His divine play."

—Amritanandamayi Ma

How Ganesha Lost His Head

Many ages ago, Shiva's wife Parvati asked her young son, Ganesha, to guard the door to the house while she took a bath inside. As fate would have it, Shiva came home from a long meditation retreat just at this moment. He'd been gone so long he wasn't aware his wife had had a child and that Ganesha was his son. And Ganesha had never seen Shiva before and didn't realize he was his dad.

Shiva was extremely irritated at the young boy who wouldn't let him into his own house. He tried to push Ganesha aside but the boy was incredibly strong. Finally Shiva cut off the boy's head and called out to Parvati, "Honey, I'm home!"

The goddess was beside herself when she saw that her husband had just killed their son. Realizing his mistake, Shiva ran up and down the mountain looking for Ganesha's head. It was long gone! Seeing the Divine Mother's grief, an elephant standing nearby volunteered its own head, which Shiva quickly cut off and replaced on his son's body, restoring Ganesha to life.

The story is about self-sacrifice. When we sacrifice our selfishness and egotism in service of the divine, as both Ganesha and the elephant did, we gain wisdom and immortality. And, like Lord Ganesha today who helps everyone who appeals to him, we gain the ability to be of service to all beings everywhere.

Hanuman: Monkeying Around

If you step into a Hindu home, odds are high you'll find an image of Hanuman, the monkey god. He has the head and tail of a rhesus monkey, and the body of a man. Sometimes you'll see him ripping open his chest to reveal Rama and Sita—God and Goddess—residing in his heart.

It's impossible to exaggerate how much Hindus love this passionate, energetic monkey. In fact, it's a crime to kill a monkey in India. Monkeys are considered sacred due to their association with Hanuman!

God's Army

Rama, the hero of the *Ramayana,* was at a loss when he had to attack the military stronghold of Lanka to rescue his wife Sita. Alone in the jungle with his brother, he didn't stand much of a chance against Lanka's powerful king Ravana. Then Hanuman joined the team along with a makeshift army of monkeys and bears. Keeping the image of his beloved Rama in his heart, Hanuman was able to leap across the strait between India and Sri Lanka to carry a message to Sita, imprisoned in Ravana's fortress.

Moving Mountains

During the battle with Ravana's demonic troops, Rama's brother Lakshman was seriously injured. Unless he could get a particular medicinal herb from a far-away mountain, the local physician explained, he would not be able to save Lakshman's life.

Seeing Rama's grief, Hanuman instantly raced to the mountain, covering huge distances in single leaps and bounds. But once he got there, Hanuman realized he had no idea which of the many herbs growing on the mountain was the one the doctor needed. So he picked up the entire mountain and brought it back to the battlefield! Lakshman's life was saved and Rama clasped Hanuman in a famous embrace of gratitude. Hanuman teaches us that when loving and serving God is the focus of our lives, the impossible becomes possible.

Now when you enter a Hindu home and see a picture of a monkey carrying a mountain, you'll know what it means.

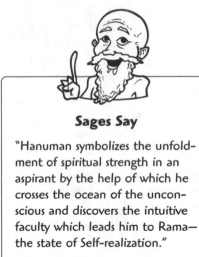

Sages Say

"Hanuman symbolizes the unfoldment of spiritual strength in an aspirant by the help of which he crosses the ocean of the unconscious and discovers the intuitive faculty which leads him to Rama—the state of Self-realization."

—Swami Jyotir Mayananda

Murugan: The Spear of God

Shiva is immensely popular in South India. So is Vishnu, called Mal ("the Great One") by Tamil-speaking Indians. But Murugan, the youthful warrior god, is uniquely South Indian. He is spectacularly handsome and courageous, not to mention a great dancer! His priests, called Velans, launch into a frenzied dance in an attempt to connect with the god and channel his wisdom and power.

Murugan is usually shown carrying his favorite weapon, a death-dealing spear. He is quick to protect his devotees and generous in granting boons.

As northern and southern Indian cultures amalgamated over the millennia, Murugan became increasingly identified with Skanda, the six-headed warrior son of Shiva. Skanda has six heads because as an infant he was nursed by six surrogate mothers, the six brightest stars of the Pleiades. The constellation Pleiades is called Krittika in Sanskrit, so Skanda is widely known as Kartikeya.

Skanda and Murugan are both shown riding peacocks. The connection between virile young men strutting their stuff and male peacocks flaunting their feathers is obvious to the Hindu imagination.

Quick Quiz

1. The three great gods of Hinduism are …
    a. Father, Son, and Holy Ghost.
    b. Brahma, Vishnu, and Shiva.
    c. On vacation in Bermuda.

2. Vishnu has incarnated on Earth as …
    a. Rama and Krishna.
    b. An elephant-headed deity called Ganesha.
    c. Mahatma Gandhi.

3. The Shiva linga represents …
    a. A dangerous poison churned from the Milk Ocean.
    b. The male sex organ.
    c. Pure consciousness beyond form.

4. Hanuman is honored by Hindus because he …
    a. Leaps tall buildings in a single bound.
    b. Demonstrates perfect devotion to God.
    c. Is a sacred monkey.

Answers: 1 (b). 2 (a). 3 (c). 4 (b).

Surya: The Divine Sun

You don't have to visit an Indian temple to see one of Hinduism's most respected gods. He goes galloping over your head in his shining chariot every day of the year. If you'd ever spent a night freezing in the cold winters of northern India, you'd definitely understand why Lord Surya's appearance over the eastern horizon each morning is so welcome!

Surya, the Sun, is the source of prana, life energy, in our world system. His total selflessness, pouring forth his blessings to all beings day in and day out, without expectation of any reward in return, is the perfect example of true sainthood.

The Sun's Difficult Marriage

Surya's wife, Sanjna, however, was not happy with her husband. He was so bright she couldn't bear to look at his face! So she ran away, leaving a substitute who looked exactly like her. Surya eventually became suspicious and went looking for his wife. She took the form of a mare to escape from him, but he took the form of a stallion, chased her, and impregnated her by breathing on her. Their sons were twin horsemen called the Ashvins.

When Sanjna confessed that she couldn't stand his intense brightness, Surya had his radiance surgically whittled down to a fraction of its original intensity, and the couple lived happily ever after.

The Meaning in the Myth

According to the Hindu tradition, the true light is the Inner Sun, the presence of divine being within us. Sanjna is the soul (her name means "the one with knowledge") who at the dawn of time fled from her divine consort, whose supreme light was too much for her to assimilate. She escaped down into the material world in the form of a horse (horses represent prana, or life energy in Hinduism). When spirit impregnates the life force, the Ashvins or celestial wisdom and healing power are born.

The Inner Sun yogis experience in deep meditation is only a fraction of a fraction of the light of the Supreme Reality. The Lord of the Universe moderates his brilliance to a level the meditator can withstand. By merging in that inner light, the soul begins its journey home to its true mate, the Lord of Light.

The Least You Need to Know

➤ Brahma, Vishnu, and Shiva are the three main gods of Hinduism.

➤ Ganesha is famous for the "Milk Miracle" he performed in September 1995.

➤ Hanuman, the monkey god, symbolizes perfect devotion.

➤ Murugan is the warrior god of South India.

➤ The Sun is honored as an important deity by Hindus.

Chapter 13

Meet the Hindu Goddesses

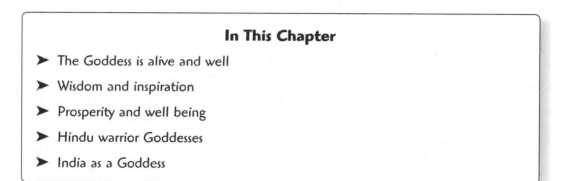

In This Chapter

➤ The Goddess is alive and well

➤ Wisdom and inspiration

➤ Prosperity and well being

➤ Hindu warrior Goddesses

➤ India as a Goddess

In ancient times, the Goddess was worshipped throughout the planet. Over the last two thousand years, male-dominated religions have stamped out the worship of the feminine face of spirit everywhere in the world. Everywhere, that is, except India. The Hindu tradition is the one world religion where the Goddess is still honored on a massive scale.

Nirguna Brahman, the Supreme Reality in Hinduism, transcends gender. But when the Divine Being takes form, It assumes both male *and* female attributes. In fact, to many Hindus, since the Divine gave birth to us out of its own being and nurtures us like a caring mother, it must be a Goddess. To Hindus, we are not apart from God as the Judeo-Christian-Islamic traditions maintain. Instead, we are a part *of* her.

I'd like to introduce you to some of the most popular goddesses in Hinduism. If you travel in India, or visit a typical Hindu home, you'll find images of the Mother of the Universe everywhere. To fully appreciate Hinduism, you must understand that the Goddess is alive and well in Hindu culture.

Shakti: Feminine Power

There is a widespread belief in the West that women are inherently "passive" and men are naturally "active." To the Hindu mind, this belief is clearly nonsense. In the Hindu tradition, active power is always thought of as feminine while passive stability is masculine. Hindus know that women get just as much of the work done in the world as men do, if not more. And what male warrior is as fierce and furious as a mother protecting her young?

The Sanskrit word for power or energy is *shakti*. Shakti is also the generic name for the Goddess, so her worshippers are called *Shaktas*. No male deity can accomplish anything without his Shakti, his female consort. She is his strength and power of accomplishment. Some goddesses are married. Others are independent feminine powers of limitless intelligence and capacity.

New Word Alert!

Shakti is the Goddess. **Shakti** also means power, energy, or the illuminating power of consciousness.

A **Shakta** is a devotee of the Goddess.

Sages Say

"You are the swan gliding over the pond of creative energy, waves and waves of creative force emanating from Your form! Radiant Goddess resplendent in white, dwell forever in the Kashmir of my heart!"

—*Sarasvati Rahasya Upanishad*

Sarasvati: The Hindu Muse

The Greeks had their muses, goddesses who inspired music and poetry, drama and science. In Hinduism, this role is filled by Sarasvati, perhaps the oldest goddess in the world who is still widely worshipped. The Veda never tires of praising her.

Artists and scientists have long noted that some of their greatest works or intellectual insights seemed to mysteriously appear fully formed in their minds. Beatle Paul McCartney reports that he first heard the melody for "Yesterday," one of the most popular songs of all time, in a dream. To Hindus, these are gifts from Sarasvati, the divine muse.

Hindu musicians chant to Sarasvati and prostrate before their musical instruments before beginning a concert. Children pray to Sarasvati for help with their schoolwork. Speakers invite her to "dance on their tongues" before giving a lecture.

Sarasvati is always dressed in white, the color of pure illumination. In one of her four hands she holds a book, showing her command over all intellectual knowledge. Another hand holds a rosary, since she is also the source of all spiritual knowledge. Her two remaining hands hold a vina, an Indian instrument that looks like a sitar. This means that she is the source of the sound vibrations or primeval waves of energy that form the universe.

Sarasvati is the wife of Brahma the Creator. While Brahma's worship has all but vanished from Hinduism, Sarasvati is still worshipped in virtually every Hindu town and village. She is the inner source of creative intelligence, wisdom, and artistic inspiration.

Lakshmi: Showers of Gold

The goddess of wealth never lacks for devotees, as I'm sure you can imagine! Lakshmi is wrapped in a beautiful red sari. Showers of coins stream from two of her hands, signifying the material blessings that pour out of her. These include not only prosperity but health and a joyful, harmonious family life. Her two other hands hold lotuses, reminding us that her greatest boons are not material but gifts of the spirit. These are the only blessings of lasting value.

Lakshmi is so well loved because of her extremely kind nature. Her husband, Vishnu, administers justice, but Lakshmi is incapable of punishing anyone. She is so softhearted that if you find yourself in trouble with Vishnu, you can run to Lakshmi and ask her to help out. She'll do everything she can to get Vishnu to ease up on you. In this respect, she's much like Mary, mother of Jesus, in Roman Catholicism. She intercedes for you with God.

In times of crisis, Vishnu incarnates on earth in human form. In Hinduism, you can't have God without the Goddess. So wherever he shows up, you can count on Lakshmi turning up, too. When Vishnu came as Rama, Lakshmi came as his wife, Sita. When Vishnu manifested as Krishna, Lakshmi came as his wife, Rukmini. Male and female must work together harmoniously in order for universal balance to be maintained.

Parvati: Divine Wife and Mother

Parvati is the dark-colored wife of the god Shiva, and the mother of the deities Ganesha and Skanda.

According to legend, Parvati was a young girl raised in the Himalayas who did years of intense austerities in order to win Shiva as her husband. She sat down in the forest and swore not to budge until Shiva materialized and asked her to marry him. This was a tall order because Shiva was a widower who had no desire to remarry.

God the Widower

How did Shiva become a widower?

In ages past, the seer Daksha insulted Shiva by not inviting him to a party. *All* the other gods and goddesses were invited. But Daksha didn't care for Shiva because he was a bum. He didn't have a job and didn't dress up; he just lived naked in the mountains meditating. Shiva's wife, Sati, was so upset at the slight that she committed suicide, jumping into a fire.

Shiva lost it completely. He carried his wife's body around in his arms, weeping and wailing. Vishnu couldn't allow this to continue, so he kept throwing his whirling discus at Sati's body, chopping off different parts which fell to earth. Every place a bit of the goddess's body landed is now a major pilgrimage spot for Shaktas. Eventually Shiva calmed down and disappeared into the mountains to spend the rest of the cosmic cycle in meditation.

My guru explained that many eons ago, the cosmic soul was united with the universal spirit, just as Sati was married to Shiva. But then the world soul immolated itself, leaping into the ever-burning fire of energy from which the material worlds are made. The cosmic soul was then sliced into many different pieces, like you, for example, and me. How can the soul return to her divine lord, the Supreme Spirit?

It's News to Me!

This world tears God apart! Egyptians believed Osiris was hacked to pieces by his evil brother Seth. The Greeks believed Orpheus and Dionysus were torn to shreds, too. The Hindus speak of the Goddess being sliced to bits. Hindu gurus believe these stories point to the same mystical truth. As the Veda says, consciousness was once a unified field of awareness that split into units of consciousness like your soul and mine. The goal of spiritual practice is to reunite our awareness with the infinite.

Getting God Back

Sitting in the forest Parvati, who had been Sati in her previous life, swore she would not let her mind shift away from the lotus feet of Lord Shiva for even an instant until he appeared before her. "If my mind should waver, may I lose him forever!" she vowed. So there she sat through monsoon rains, forest fires, elephant stampedes, and just about every other form of botheration you can picture. Parvati kept her mind fixed on God alone.

Then one day, she heard a small child screaming in terror. Immediately she jumped up and raced to help. But there wasn't any child. Instead Shiva materialized in front of her. "You promised you wouldn't let anything distract you from meditating on me!" Shiva complained. "I created this illusion to test you." And then he smiled. "Just now you showed that you would give up even what you want most in the world, union with me, to help the helpless. I see now that you really are fit to be my wife!"

Shiva and Parvati are living happily ever after at their mountain retreat in Tibet. But Parvati has shown us the way back to God: continual loving meditation on his divine form, and self-sacrificing service to our fellow humanity.

Durga: Take No Prisoners!

At one time, Durga was worshipped all the way from India to Rome. While she has been forgotten in today's Christian and Muslim cultures, she is still the great warrior goddess of Hinduism.

You can recognize Durga immediately because she's always shown riding on or standing beside a lion or tiger. She holds a host of weapons in her many hands. Often she's pictured attacking a buffalo demon named Mahisha. Look at her face: You'll notice that even in the thick of battle she always appears completely calm.

The Glory of the Goddess

I told you earlier the most popular scripture in Hinduism is the *Bhagavad Gita*. A close runner-up in popularity is the *Devi Mahatmyam*, which means "Glory of the Goddess." Millions of Hindus can recite sections from it by heart. It's the story of a king and a merchant who have been betrayed by their families and friends and have lost everything they own. Deeply disillusioned, they go to the sage Medhas for spiritual counseling.

Medhas explains that most people are deluded by the Goddess's great power of maya. They fail to see their unity with all creation and with each other. Instead they selfishly strive to enrich themselves without regard for how others may be harmed in the process. Medhas advises the two men to worship the Goddess in the hope that she will reveal to them her other great power: the power to grant enlightenment. They beg Medhas to tell them more about this wonderful Goddess.

Sages Say

"When we remember You in times of crisis, You instantly remove the cause of our fear. When we remember You in contemplation, You grant us the highest state of meditation. Oh Mother, You dispel suffering, poverty and fear! Who but You is so compassionate, that You rush at once to help everyone who calls to You?"

—*Devi Mahatmyam* 4:17

The Demon Slayer

Medhas tells a series of stories about Durga's battles with an assortment of evil demons. Blood and gore are described with relish as Durga finishes them off—the poor devils don't stand a chance! These demons are unhelpful qualities in ourselves, such as hatred, anger, greed, depression, conceit, and misuse of our natural abilities.

The *Devi Mahatmyam* promises that anyone who hears these stories will be cleansed of their sins. This is not just a fast and loose sales pitch. Many devotees experience a profound sense of catharsis from hearing how the Divine Power purifies the psychic atmosphere of these malignant forces. Even if you don't grasp intellectually that Durga's battle is an inner one, the story is told so vividly that you feel it going on inside you. This has been called "therapeutic myth," the process of addressing your inner conflicts through vivid mental imagery. When the Goddess triumphs in the end, you feel like you yourself have won an important battle.

Sages Say

"The people of India do not deny the evil side of the world. They take that also and adorn the Mother on the one hand with evil ... on the other hand they represent Her as overflowing with blessings. In times of distress they face danger bravely, and pray to Her with unflinching faith and whole-hearted love, recognizing Her grandeur and divine power even behind misfortune and calamity."

—Swami Abhedananda

Guidepost

Next time you see a picture of the goddess Kali, look *very* closely at the garland of skulls she wears around her neck. One of those decapitated heads is *yours!* Kali is the bitter enemy of egotism. In the course of each person's life, she finds a way to lop off our conceit and self-importance. *Ouch!*

Medhas' two students now enthusiastically propitiate the Goddess. Eventually she appears to them both and asks what boon they prefer. The king wants his kingdom back and is granted a vast empire. The merchant, however, has developed a taste for the higher things in life after months of worship and austerity in the woods. So he asks for the highest thing he can think of: spiritual liberation. With great delight, Durga grants his request.

Kali: The *Really* Scary One

One of the demons Durga fought in the *Devi Mahatmyam* was called Raktabija, which means "drop of blood." Whenever she attacked him, each drop of Raktabija's blood turned into a clone of himself as soon as it touched the ground.

This was the only demon actually capable of holding his own against the Mother of the Universe. For one moment the Divine Power frowned. From her knit forehead leapt the most terrifying Goddess ever: Kali!

Kali stuck out her long tongue and drank up every drop of Raktabija's blood before it could touch the earth. And then she ate him!

The battles being described here are purely internal. Your guru will help you understand that Raktabija is the mind's ability to keep generating negative thoughts and bad habits without end. The only way to stop this proliferation is to catch each thought before it has a chance to take root in the fertile field of your unconscious. If you invoke her, Kali will help you clean out the garbage stored in the basement of your subconscious. The process is full of grace, but it's not always pleasant!

The Bloodthirsty Goddess

Kali is a very distinctive-looking goddess. She's half naked, though she does wear a garland of skulls and a belt of hacked limbs. She's waving a lot of very scary-looking weapons around in the air, and her tongue is stuck out to suck up any negative thought that passes through your mind.

Westerners will sometimes say, "I'm getting in touch with my inner Kali. I'm really connecting with my anger!" But Hindus do not experience Kali as an angry goddess. On the contrary, they recognize Kali as the slayer of duality. If we're angry at someone, it's because we're seeing them as an enemy, as someone apart from ourselves. It's that sense that anyone or anything exists other than divine consciousness that Kali is determined to destroy. If there's anything less than pure love inside us, sooner or later, in this life or the next, Kali will hack it out of us!

The Divine Protectress

Though she's juggling a lot of terrifying weapons, you'll notice that two of Kali's hands are empty, making strange-looking gestures. One of those gestures means "Don't be afraid!" The other signifies "I will protect you!"

Though Kali is a scary-looking goddess, Hindus do not think of her as frightening. Instead they see her as their loving mother who corrects them when they make mistakes and who races to protect them when they're in trouble. When you visit a Kali temple, you will not find devotees cringing in terror before her. What you *will* find is men and women eagerly trying to catch a glimpse of their beloved Divine Mother at the front of the temple, and singing and dancing with ecstatic devotion.

You'll usually see Kali dancing, too, on top of a prostrate male body. That's Lord Shiva, pure divine awareness. He gazes up at her in rapture, much like her Hindu devotees.

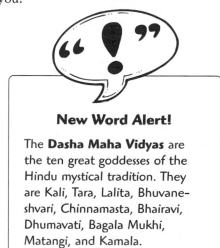

New Word Alert!

The **Dasha Maha Vidyas** are the ten great goddesses of the Hindu mystical tradition. They are Kali, Tara, Lalita, Bhuvaneshvari, Chinnamasta, Bhairavi, Dhumavati, Bagala Mukhi, Matangi, and Kamala.

Lalita: The Supreme Seductress

If you start pursuing serious spiritual practice in a Hindu community, sooner or later you'll hear about the *Dasha Maha Vidyas,* the ten great goddesses of the Hindu yoga tradition. These are the special forms of the Great Mother worshipped privately by the yogis and mystics, as opposed to goddesses like Lakshmi or Durga worshipped more openly by the public.

Lalita is one of these esoteric goddesses. Her name means "She who plays"—the universe is her playground. She's also called Maha Tripura Sundari, "the most beautiful girl in all the worlds," Raja Rajeshvari, "the supreme sovereign empress of the universe," and Kameshvari, "the goddess of love."

The Goddess in the Moon

Kali is worshipped on the day of the New Moon. Its waning cycle represents her action in our lives, as she strips us of anything we value more than her, including finally our life itself. She is dark as the invisible Moon, the embodiment of the destructive power of time. She stands for the loss of every material thing, revealing nothing in the end but the pure existence of spirit itself.

Lalita, however, is worshipped on the Full Moon. Its waxing cycle represents her activity as she helps us expand the field of our loving awareness to include everyone around us, then all of manifestation in a crescendo of bliss. Kali takes everything away but spirit. Lalita reveals that everything *is* spirit.

Guidepost

Want to pay your respects to Mother India? The Bharat Mata Temple is about a mile south of the Varanasi train station in Benares. Non-Hindus are welcome. While you're in town, stop by the New Vishvanath Temple at Benares Hindu University. There you'll get a full education in Hindu spirituality just by reading the beautifully decorated plaques on the wall. Visit the Shiva linga inside, and you'll receive a blessing from the priest who worships there all day.

With Lalita you have your cake and eat it, too. She is supreme love, supreme beauty, and cosmic consciousness. While Kali takes everything away, Lalita gives us everything we desire. She is the force of desire itself.

You understand, of course, that the New Moon and the Full Moon are not two separate things. There's only one Moon! In the Hindu tradition, we recognize that ultimately Kali and Lalita are the same Goddess. Loss and gain blend together in the epiphany of enlightenment.

Consciousness and Power

Some Hindus speak of Shiva and Shakti, God and his power. Lalita represents a state of consciousness in which there is no distinction between spirit and matter, consciousness and energy. Pure consciousness *is* pure energy and is continually spontaneously pouring forth the "play" of life. Lalita is constantly forming new universes through which her infinite glory manifests. And she is constantly calling back the souls wandering in these worlds into the wonder of her supremely blissful being.

Quick Quiz

1. Hinduism is the one world religion in which ...

   a. The Goddess is still honored.

   b. Worship of a male God is forbidden.

   c. Ice cream socials are sanctioned.

2. Sarasvati is the goddess of ...

   a. Wisdom and creative energy.

   b. High-fashion clothing and photography.

   c. Cooking and cleaning.

3. The goddess Durga is poised to attack ...

   a. Non-Hindus.

   b. The unwholesome qualities in ourselves.

   c. Lions and tigers and bears.

4. Parvati demonstrates that we can attain union with God by ...

   a. Committing suicide.

   b. Sitting alone in the forest.

   c. Meditating and serving others.

Answers: 1 (a). 2 (a). 3 (b). 4 (c).

Bharat Mata: Mother India

The Bharat Mata Temple in Benares is one of the most unique temples in the world. Instead of a traditional statue of an Indian deity, it contains an enormous three-dimensional relief map of Greater India from Afghanistan in the west to Burma in the east, from the Tibetan plateau in the north to Sri Lanka in the south. The topographically correct map, made of colored marble tiles, gives a vivid sense of the vast expanse of Hindu culture and the dramatic contrast in altitude between the high Himalayas and the plains of the Deccan.

A colorful poster in the temple shows Bharat Mata, "Mother India," in the form of a mature goddess presiding over a satellite image of the Indian subcontinent. The temple is new by Indian standards. It was inaugurated by Mahatma Gandhi.

Hindus, like native peoples everywhere, have a profound connection with the land they live on. The planet itself is Bhu Devi, Mother Earth. Bharat Mata is more than the land itself, however. She is the very consciousness of the culture, the magic, sanctity, despair, and self-renewal of the ageless Hindu civilization. At this remarkable temple the people of India honor their own enduring spirit.

Ganga Ma: Mother Ganges

Hinduism is so incredibly old it remembers a time when the Ganges River didn't exist! The ancient hero Bhagiratha had to go up into the Himalayas and bring Ganga down from her home in the glaciers to the plains of north India.

When the Ganges first came cascading down from on high (some texts say her source is actually in heaven!) the force of her landing would have destroyed the Earth. So Shiva caught her in the locks of his hair and eased her gently to the ground. In many paintings of Shiva, you'll see streams of water pouring down his head. That's Mother Ganga!

In Vedic times, the Sarasvati River was the largest and most sacred river in India. She dried up about four thousand years ago. At that point much of the sanctity associated with the Sarasvati was transferred to the Ganges, which has been Hinduism's holiest river ever since.

It's News to Me!

Can a river fall in love with a city? The Ganges runs eastward about 1,200 miles from her source in the Himalayas to the Bay of Bengal. At only one point does she turn around and head back west. That's at Benares, the city sacred to Lord Shiva, who gently helped Mother Ganga down when she first fell to earth. The Ganges swings around to lovingly embrace Shiva's holy city, and then resumes her course to Bengal.

Hindus go to the Ganges not just to wash their clothes but to wash away their sins. Baptism is an extremely ancient rite in Hinduism, one that you engage in as often as possible since there are always new sins to wash off!

Visits from Mother

Many of us in the West have heard of the Virgin Mary's many appearances—at Fatima for example, or Lourdes, or more recently at Medjegorje. What we don't hear about is the Divine Mother's visits to other cultures like China or India. Showing up as the mother of Jesus wouldn't do much good in a Chinese village, where many people haven't heard of Mary. So there she'll show up as Quan Yin, a goddess the people instantly recognize.

Some of my American friends and I stopped at a Kali temple in the village of Rajpur in Bengal. As soon as we entered the grounds, we felt electricity in the air. We sat down to meditate and each of us was transported into extraordinary states of meditation. We all distinctly felt the magic, the tangible presence of spirit, and asked what was going on.

The locals then explained that at this very site the Divine Mother, in the form of the goddess Durga, had been appearing to a Hindu villager named Baba Dulal. They took us to the spot, marked by a sacred tree, where he had repeatedly seen the Mother of the Universe. Her presence was still palpable. It was as if we should still smell her perfume!

To Hindus, the Goddess is not a metaphor or a political statement. She is the Supreme Being itself who gives birth to us, nurtures, educates, and protects us. Who lifts us into her lap during meditation. And who blesses us with shakti, the illuminating power of consciousness, when it's time for us to leave the playground of this world and return home to an inner realm of light.

The Least You Need to Know

➤ The Goddess is still widely worshipped in Hinduism.

➤ Sarasvati is the goddess of wisdom and divine inspiration.

➤ Lakshmi is the goddess of prosperity and well being.

➤ Durga and Kali are Hinduism's two fierce warrior goddesses.

➤ Lalita represents pure consciousness and energy.

➤ India itself is worshipped as a goddess.

Chapter 14

Avatars: Gods in Human Form

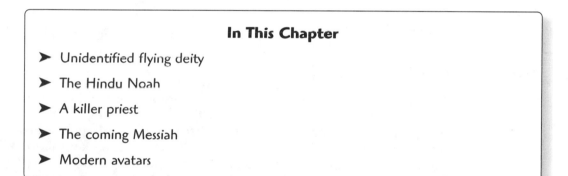

In This Chapter

➤ Unidentified flying deity

➤ The Hindu Noah

➤ A killer priest

➤ The coming Messiah

➤ Modern avatars

Many ancient cultures believed that God would visit Earth in human form. (Greeks and Romans thought Dionysus was a god-man.) Or that some men and women were so special that they elevated themselves to divine status. (Hercules and Perseus were two such men-gods.) Christianity picked up the theme, though it claimed that Jesus was the only legitimate instance.

Hindus have long believed in divine incarnations called *avatars*. Avatars are immensely popular in India. In fact, much Hindu devotional practice is centered on these beloved figures. Let's look at God and Goddess's interventions in history, when Hindus say he and she assumed a physical form to save the world.

Hindu Saviors

It's Vishnu's job to keep the world in running order and protect the innocent. His ten incarnations are the best-known avatars. Surprisingly, the human form is not his only uniform. He'll assume whatever shape is called for under the circumstances.

For example, when the demi-gods and demons wanted to churn the Milky Ocean to produce the nectar of immortality (see Chapter 12, "Meet the Hindu Gods"), they found a mountain they could use as a churning rod and a gigantic snake they could use to spin the rod. But there was no base strong enough to rest the mountain on. Vishnu obligingly assumed the form of a huge turtle, and the churning rod, Mount Meru, was balanced on his shell.

New Word Alert!

An **avatar** is an incarnation of God or the Goddess.

This myth may seem less odd when you learn that in Hindu astronomy the bare shell of the turtle refers to the south celestial pole, a comparatively vacant part of the sky where there are few bright stars. The churning motion represents Earth's precessional cycle, an astronomical phenomenon the Vedic sages often referred to.

Visitor from Outer Space

Another time Vishnu averted a disaster of cosmic proportions. The landmass of the planet Earth was disappearing beneath the sea. Suddenly a great being shaped like a boar appeared in the sky. With a roaring cry it crashed into the Earth, plunged beneath the ocean, and used its mighty tusks to heave the landmass back up above the water. The boar was so virile it impregnated Mother Earth, who had fallen desperately in love with her rescuer. A great mass emerged from her belly and roared off into the sky. The son of Mother Earth and her celestial savior was the planet Mars.

More than a few commentators have noted that the story of the boar avatar sounds uncannily like an asteroid hitting the Earth, perhaps after sea levels began to rise at the end of an Ice Age.

A Fishy Avatar

The *Matsya Purana* tells an amazing story I'm positive you'll find interesting.

Long ago a man named Manu was bathing in a river when he accidentally cupped a small fish in his hands. The fish begged him to take him home because a river full of hungry big fish was not a safe place for a tasty little fish.

Manu placed the fish in a bowl of water but it quickly outgrew its new home. Manu kept transferring the fish into larger containers until finally it grew so large that it would now be perfectly safe in the sea. As he released the fish into the ocean it thanked him for his kindness and warned him, "Very soon the entire planet is going to be destroyed in a flood. Build yourself a boat and put two of every kind of creature into it, and seeds of all types. Better hurry!"

Manu quickly obeyed. Soon a tremendous flood blanketed the world with raging waters. The fish reappeared, with a horn on its head this time. Manu tied his floundering vessel to the fish, which towed him to the safety of a nearby mountain. When the waters subsided Manu repopulated the world, which is why we're called the race of man, or of Manu. By now he had figured out that the fish was none other than Vishnu himself, come to save humanity from total destruction.

The Fish Messiah reappears in ancient Zoroastrian mythology where he advises Yima, the first man, to release a dove to see how low the waters have ebbed. He shows up again in a Sumerian tablet dated to 1750 B.C.E. Previously scholars had thought the Sumerian version of "Noah's Ark" was the oldest. With the redating of early Vedic and Zoroastrian texts, it's now much more likely the Hindu myth is by far the most ancient version of this famous story.

Tallest Dwarf in the Universe

An extremely ancient myth about Vishnu tells of his famous "three steps." The egotistical king Bali had built a huge empire. It was time to put him in his place. A dwarf showed up at his door asking for a gift. Bali may have been conceited, but he was also generous. "Anything you want."

"I want as much land as I can cover in three strides," the dwarf said.

Bali said sure. The dwarf took one step—and covered the entire Earth. He took a second step—and covered all of heaven. "You owe me one more step," he told the king, "but there's no more space in the universe. Where should I put my foot next?"

Bali was no idiot. He recognized now that he was in the presence of the Lord of the Universe.

It's News to Me!

The Dogon people from the West African republic of Mali are famous for their claim that "fish people" from outer space provided them with their advanced knowledge of astronomy. They do appear to have known about double star systems long before modern astronomers discovered them. According to the Babylonian historian Berossos, the fish-man savior *Oannes* is supposed to have taught humanity the arts and sciences at the beginning of time. Fish-men teachers are also often depicted in Assyrian art.

Sages Say

"Vishnu strode across the universe. Three steps He took, and all the worlds were just the dust raised by His feet. In deepest meditation the great souls look up to that lofty place where Vishnu reigns like an eye in heaven."

—*Rig Veda* 1:22.17,20

"Here," he said, offering his own head. The "dwarf" stepped on Bali's face, crushing it into the Earth.

It's News to Me!

Was Buddha an incarnation of Vishnu? Not according to Buddhists. But Hindus can make room for just about anyone in their religion, and even the renegade Indian guru Buddha found a place in their pantheon. Too many people were becoming enlightened by following Hinduism. To prevent the world from being depopulated, some Hindus say, Vishnu assumed the form of Buddha and misled millions into abandoning the Veda. Hindus believe Buddha was Vishnu at his most mischievous.

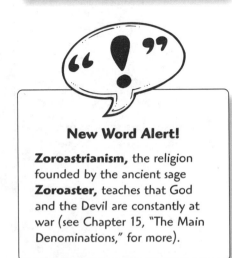

New Word Alert!

Zoroastrianism, the religion founded by the ancient sage **Zoroaster,** teaches that God and the Devil are constantly at war (see Chapter 15, "The Main Denominations," for more).

There is, of course, a moral to the story. Bali is the human ego. Vishnu is all-pervading spirit. Before the Supreme Being the mature ego must surrender, no matter how great a king or queen it formerly imagined itself to be. For magnanimously admitting defeat, Bali was ultimately generously rewarded.

The Lion Man

Vishnu often incarnates to teach kings gone bad a good lesson. In this story, it's Hiranya Kashipu, whose military exploits are terrorizing the earth. Worse, Hiranya Kashipu is also persecuting his innocent son Prahlada, who is a guileless devotee of Vishnu. Well, this is the straw that broke the camel's back!

The evil king had won a boon that he could not be killed at day or night, inside or outside, by man or by God. But no king is more clever than Vishnu. At twilight (neither day nor night) as Hiranya Kashipu stepped through a doorway (neither outdoors nor indoors), a statue of a half-man, half-lion (neither human nor God) fell on him, ripping him to pieces.

Zoroastrianism is closely related to Vedic religion. Interestingly, in the Zoroastrian tradition, the image of a half-man, half-lion represents the all-consuming force of time. As the Zoroastrians were long the Hindu hostile neighbors, it's possible Hiranya Kashipu was opposed to his son worshipping Vishnu because he was a follower of *Zoroaster,* who rejected the Hindu tradition.

Parashu Rama: An Axe to Grind

Parashu Rama was a hot-tempered guy. How hot tempered? Well, his name means "Rama with an axe." If that brings to mind a certain genre of horror movie, your image isn't far off the mark.

Brahmin priests aren't axe murderers as a rule, but there are exceptions to every rule. In Parashu Rama's

time, the warrior caste was out of control. They were rampaging through the countryside, killing and exploiting innocent people (a definite no-no in Hinduism's strict
code of conduct for warriors). When a soldier assaulted his father, Parashu Rama went
berserk. Though he was a brahmin himself and not supposed to fight, Parashu Rama
picked up an axe and killed the soldier.

But he didn't just kill that warrior. He killed *all* the warriors. But he didn't just kill all
the warriors. He broke into their homes and killed their wives and children. And he
didn't just do this once. Anytime he heard there was a surviving warrior anywhere,
he rushed there and killed him and his family. Parashu Rama's goal was flat-out geno-
cide. He didn't just want to wipe out the present evil race of violent men. He wanted
to expunge the fighting class forever.

The story of Parashu Rama is probably based on historical fact, perhaps a brahmanical
uprising against the corrupt warrior caste. But obviously no ordinary priest could
achieve what Parashu Rama did and live to tell the tale. The fact that he was so successful could mean only one thing: He must have been an incarnation of Vishnu,
come to purify the world.

The Himalayan Master

The *Tripura Rahasya* tells the poignant story of Parashu Rama's inner struggle. He realized that he was mentally ill. His anger was out of control, and he was a danger to
everyone around him. He sought out various gurus
for counseling, but they were all too scared of him
to teach him. So they sent him to the Himalayas to
seek help from Dattatreya, the greatest spiritual
master of them all.

Dattatreya was so awesome that Hindu tradition
would designate him an incarnation of Brahma
and of Vishnu *and* of Shiva all at once! As he approached the master's hermitage, Parashu Rama
found other would-be disciples running in the opposite direction. "Don't bother with Dattatreya,"
they advised him. "He's a fraud!" But our axe mur-
derer had come too far to turn back now.

Entering the ashram Parashu Rama saw Dattatreya
sitting with a jug of wine on one knee and a nubile
young woman on the other. No wonder the other
seekers had left in such a hurry! But Parashu Rama
noted the light of Self-realization glowing in the
guru's face and wasn't fooled. Instead he prostrated
before the master and begged for his help.

Sages Say

"A man without spiritual wisdom
is like a frog in a well. The frog
thinks its dark, damp well is the
entire universe. It never leaps
out into the light. In the same
way a man who has never developed his spiritual awareness
thinks this world is the whole of
reality. He dies in ignorance,
never having seen the light."

—Dattatreya in the *Tripura
Rahasya 2:79–81*

Peace of Mind

In passages of extraordinary beauty, Dattatreya introduced Parashu Rama to the Goddess within. By learning to see the Goddess of beauty and bliss inside himself, Parashu Rama overcame his violent tendencies and finally found peace.

Parashu Rama is also honored for leading a community of north Indians to colonize the south. The Vedic god Varuna promised him as much land as he could cover with an arrow shot. Then realizing Parashu Rama was so strong his arrow might fly over the entire earth, Varuna sent an ant to gnaw loose his bow string. Because the bow was damaged, Parashu Rama's arrow only flew as far as the southern tip of India.

Thousands of years later, Parashu Rama is still enthusiastically worshipped in South India. I have been told these days he lives quietly in a cave in Central India.

Sages Say

"A jack ass chases a she-ass no matter how many times she kicks it. Just so the ignorant man pursues worldly pleasure, no matter how much grief it causes him."

—Dattatreya in the *Tripura Rahasya* 2:84

Rama: Avatar Unaware

Could God ever forget he was God? Amazingly, according to many Hindus, he could!

Through intense spiritual practices the king Ravana won a boon from Shiva that no god or any other supernatural being could defeat him in battle. They say power corrupts, and with that kind of power Ravana went a little crazy and started terrorizing heaven and earth. Problem: Ravana was so formidable it never occurred to him to ask Shiva that a mere human not be able to kill him either.

Guidepost

Confused about the violence in Ayodhya? Sad to say the city where Rama was born is now a battleground between Hindus and Muslims. In the fifteenth century, a Mogul emperor horrified Hindus by building a mosque over the spot where Rama was born. In December 1992, militant Hindus destroyed the mosque. Today the matter rests with the Indian court system which is searching for a peaceful resolution to an issue almost every Indian—Hindu or Muslim—feels extremely passionate about.

So it was up to Vishnu to set matters right, but the only way through the loophole in Ravana's contract with Shiva was that Vishnu would have to renounce his divine identity and come to earth as a mortal man.

God and the Flying King

Vishnu was born as Rama in the city of Ayodhya where he set an example as the perfect son, perfect husband, and perfect king. All the while not realizing that he was God incarnate! And not realizing what he was getting into, Ravana kidnapped Rama's wife, Sita (who was the goddess Lakshmi incarnate, though she didn't realize it either), hoping to force her to marry him.

Rama came after Ravana and eventually destroyed both the demon king and his capital city. Ravana had a huge, highly trained army at his disposal as well as every technological advantage. He even had a flying machine called a vimana, the Vedic equivalent of a helicopter, with which he could drop in unexpectedly on his victims.

Rama had only a motley army of monkeys and bears (perhaps this was a colorful way of describing some simple tribal people of southern India), and bows and arrows. Yet his love for Sita was so strong he managed to defeat Ravana's vastly superior forces. The story is told in loving detail in the Hindu epic *Ramayana*.

Who's an Avatar?

Some avatars are "full" avatars, fully aware of their divine nature from birth. The late Anandamayi Ma, believed by many to have been an incarnation of the goddess Kali, reported that she was fully conscious from birth. She even described details from her earliest infancy that ordinarily a child couldn't possibly remember. She said she didn't experience the world piecemeal, but "all at once," without any limitations on her awareness. She proved again and again that she accurately knew exactly what was happening with devotees in other parts of India.

It's News to Me!

Did the ancients have airplanes? Or hot air balloons maybe? To this day, scholars speculate whether the vimana, which is mentioned often in early Hindu texts, was just science fiction, or whether early Indians actually had some kind of flying vehicle. No drawing of what a vimana might actually have looked like has survived.

Sages Say

"An Incarnation of the Godhead and, to a lesser degree, any theocentric saint, sage or prophet is a human being who knows Who he is and can therefore effectively remind other human beings of what they have allowed themselves to forget: namely, that if they choose to become what potentially they already are, they too can be eternally united with the Divine Ground."

—Aldous Huxley

Some incarnations, like Rama and Sita, may be "partial," where God and Goddess retain some of their divine powers but are not fully aware of their divinity. Others, like Parashu Rama, had forgotten their divine status completely and lost themselves in the world play until reawakened by an inspired guru.

Many Hindus sincerely believe their own guru is a special incarnation of one aspect or another of the divine. A guru may be an incarnation of divine wisdom or an embodiment of divine love. A number of truly remarkable modern women, like Anasuya Devi from Jillellamudi and Amritanandamayi Ma from Kerala, are felt by many Hindus to be actual incarnations of the Mother of the Universe.

An important point to remember here is that in a sense, *we're all avatars*. Each of us incarnates a portion of divine consciousness, though most of us (like Parashu Rama) have completely forgotten it. The fundamental distinction between a great avatar like Rama or Krishna and the rest of us is that we're "average" souls working our way *up* to divine status. The great avatars start from the top, working their way *down* to our level of consciousness.

Krishna: He's So Divine!

No Hindu contests Krishna's level of consciousness. He was a full avatar of Vishnu, completely conscious of his divinity from birth. Every day of his life was full of miracles. He embodied Godhood at its most loving, most wise, and most fun.

According to the Bible, King Herod heard of the birth of a future king and was paranoid enough to send out troops to kill newborn male infants. The circumstances around Krishna's birth were so similar that Christian theologians at first thought the Hindus had stolen parts of the story of Jesus' birth—till they discovered that Krishna's story was centuries older.

The Butter Thief

A sage had told the malicious king Kamsa that his nephew would kill him and take his throne. No problem: Kamsa simply had each of his sister's children killed the moment it was born. But sister Devaki and her husband Vasudeva managed to slip their eighth infant to safety. Little Krishna grew up in the village of Vrindavan, where he made a charming nuisance of himself. He was always finding ways to get his little fingers into his foster mother Yasoda's tasty fresh butter. Which is why to this day you'll hear Hindus, with tears of affection streaming from their eyes, call Krishna *damodara*, "the butter thief."

Kamsa's assassins were always lurking nearby but somehow the little toddler turned the tables on them all. Kamsa never did catch the boy destined to be his undoing.

The Dance of Love

The stories of Krishna's boyhood in Vrindavan are some of the most delightful—and most sensual—in Hindu spiritual lore. It's not surprising that Vrindavan is one of the most popular pilgrimage sites in India today! It was here Krishna grew up looking after the cattle. In Hindu art, he is often depicted as a loving tender of cows, much as Christians picture Jesus as the good shepherd.

Krishna was so devastatingly attractive that all the women of the village fell helplessly in love with him. Most of them were simple milkmaids (*gopis* in Sanskrit), who made their living selling fresh milk. At night, Krishna would wander out into the forest and play enchantingly on his flute. The gopis would slip out of their homes (sometimes out of their husbands' beds!) to rendezvous with their divine lover.

The *Rasa Lila* is Krishna's mystical dance, a bewitching scene depicted again and again in Hindu art. One night, to satisfy the desires of all the women in love with him, Krishna temporarily "cloned" himself into dozens of Krishnas. Then he danced through the night with every one of the gopis at the same time. Each of them innocently believed she alone enjoyed his love! This beautiful story makes the point that while members of different sects and religions believe God is theirs alone, in fact God dances with his lovers everywhere, in all times and all places.

King of Mathura

As a young man, Krishna left Vrindavan to fulfill his destiny in Mathura, where he overthrew the vicious king Kamsa. But back in his village, the gopis pined for him night and day, especially Radha, his favorite girlfriend. Krishna never returned to Vrindavan. But the gopis ached for him every moment of their lives, until they actually began to see him in everyone and everything around them. Merging in Krishna's true Self, the all-pervading consciousness of Vishnu, they each attained enlightenment. Many Hindus still cherish the memory of the gopis as the greatest devotees who ever lived.

New Word Alert!

Damodara means butter thief. It's an affectionate name for the mischievous child Krishna.

A **gopi** is a milkmaid. The gopis of Vrindavan have been immortalized as Krishna's most lovelorn devotees.

The **Rasa Lila** is the dance of love. Krishna danced all night with all the gopis of Vrindavan at once. Each believed Krishna was hers alone.

Sages Say

"Krishna, You shine among a thousand milkmaids like the Moon amid the stars. You fulfilled the pure desires of the holy women of Vrindavan. I want You too—please don't hold Yourself aloof!"

—Mira Bai

Krishna eventually became king of Mathura. As the *Mahabharata* relates, he would go on to help his friend Arjuna win the disastrous war against the Kauravas. The *Bhagavad Gita,* one of the wisest and most powerful scriptures in the world's spiritual literature, recounts Krishna's advice to Arjuna as Arjuna confronts the consequences of human evil and the inevitability of death.

Once, when hundreds of women from a nearby kingdom were carried off by a pillaging army, Krishna rushed to the rescue. After he'd saved them the women cried that their husbands and fathers wouldn't accept them back because they were "impure" now that they'd been raped. Krishna called for a priest and married them all on the spot. It's easy to see why Krishna is so popular with women devotees to this day!

Krishna may well be the single most beloved figure in the history of Hinduism. He's more loved than Vishnu himself even though he's supposed to be just one of Vishnu's ten major incarnations. The character of Krishna combines unsurpassed wisdom with masculine charm and heroic deeds. He towers over the centuries as a Divine Man for all time.

Quick Quiz

1. Vishnu stepped on Bali's head …

    a. Because Bali's skull was Vishnu's shoe size.

    b. By accident when the lights went out.

    c. To teach him humility.

2. Manu is famous for …

    a. Repopulating the Earth after the flood.

    b. Rajput miniature paintings.

    c. His fried fish recipe.

3. The most beloved figure in Hinduism is …

    a. Ravana, king of Lanka.

    b. Krishna, king of Mathura.

    c. Indira Gandhi, prime minister of India.

4. The boar avatar …

    a. Bore Mount Meru on his back.

    b. Lifted the earth's landmass with his tusks.

    c. Digs for truffles on Full Moon nights.

Answers: 1 (c). 2 (a). 3 (b). 4 (b).

Kalki: The Future Liberator

Vishnu's most dramatic incarnation is yet to come. At the end of the Kali Yuga, the cycle of darkness in which the world is presently languishing, Vishnu will incarnate in the form of Kalki the liberator. He will be a military commander who will "liberate" the world from evil and inaugurate a new cycle of truthfulness, justice, and universal goodness.

It is difficult to say where the legend of the Kalki avatar originated. It seems to be an extremely ancient myth, shared by the Persians, the Jews, the Christians, the Tibetans, and many Central Asians. Even the Native Americans had their version named Kukulkan!

The Least You Need to Know

➤ Avatars are incarnations of God and the Goddess.

➤ Vishnu incarnates to save the world at times of special stress.

➤ Vishnu saved Manu from a deluge that flooded the entire Earth.

➤ The heroes Parashu Rama, Rama of Ayodhya, and Krishna were avatars.

➤ Some of the greatest saints are considered divine incarnations.

➤ The Kalki avatar will restore righteousness at the end of this world cycle.

Chapter 15

The Main Denominations

In This Chapter

➤ Major Hindu sects

➤ Vishnu's devotees

➤ Shiva's nonconformists

➤ Goddess myth and gospel

➤ Hinduism and its discontents

There are so many thousands of Hindu sects that religious scholars despair of ever getting them all straight. Still, if you walk into a Hindu home, odds are high that the family members belong to one of three major groups:

➤ Vaishnavas: devotees of Vishnu

➤ Shaivites: devotees of Shiva

➤ Shaktas: devotees of Devi, the Goddess

Let's have a look at Hinduism's major denominations. Then we'll take a quick peak at some very important sects which broke from Hinduism to start their own religions.

Vaishnavas: "Hare Krishna!"

The Vaishnavas are the largest denomination in India and have numerous subsects. Devotion to Lord Vishnu and his avatars (especially Krishna and Rama) is their keynote. In addition to the Veda, they hold particularly sacred the *Bhagavad Gita,* the *Bhagavata Purana* (which contains many enchanting stories about Krishna), and various compendiums of religious lore, such as the *Vishnu Samhita*. There is also ecstatic devotional poetry, such as the erotically charged *Gita Govinda,* which compares a devotee's yearning for God with a young woman's intoxication with her lover.

A Personable God

Many Vaishnavas believe God has six special qualities: all knowledge, all power, supreme majesty, supreme strength, unlimited energy, and total self-sufficiency. So he's not just a transcendent undifferentiated mystical blur, but an actual divine person. Vaishnavas like to use one of the oldest Vedic names for God, *Purushottama,* which means "the ultimate person." Or, as the Hare Krishnas put it, "the Supreme Personality of Godhead."

For most Vaishnavas, the divine Self inside ourselves is the same as but not equal to Vishnu. Spiritual liberation means merging into God, but not in the same total sense that Shankaracharya taught. We merge in God without losing our individual nature, for we are meant to be his companions for all eternities. And even though we may enjoy his bliss when our awareness bathes in his, we do not share his infinite power. Only God can create a universe. We hang out in the worlds he places us in. We don't create new worlds ourselves.

Hanging Out with Vishnu

While Vaishnavism recognizes the importance of meditation practices, its emphasis lies primarily in religious devotion and morality. The word *bhava* is the key to understanding Vaishnava spirituality. It means emotion, or more specifically the overwhelming joy and love that arise from living life in active companionship with God.

While some Hindus focus on deep meditation and others on philosophical contemplation, Vaishnavas are often suspicious of too much head stuff. It's that

Guidepost

Shaven-headed young men in orange robes approach you at the airport chanting "Hare Krishna! Hare Hare!" *Who are these people?* The "Hare Krishnas" are devotees of the late Bhaktivedanta Prabhupada, who showed up penniless in the streets of New York back in the mid-1960s. This Vaishnava guru was already in his 70s when he began his hugely successful teaching mission to the West. He was following in the tradition of the fifteenth-century Bengali saint Chaitanya, who also liked to sing and dance in public streets.

juice in the heart called love that gives spiritual life its zip. Vaishnavas love to recount the story of Rama's passion for his wife, Sita, or to sit contemplating Krishna's beautiful features and amorous adventures. Deep feelings of religious ecstasy cleanse the mind and propel the heart toward living companionship with Vishnu here and after death.

For some Vaishnavas, God's wife is just as important and maybe even more important than he is. This is Lakshmi, who you've already met in Chapter 13, "Meet the Hindu Goddesses." Many Vaishnavas call her Sri (pronounced shree), which literally means "auspiciousness" or "all good things." She is the supremely compassionate one, the beloved World Mother who looks after us kids and guides us home to Dad.

Heaven Full of Saints

The spiritual sky of Vaishnava spirituality is alight with a brilliant array of stars: saints of the highest magnitude. Some of the most famous were the 12 *Alvars,* who lived in the eighth and ninth centuries C.E. in the south of India. Their hymns were saturated with love for the divine, bemoaning their separation from the Lord (usually in the form of Krishna) and celebrating those moments of merger when they experienced his living presence.

The Alvars had such an enormous impact on Hindu spirituality that across the subcontinent Hindu intellectuals were forced to rethink their philosophical systems to accommodate a personable God. They also had to work in the intense devotion that the Alvars showed can transport a soul to highest states of mystical ecstasy.

Closer to our own time the Bauls of Bengal frankly call themselves "madmen for God." Many are minstrels who travel through the countryside singing and dancing. If you hear a Baul even once, you'll never forget the experience. They sing with such passion you half expect their hearts to split open!

New Word Alert!

Purushottama means "the Supreme Person"—God or specifically Vishnu.

Bhava is intense religious emotion or spiritual ecstasy.

Alvar means "one who dives deep" and refers to the 12 great South Indian Vaishnava saints of the eighth and ninth centuries.

Merging in the Temples, Singing in the Streets

Names of certain Vaishnava saints will come up not infrequently in your conversations with orthodox Hindu families. Here is a primer listing a few of the most loved saints from the last 1,500 years or so (the dates given here are historians' approximations):

➤ Antal (725–755). One of the most famous of the Alvars, she so adamantly insisted she would have no husband but God himself that her family actually took her to the Vishnu temple at Srirangam for the marriage ceremony! It's said that there she physically merged into the image in the temple, her love for him was so intense.

➤ Jnanadeva (1275–1296). The child author of the *Jnaneshvari,* which is a commentary on the *Bhagavad Gita* and perhaps the greatest spiritual classic of Maharashtra. At the age of 21, Jnanadeva had himself entombed alive so that he could close out his life focused exclusively on attaining union with Krishna.

➤ Mira Bai (1498–1546). A Rajput princess whose ecstatic songs to Krishna are still sung throughout India. She caused a stir of divine fervor everywhere she traveled singing of her love. At her death, she merged into a statue of Krishna at Dvaraka.

➤ Chaitanya (1486–1533). Regarded by many Hindus as the incarnation of both Krishna and his lover Radha, Chaitanya made his way through much of India chanting Krishna's name and dancing in the streets. And triggering a massive social movement of religious devotion!

Sages Say

"O Lord of all living creatures! Your behavior is so audacious! But who can match Your courage? You remain in bliss even as the stars tumble from heaven and the entire universe disintegrates. Even the sages are stricken with terror as the world systems are destroyed. Yet—all alone—You laugh with delight!"

—*Shivananda Lahari* 34

➤ Tulsi Das (1532–1623). A homeless child taken in by the guru Ramananda, he grew up to compose some of the most loved poems in Hindu spiritual literature. His retelling of the story of Rama and Sita, called the *Rama Charita Manasa,* actually replaced the original *Ramayana* in popularity among Hindus.

➤ Tukaram (1600–1650). A destitute farmer who became one of Hinduism's most inspired poets. Though physically assaulted by a jealous detractor (who poured boiling water over him!), he forgave the man and later healed him of an incurable illness.

➤ Anandamayi Ma (1896–1982). A saint so amazing other saints came to prostrate before her. Illumined from birth, she lived in God consciousness, traveling around India wherever God directed her. From an inner space of luminous clarity, she shared her experience of the unity of all things.

Anandamayi Ma, one of the most extraordinary Vaishnava saints of the twentieth century.

Shaivites: "Om Namah Shivaya!"

You can identify the Shaivites by the three lines of ash running horizontally across their foreheads. Or by the lingam (a small conical stone) many of them wear around their necks. While the Vaishnava holy men usually have shaved heads, the Shaivites have a full head of hair, sometimes matted and wrapped around their skulls like a turban.

Even if you've never met a Hindu in your life, you still may have heard friends of yours come home from their yoga classes repeating the most sacred Shaivite mantra, "Om namah Shivaya." It means "With loving reverence, I bow to the Supreme Consciousness." In this tradition, the Supreme Being is called Lord Shiva.

Pashupati: Lord of Beasts

Of the major subsects of Shaiva Hindus, the Pashupatis are the most notorious. *Pashupati* means "lord of domesticated animals." Most people, these Shaivites say, are like cows with rings through their noses. They're led here and there by social conventions and by their own hopes and fears. The Pashupati practitioners break with social norms and often behave in the most outrageous and upsetting ways—on purpose. They're trying to set their inner world upside down so that they can shake themselves loose from past mental conditioning and begin to move through the world with true freedom.

There are five stages of practice according to this tradition. First is the conventional spiritual aspirant, who meditates and tries to do good. If these aspirants progress, they'll reach the second stage of genuine sainthood. They follow rigorous moral standards and are exemplars of compassion, wisdom, and selfless service. By Pashupati standards, the average saint we recognize in the West is at the second of five levels of spiritual attainment.

Guidepost

Some crazy people are, well, crazy. Others may actually be enlightened! In India great saints sometimes act crazy to get supplicants—people who show up demanding miracles and favors—to leave them alone.

The problem with being a Stage 2 saint is that you attract needy souls who waste your time with their constant demands and sycophants who inflate your ego with their constant praise. So at the third stage, practitioners are advised to act outrageously, leaping around and shouting as if they're crazy. They make sexual advances on anyone and everyone and break their promises. The crowds of devotees and well wishers who surrounded them in the past now quickly vanish, and the yogi is free to move on to higher practices.

In the fourth stage the aspirants are more "there" than "here." Though still inhabiting a physical body, their awareness is centered in the world within. To normal people, they may seem distracted or even catatonic. Stage 5 is the level of real mastery, where the adept remains centered in the highest consciousness but now acts in the material world for the benefit of all beings, helping to free others from their "nose rings."

Vira Shaivism: Path of Heroes

The Vira Shaivites also behave horribly by conservative Hindu standards. One of their greatest saints, a twelfth-century brahmin from Karnataka named Basava, was one of the great religious reformers in Hindu history. He led the Vira Shaivites in rejecting caste distinctions (a major no-no in Hinduism), honoring women as full equals of men and respecting all forms of honest labor including the lowest and dirtiest.

Vira means hero. A Vira Shaivite is as dauntless and alert in his or her spiritual life as a soldier in the thick of battle.

Vira Shaivites wear a linga, the symbol of Shiva, on their bodies. They consider it his living presence. By keeping it close, they make their bodies Shiva's living temple. A second form of linga exists in the heart. When the kundalini rises from the bottom of the spine illuminating the energy of the heart center, this linga is directly experienced. The third linga is in the brain. When the kundalini activates the center at the top of the head, union with Shiva is experienced. You merge into the linga of pure consciousness.

Vira Shaivites compare the *jiva,* the individual soul, and Shiva, the cosmic being, to a river and the ocean. There is definitely a difference between the two, as anyone can see. But at the time of enlightenment, the soul merges into Shiva like the river pouring into the sea. At that point, it becomes impossible to distinguish between the two.

New Word Alert!

Pashupati is "lord of bound animals"—Shiva.

The **jiva** is the individual, reincarnating soul.

Vira means hero. It's related to the English word virile.

Shaiva Siddhanta: Loving Shiva

Shaiva Siddhanta also shows more flexibility in matters of caste, gender, and ethics than the generally more socially conservative Vaishnavas. It is the most commonly practiced form of Shaivism in South India today. Devotees of this tradition value the *Tiru Murai* even more than the Veda. This exquisite collection of Tamil hymns to Lord Shiva was compiled by Nambiyandar Nambi in the eleventh century.

Shaiva Siddhanta is famous for its 63 Nayanars, Tamil poet saints who lived between 700 and 1000 C.E. Their poetry extols Shiva's extraordinary grace and compassion. Until their arrival on the scene, both Buddhism and Jainism had made substantial inroads in South India. The Nayanars won back the hearts of the people and reestablished Lord Shiva as South India's premier god. Let me introduce you to a few of these exceptional saints:

➤ Appar (600–681) converted from Jainism to Shaivism. The local Jain king had him thrown into a vat of poison, tried drowning him, and drove an elephant to attack him. But by remembering the holy mantra "Namah Shivaya," Appar survived every assault. The king was so impressed he converted to Shaivism himself.

➤ Sambandhar (644–660) was known for the miracles he accomplished in Shiva's name. It was said he was so adept he could raise the dead even after they were cremated! Like Appar, he taught that ultimately Vishnu and Shiva are the same Divine Being.

➤ Sundar (716–735) went blind as a young man. He complained angrily to Shiva who, after all, according to myth, had three good eyes! Shiva restored his eyesight. In fact, Shiva loved the boy saint so much he is said to have shared his wife, Parvati, with him!

201

Kashmir Shaivism: The Naked Lady

Kashmir Shaivism is the best known form of Shaivism in the West today. It was popularized here by Swami Muktananda and his successor Gurumayi Chidvilasananda in the second half of the twentieth century. It emphasizes that we're already enlightened. We just need to remember that.

Pratyabhijna means recognizing one's true identity and is the key to the Kashmiri system. At the center of our being lies undying divine awareness. When we clear the impurities out of our minds and stop being distracted by our desires, the light of pure awareness shines through. Then we experience our real nature as Shiva.

Lalleshvari (fourteenth century) is one of the best-known saints of this tradition. She walked out of an abusive marriage and spent the rest of her life wandering naked through the countryside, absorbed in love for Shiva and performing advanced yogic practices.

New Word Alert!

Pratyabhijna means Self-recognition, recollecting the divine consciousness in oneself.

A **Nayanar** is one of the 63 great Tamil poet saints of the Shaivite tradition.

Sages Say

"Meditate on the divinity within yourself. Drink the nectar of love that pours continually from Shiva's heart."

—Lalleshvari

Shaktas: *"Jai Ma!"*

There's a famous saying in India. "When you're in public, be a Vaishnava. When you're in private, be a Shaivite. But in your heart, always be a Shakta." The advice is to behave like a conventional religious person with the masses. With a circle of friends you may explore your more radical spiritual insights. But when all is said and done, there ain't no lap more comfortable than Mom's!

Shaktas worship the Mother of the Universe as both the Supreme Consciousness itself and its power. Its power is the will and energy that creates, nurtures, and finally dissolves away the worlds. Some Shaktas, called Kaulas, engage primarily in ritual practice. Others, in the meditatively oriented Samaya tradition, focus exclusively on inner work. The Mishras do some of both: ritual to channel one's physical energy and focus the mind, and meditation to plunge into the inner depths where Devi, the "radiant goddess," resides.

In heavily Shakta parts of India, like Bengal or Assam, you'll hear Hindus shout *"Jai Ma!"* It literally means "Hurray for Mom!" and has an energy something like "Hallelujah!" Worship of the Divine Mother permeates every aspect of Hindu spirituality. Even Vaishnavas and Shaivites don't worship a male God exclusively like Christians and Muslims do. The feminine divine is always also honored even when the male aspect of the Supreme Being is emphasized.

Debunking Indiana Jones

Unfortunately, the little most Westerners know about the Hindu Goddess tradition is what they learn from fiction like *Indiana Jones and the Temple of Doom*. Harrison Ford is called upon to rescue struggling victims about to be sacrificed to a horrible, multi-armed female deity. There is no way to sufficiently express how offensive this depiction of Goddess spirituality is to Hindus!

Europeans of the Victorian era also mistakenly believed that Shaktas engage in drunken sex orgies. No such luck! These myths got started from rumors based on real tantric practices, though. A Shakta would purify himself or herself for weeks, fasting and chanting a Goddess mantra millions of times. Then under the close supervision of a Shakta master, the aspirant would drink high-proof liquor, strong enough to knock the socks off even the sturdiest drinker, much less a teetotaler like most Hindus.

The point of the practice was to learn to face death consciously. Most people die in a state of unconsciousness, which is bad news from a Hindu point of view because you want to be alert so that you can direct the stages of the after-death process. By learning to maintain awareness despite the stupefying effects of strong liquor, the Shakta is training to remain conscious during the process of death itself.

Guidepost

Ladies, if you're concerned about being carried off screaming to be offered to a bloodthirsty Hindu goddess, relax! Only males are offered to the goddess. And it's usually male goats at that. At almost all Goddess temples these days, however, flowers and fruit are the offerings of the day.

God or Goddess?

Philosophically Shaktism is very close to Shaivism. In fact the two are often considered brother-sister traditions. Their doctrines are essentially identical. However Shaivism emphasizes the consciousness or Shiva aspect a little more. Shaktism emphasizes the energy or active facet of the divine slightly more.

In the end, Shaivites admit Para Shiva, the highest form of Shiva, contains both Shiva and Shakti. Shaktas say Sadakhya, the highest form of the Goddess, contains both Shiva and Shakti, consciousness and energy. Same difference. Consciousness *is* energy—living self-awareness.

The Lousy Accountant

One of the most famous Shakta saints of recent centuries was Ramprasad Sen, who lived in Bengal in the eighteenth century. He was on fire with passion for the goddess Kali and neglected his work as an accountant so badly his boss fired him! But when

203

his boss read the beautiful lines of poetry Ramprasad had scribbled in the account books, the businessman was astute enough to realize his clerk was a burgeoning saint. He encouraged Ramprasad to give up accounting and devote his life to spiritual practice. And he sent a generous stipend home to Ramprasad every month so that his ex-employee could actually afford to do so!

Ramprasad is famous for poems in which he approaches the Mother of the Universe like an innocent child. Or like a petulant child at times! Speaking of his meditation practice he writes:

> Mother Kali, You dwell in cremation grounds
> so I've made my heart a burning pit
> where You can dance.
> One desire burns in the conflagration of my life:
> To watch Your blazing dance!
> I sit here still as death in my funeral pyre,
> looking for You with eyes closed.

Quick Quiz

1. The three main sects of Hinduism are …
   - **a.** Buddhism, Sikhism, and Jainism.
   - **b.** Shaktism, Shaivism, and Vaishnavism.
   - **c.** Tantra, yantra, and mantra.

2. Followers of Vaishnavism approach God with …
   - **a.** Fear and trepidation.
   - **b.** Love and joy.
   - **c.** Long lists of complaints.

3. The Shaiva Siddhanta saints taught that Vishnu and Shiva …
   - **a.** Are bitter enemies.
   - **b.** Are ultimately identical.
   - **c.** Are related on their mothers' side.

4. *Indiana Jones and the Temple of Doom* …
   - **a.** Portrays a startlingly accurate vision of Goddess worship.
   - **b.** Grossly distorts Hindu Goddess spirituality.
   - **c.** Was #1 at the box office in Bombay cinema for nearly a year.

Answers: 1 (b). 2 (b). 3 (b). 4 (b).

Hindu Spin-Offs

From time to time, great spiritual masters left the Hindu fold to start their own traditions. Hindu policy is so liberal, Hindus are allowed to believe just about anything, so what do you have to do to be excluded from Hinduism? Refusing to accept the Veda as divinely inspired and breaking with the caste tradition entirely will do the trick.

A number of important Hindu sects splintered from the Vedic fold to form their own faiths. Hinduism has no less than four world-famous stepchildren.

Breaking with Tradition

Buddha was disgusted by the Hindu priestly caste, in whose rituals he had little faith. He rejected the authority of the Veda, the value of worshipping deities, and the concept of an immortal soul. Most of Buddha's teachings and practices, however, retain a strong Hindu flavor.

Mahavir, who lived around the same time as the Buddha and whose life paralleled Buddha's in a number of surprising ways, also rejected the Veda. His spiritual tradition, which strongly emphasizes nonviolence, is called Jainism.

The Sikh tradition started in the Punjab in the twelfth century C.E. It emphasized devotion to God and guru, and later to the *Adi Granth*, the collection of beautiful hymns that eventually took the place of a human guru. Combining Hindu and Muslim ideals, the Sikhs became known for their military valor.

It's News to Me!

From the third century C.E. up till just a few centuries ago, Manichaeism was one of the great world religions, practiced from Europe to China. It taught that we are beings of light who must purge ourselves of association with matter in order to merge back into the divine light. (Both Christian and Muslim authorities made the extermination of Manichaeism a top priority, which is why you don't see Manichaeans hanging around anymore.) It's startling to find Manichaean literature filled with Sanskrit terminology. This is because Mani, the founder of that religion, traveled to India to study with Buddhist and Hindu masters. Mani, who was born in Babylon in 216 C.E., helped introduce many Eastern ideas into Europe, where they still echo in Europe's Gnostic underground.

The Zoroastrian Connection

Zoroastrianism is immensely ancient. According to the Hindu tradition, Zoroaster would have lived long before 4000 B.C.E. (He is mentioned as an ancient renegade teacher several times in the *Rig Veda,* which was composed somewhere around 4000 B.C.E.) Aristotle, the ancient Greek philosopher, confirms that the Persians of his time dated Zoroaster to around 6000 B.C.E. (Western scholars have been extremely reluctant to accept such ancient dates for Zoroaster.)

Zoroaster is one of the most important figures in religious history. When he broke with Hinduism, he established a new set of beliefs which much later would work their way into Judaism and from there reincarnate in Christianity and Islam. These ideas include the linear nature of time with history ending on Judgment Day, the resurrection of the physical body, and the promised return of a savior to inaugurate a millennial period of peace on earth. He also taught the existence of the Devil, a malevolent being nearly as powerful as God.

Hindus accept a modified version of the story of the returning savior. None of Zoroaster's other ideas is accepted in Hinduism.

The Least You Need to Know

➤ The three major sects of modern Hinduism are Vaishnavism, Shaivism, and Shaktism.

➤ Vaishnavas believe in the loving personal God Vishnu.

➤ Some Shaivites are radical in their approach to enlightenment.

➤ Shaktas worship the Goddess as the active, creative power of Divine Reality.

➤ Four great religions splintered off from Hinduism: Buddhism, Jainism, Sikhism, and Zoroastrianism.

Part 4
How Hindus Live

Hindus live in a tightly ordered, hierarchical world with clear moral values. Although India is technically a secular state, for practicing Hindus there is no such thing as a secular life. Everything occurs within the context of religion. Sacraments for every Hindu begin before birth and continue after death. Holy days are frequent. Activities are oriented, directly or indirectly, toward the ultimate goal of Hindu spirituality: liberation of the soul from the bondage of karma and rebirth.

Mother India herself is sacred. You can't travel far without reaching one pilgrimage center or another. Temples appear everywhere, though the most familiar one is right in each Hindu's own home.

Here is how the saints and sages of the Eternal Religion counseled Hindu men and women to structure their society—and how to live with each other and find peace with themselves.

Chapter 16

A Classy Religion

In This Chapter

➤ The structure of Hindu society

➤ Why we're here

➤ Phases of life

➤ Women's experience

Hindu culture is tightly structured. Everyone knows where they belong—and where they don't. If you're a Hindu, many of life's choices are made for you. What your job will be. Who you'll marry. The class of people you'll hang out with.

For those of us who've grown up in the individualistic West, where our right to self-determination is a paramount value, the hierarchical societies of the East may seem stifling, even inhumane. Yet many Hindus would not trade their way of life for ours. Hindus who move to the West often complain that compared to home, Western culture seems cold and selfish.

Let's look at the way Hindu society organizes itself, and the religious purpose for this way of life.

What Turns You On?

What turns people on? The Hindu sages noted that there are basically four distinct personality types.

The first type is people whose primary passion in life is power. They feel most alive when they're controlling others. They would be miserable if they couldn't express their need to be in charge.

Guidepost

Ever feel like an outcast? Sad to say, the outcastes of India probably feel even worse. Mahatma Gandhi renamed this group of people Harijans, "the children of God." Outcaste status was outlawed in 1950. Today all Hindus are equal before the law.

Another personality type is mostly motivated by material things. These folks want to be wealthy. Their satisfaction comes from producing or owning things. Their worst fear is poverty. Or sometimes simply having less than other people do.

The third kind of person is oriented more toward the inner world. It's ideas that turn them on, and internal experiences like spiritual visions. Give them a book, have them teach a class, or let them sit quietly thinking or meditating, and they're happy as ducks in a pond.

Then there are your burger flippers. These are the people who don't particularly want to rule the world. And they aren't money hungry enough to work their way up to a top-paying job. They don't necessarily long to be the world's leading philosophers either. They're content to wash dishes and sweep the floor, then go home and relax with friends and family.

Four Classes of Hindu Society

The sages gave each of these types a name.

➤ *Kshatriyas:* motivated by power
➤ *Vaishyas:* motivated by material objects
➤ *Brahmins:* motivated by knowledge
➤ *Shudras:* unmotivated people

The kshatriyas are your kings and queens. They're your top-level executives and administrators. They're also your military and police personnel, the ones who use force to keep order. For most of its history, India was a patchwork of numberless little kingdoms. So the kshatriyas were primarily your maharajahs and maharanis, your princesses and dukes and their families, and the warriors they retained to help protect those they ruled and conquer those they didn't.

Vaishyas are your business people, trades people, artisans, farmers. Your skilled labor. Brahmins are priests, counselors, educators, philosophers. In India until fairly recently, brahmins were primarily responsible for preserving the Veda and were valued as ritual specialists. Today more brahmins are moving into other fields, such as politics, administration, and medicine. Shudras are your unskilled laborers.

Originally the *varnas,* or four castes as these groups are called, were somewhat fast and loose designations. But in India as in much of the rest of the world, children learned their trade from their parents. So over the course of time your caste status became something you inherited from your parents rather than an innate inclination you brought with you from your past lives.

The Hierarchy of Being

The three upper castes (all except the shudras) are called twice born in Hinduism. The first birth occurs when the infant burst hollering from its mother's womb. The second birth occurs at initiation, the Hindu version of the Christian rite of confirmation. At this time, the child is inducted into formal spiritual practice. Shudras do not receive this initiation probably because originally they were not considered focused and serious enough to stick with a spiritual discipline. In real life, of course, many shudras are highly spiritual. Many great saints have come from the shudra caste.

The four castes are very broad groupings. Most Hindus actually think of themselves in terms of their subcaste and clan. There are over 3,000 human subcastes in Hinduism. This system represents the hierarchical nature of souls in the universe, so there are nonhuman subcastes, too. Animals, plants, even insects have their subcastes. So do gods and demons!

It's News to Me!

There are four basic castes or classes, called **varnas,** in Hindu society: priests, administrators, skilled labor, and unskilled labor. They're broken down into **jatis** or subcastes, a Hindu's specific social group, which comes with a preassigned level of social status and religious purity. In theory all souls are created equal. In material manifestation, though, souls have vastly different experiences based on their karma and how long they've been incarnating on a particular planet.

Outsiders

Not everyone in the world fits into the four-caste system. There were people who left the system voluntarily. And there were people who left involuntarily. Finally, there were people who were never in the system to begin with.

The *panchamas* are the famous outcastes of India. These are people, or descendants of people, who committed some serious infringement of caste regulations that led to their being ostracized from orthodox Hindu society. A person could become a pariah, for example, by marrying outside their social group. (Remember that until about the twentieth century, this kind of thing wasn't so unusual in Western countries either.) Hindus who adopted a new religion, like Buddhism or Jainism, met with disapproval, too.

People who performed unsanitary types of jobs were also considered "untouchable." These were people who cleaned dirty areas like lavatories or who handled dead animals or dead people. Perhaps the ancients noticed that these people were a source of contagion (of viruses and bacteria we'd say today) and started keeping a distance from them.

New Word Alert!

The **panchamas** are the out-castes, excommunicated from orthodox society.

Mlecchas are foreigners.

Guidepost

Is that Hindu holy man you just met in the road an enlightened master? Unfortunately, some of the sannyasins you see are not real spiritual aspirants but people who don't want to work. They know that posing as a holy man can be a ticket to a free meal. Some just spend the day smoking hashish and soaking up the Sun.

Mlecchas are foreigners, people who never were Hindus to begin with. Generally Hindus have tended to be somewhat suspicious of foreigners. Until only recently, many Hindus considered it a calamity to have to leave India and live with mlecchas. This makes sense because for most of their history Indians enjoyed a high standard of living compared to many other cultures.

Renouncers

Some people step outside the caste system on purpose. These are the *sannyasins,* the wandering holy men and women of Hinduism. Caste law applies only to Hindus of this world. Sannyasins have given up the comforts and luxuries of home and family to wander freely without any possessions or worldly responsibilities. They are focused only on Self-realization and are considered "in this world but not of it." Caste regulations don't apply to them, yet they are among the most highly respected members of Hindu culture.

Some sannyasins are swamis, who have formally taken vows in one of the renunciate orders. Don't expect to go to their headquarters and get a list of all the swamis, though. Things are not done in an organized way in India. They're done in an *organic* way. Someone who's a swami initiates you in his or her order without necessarily registering your name anywhere. You put on the orange robe of a swami, and you're in business. Recently there was an attempt to begin keeping order in the orders, but the resistance was so fierce the effort collapsed. How can you expect someone who's renounced the world to worry about whether their name is listed in the ledger in some administrative building?

Quite a few of the sannyasins wandering India are not swamis but have simply renounced worldly life with the blessing of their guru or even on their own. They beg for food once a day or get a free meal at the local temple. Typically they move along from one pilgrimage spot to the next since staying in any one place for longer than a few days (except during the monsoon season when travel is impractical) is seen as a potential source of attachment. They do their daily ritual practice, chant, meditate, and sometimes teach or hang out with fellow renunciates.

What's Life For?

According to Hinduism, there are four main goals in human life.

➤ *Dharma:* Fulfilling your purpose

➤ *Artha:* Prospering

➤ *Kama:* Having fun

➤ *Moksha:* Getting to know God

Let's take a brief look at each.

Doing Your Dharma

In this context, dharma means doing that which you were meant to do, doing it ethically, and doing it to the best of your capacity. Generally it refers to one's career. One person's dharma may be to manufacture tires. Another person's dharma could be to sing professionally, or lay foundations, or practice medicine.

In Hindu culture, often your dharma was determined by the family and clan you were born into. If you were born in a family of stone masons, your fulfillment in life would come from working with stone. If your mother was a washerwoman, you would probably be a washerwoman, too. Though for most women, the primary dharma was being a housewife and mother.

Arjuna's Dharma

In the *Bhagavad Gita,* Lord Krishna urges Arjuna to pick up his bow and go to war. This was because Arjuna had been born into a kshatriya family of kings and warriors. His brother's kingdom had been illegally taken over by a tyrant. It was not the dharma of the priest or the stone mason to stop

Sages Say

"Respect your mother as if she were a goddess. Respect your father as if he were a god. Respect your guest like a deity. Any work you do, do it perfectly. Whatever you do, do only good."

—*Taittiriya Upanishad* 1:11.1–2

the evil tyrant. As a defender of justice, it was Arjuna's job to ensure that the king-dom was returned to its rightful ruler.

Even though Arjuna didn't want to fight, Krishna insisted he must fulfill his dharma. The Hindu view is that even if the stone worker would rather be a World Federation wrestler, he should stick with the professional responsibility he was born into. This attitude is incomprehensible to many Westerners. But in India (as in many Asian cultures), the welfare of society as a whole outweighs the individual's own preferences. Traditional Hindus believe that it is by fulfilling their duty, not by fulfilling their fantasies, that people hold their society together.

Paying Your Debts

There is also a general dharma incumbent on all human beings. Each of us has five duties or debts we need to repay:

1. We must fulfill our obligations to the gods for their many blessings by honoring them with the appropriate rituals.

2. The tremendous debt we owe to our parents and teachers must be repaid by supporting them and by having children and passing on our knowledge in turn.

3. We fulfill our duty to our guests by treating them as if they were deities visiting our home.

4. We have a debt to all other human beings as well. This can be repaid by treating each with the respect he or she is due.

5. Also, we have an obligation to all other living beings. We must offer them our good will and food or other types of help when appropriate.

There are two central preoccupations in Hinduism: freedom and responsibility. While tantrics, ascetics, and renunciates launch into the freedom of spirit, Hindus who choose to remain in the workaday world are very conscious of their karmic debts and the profound interconnection and interdependence of the living beings in the many different planes of reality. Dharma defines their place in the world order and shows them how to live together in mutual respect and support.

Making Money

In the Hindu religion, getting rich is considered an entirely appropriate human be-havior. In fact, some holy texts advise us to make as much money as we can with our two hands. And then to give it away with *ten* hands to those in need!

There's an important caveat here. Remember how in the list of goals of human life, dharma came first? This means that while we are free, and even encouraged, to make money, it must be done within the context of dharma. Our way of making a living must be ethical. Dharma not only means our duty in life, it also means righteousness. Morality is the basic underpinning of society.

Making Love

Hindus' attitude toward sex is perplexing to many outsiders. No one can fail to notice the expansive variety of sexual postures assumed by half-naked statues that decorate the outside of many Indian temples! Yet to outward appearances, many if not most Hindus are quite sexually conservative. Not only women, but men are often still sexually inexperienced on their wedding night. And it seems overly prudish to Westerners that many Hindu women remain dressed even while bathing! (This was also the practice in much of Europe till fairly recently.)

Sexuality is celebrated in Hinduism, but generally within the context of marriage. By confining one's amorous adventures to a spouse, the sexual drive is expressed in a healthy manner and yet also disciplined. There have, of course, always been otherwise outstanding Hindus who did not live by these norms. A few parts of India have been known for their more relaxed attitudes toward sexuality. Today as Western influence becomes more pervasive, sexual experimentation is increasing among Hindus generally.

Moksha: The Ultimate Goal

The basic goal of life on which the others are founded is dharma: morality especially as it expresses itself in the fulfillment of one's duties. But the ultimate goal of life is moksha, enlightenment. The previous three aims are understood with this very much in mind.

It's News to Me!

The *Kama Sutra*, a manual on aesthetics, etiquette, and sex, is considered a sacred text, not pornography, in Hinduism. It was written by a monk! Kama, incidentally, refers to many forms of sensual pleasure (including, for example, flower arranging), not just sexuality.

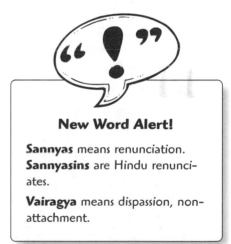

New Word Alert!

Sannyas means renunciation. **Sannyasins** are Hindu renunciates.

Vairagya means dispassion, nonattachment.

Prosperity and pleasure are great. Just about everybody wants them. But they don't last forever. After eight or nine decades at the most, the soul loses both as its physical body crumbles away. If your pursuit of the good things in life hasn't been from the perspective of the supreme good, then death can be a horrendous experience. Being cut off from the people and things we're attached to is wrenching.

Death is less of a trauma if during our lives we've been practicing the premier Hindu spiritual discipline of *vairagya*, dispassion. Western students sometimes think vairagya or nonattachment means stifling our emotional nature and cutting ourselves off from relationships. In fact it means expanding them.

Truly dispassionate people are the most loving folks you'll ever meet. They don't just love their family members and friends. They love everyone and everything. The divine inner nature, which is love itself, is allowed to shine in all directions, embracing everyone without particular attachment to one individual or another.

Sages Say

"Your skin wrinkles and your hair turns grey. Your teeth fall out and your hands shake. Still you are tortured by desire. Your children bring you grief. You find no comfort in wealth. Everything is passing away. Give up clinging to things that disappear. Free yourself to enter the peace and joy within yourself."

—Shankaracharya

As human beings we naturally love our children, our family and friends. Hinduism suggests though that we not get overly attached to our attachments. At some point, we will have to let every one of them go. If we bear this in mind through life, death becomes an expansive experience, not a fearful ending. We look forward to—and work toward—an illumined state of consciousness that enfolds all our fellow beings in a state beyond time.

Metamorphoses

The Hindu life course is specifically structured so that each individual has an opportunity to go for the gold, to reach for spiritual liberation before death. If all goes according to plan, life metamorphoses through four stages:

1. *Brahmacharya:* Student life
2. *Grihastya:* Married life
3. *Vanaprastha:* Intensive spiritual practice
4. *Sannyasa:* Letting go

Brahmacharya literally means "walking with God." During these years, the student receives cultural, vocational and religious training. You'll also hear the term brahmacharya used to mean celibacy since Hindus weren't supposed to have sex before marriage.

Marriage is a Very Big Deal in Hindu culture. A small number of individuals renounce the householder life and go directly from brahmacharya to sannyasa, devoting their entire lives to the spiritual quest alone. But the vast majority of people are expected to practice spirituality within the context of raising a family. Remember that having children was one of the five sacred duties required of Hindus. Even parents of some of the greatest saints India has ever known, like Shankaracharya and Ramana Maharshi, tried to pressure them into married life to meet the social norm—and so that they'd support them in their old age.

When a couple got on in years, they'd retire as we do in the West. But rather than moving to Florida and fishing all day, they'd go live in a hut in the forest to pursue intensive spiritual practices. Vanaprastha literally means "living in the woods."

As death approached, Hindus (especially males) would renounce even the little hut and go wandering on pilgrimages, living on whatever handfuls of food strangers would offer. This was the act of letting go preparatory to final release when the body itself dropped away.

In Western culture, people are very rarely prepared for death. Hindus spend the last years of their life specifically preparing for this transition. Though these customs are gradually losing their hold on the culture, you will still find temples where the aged have gone to spend the last months of their lives chanting God's name and praying. Many temples specifically accommodate these retirees with a minimum of food and shelter so that they can close out their lives with God.

Quick Quiz

1. The four castes are …

    a. Earth, water, fire, and air zodiac signs.

    b. Priests, leaders, business people, and unskilled laborers.

    c. Tinkers, tailors, soldiers, sailors.

2. The Hindu goals of life include …

    a. Mastering a musical instrument.

    b. Moving to Silicon Valley and opening a software firm.

    c. Enlightenment.

3. As orthodox Hindus get older they …

    a. Devote themselves full time to spiritual practice.

    b. Start taking supplements and working out more.

    c. Move to Florida to go boating and fishing.

4. Sannyasins are …

    a. Hindu hippies.

    b. Wandering holy men.

    c. Ottoman Turks who terrorized the Crusaders.

Answers: 1 (b). 2 (c). 3 (a). 4 (b).

Women First

In Hindu India, the role of women is perceived very differently than in North America. Take the first 50 years of India's existence as an independent nation following its emancipation from Britain. For one third of that time, India had a woman prime minister. In the United States, at least up till the moment I'm writing, if Americans so much as had a strong first lady, half the country would become apoplectic!

Perhaps the reason Hindus seem to feel more comfortable with a female commander-in-chief than North Americans is because they're constantly exposed to images of powerful goddesses. And the Hindu national epics are full of accounts of intelligent, politically influential women. Or maybe it's because the archetypal role for a woman in India is mother rather than sex object as in the West. You might trust your mother to run the country, but you'd probably hesitate to have a sex kitten do so!

If you cross the border from Hindu India into Muslim Pakistan, you'll instantly feel the different cultural climate. In most of India, women can travel comparatively free from fear. In Pakistan, a woman needs to be covered from head to toe in a heavy robe or accompanied by a male guardian. Otherwise she may find herself in serious trouble.

Declining Status

Nevertheless, there's no question women have lower status than men in Hinduism. The difference in status was almost certainly not so dramatic in the distant past.

Hindu scriptures written centuries ago describe women teachers and philosophers and show women receiving initiations they are denied today. The Veda itself includes women among its highest seers.

Some of the unfortunate problems women experience in Hindu culture today may be due to 1,500 years of nearly continual invasions from the north, beginning around 500 B.C.E. To protect mothers, wives, and daughters, women were increasingly confined inside the house, cutting back their wider social roles.

But the worst problems Hindu women experience are due to the horrible practice of selling sons. Though outlawed in modern India, sadly this custom is still widely practiced.

Selling Sons

The dowry system probably did not start out as a bad thing. On the contrary, its original purpose was not to demean women but to support them. In Hindu culture, most women leave the birth home when they marry and become part of their husband's family. The dowry ensured that they brought their own financial

It's News to Me!

When Hindus list men and women's names, out of respect for the female gender, they usually list the woman's name first. That's why when Hindus refer to the avatar Rama and his wife, Sita, they'll say "Sita-Ram." Or when they talk about Krishna and his lover Radha they'll say "Radha-Krishna." Rama himself (Ram in Hindi) is sometimes actually called Sita-Ram, signifying that he's the man privileged to have Sita for a wife.

resources with them—money they could use to support themselves and their families if their husband died or abandoned them.

Hindu males, however, stay with the birth family. The eldest son is particularly important since he's responsible for looking after the welfare of his younger siblings, for supporting his parents when they retire, and for conducting the parents' funeral rites.

While men receive their inheritance when their parents die, women receive theirs when they marry. This means that each time a daughter marries, her family sustains a substantial loss of income. There's financial loss in both cases, but families only feel it when the girl marries because the son keeps his money within the family.

This system has become grotesquely distorted. It has evolved from sending a daughter away with some worldly goods, to would-be in-laws demanding huge sums of money from parents looking for husbands for their girls. "If she's joining our family, she better bring plenty of income with her!" In other words, these parents sell rights to their sons for exorbitant prices.

The disastrous social consequences are that Hindu families go bankrupt financing the weddings of their daughters. Many families just can't afford to have girls. Now that tests to check the sex of a fetus are available, some Hindus opt for abortion if the fetus is female. That it should come to this is bitterly ironic since Hindu scriptures uniformly condemn abortion.

The opposite practice, of demanding money for a daughter, was strictly forbidden in Hindu law. It smacked too much of prostitution.

Manu and Woman

Manu the ancient Hindu lawgiver is leery of granting women independent status. He prefers that they be supervised either by a father or a husband. This way there's no question who is a baby's dad.

But Manu's impression of women wasn't all bad. "Men who wish for good fortune must always honor women," he wrote. "The gods shower happiness and prosperity wherever women are venerated. But in those lands where women are not respected, misfortune surely befalls."

It's News to Me!

Some parts of India, such as large sections of Kerala, are matrilineal. In these communities, males marry into the wife's family rather than vice versa.

The Least You Need to Know

➤ Hindu society is divided into four castes made up of over 3,000 subcastes.

➤ The goals of Hindu life are ethical work, wealth, pleasure, and spiritual illumination.

➤ The four stages of Hindu life are study, marriage, retirement, and renunciation.

➤ Women are highly respected in Hindu culture but don't always have an easy lot in life.

➤ Hindu life is specifically structured to accommodate spiritual growth.

Chapter 17

The Ten Commitments

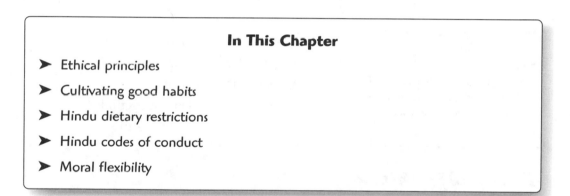

In This Chapter

➤ Ethical principles

➤ Cultivating good habits

➤ Hindu dietary restrictions

➤ Hindu codes of conduct

➤ Moral flexibility

The ultimate goal of Hindu spirituality is liberation from the wheel of rebirth. But while we're still riding up and down on the wheel, there's a practical matter we need to attend to. How do we live in this world? How should we conduct ourselves?

Moral principles are the foundation of every religion. Not everyone is capable of becoming enlightened in this lifetime just as very few of us have the stuff to become gold medal Olympic athletes. But all of us have to live together on this planet. And most of us are concerned about living at peace not only with others but also with ourselves and with God. Our ethics shape both our inner and outer worlds.

Different religions hold many moral principles in common. Other ideas about what constitute virtuous actions are startlingly different. We've already looked at one major difference between Hindu beliefs and Christian and Islamic principles. Christians and Muslims feel morally obliged to convert other people to their religions. Hindus feel respect for other faiths is a more appropriate moral position. Let's look at the basic ethical tenets of Hinduism. We'll see how they agree with and how they diverge from contemporary Western views.

Five Things to Definitely Avoid

I recently returned from Prayag, the area near Allahabad where the second century B.C.E. sage Patanjali had his ashram. He was a spiritual genius of the first magnitude whose books on yoga science, medicine, and grammar are Hindu classics. His presence is still strongly felt there and legends about the great master abound.

It's News to Me!

Snake temples at Prayag honor the sage Patanjali's yogic mastery. His name means "gift of a snake." It signifies that Patanjali had mastered the kundalini, the serpent-like energy in the subtle body.

One of Patanjali's many contributions to Hindu culture was a set of Ten Commitments. It's a famous list of basic do's and don'ts that define what it means to be an ethical person. It spells out a fundamental commitment to spiritual life. It's the perfect place to begin our consideration of Hindu morality.

Patanjali began by listing five *yamas*, things that no one should ever do:

1. *Ahimsa:* Do not harm anyone.
2. *Satya:* Do not lie.
3. *Asteya:* Do not steal.
4. *Brahmacharya:* Do not overindulge.
5. *Aparigraha:* Don't be greedy.

Ethics 101: Ahimsa

Ahimsa literally means nonviolence. It may ring a bell because it was the famous codeword of Mahatma Gandhi's movement of nonviolent resistance to the British occupation of India. Ahimsa means not hurting others and not hurting yourself.

There are some situations where causing harm cannot be avoided. In the well-known example from the *Mahabharata*, Krishna advises Arjuna to take up arms against a prince whose evil actions must be stopped. Note that Krishna makes this suggestion only after multiple attempts at peaceful negotiation have failed.

Hindus are generally a peace-loving people. Yet only a minority go so far as to say that even in cases of self-defense or protection of the innocent, violence must always be avoided. Hindus generally acknowledge that the ahimsa movement worked because Mahatama Gandhi was defying the British. If he had been up against the Nazis, the outcome might have been different.

Nevertheless, practicing Hindus take ahimsa quite seriously. A Canadian friend of mine was mentioning how each time he would leave the home of a Hindu friend she would hand him a sweet and say to him, "If I have offended you in any way during your stay in my home, please forgive me." This was a woman of extraordinary kindness who he couldn't even imagine doing anything offensive! Yet it was important to her to ensure that if she had inadvertently harmed anyone, she clear the air at once.

Honest Indian: Satya

You'll notice that Patanjali's instruction not to lie comes *after* his advice not to harm anyone. Hindus are very conscious that speech can be hurtful, even when—perhaps especially when—it's true. In a society where so much depends on group dynamics, good Hindus take care to ensure that their speech is kind and helpful. Even when this means bending the truth a little.

Not Taking What's Not Yours: Asteya

Taking something that doesn't belong to you is wrong according to Hinduism. (So is hoarding something you don't really need that someone else does need!) Yet the command to practice asteya, nonstealing, was never enforced as strictly in Hinduism as it was in the West. In medieval Europe, a starving man could be hanged for stealing a loaf of bread.

Hindus were a lot more flexible about this kind of thing. In a country with an increasing number of hungry people, it has long been acknowledged that sometimes you have to do what you have to do to keep body and soul together. Punishment for poor people stealing something they urgently needed like food or clothing was not severe, and sometimes wasn't enforced at all. Gratuitous theft, however, was viewed less tolerantly.

Control Yourself! Brahmacharya

All Hindus are supposed to practice brahmacharya, celibacy. Fortunately, celibacy has a broader meaning for married couples! Husbands and wives who are faithful to each other are considered the equivalent of celibate. But brahmacharya means more

Guidepost

Most humane people accept ahimsa as a value. But how non-violent should you be? Some of India's Jains took ahimsa so literally they would wear a piece of cloth over their mouths to avoid accidentally inhaling an insect. They would sweep the ground in front of them as they walked to avoid stepping on a worm.

Guidepost

Important! While stricter rules are reserved for renunciates, Patanjali's Ten Commitments are meant for everyone, including ordinary people living out their lives in the world. It is not indulgence in the usual pleasures of life he is forbidding. It is *overindulgence* he is warning about!

than avoiding extramarital sex. It also means avoiding any kind of sensual overindulgence. Not giving in to gluttonous impulses for a second or third bowl of ice cream is a form of brahmacharya, for example.

Give Up the Greed: Aparigraha

Patanjali took a dim view of greedy, possessive people. In Hinduism the emphasis has always been on acquiring things of lasting value. In a religion that believes in reincarnation, this means collecting things you *can* take with you. Everything you own is lost at death. What you can carry with you into the next life is generosity of spirit, devotion to God and Goddess, fearlessness, and all the good karma you've acquired through your loving and selfless acts. Greedy behavior can't benefit you for more than one lifetime. Generosity benefits you forever.

Five Things to Definitely Do

Patanjali then spelled out five *niyamas,* the things everyone *should* be doing:

1. *Saucha:* Cleanse yourself.
2. *Santosha:* Be content.
3. *Tapas:* Discipline yourself.
4. *Svadhyaya:* Study.
5. *Ishvara Pranidhana:* Surrender to God.

New Word Alert!

A **yama** is a moral restraint, something you shouldn't do.

A **niyama** is a moral observance, something you really ought to do.

Keep It Clean: Saucha

Hindus strongly believe in internal purity and external cleanliness. It's not unusual to find orthodox brahmins bathing repeatedly throughout the day. (This is more understandable if you keep in mind the heat and dust of India.) But a dirty body is the least of problems on the spiritual path. Meditation is the Hindu method for cleaning out the gunk in the mind, which is a far more serious obstruction to spiritual progress. And through japa, constant repetition of the God's or the Goddess's name or of a sacred mantra, the mind remains full of pure vibrations throughout the day, rather than polluting itself with erotic fantasies and gossipy internal jabber.

Constant Craving: Santosha

"Be content. But not satisfied!" the late Swami Rama Bharati used to tell me. He was reiterating the old truism that the wealthiest person is the one who's content with what he or she has. Constant craving for more things, more success, more sex, and more premium-grade ice cream transports us out of the present into a continual uneasy relationship with a fantasy future in which we hope things will be better. But God—in the form of the deepest states of consciousness—can be experienced only in the present moment. When the mind stops being distracted by what it hasn't got, it can start attending to what it *does* have—the living presence of divine being within itself.

Yet complacency is also a spiritual pitfall. So the swami warned against feeling smug or self-satisfied, feeling that you'd gotten as far spiritually as you need to go until you've actually reached the final goal. Enlightenment is an attainable goal to those who sincerely strive and connect with divine grace, according to Hinduism. "You can do it! You will do it! Do it now!" Swami Rama would shout.

Sages Say

"The mind is in a constant state of agitation, and tranquility is only possible through the cultivation of contentment. But contentment should not lead to slackening of effort. Rather effort should stem from a sense of duty and service instead of from discontent."

—Swami Rama Bharati

Discipline Yourself: Tapas

Tapas actually means heat but is used in the Hindu tradition to signify the red-hot focus of concentrated attention. The Veda says God created the universe through tapas through the force of concentrated will. Hindus practice focusing the will through self-discipline and austerity. A well-disciplined body and mind, like a lovingly cared for yet carefully trained horse, can carry us to the goal.

Self Study: Svadhyaya

Svadhyaya means study that leads to Self-realization. Patanjali is encouraging Hindus to study the sacred scriptures. They should study the wisdom the sages embedded in the great myths of Hinduism. And no doubt also study classic works like Patanjali's own *Yoga Sutras*. These books generate enthusiasm for spiritual practice and help dispel doubts.

But svadhyaya has a second meaning. Ultimately self-study is more important than scriptural study. One can read holy books for lifetimes without getting enlightened. Ramana Maharshi lay down on the floor and studied himself intensely for just a couple of minutes and achieved enlightenment. It's in the direct living experience of divine being that moksha, the fourth and final goal of life, is achieved. It can only come from diving within one's own self to make the actual connection with divine being. Then the circuit is closed, and the electricity of inner illumination starts to flow.

Ishvara Pranidhana: Keep God in Mind

Surrender to God means making God your top priority. Most people surrender their minds to their jobs or their relationships or their TV set. Patanjali says focus on inner truth. And don't worry so much. Do your level best, then surrender to God's will and let things flow. The universe is going to flow its own way anyway, no matter how much you resist!

Antidotes to Bad Behavior

Patanjali was quite aware that listing a code of ethical conduct and getting people to actually follow it are two different undertakings. So he offered some practical advice on how to turn your personality around if it wasn't already heading in the right direction.

In Hinduism, it's not enough that you don't harm anyone else if in your heart you'd still really like to smack them. Thoughts are things, and negative thoughts may hurt the person you hate if they're strong enough. And they certainly hurt you! The increased blood pressure, churning stomach, and grinding teeth can't be doing you any good.

Patanjali advises that when you're in the throes of a destructive emotional complex or feel trapped by a bad habit, you "cultivate the opposite." If you hate your brother-in-law's guts, sit down for a set time every day and focus intently on sending him your good wishes. If his personality aggravates you so much you can't visualize his face without starting to froth at the mouth, then beam your best wishes to his innermost soul, which is free from the personality characteristics that irritate you so much.

Patanjali suggests that rather than wrestling with a bad habit that undermines your spiritual progress, work on developing a good habit. One that counterbalances the unhealthy one. For example, if you're having trouble cutting back your unrestrained indulgence in oily curries and Indian sweets, then go out and get some exercise every day.

Holy Cow! What Hindus Do (and Do Not) Eat

Speaking of curries, what do Hindus eat? Hindu dietary habits are tied in with Hindu ethics and social codes. Because ahimsa is a prime moral value, many Hindus are vegetarians. Yet culinary restrictions vary from one social group to another. Most brahmins will not eat meat because they refuse to incur the bad karma of needlessly killing a defenseless animal. Kshatriyas, the warrior caste, have much more liberal attitudes toward hunting and eating flesh since killing is allowed for in their profession.

Many (though by no means all) Hindus are vegetarian, especially in South India. If you're having Hindus over for dinner, it's a good idea to assume they don't eat meat, fish, fowl, or eggs. Dairy products are fine and are a staple of the Hindu diet. But no beef under any circumstances, please! Cows are beloved animals in India. Killing and eating them is unthinkable to Hindus.

Your guests may surprise you, though, and admit they do eat some forms of flesh. Some Hindu communities, especially those along India's coasts, are okay with eating fish. Eggs are a source of protein in many areas. In quite a few Indian restaurants these days you'll find entrees including chicken or goat meat. (The goat may be listed on the menu as "mutton.")

It's News to Me!

Hinduism actually has a culinary theology! The Veda says, "Food is God." The most widely recited table prayer affirms that food is divine energy being offered back to the divine energy comprising our bodies. Eating is consciousness experiencing itself!

Pass the Curry! Skip the Wine!

Many Hindus live on *dahl* and *chai*. Dahl is a soupy dish of heavily spiced, oily, well-cooked beans. Indians use few of the beans Westerners are most familiar with. They generally cook mung beans, chick peas, and other South Asian varieties of beans and lentils. Dahl is usually served with rice, especially in the south. In the north, you're more likely to have your dahl with an unleavened flat bread called *chapati*, which is made from wheat. A spicy vegetable dish and maybe some yogurt come along with your typical Hindu meal.

Guidepost

Don't ever hand a Hindu a tray of food—or anything else for that matter—with your left hand. It's considered horribly insulting. Hindus don't have toilet paper. The left hand has uses in Hindu culture that disqualify it from handling other people's food!

Some Hindus refuse to eat certain types of foods, like garlic or onions, which are considered too unsettling for people trying to calm their minds for meditation.

In orthodox Hindu society, with some exceptions, alcohol is strictly forbidden. In the past few decades, Western influence has helped break down this prohibition in many communities—with catastrophic consequences. It's becoming tragically common to see Hindu men taking their meager earnings to the bar to drink with their friends.

This leaves precious little money for their wives and children. Hindu saints and gurus are calling with increasing urgency for a return to the traditional practice of abstaining from alcohol.

Chai is the Indian national beverage. Some spiritual practitioners rely on its stimulating effects to help them sit up meditating through the night. Chai is tea leaves steeped in scalded milk, or in a mixture of hot water and milk. Those who can afford to add spices like cardamom or cloves. And plenty of sugar!

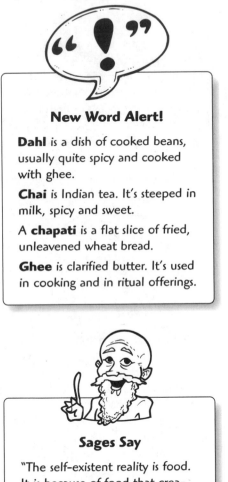

New Word Alert!

Dahl is a dish of cooked beans, usually quite spicy and cooked with ghee.

Chai is Indian tea. It's steeped in milk, spicy and sweet.

A **chapati** is a flat slice of fried, unleavened wheat bread.

Ghee is clarified butter. It's used in cooking and in ritual offerings.

Sages Say

"The self-existent reality is food. It is because of food that creatures are born. It is food that sustains them. And at death, creatures themselves become food."

—*Taittiriya Upanishad 3:2*

Spice Capital of the World

Hindus like their food spicy. Since time immemorial, the Indian subcontinent has been virtually synonymous with delectable spices. A typical bean dish may be prepared with chilies, turmeric, cloves, cinnamon, coriander, peppercorns, cardamom, bay leaves, mace, and lots of cumin.

Hindu food is often quite oily by American standards. Traditionally Hindus use lots of *ghee*. Ghee is made by simmering butter and skimming away the milk solids. It's an important staple of both human and divine diets. Generous helpings of ghee are offered into the sacred fire during religious rituals since the gods love the taste. Also it helps Agni, god of fire, burn that much brighter. Today, unfortunately, cheaper oils that spoil more readily in the Indian heat have found their way into the Hindu pantry.

Hindus have a saying: "He who eats alone, eats in sin." Food is meant to be shared. Even those who have no choice but to eat by themselves will take a handful of food to scatter to wild animals outdoors before sitting down to eat themselves. In traditional Hindu households, families would not eat before first offering their food to the image of the divine in their household shrine and then offering at least a cupful of grain to the poor in their community.

Laying Down the Law

Hinduism is similar to Judaism in another respect besides having dietary regulations. Both traditions involve every aspect of life. There are rules and regulations for every group in society for every part of the day and year.

There is a vast literature on Hindu codes of conduct. One of the most important is the *Manu Smriti,* written perhaps three or so centuries before the Common Era.

Who's In Charge?

The *Manu Smriti* or *The Lawbook of Manu* is unreservedly patriarchal. Men are for the most part in charge in Hindu culture, though women generally control household affairs. Since sons stay in or near the birth home, a Hindu man often defers to his mother as long as she's alive.

Manu considers brahmins the most prestigious caste, which may not be too surprising since Manu was a brahmin. Authoritative textbooks on Hindu politics, written by kshatriyas, consider kshatriyas the preeminent caste. But most Hindu scriptures depict kings offering tremendous respect to their brahmin priest counselors. In Hinduism, spiritual power is real power. It deserves and often gets real respect.

Manu explains who you can or can't eat with and who you can and can't marry depending on your caste. Punishments are allotted for—crimes like killing a priest or a cow. (In ancient times, cows were the basis of the Hindu economy. You didn't ask a person how much money he had. You asked how many cows he had!)

Manu also delineates various ways a person becomes psychically polluted. It's inauspicious to be anywhere near a corpse, for example, and rites of purification must be performed afterward.

It's News to Me!

Manu the Hindu lawgiver was vehemently pro-environment. Denuding, polluting, or otherwise damaging the environment was considered such a serious offense in Hinduism a person could be excommunicated for killing trees!

Clearing Your Conscience

How can you clear your conscience when you've done something you know is wrong? Manu says, "Confess your misdeed and sincerely admit you're sorry. Then by performing some austerity, giving a generous gift, or by reciting holy mantras, you can free yourself from the evil karma. If your repentance is absolutely sincere, your guilt will be erased. But there is one condition. You must never repeat that mistake again."

Quick Quiz

1. Ahimsa means ...

   a. Not hurting others or yourself.

   b. Being content but not satisfied.

   c. Telling the complete truth, even when it hurts.

2. Brahmacharya means ...

   a. No one should ever have sex.

   b. Sex should ideally be confined to marriage.

   c. Having sex with anyone you want is fine as long as you're practicing Tantra.

3. The sage Patanjali ...

   a. Listed Ten Commitments for spiritual life.

   b. Wrote *The Lawbook of Manu*.

   c. Has ashrams around the world where he teaches Tantra.

4. In a traditional Hindu home, alcohol is ...

   a. Served with every meal.

   b. Reserved for tantric sex orgies.

   c. Forbidden.

Answers: 1 (a). 2 (b). 3 (a). 4 (c).

Changing Tides

The past thousand years have been the most traumatic in Hindu history. (Hindu history is so long, a thousand-year period is just a short segment!) The Moghul invasions and later the British conquest put Hindus on the defensive and shook their institutions to the core. In some cases, fundamental values flew out the door in the face of violence, oppression, and the resulting massive poverty.

Westerners visiting Hindu areas are unlikely to be impressed with some current Hindu values, unfortunately. Visitors in past centuries marveled at the peacefulness, prosperity, and moral rectitude of the people. Today, sad to say, corruption is endemic. From government offices to some of the holy temples themselves, you're likely to find a hand clutching at you demanding baksheesh, bribes. The condition of Hindu women has deteriorated shockingly. Attempts to raise the status of outcastes have met with only modest success.

Beggars are everywhere and even some gurus (traditionally Hinduism's most sacred vocation, second only to parenthood) are on the take. Some Hindu groups, fed up with the Muslim minority, are developing a strident anti-Muslim militancy unfamiliar to Westerners who visited India only a few decades ago.

Throughout the subcontinent, Hindu teachers are calling for a return to their religion's eternal values: tolerance, purity, generosity, and love for the divine in all its manifestations.

The Hindu Heart

Hindus remain among the most friendly and hospitable people on Earth. "The guest is God," is a fundamental Hindu value. Many of us visitors can testify that Hindus behave as if this is literally true!

The caste system, which in some ways seems so contrary to the Hindu spirit of toleration, has actually served to protect the fantastic diversity of communities you'll find in India. Nowhere else can you find so many radically different subcultures in such a confined area. The subcastes are something like the trade guilds of medieval Europe, which isolate—but also protect and promote—the community.

Sages Say

"The good Hindu should continually recite the holy scripture. He should be self-controlled, kind, and tranquil. He desires to give, not to receive. He is loving toward all living things."

—Manu Smriti

Yet there's no question that some of the moral values that define Hinduism sit uneasily in today's world. While Patanjali's Ten Commitments still make sense, there are passages in Manu's 2,300-year-old law codes (especially those disparaging toward women and the lower classes) that make some modern Hindus flinch. One of the major challenges for Hindus in the twenty-first century is to decide which of their values reflect the biases of days gone by and which really are eternal.

The Least You Need to Know

➤ The sage Patanjali listed Ten Commitments that Hindus serious about spiritual life need to make.

➤ The fundamental value of Hindu ethics is nonviolence.

➤ Many, but by no means all, orthodox Hindus are vegetarians and teetotalers.

➤ *The Lawbook of Manu* and similar manuals define orthodox Hindu behavior.

➤ Values are rapidly shifting in India today.

Sacraments and Holy Days

For Hindus, one advantage to having so many gods and goddesses is that there are lots of holidays. One deity or another is always being honored. This makes for plenty of festivals, lots of good food, and warm relations between humans and gods.

In addition to public holidays, there are numerous private holy days. Hinduism has 16 major sacraments and a couple dozen minor ones. Let's have a look at some of the most important days in the Hindu calendar and in a Hindu's life. Then you'll know when to send your Hindu friends "Happy Divali" cards!

Living Life Holy

All of nature, and all of time, are sacred in Hinduism. Among traditional Hindu families, there is no radical distinction between sacred and secular as we have in the West. In the morning, you get up and put your feet on the Earth, who is a goddess. You go outdoors and greet the Sun, who is a god. You are surrounded by divinity.

The Sanskrit word *samskara* means a groove in the mind, a deep impression made in consciousness. The Hindu sacraments, also called samskaras, are special rites in which a Hindu's connection with the pervading divinity is formally reaffirmed. A new groove formed in the soul orients it toward God as another stage in life begins.

Rite from the Start

Sacraments begin before a soul is even conceived. Orthodox couples consider the moment they consciously decide to have a child to be a sacramental time of great auspiciousness. The *Upanishads* contain special mantras for would-be parents to recite in order to invite intelligent, devoted, and highly evolved souls into the wife's womb.

Sexual relations then are engaged in with full conscious intent to conceive a child. A special rite is actually performed at what the parents assume to be the moment of conception. Many Hindus believe that the state of their minds at the moment they conceive a baby will influence the child's development. Couples whose minds are preoccupied with physical sensations will produce passionate children. Couples who keep their minds in loving and clear states will invoke the entrance of more spiritually advanced souls into their family.

Birth itself is a sacrament. The birth rite is called *jatkarman,* which means the act of birth or the birth of action, depending on your point of view. Paradoxically, for Hindus biological events like giving birth are both sacred and polluting. So rites blessing and celebrating the event are joined with rites to purify the physical and mental environment of the suffering and shedding of blood that accompanied childbirth.

New Word Alert!

Samskara is a tendency in the mind and personality; also, a Hindu sacrament.

Jatkarman is the sacramental rite performed at the birth of a Hindu baby.

Childhood Passages

Several important sacraments are performed during childhood. Usually sometime between the third and sixth week of life, the child is formally given its name. The parents may take the infant to their local temple for this special event or do it at home. Often an astrologer is first consulted to help select an auspicious name reflecting the cosmic energy at the moment of birth. Then the father whispers the child's name into its right ear.

The first time the child is taken outside the house its universe expands exponentially. The first time he or she takes solid food marks the beginning of the end of its dependence on its mother's breast. Both these events are considered major rites of passage by Hindus. They're witnessed and celebrated by relatives and consecrated with mantras.

Hindus also consecrate their children's first haircut, which would occur some time before the age of three. The head is shaved, symbolizing purity. Some Hindus like to believe this also helps to shave off some of the bad karma from previous lives.

Ear piercing (for both sexes!) is also a sacramental event and usually is scheduled when the child is around a year old, though it may not occur till age five. Hindus believe that certain points in the physical body relate to particular energy centers in the subtle body, much like the Chinese acupuncture points. Therefore, Hindu-style ear piercing is believed to benefit the baby's health.

One of the most important sacraments occurs between the ages of four and seven. This marks the inauguration of formal academic study. A parent, priest, or guru holds the child's finger and guides it through grains of uncooked rice sprinkled across a plate. With the tutor's help, the child spells out a letter of the alphabet for the first time. This is an extremely charming and auspicious event to which Sarasvati, the goddess of education, is invited.

Young People's Initiations

The one Hindu sacrament people in the West have heard of, if they've heard of any of them at all, is the investiture of the sacred thread. This initiation is reserved for boys of the brahmin, kshatriya, and vaishya castes. Without this rite, an upper caste boy cannot study the Veda or marry. The sacred thread is hung over the boy's left shoulder and swings around his right torso. Depending on the boy's caste, this ceremony may take place between the ages of nine and fifteen.

The boy is now initiated in the Gayatri mantra, the most sacred mantra in the Veda. He is then considered "twice born," since this spiritual initiation is the equivalent of a second birth. His initiators invoke the gods' and goddess' blessings for this extraordinarily important event.

In olden times, following this critical event, the boy would be sent away to live and study with his guru until he reached marriageable age. In some communities today, the significance of this rite has shifted and a young man might not receive his sacred thread till his early twenties, immediately before marriage.

Another rite for boys only occurs when the adolescent shaves for the first time. This sacrament is less serious in tone than the investiture of the sacred thread. Gifts are exchanged all around. Once he's relaxed and in a good mood, the boy is asked by his smiling but not joking elders to remain celibate till marriage!

Sages Say

"With loving reverence we bow to the Inner Sun, the most splendid light in all the worlds. Please illuminate our minds."

—The Gayatri Mantra

The equivalent sacrament for women occurs at the time of a girl's first menstrual period. She is closed away in a dark room for several days to adjust to her new status as a potential mother and to think seriously about the responsibility this entails. Friends come by to advise and tease her. Then she emerges for a ritual bath and a feast of celebration. Sometimes her female relatives will take the young lady to the local temple and wave lights around her as if she were the Goddess herself. She has just grown into one of the Goddess's most amazing powers: the ability to produce new life.

A Wedding to Last Forever

For many Hindus, the wedding is the most important sacrament of their lives. Hindu weddings go on for days. Even the abbreviated modern versions run on for many hours. The marriage is expected to last a lifetime (at the very least!). Widows seldom remarry in India. Widowers are free to remarry but since grooms are often a fair bit older than their brides, it's more common for husbands to predecease their wives.

Guidepost

Don't ask a swami to perform your wedding ceremony! Hindus believe you can't give what you haven't got. Since a swami isn't married, he can't give you the state of marriage. In India, it's inauspicious if a swami shows up at your wedding. He represents renunciation of worldly life and infertility—a bad omen for newlyweds!

Hindu marriages are almost always arranged by parents. Even today when many young Hindus are immigrating abroad looking for better job prospects, they'll travel back to their village in India to marry the partner their parents have selected. In north India particularly, the bride and groom may never have met before!

In making a suitable match, parents consider the prospective spouse's subcaste and clan, profession and financial status. Horoscopes are carefully compared. Then an astrologically auspicious date is selected and the festivities begin.

The heart of the long ceremony occurs when the bride steps three times on her in-laws' grinding stone, symbolizing her entrance into their household. Then the couple walks around the sacred fire seven times during which incalculably ancient Vedic mantras are chanted. The groom offers his new wife half of all his good karma. The bride offers back half of her bad karma. As you can see, Hindu women drive a tough bargain. But most Hindu men agree to the deal!

Life After Death

Hindu sacraments begin before a child is born, continue throughout life, and go on even afterwards. There are two major types of rites for the dead. One kind is for dead people who've left their bodies. The other is for dead people who're still very much alive.

Honoring the Departed

A funeral is always a painful and sobering event. Final rites involve bathing and anointing the body and shaving it if the body is male. The corpse is wrapped in a shroud and carried to the cremation grounds, usually within hours of death. Hindus most often burn the dead, then offer the remains to the earth or a river. Children and sometimes pregnant women are buried rather than cremated. Poorer people, who may not be able to afford the expense of cremation, may also bury their dead. Often saints are buried in special mausoleums rather than cremated. These tombs, the famous *samadhi* shrines of India, often become popular pilgrimage sites.

Final rites, called *shraddha,* conclude with the offering of rice balls to the departed. You wouldn't want to send them on their way without something to eat! Some Hindu families continue making food offerings for years after the death has occurred. Attitudes toward the dead can vary greatly from community to community or from home to home. Some people greatly fear hauntings and hope the spirits of the dead will quickly depart. Others rely on the continuing advice and blessings of the dead, as indicated in the omens spirits use to signal their suggestions to loved ones left behind.

New Word Alert!

Shraddha *is the sacrament performed for the dead.*

A **samadhi** *shrine is the burial place of a saint. Samadhi also means an intense state of meditative absorption.*

Performing Your Own Cremation

One of the most important sacraments is performed by only a small number of Hindus. These are the sannyasins, the Hindu renunciates. When they take formal vows of renunciation, Hindu men and women perform their own cremation, burning themselves in effigy.

From the point of view of their families, sannyasins really are dead. The cremation marks the end of the old personality with all its ties of friendship and family, all its attachments and responsibilities. The renunciate then enters a river and emerges naked, symbolizing his or her spiritual rebirth. The guru waiting at the bank gives the renunciate a new name and the ocher robe of a world renouncer.

The orange robe is the color of fire. It stands for the fiery immolation of the person this individual used to be and for the fire of spiritual awareness in which he or she now lives. Most sannyasins then begin a homeless life of wandering, begging, and

It's News to Me!

When Hindu renunciates physically die, they are usually not cremated. This is because when they took their vows of renunciation, they already cremated themselves. You can't burn them twice! Most often their corpses are offered to a river.

one-pointed focus on Self-realization. Some join ashrams or welfare organizations and commit themselves to a lifetime of teaching or selfless service.

Linking Up

There are numerous other Hindu sacraments besides those I've described here. Some are rarely practiced anymore. Others are performed only regionally. Yet the sacraments are an extremely important expression of Hindu life. Not every Hindu is versed in the intricacies of Upanishadic philosophy or can chant whole books from the Veda. Yet every one feels connected to the wider Hindu community and to the fountain of blessing force flowing from higher levels of reality, through the samskaras, these ancient holy rites.

Sacred Time

Next you're going to read about the most popular Hindu holidays. But I've got a problem here because I can't tell you exactly when these holidays are! That's because most Hindus use a lunar calendar, the calendar based on the phases of the Moon. That's different from our Western solar calendar, which is based on the solstices and equinoxes, pivotal points in the Sun's yearly journey through the ecliptic.

Because of this discrepancy, dates from the Hindu calendar seem to hop around on our Western calendar. This is the reason your Hindu friend who celebrates her birthday in October one year may have a birthday party in November the next year! I'm tacking in an East/West calendar wheel, so you'll have at least a general idea how the two calendars interface.

The Festival of Lights: Divali

According to legend, it was on this night thousands and thousands of years ago that the hero Rama and his wife, Sita—freshly rescued from the tyrant Ravana—returned to their home capital of Ayodhya after fourteen years of exile. The city exploded with joy! Citizens came racing into the night carrying portable lamps to celebrate the safe return of their dearly loved king and queen.

If you can only attend one festival in India, Divali is the one to see. Like many Hindu holidays, it actually goes on for days. Why celebrate one day when you can party all week? Though this holiday isn't all play and no work. For many Hindus, it's a time for cleaning out the house and buying new things for the home. Business people start up new ledger books on this holiday. It's time to move out the old and start afresh!

Divali, or Dipavali as it's also called, occurs in October or November. It means "the festival of lights." You'll see why on the New Moon night. As the Sun slips over the western horizon, all over India villagers light small clay lamps, leaving them on their windowsills and in the roads. They also float millions of makeshift lamps down the rivers. In the cities, Hindus hang out strings of electric bulbs. The entire subcontinent

238

is lit up with cheerful twinkling lights. The effect is so spectacular—and so heart-stoppingly beautiful—you'll never forget the sight till the end of your days.

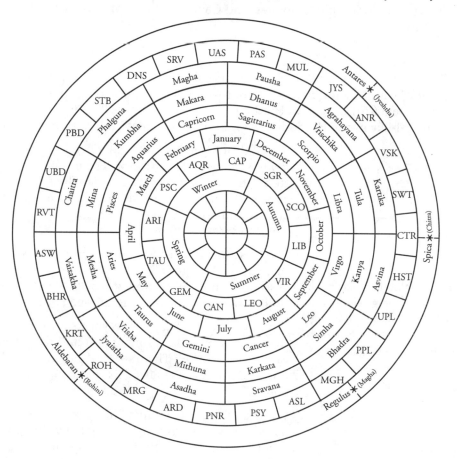

Calendar Wheel

- Western Seasons
- Western Sun Signs
- Western Months
- Constellations
- Hindu Sun Signs
- Hindu Months
- Hindu Moon Signs
- Bright Zodiac Stars

Moon Sign Abbreviations

"P." is for "Purva", "U." for "Uttara"

ASW	Ashwini	MGH	Magha	MUL	Mula
BHR	Bharani	PPL	P. Phalguni	PAS	P. Ashadha
KRT	Krittika	UPL	U. Phalguni	UAS	U. Ashadha
ROH	Rohini	HST	Hasta	SRV	Shravana
MRG	Mrigashiras	CTR	Chitra	DNS	Dhanishtha
ARD	Ardra	SWT	Swati	STB	Shatabhishaj
PNR	Punarvasu	VSK	Vishakha	PBD	P. Bhadrapada
PSY	Pushya	ANR	Anuradha	UBD	U. Bhadrapada
ASL	Ashlesha	JYS	Jyeshtha	RVT	Revati

© 2001 Johnathan Brown

The Western solar-based calendar in relation to the Hindu lunar-based calendar.

Firecrackers (and these days fireworks) go off everywhere. Dainty foods, especially sweets, are offered to the deities. This is a night to connect with Lakshmi, the goddess of prosperity and domestic happiness, and Ganesha, the elephant-headed god of wisdom and success.

Holi Day

Holi is New Year's Day for many Hindus. (Not for all Hindus. Some communities have still other calendars!) But for all Hindus, it's time to celebrate. This is the craziest, most carnival-like of the Hindu holidays. In happens in late February, early March.

Sages Say

"Clothed in light, glittering like priceless gems, You, the grace-filled World Mother, uphold the entire universe! To Goddess Lakshmi I bow again and again with gratitude and awe!"

—Maha Lakshmi Stotram

Guidepost

I hope you're not wearing your good clothes if you're with Hindus during Holi! Out come the water guns and you're covered from head to toe with colored water or red powder. Let me tell you from personal experience, it's not easy to wash out!

How did Holi get started? Well, once there was a demoness named Holika who was so mean-spirited she ate a little boy or girl every day! Finally a sannyasin passing through the area saw a poor widow weeping bitterly and asked what the problem was. "Holika is going to eat my only son!" she wailed.

The holy man devised a plan. When Holika showed up that day, he brought all the children together to shout obscenities and throw mud at her. The ruse worked. Holika was so humiliated she dropped dead of shame!

Anyway, that's the reason everyone's running around shouting insults and throwing dirt and red powder at each other on Holi! There's lots of singing and dancing. And mean old Holika gets roasted in a roaring bonfire!

While all Hindus participate in these festivals, Divali has a vaishya feel, as if it was originally thought up by business people. Its focus is on prosperity, happiness, and success. Holi has more of a shudra atmosphere. It's time for the working class to let loose a little and vent. They shout their real feelings at their employers and neighbors. The next day everything is forgiven and forgotten!

Honor Thy Sibling

In ancient times, the gods got themselves in a pickle. They were losing their war against the demons so badly that Indra, warrior king of the deities, was completely unnerved! Indrani, his peerless wife, saved the day. She tied a beautiful magical bracelet around Indra's wrist, and the next day Indra led the gods to an easy victory.

Rakhi Bandhan is celebrated around July or August. It means "bond of protection." On this day, sisters tie multicolored bracelets around the wrists of their brothers. It means from now on, their brothers will have to protect them, no matter what!

While the festival is lighthearted, the commitment signified by the *rakhi* or protective bracelet is not. There are stories of women being harassed by amorous suitors who ended the problem by sending the man a rakhi. It means she sees him as her brother and from now on he's responsible for protecting her virtue, not trying to make off with it!

In some parts of the country, women tie the colorful bracelets around their uncles' wrists, too. Sections of Hindu culture are matrilineal, which means uncles even more than fathers are responsible for a woman's welfare.

Celebrating Spirit

Some holidays like Holi are raucous. Others like Divali have a mercantile flavor, somewhat like our Christmas, which also involves making lots of purchases and hanging out strings of light. Rakhi Bandhan is more private, a family rather than community event. Still other festivals are devoted to spirit and are celebrated with fasting rather than feasting, with meditation rather than merrymaking.

Shiva's Night

Shiva Ratri occurs in November or December for some Hindus. Others celebrate it in February or March. This night is sacred to Shiva. Devotees honor it by sitting in meditation with Lord Shiva himself. They fast all day (they may take some fruit and water) and hold vigil all night.

The Shiva linga at the temple or in one's home shrine is bathed with milk, honey, and water and offered particular types of fruit and leaves that Shiva especially likes. Celebrants chant holy mantras like "Om namah Shivaya!" They sing hymns, often accompanying themselves on the harmonium. You may find some devotees seated around the sacred fire, tossing offerings of grain into the flames as they chant Shiva's name. Many simply meditate all night.

New Word Alert!

A **rakhi** is a bracelet girls tie around the wrists of their brothers and uncles, calling for their protection.

It's News to Me!

Harmoniums or hand organs were introduced into India by European invaders. They (the harmoniums, not the invaders) became immensely popular and are still frequently used to accompany devotional singing. Some Hindu melodies are impossible to play on this instrument, so musicians glide their fingers along the keyboard rather than playing individual notes. This approximates the feeling of the original Indian music.

Happy Birthday, God!

Just as Christians celebrate the birth of their savior Jesus Christ, Hindus celebrate the days their most popular divine incarnations were born. The birthdays of the avatars Rama and Krishna are cause for special festivities. The delightful elephant-headed deity Ganesha also gets his own special festival.

Rama Navami

Rama Navami, Lord Rama's birthday, is a huge pan-Indian celebration. It's celebrated in or around April. Some Hindus will fast for the nine days leading up to the big day. In many communities, recitations of the *Ramayana* are organized. Folk dramas enacting favorite scenes from the lives of Rama and Sita are enthusiastically staged.

Krishna Jayanti

Krishna's birthday, called Krishna Jayanti, occurs in July or August and is an enormous national celebration. Much as Jesus was born rather humbly in a manger, Krishna was born in a prison cell! His parents were being held captive in a Mathura jail by the tyrant Kamsa. Krishna's father managed to get the baby to safety while the prison guards slept.

Krishna was born at midnight. At the stroke of midnight on every Krishna Jayanti, Hindus blow their conches, clang their bells, and shout Krishna's praises at the top of their lungs! Then they break their fast, sitting down to a feast including plenty of sweets.

Ganesha Utsava

Rama and Krishna were both avatars of Vishnu, so they had actual birthdays you can find on a calendar. Identifying Ganesha's birthday is a little trickier. You'll remember he's the god with the elephant head and a taste for milk. His special day, Ganesha Utsava, is held in August or September and is a time of great rejoicing.

On the final days of the celebrations, statues of Ganesha, which were made specifically for worshipping during this festival, are carted down to a nearby river. Then they're immersed till the lightweight materials they're made of dissolve away. The ritual immersion of images of deities is a reminder that at the end of the universal cycle even the gods themselves will dissolve back into the all-pervading consciousness of the Supreme Reality.

Quick Quiz

1. For Hindus, marriage is ...

    a. A time of deep sadness.

    b. An excuse to get drunk.

    c. The most important sacrament.

2. Sannyasins perform their own cremation ...

    a. By burning themselves alive.

    b. And then assume a new spiritual identity.

    c. To avoid paying taxes.

3. The Festival of Lights commemorates ...

    a. The destruction of the demoness Holika.

    b. Rama and Sita's return home.

    c. The discovery of electricity.

4. On Holi you're likely to ...

    a. Be squirted with colored water.

    b. Sit up all night meditating.

    c. Deck the halls with boughs of Holi.

Answers: 1 (c). 2 (b). 3 (b). 4 (a).

Victory on the Tenth Day

Dassera isn't just a holiday. It's a whole holiday season! It's ten straight days of celebrations held in September or October. The first part is called Nava Ratri ("Nine Nights"). Three days and nights each are devoted to the worship of the great goddesses Durga, Lakshmi, and Sarasvati. Nava Ratri commemorates, among other things, Rama worshipping the warrior goddess Durga before setting off to battle the evil king Ravana. Rama won Durga's favor, which made him invincible even though he was vastly outnumbered by Ravana's better trained troops.

The final day of the holiday is called Vijaya Dashmi ("Victory on the Tenth Day"). Rama's fantastic victory over Ravana is celebrated with parades and fanfare. Enormous, odd-looking effigies of Ravana (after all, he had ten heads!) are set on fire to signal the triumph of justice over injustice. Nava Ratri is the favorite festival of the year in Goddess country—the northeastern part of India. This is an especially auspicious time to approach the Divine Mother for blessings and special favors.

243

Saris for Spring

Hindu communities have their own regional festivals as well. In Tamil Nadu in the south there is Pongol sometime around January, celebrating the rice harvest. During Naga Panchami, also held in the south, snakes are honored and fed. (Few Hindus use pesticides. Snakes have always done just fine for pest control.) In the north, Vasant celebrates the arrival of spring. You'll know it's Vasant when all the women you see are wearing bright yellow saris!

In one month it's time to plant. In another it's time to harvest. But in Hinduism it's always time for God. Sacraments and holy days help keep mortals and eternity in close touch. That's something to celebrate!

The Least You Need to Know

➤ Hinduism has many sacraments, beginning before conception and ending after death.

➤ Marriage is the most important sacrament for most Hindus.

➤ Religious renunciates perform their own cremation, and then take a new identity.

➤ Favorite Hindu holy days include the Festival of Lights, and Rama and Krishna's birthdays.

➤ On Shiva Ratri, Shiva's devotees stay up all night meditating and worshipping.

Chapter 19

Temples and Sacred Sites

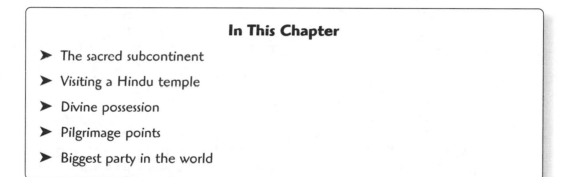

In This Chapter

➤ The sacred subcontinent

➤ Visiting a Hindu temple

➤ Divine possession

➤ Pilgrimage points

➤ Biggest party in the world

Few North Americans have a sense for the sanctity of the land. There may be a few places like the Grand Canyon or Niagara Falls that evoke a sense of awe. But an appreciation of the inherent holiness of the land itself—such as the Native Americans have—is largely missing from the children of immigrants who now dominate North America.

The Hindu attitude is dramatically different. To them the planet itself is Bhumeshvari, "Mother Earth" —a living Goddess. And India is Jambu Dvipa, "Rose-Apple Island," the holiest place in the world.

The entire Indian subcontinent is dotted with temples and sacred sites. Within a day's walk of virtually any spot in India you'll find at least one holy center. Hindu renunciates spend their lives circling India, stopping at another pilgrimage point or famous temple each evening. These places are magnifying lenses for the spiritual energy of the land itself, the Hindus' beloved Mother India.

Take Off Your Shoes!

You'll have to take off your shoes before you enter a Hindu temple. You're not allowed to drag in the dirt from the outside world, either on the soles of your shoes or in your own soul. Outside all large temples you'll find a shoe stall where you can store your shoes for a few pennies. You're expected to leave your worldly thoughts behind too though there's no convenient place to store them!

You should also dress modestly. Ladies, in Hindu culture this means the bosom, upper arms and legs should not be exposed. So no halter tops or shorts. Gentlemen, clothes should be clean and untorn, with your legs covered. Please leave leather items at home. It is considered a desecration to bring objects made from butchered cows into a Hindu temple.

Guidepost

It's appropriate to circumambulate a Hindu temple several times before you enter. This means walking around it, keeping the temple to your right. You're going to meet God or the Goddess inside. Use the time to prepare yourself for a beautiful spiritual experience.

Come bearing gifts! God and Goddess have filled your life with blessings. It's only appropriate that you bring a present as an expression of your gratitude. Fruits like mangoes, coconuts or bananas are good. So are handfuls of flowers. Rupee notes go down particularly well. Foreign currency will not be turned away! If it wasn't convenient to bring anything with you, don't fret. You'll be met at the temple door by plenty of helpful vendors who'll cheerfully sell you every kind of offering appropriate at that temple.

Be careful not to stumble as you walk in. There's a raised step right before you enter. (Don't worry—after you've fallen a few times you'll start remembering it's there!) You may want to bow and touch this step with the fingers of your right hand. Then touch your fingers to your forehead and heart. Even the dust from the steps of a holy temple carries a blessing!

Worshipping in a Hindu Temple

If you've timed your visit right, Goddess or God will come out and greet you. Ask in advance what the deity's office hours are. You don't want to get there before the murti, the divine statue, has had a chance to bathe, dress, and have a bite to eat—with a little help from the priests. Dressed up in fresh clothes and weighed down with numerous garlands of fragrant flowers, the deity will see you now.

You are admitted into the holy of holies and a screen is pulled away so you can see the deity and he or she can see you. At busy temples, you may have only a moment in the divine presence before you're waved out so the next group of devotees can squeeze in. At smaller community temples you can stay for the full service, however. This may include devotional singing and devotees dancing before the divine image. These are slow, very stylized dances, quite restrained by Western standards.

A Hindu temple.

© *Hinduism Today*

A priest or devotee will offer objects like a fan, a fly whisk, and incense. If it's a goddess, a few accessories she especially enjoys may be brought out, like a mirror to help her check her makeup!

The main event is *arati,* the ritual waving of lights before the deity. A brass tray filled with camphor candles is waved in circles before the deity. Then a temple officiant carries the tray around to each worshipper. Pass your hands quickly through the flames (it doesn't hurt!) as you waft the sacred fire's blessings toward yourself

Receiving Your Blessing

The temple assistant will come around with several more items for you. He or she will pour some holy water into your cupped right palm. Hindus drink the water, then run their right hand over their heads, distributing the blessing force. Don't tell anyone I said this, but if you're in a Hindu temple in India, as opposed to another country where you're sure the water is amoeba-free, you may be

It's News to Me!

Devotees of Vishnu mark their foreheads with sacred designs etched with white clay. Followers of Shiva streak ash across the top of their faces. If the temple priest marks your forehead with red cosmetic powder, he's a devotee of the Goddess.

better off discretely pretending to drink it, and then rubbing it into your hair. You'll get the blessing just the same!

Temple personnel will also come around to mark your forehead. This *tilak* is a sign that you've received the deity's blessing.

Don't leave without *prasad*. Some of the gifts devotees have brought to the temple will be returned to you, blessed by the deity. Usually this is an article of food or a handful of flowers. This is a token of the Goddess or God's affection for you. It's considered quite holy. Amazing healings have been attributed to the power of prasad!

Inside and Outside the Temple

Just a point or two about the Hindu temple itself. Westerners sometimes find Indian temples a bit hard on the eye. The outside of many temples is covered with so many figurines it's exhausting to look at. At the bottom are demons and animals, at the middle story humans are portrayed, and higher up are numerous figures of gods and goddesses at work and play. Then you walk into the temple itself—and it's practically empty!

Do you get the point? The outside of the temple represents our outer life and the infinitely varied external manifestation of the divine. The inside, or *garbha* (which literally means "womb"), stands for the interior of the soul, and for the unmanifest reality, in which only Pure Consciousness itself is present. In some temples, there's nothing inside but the image of God or the Goddess itself.

Outside the many. Inside the One.

New Word Alert!

Arati is the ritual waving of lights before a Hindu deity.

Prasad is food or some other offering you've brought to the image of a Hindu god or goddess. It's returned to you with blessings.

A **tilak** is the mark Hindus wear on their foreheads.

Altar in the Living Room

In the West, we think in terms of the separation of Church and State. Most of us also tend to think of a church, synagogue, or mosque as the place we go to worship and home as the place we go to watch TV. The situation is *totally* different for Hindus. The center of the Hindu religion is *not* the temple. It's the home.

Hindus go to the temple for festivals or consecrations or to ask for special favors from the deity. No sermons are delivered there. You don't go there to get lectured to or be educated in your religion. You just go to pay your respects to the temple deity. The real worship goes on right in your own house. So does your religious education, which comes from your parents and elders. Or you may go to your guru's home to study with him or her.

Every Hindu home has its own shrine where images of the favorite family deities are installed. The family (or at least the women, who are in charge of household activities) worship before these deities every day, waving lights and offering incense and food. In fact, good Hindus won't touch their meals till the food has first been blessed by the household gods.

The home shrine may contain small statues of popular deities like Krishna, Lakshmi, or Shiva. Or there may be pictures and even inexpensive color posters of the Hindu gods and goddesses. These are not considered less holy than metal or stone statues. The divine presence has been invoked in these articles and Hindus treat them as living representations of the deity.

The household shrine saved Hinduism during the Muslim takeover. Fanatic Muslim leaders destroyed almost every major temple in northern India in an effort to exterminate Hinduism. They failed because the most important temples were in peoples' homes. Most Hindus remained faithful to their religion despite tremendous pressure to convert to Islam. When calmer Muslim governors, and later the British, headed the country, the great Hindu temples were rebuilt.

Hindu Hot Spots

If this entire book was devoted just to listing holy sites in India, and I somehow managed to limit myself to only two paragraphs for each one, we still could barely skim the surface of the thousands of pilgrimage spots in India. When Hindus talk about India as a holy land, they're not kidding!

Let's take a quick tour of the subcontinent. I'll introduce you to a few of the most special places in India and what each one represents for Hindus.

The Navel of the World

Let's start at the extreme north, a little way across the present Indian border into Tibet. Ironically, this northernmost tip of Hindu culture was considered the *center* of the Hindu world by the ancients. I'm talking about Mount Kailas, an amazing mountain that seems to spring up out of nowhere in the Tibetan plateau. Its striking conical shape reminds Hindus of a Shiva linga. Lord Shiva and his wife, Parvati, are said to have their main residence at the top of the mountain. It's so sacred no one would even think of climbing it. You might disturb Shiva in his meditation!

Sages Say

"There are no other mountains equal to the Himalayas! There you will find Mount Kailas and Lake Manasarovar. Dew disappears in the morning Sun. In the same way, sin vanishes instantly at the stunning sight of the Himalayas."

—The *Ramayana*

Within walking distance from Kailas are two sacred lakes. Remarkably, Manasarovar is shaped just like the Sun. And Raksas Tal is shaped like a crescent Moon. In a sense, Kailas really is the center of the world. The Indus, Sutlej, Brahmaputra, and Karnali rivers—some of the greatest rivers of Asia—all start up in this region.

Kailas is the holiest mountain in the world. It's sacred not just to Hindus but also to Buddhists, Jains, and the native Tibetan Bonpos. Even during the most brutal part of the Chinese occupation, Hindu pilgrims risked their lives trying to reach this legendary mountain. Today the political situation has calmed down somewhat. But the mountain rises from a barely breathable altitude of 15,000 feet (add 22,028 feet on top of that if you want to measure the peak). In addition, the plateau is riddled with killer hail and sandstorms, making this one of the most difficult spots in the world to get to. Perhaps that's why pilgrims who actually reach this holy place are said to gain tremendous merit.

New Word Alert!

A **ghat** is a set of steps leading down to a river. Many Hindus bathe, wash their clothes, worship, and perform cremations at ghats.

Sages Say

"Worship the feet of Lord Shiva! They will destroy your evil karma. They will grant you presence of mind. They will bestow unending joy. But you must understand that Shiva's feet are Consciousness itself!"

—The Natchintanai

City of Light

One of the best things about being a tour guide is I get to pick our stops. The next point on our itinerary is Benares, my favorite city in India. There is archeological evidence suggesting that this is the oldest continuously inhabited city in the world. Kashi, "the City of Light," as Benares is also called, is mentioned even in the ancient Veda!

Benares has been one of the intellectual capitals of India since time immemorial. Today it's home to four universities, including the largest residential university in Asia.

Even more important, it's Lord Shiva's favorite city! Hindus fortunate enough to die here are shuttled directly to the highest heaven, thanks to Shiva's gracious intervention. This is the final stop for many of Hinduism's elderly, who stream into the city hoping to take advantage of Shiva's good nature and pass away here on Shiva's deluxe train to heaven. If you take the spectacular boat ride down the Ganges here, you'll see the famous burning *ghats* on the west side of the river where older pilgrims who got their timing right are being cremated.

On some maps, Benares is still called by its older name, Varanasi. The ancient city was bounded by the Varuna River on its north and the Asi River (now a creek) on its south, with the Ganges running along its western shore. Here's a secret the yogis will share with you. The Varuna stands for the right *nadi* or "inner river of energy" in the subtle body. The Asi is the left nadi. The Ganges stands in for the central canal in the subtle body through which the kundalini energy flows. If at the moment of death you can balance the subtle energy flowing through these nadis, then you will indeed enter "the city of Shiva." This is the center of highest consciousness at the top of the brain. If you hold your awareness here throughout the death process, you'll experience the light of liberation. Then your karmas will burn away in the cremation ghat of divine awareness.

City of Tents

What if you threw a party and 70 million guests showed up? In India it happens! Every three years a festival called the Kumbha Mela is held at one of four sites: Prayag at Allahabad in north-central India, Nasik on the west coast, Ujjain a little northeast of Nasik, and finally at Hardwar in the Himalayas. The festival rotates between these four centers, so each city gets to sponsor the Mela every 12 years.

Tens of million of Hindus attend these fairs. Every possible Hindu sect is represented. They get together in an atmosphere of mutual respect to worship in their own way. Holy men and women pour out of their retreats in the Himalayan mountains and forests to join the common people in a celebration of spirit.

The Kumbha Mela at Prayag (where the Ganges and Yamuna rivers meet) is the biggest of all. It's generally held in January–February when the two rivers partly dry up. The Indian army is sent in to construct a city of tents in the dry river basin. Pilgrims live in the tents for free. Spiritual leaders from all over the country build makeshift ashrams there for the six-week festival. Programs go on 24 hours a day, and food is distributed free to all comers.

Seventy million people turned up for the Kumbha Mela at Prayag in January 2001. It was the biggest collective event in world history! Ordinarily you can't see even the largest cities (like Tokyo with a population of a mere 34 million) from outer space. This Kumbha Mela was so huge that satellite photographs picked up the massive crowds!

New Word Alert!

A **nadi** is a current of energy in the subtle body. This is the subtle equivalent of the physical nervous system in the pranic body.

Garbha means womb, matrix, or the inner sanctum of a temple.

It's News to Me!

Kumbha Mela means "Festival of the Pot." Ages ago the celestial physician (the constellation Aquarius, called Kumbha in India) accidentally spilled his pot of divine nectar. A few drops splattered in Nasik, Ujjain, and Hardwar, but most of it poured out in Prayag. At the astrologically auspicious time of the Kumbha Mela, you can taste the nectar of immortality as it drips from heaven!

I attended the 2001 Kumbha Mela myself. It was absolutely one of the most powerful spiritual experiences of my life. I can hardly begin to express the effect of having 70 million human beings together in one place, all praying, chanting, and meditating with each other in an atmosphere of harmony and mutual support. It was like spending a month in heaven!

The Busiest Temple in the World

What is the one most visited pilgrimage site in the entire world? Rome? Mecca? Guess again! If you guessed Tirupati in Andhra Pradesh in South India, you win a cookie and a bowl of ice cream!

The Sri Venkateshvara Temple at Tirupati is the wealthiest in the world, bringing in about $6,000,000 *per day.* Some 30,000 devotees show up every day of the year. They climb 10,000 steps (you read right—I said *10,000 steps)* to reach the temple at the top of the hill. There they are offered the opportunities to donate all their gold and valuables and have their heads shaven clean. (Both men and women leave Tirupati bald.)

Devotees then shuffle forward in an agonizingly slow line leading to the inner sanctum. Many of them are singing hymns, chanting holy texts, or repeating their mantra. Finally they reach Vishnu himself, who is appearing as Sri Venkateshvara in the form of a black stone statue covered with priceless jewels.

It's said that any wish you make before Sri Venkateshvara *must* come true. Stories abound of extraordinary miracles and healings experienced by Hindus who visit this shrine. Many devotees return with even more expensive gifts for Sri Venkateshvara to express their gratitude for the boon he granted on their last visit. There's no stronger endorsement for a Hindu deity than this kind of repeat business!

Sages Say

"The satisfaction of getting revenge lasts only for a moment. The glory of forgiveness lasts forever."

—*Tirukural* 156

The Statue of Liberation

The United States has the Statue of Liberty. India has Saint Tiruvalluvar. At Kanya Kumari, the very southernmost point of India, you can see the Indian Ocean, the Arabian Sea, and the Bay of Bengal with one sweep of the eyes. You'll also see the spectacular 133-foot statue of Tiruvalluvar towering over the shoreline.

At 151 feet, the Statue of Liberty is a bit taller, but it's only a third the weight of the 7,000-ton Indian statue, which was sculpted by hand by over 150 stone workers. The statue is spanking new, having been completed in the year 2000.

Tiruvalluvar wrote a Tamil spiritual classic called the *Tirukural* ("Holy Verses") some 2,200 years ago. It's one of the greatest masterpieces on religious ethics in world literature. The 1,330 verses of the text are inscribed around the pedestal of the statue.

The Statue of Liberty represents American's highest value and its lasting contribution to world culture: the commitment to personal freedom. The stone statue on India's southern shore represents India's greatest value and *its* greatest gift to the world: a religious tradition devoted to freedom from ignorance, suffering and the wheel of rebirth.

While we're here, take note of the Vivekananda Memorial a few hundred yards away. It was on this rock Swami Vivekananda was sitting when he had a vision of his late guru, Ramakrishna, standing out on the water. Ramakrishna was urgently signaling him to step out into the ocean. Vivekananda took this as a sign that he was supposed to cross the Atlantic and begin teaching Hinduism in America. In 1893, he made the crossing and first introduced modern Westerners to Indian religion.

Krishna's Playground

Swinging back up the western side of India, we have to pause in the holy cities of Mathura and Vrindavan, where many of the enchanting episodes in the life of Lord Krishna unfolded. Krishna was born in Mathura and later reigned there as king. But his childhood romances all occurred in Vrindavan (Brindavan in Hindi), about six miles to the north.

Mathura has been a great city for thousands of years, and was known even to the ancient Greeks following Alexander's visit. But it's hard to get a feel for what the rural area of Vrindavan must have been like 3,500 years ago when Krishna was tending cows there and devastating the milkmaids with glances from his foxy eyes. Now there's so many temples and shrines built in his honor that he wouldn't recognize his old town if he dropped by!

About three million Krishna devotees make the pilgrimage to Vrindavan every year. It's a very active center for religious devotion with singing, ecstatic dancing, worship, and meditation going on at all

Guidepost

Don't be offended if you're denied entrance to a Hindu temple. A number of non-Hindus have behaved so disrespectfully in some temples that the priests have closed the doors to foreigners. The problem isn't you and it isn't the priests. It's immature foreigners whose disdainful behavior spoils the experience for everyone.

Sages Say

"There is just one place where man meets God—right within the heart He dwells as the innermost self. He who seems to be the farthest is the nearest of all."

—Swami Satprakashananda

hours of the day and night as pilgrims seek to recapture the feeling of being in Krishna's living, loving presence.

Seeing the Saints

If Westerners are going to make a pilgrimage all the way to India, often it's the saints, not the temples, they're there to see. Connecting with great yogis and sages is not as easy as you might think. Contrary to popular mythology, you're unlikely to get off the plane at Delhi and find a guru waiting for you, crying breathlessly, "My child, at last you have come!" Most real gurus deliberately play hard to get, because life is short and they only have time for the most serious students. Trusting the flow of karmic forces, they know the legitimate devotees will be guided to the right teacher.

But if it's holy people you want to see, I recommend you make your way to Rishikesh in Uttar Pradesh. There no matter how bad your karma is, you're sure to run into at least a couple of saints.

Rishikesh is about a dozen miles north of the holy city of Hardwar, where the Ganges bursts through a breathtaking gorge to begin its descent into the Indian plains. Rishikesh is less congested than Hardwar, so more sadhus congregate there. It's also where pilgrims come to begin the long trek up to the holy sites of Badrinath, Kedarnath, and Gangotri. These three areas are tougher to get to but serious spiritual practitioners make their way there to bask in the beauty and purified atmosphere of the Himalayas while they worship and meditate.

You'll find plenty of ashrams in Rishikesh. However, for a place that used to be awfully secluded, there's a lot of construction going on these days and it's not as quiet as it used to be. With the modern world encroaching on all sides, it's getting harder to find a quiet, isolated cave to do your spiritual practice in the traditional manner.

The Goddess Drops In

Divine energy doesn't just center itself in places. It also comes through people. Divine possession is commonplace in Hindu culture. The Goddess in particular is fond of selecting special women as her mouthpiece.

When people in the community experience a crisis, they may go to the Goddess's franchise representative, a local village woman who then goes into trance. The Goddess speaks through her, offering advice and blessings. The woman temporarily becomes a living temple through which divine grace radiates.

Divine being is not a theoretical abstraction to Hindus. It is really present in the temple and in the land. It even speaks to Hindus directly through a human oracle when receiving specific instructions is critical. While temples and sacred sites can be focal points for divine energy, the most fluid conduit for divine grace remains the human heart.

Quick Quiz

1. Camphor candles are waved in Hindu temples ...

    a. So you can see your way in the dark.

    b. To express devotion to the deity inside.

    c. To send messages to priests hiding behind a screen.

2. The most popular pilgrimage place on Earth is ...

    a. Mecca.

    b. Tirupati.

    c. Graceland.

3. At the southernmost tip of India is an enormous statue of ...

    a. Mother Teresa.

    b. Swami Vivekananda.

    c. Saint Tiruvalluvar.

4. Hindu temples are mostly empty inside ...

    a. Symbolizing the unmanifest reality.

    b. To make them easier to clean.

    c. Because Hindus are too poor to decorate them.

Answers: 1 (b). 2 (b). 3 (c). 4 (a).

The Least You Need to Know

➤ Hindu temples are constructed to represent inner and outer realities.

➤ Hindus worship primarily not in temples but in their own homes.

➤ India contains the most popular pilgrimage sites in the world.

➤ The Kumbha Mela attracts as many as 70 million pilgrims for a six-week festival.

➤ "Divine possession" allows people to channel advice directly from the Goddess.

Part 5

God's House Has Many Doors

According to Hinduism, there are many entrances to God's house. Let's look at some of the ways inside taught by the Hindu sages. There's the door for people with dynamic personalities who've always got to be doing something. There's another door for people who are all heart. And still another for those who are mostly in their heads. Then there are entrances for technique-oriented people who prefer a systematic approach to spirituality.

Hinduism is not a "one size fits all" religion. Whatever your personality, whatever your circumstances in life, whatever your skills and abilities, the Divine Being will find a way to guide you to the highest point in the universe.

Chapter 20

The Path of Action

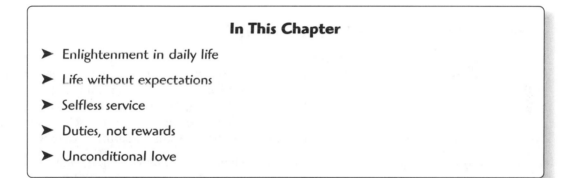

In This Chapter

➤ Enlightenment in daily life

➤ Life without expectations

➤ Selfless service

➤ Duties, not rewards

➤ Unconditional love

Usually when we in the West picture Hindus, we think of the renunciates. We imagine the orange-robed swamis or the naked *babas*. But the vast majority of Hindus are ordinary lay people raising children within the context of the extended family system. Getting up each morning to work.

In Buddhism, it's pretty much understood that if you're serious about spiritual life, you renounce the world and go off to be a monk or nun. The role of lay people is to support the monastics until they build up enough good karma to become monastics themselves. But in Hinduism, working people are just as capable of enlightenment as swamis. Most of the Vedic rishis, the sages who composed the holy Veda, were married and worked for a living.

Renunciates are free to devote their full attention to the quest for Self-realization. Lay people have more balls to juggle. Yet sacred texts like the *Bhagavad Gita* explain how working men and women can transform their daily duties into spiritual discipline—how housewives and washerwomen can become sages and how farmers and shopkeepers can become spiritual masters.

Getting Sacrificed

The word karma comes from the Sanskrit root *kri* which means "to do." You perform some sort of work, and you get paid for it appropriately. Your reward is pleasant or unpleasant depending on the nature of your actions. It's big or small depending on the intensity of your actions.

However, your paycheck doesn't always arrive right away. The reward for your good and bad actions may come after death or in a future incarnation. But come it will. Every expenditure of energy—whether it's a physical act or even a thought—has an inevitable and proportionate effect. The law of cause and effect doesn't just apply in physics and economics. It works in the moral universe as well.

Some Hindus sages asked themselves how we can use this law to our advantage. Others asked how we can get out of it!

Paying Your Way into Paradise

According to the Veda, at the beginning of time Prajapati, the Supreme Being, performed the first act of karma. He sacrificed himself in order to create us. He sacrificed his original state of perfect unity and bliss, splitting his body into the component parts of the material and subtle worlds, and splitting his consciousness into the infinite number of souls inhabiting these worlds.

God set the example for how we ought to live. Our lives should also be based on the principle of self-sacrifice. For yogis who want to return to him, this means reversing the process and sacrificing their individual selfhood back into his Supreme Consciousness.

But most orthodox Hindus are by no means ready to renounce everything they have and everything they are. They would rather continue enjoying life right here, have a sublime experience in a heaven world after death, and finally, after a long and enjoyable stay in heaven, come back for another shot at a pleasant and fulfilling life on Earth.

How to earn brownie points for a healthy and happy life here and an extended, enjoyable vacation hereafter? Easy. You fulfill your social obligations conscientiously. And you perform lots and lots of rituals to the gods. This fills up your karmic credit account with

Sages Say

"The gods need our help as much as the Sun needs us to hold up a candle to light its way. The real reason we make offerings to the gods is to cultivate the spirit of self-sacrifice. We contemplate the divine qualities of the gods and goddesses in order to become more like them, generous, pure and selfless."

—Amritanandamayi Ma

chits you cash after death. The deities you worshipped are now karmically obligated to ensure you get the nicest bungalow in heaven and have a pleasant stay.

Ritual action involves manipulating the law of karma to our advantage. We do good, good comes to us. We benefit the divine forces by sacrificing to them, and they reciprocate by looking after our welfare. Everybody's happy.

Alternatives to Heaven

The path of Karma Yoga, explained by Krishna himself in the *Bhagavad Gita,* turns this whole tradition on its head. Karma Yoga, the path of action, is not about working with the law of karma to create as happy and fulfilling a future as possible. It's about throwing out the karmic process altogether. Its goal is *mukti,* freedom, not *svarga,* heaven.

Remember we talked about the different schools of Indian philosophy (see Chapter 9, "Truth Is a Multi-Layer Cake")? One of the most important was Sankhya. The Sankhya yogis saw both this world and the next as full of suffering. Disease, decrepitude, and death lay everyone low. Evil people and demons like those that cause disease make life miserable for everyone. Besides, you no sooner find something that makes you happy than you start to worry about losing it. Or you get bored with it and start wanting something else.

Heaven is highly overrated, according to these yogis. Even the great souls in the most comfortable bungalows in heaven are constantly looking over their shoulders. They know that when their pool of karmic credit runs dry, it's back to the salt mines on Earth.

If you want to play the karmic game, fine. Hinduism's got plenty of rituals to help you get what you want and plenty of priests who'll perform them for you. But when you start getting tired of being jacked around by life, when chasing after one thing you desire, then another, and then another, finally starts to wear you down, you've got to ask, "Is there a way to turn off the treadmill?" Then Sankhya yogis like Krishna himself show you how to short-circuit the karmic cables that bind you to the endless, repetitive, and ultimately futile attempt to find lasting happiness in the material world.

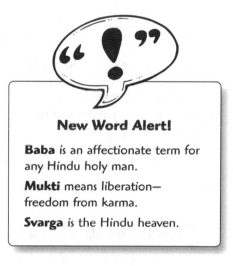

New Word Alert!

Baba is an affectionate term for any Hindu holy man.

Mukti means liberation—freedom from karma.

Svarga is the Hindu heaven.

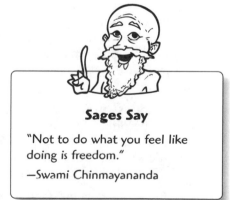

Sages Say

"Not to do what you feel like doing is freedom."

—Swami Chinmayananda

Renouncing the Fruit

You can't get out of doing things. Yet actions have karmic consequences you must experience sooner or later. Karma Yoga gets you out of this double bind. It's simple to understand, but it's tough to practice. It involves cutting the link between cause and effect. You snap the chain of causation in two.

It's News to Me!

People often think of Buddha as sitting under a tree and achieving enlightenment all by himself. The historical reality is that he studied under two Hindu gurus first. One was a Sankhya yogi. The Sankhyas emphasize how painful life is. This may be why the First Noble Truth Buddha taught was "Life is full of suffering."

"Surrender the fruits of your actions to Me," Krishna tells Arjuna in the *Bhagavad Gita*. "Perform your duty without any expectation of reward. Do what you have to do because it's the right thing to do. Not because there's something you want out of it."

If we renounce the fruits of our actions, sacrificing the results to God, we are no longer emotionally bound to suffer or benefit from our actions. We do our job to the best of our ability because that is the work God has put in front of us. Not because we want to be successful or because we need a paycheck. We don't worry about money or success because we've given our lives to God. Let him worry about it!

Then when our biweekly paycheck arrives or we get credit for our excellent work, we count these as gifts from God, not as something that we somehow inherently "deserve." It was God who gave us the intelligence and energy to do the job in the first place. Why shouldn't he get the credit?

Conquering Through Surrender

Karma Yoga involves actively engaging in life, fulfilling our dharma whether that's being a housewife, a police officer, a camel trainer, or a silk merchant. We do the best we can because our everyday actions are our form of worship. Our work—be it ever so humble—is no less valuable spiritually than the inner work a yogi does sitting in meditation—provided that we do it with awareness and without demanding anything in return.

The key to transforming work into worship and external activity into internal purification is attitude. When we simply do the best we can and leave the results to God, we become free. We raise our children to the very best of our ability, but how they turn out is in God's hands. We sow a crop of grain and tend it carefully, but whether there's a bountiful harvest or a flood that wipes it all away is up to God. He carries the burden of our existence. We are free!

In Karma Yoga, we sacrifice our attention. Thoughts that would ordinarily run toward fantasies about the future or romantic liaisons or irritating memories are instead directed to God. "This action is for you, Lord. And this one. And this one too."

Highway to Heaven

Karma Yoga brings peace through action. The paradox is that while the surrendered soul becomes free from worry about the results of his or her actions, those results still occur.

The law of karma still operates in the outer world. But we are psychologically free because our inner world remains unpolluted by the aggravation caused by unrealized expectations or delayed rewards. Or by fear about what may or may not happen. If we're karma yogis, our bodies go through the motions of fulfilling our duties and reaping the consequences. But our souls remain at peace, leaving our fate to God or the Goddess, in whose providence we trust implicitly.

Yoga, not *bhoga,* is the desire of the karma yogi. Yoga here means union with the Divine Will. Bhoga means enjoyment in the world. We may well still enjoy life (with Krishna's help Arjuna won the war and enjoyed the victory, such as it was) but the good things that come to us are now seen as gifts of God's grace—not as the rightful results of our work, as something we have coming.

Sages Say

"Duty done out of selfish motives is far inferior to that done with a detached attitude. When the mind is yoked to the ultimate good through cultivation of detachment, which is the highest form of love, then one takes delight in loving all and excluding none."

—Swami Rama Bharati

Hindus consider Karma Yoga a legitimate path to spiritual liberation because it cultivates a state of desirelessness and egolessness. And when selfishness and desire drop away, so does the karmashaya, the depository of past life karma that we carry around with us in our causal body. There's no emotional glue to make it "stick" to our soul anymore. We are now free from the wheel of rebirth and don't have to reincarnate again, unless we want to for the sake of helping others.

Freedom from Morality?

If you can free yourself from karma, that means you can get out of punishment for bad karma, right? So then you could go out and do all the evil things you've ever fantasized about and not suffer the consequences, right?

A small number of Hindu practitioners have experimented with this perspective. (Hindus have experimented with *everything!*) In theory, if you've got Karma Yoga down to an art, you can get away with murder. There are, however, two major problems with this approach. The first is that if you're still hankering to commit unethical actions, it's unlikely your level of surrender to God is very deep. Without total surrender, you could find yourself in serious do-do karmically.

The second catch (and it's a big one) is that the consequences of your actions still play out. Some years ago, an American-born Tibetan Buddhist teacher decided he was so far beyond the reach of karma and morality that he could freely have unprotected sex with as many of his students as he wanted. Perhaps in his mind he remained in a free and clear state. But on the physical plane he and the disciples he slept with (and their spouses) died of AIDS because of his irresponsible behavior.

The Potter's Wheel

Remember that Karma Yoga arose out of the Sankhya tradition, which splits spirit and matter in two. From this perspective it's the inner spirit that's free from karma, not the outer body. By surrendering to God and acting from the space of the Inner Self, the soul is freed from karma. Inside you remain tranquil no matter how good or how bad circumstances are. But the body may still go through tribulation. Though he totally surrenders to Krishna in the *Bhagavad Gita,* Arjuna suffers horrendous losses, including the death of his son.

In Hinduism, a person who's achieved liberation is called a *jivanmukta,* which means "a soul who's free." In India, where to this day saints aren't rare, you'll see great men and women who go through life in an amazingly tranquil and composed state of mind. Nothing seems to throw them off their center. Yet karma still plays through their lives: they still get sick, still have enemies, may still be unusually lucky or unlucky.

The sages say this is because the life of an enlightened person is like a potter's wheel. When the potter finishes work, she gets up and walks away. Even so, the potter's wheel keeps spinning for a while because it still carries some momentum. Just as the potter is no longer continuing to spin the pot, a jivanmukta is no longer adding to his store of karmic merits and demerits through his desires and expectations. Yet his body keeps moving and his karma keeps playing out because of the karmic momentum of the past. Inside, however, the jivanmukta is free.

Guidepost

Why not experiment with Karma Yoga? If you're intensely aggravated at your job, for example, decide you're simply going to do the very best you can and that's it. It doesn't matter if your boss approves, if you get a raise, if there's a write-up about you in the company newsletter. Do your job well and surrender the results. You may find that you're in a much more relaxed frame of mind and that you work more effectively and efficiently.

New Word Alert!

Bhoga is worldly enjoyment.

A **jivanmukta** is a liberated soul who's still in a physical body.

Action in Inaction

Hindus believe that even the sages who appear to be doing nothing at all immensely enrich society by their mere presence. One of my mentors, Swami Rama Bharati, was raised in a cave monastery in Uttar Pradesh. He was a philanthropist who built a huge hospital facility for the impoverished villagers of the U.P., as well as providing scholarships for numerous poor students (including me!). Yet he bristled at the suggestion that his own teachers, who spent their lifetimes meditating in the Himalayas, were turning their backs on humanity. "The sages protect the world!" he insisted. "The human race would have destroyed itself long ago if not for the blessings the sages send out in their meditation! You have activists who protect the outer environment. Through their pure thoughts and well wishes the Himalayan sages clean out the pollution in the inner environment!"

In deep states of meditation, the yogi's will takes on laser-like intensity and benefits the entire world. This is the supreme Karma Yoga of the masters who appear to be doing nothing at all.

Calling Out the Troops

Swami Vivekananda's explanation of Karma Yoga is illuminating:

> Karma Yoga teaches us how to work for work's sake, unattached. The karma yogi works because it is his nature … and he has no object beyond that. His position in the world is that of a giver, and he never cares to receive anything. He knows that he is giving, and does not ask for anything in return, and therefore he eludes the grasp of misery.

After his guru Ramakrishna died in 1886, Swami Vivekananda spent several years wandering throughout India. The once great Hindu culture had been crushed by centuries of hostile foreign domination. Vivekananda found poverty, corruption, and despair everywhere he traveled.

When he returned to Calcutta, Vivekananda decided it was time to send out the troops. He called on Ramakrishna's other disciples to found a new order dedicated to the service and education of the downtrodden. Some of his fellow disciples were intensely resistant to the idea. They hadn't achieved enlightenment yet themselves. How could they guide others? Wasn't their first priority to illumine themselves before setting out to help others?

Sages Say

"This is the gist of all worship: to be good and to do good to others. He who sees Shiva in the poor, in the weak, and in the diseased really worships Shiva; and if he sees Shiva only in the image, his worship is but preliminary."

—Swami Vivekananda

New Word Alert!

Seva means selfless service.

The **third eye** is the center of intuitive consciousness in the subtle body. Find the point between your eyebrows, then move your awareness about three inches backward toward the center of your brain. This is the focus point of your inner vision.

We grow by benefiting others, Vivekananda insisted. While the concept of *seva* or selfless service has a long history in Hinduism, Vivekananda brought it into sharp focus for modern Hindus. The Ramakrishna Mission he founded would have a huge impact in India, championing the uplifting of the poor and the education of women.

Everyone's Mother

Seva is a major component of Hindu spirituality and an important expression of Karma Yoga. "Our quest for the Self starts with our selfless service in the world," says Ammachi, the great contemporary saint from Kerala.

> If all we do is sit in meditation with our eyes closed, anticipating the third eye will open, we will be disappointed. We cannot escape from the world by keeping our eyes closed. Spiritual practice is the effort we make to see the oneness of all beings in creation with open eyes. When that vision becomes spontaneous, that is Self-realization.

Ammachi (a.k.a. Amritanandamayi Ma) was born in a poor fishing village in southwestern India in 1953. From earliest childhood, she was completely devoted to God. If she caught herself walking several steps without repeating Krishna's name, she would run back and take those steps again keeping the Lord foremost in her mind.

When Ammachi was in her late teens, the Goddess herself in the form of blazing light appeared before her, commanding her to serve humanity, and then merged into her body. Extraordinary miracles began occurring all around her. A small bowl of water suddenly contained enough rice pudding to feed the village. Patients with serious diseases, such as leprosy or malignant cancers, were suddenly healed. Men addicted to gambling or alcohol mended their ways after just one visit to the radiantly loving young saint.

Sages Say

"Sitting in a dark room complaining 'It's dark in here!' is foolish. Open the door and the light will flood in. Complaining you're lonely and empty is also useless. Open the door of your heart by cleaning out your self-centered thoughts and by developing qualities like love and humility. Then God's grace will flow through you in a never-ending stream."

—Amritanandamayi Ma

Unconditional Love

Many Hindus believe Ammachi is an incarnation of the Mother of the Universe. If you have a chance to see her in action, you'll see why. When she travels, millions come rushing to see her. Her ability to connect with every single soul who comes before her is phenomenal. She radiates love, making each person feel like he or she is the one person Ammachi loves most in the world.

Ammachi, Hinduism's "supernova of spirituality."

But here's the really strange thing. At every stop in India, there's a minimum of forty thousand people waiting for Ammachi's blessing. The lines are literally *miles* long. She doesn't get up, not even to eat or go to the bathroom, till she's seen—and physically embraced—every person. Which can take *days*! And when Ammachi finally does get up, she's still as fresh and radiant as she was when she first sat down. I've seen this with my own eyes and can still scarcely believe it. Where does this lady get her batteries? I get exhausted just watching her!

Hinduism Today calls Ammachi "a supernova of spirituality." In 1993, she was named one of the top three Hindu leaders of our time. She embodies unconditional love in the most dramatic way possible, in her every action. When I interviewed her, Ammachi explained that she actually sees God in the face of every person she meets. Her limitless love, and equally limitless energy, arise from her delight in serving God in each of us.

Selfless Service

In the past two decades, Ammachi's charitable projects have expanded to include orphanages, shelters for battered women, a huge hospital complex in Kerala that provides medical care free to the destitute, schools and vocational training institutes, temples and ashrams. One of her current projects is building 1,000 new homes each year to be given free to poor families.

How can a penniless woman from a tiny Indian village inspire millions to help her build huge institutions or to give up their jobs to work unpaid for the benefit of the poor? Ammachi is the quintessential karma yogi. People see her walking her talk. She lives a life of selfless service, working 22 hours a day. Hindus—and increasingly admirers from around the world—are so inspired by her example that they want to join her work.

Hindu culture is perhaps the last place on Earth where many children, like Ammachi, still grow up aspiring to be saints. Charitable organizations abound. There is hardly an ashram that doesn't help provide free food and free medical care for the poor. Seva, selfless service, is an integral part of the Hindu tradition.

Quick Quiz

1. Karma Yoga is ...

   a. Doing your duty without desiring any reward.

   b. A series of physical postures such as the headstand

   c. The yogis' excuse for not working.

2. The goal of Karma Yoga is ...

   a. Life everlasting in heaven.

   b. Scored only if the goalie can be lured from the net.

   c. Freedom from the bondage of karma.

3. Renouncing the fruits of our actions ...

   a. Leads to irresponsible behavior.

   b. Frees us from worry.

   c. Is fine if we can still have the vegetables.

Answers: 1 (a). 2 (c). 3 (b).

Get Up and Fight!

In the *Bhagavad Gita,* Krishna describes several paths to God-realization. These are the paths of devotion, knowledge, and action. Yet given the emergency of impending war, Krishna's specific advice to Arjuna is, "Get up and fight!" But Arjuna is not to fight out of anger or desire for revenge. To fight in this mindset would incur terrible karma. Instead he must go to war because it's his duty to stop an evil tyrant from taking over the country. Whether he ultimately wins or loses isn't as important as taking the action he knows is right.

"People are trapped in the web of their own karma except when they perform their actions as worship of God," Krishna explains. "Therefore do your work as if it is a sacrament. Don't be concerned about the results. Always do your duty, but without attachment. By working honestly without anxiety about the future, you will reach the supreme state."

The Least You Need to Know

➤ Karma Yoga means performing your work to the best of your ability without concern for reward.

➤ Karma yogis rise above the karmic process by not engaging psychologically with the consequences of their actions.

➤ Selfless service is a huge component of Hindu spirituality.

➤ Hindu saints like Vivekananda and Ammachi taught selflessness through their living examples.

➤ Even sitting alone in meditation, yogis are able to transmit blessings throughout the world.

Straight from
the Heart

In This Chapter

➤ Hindu devotionalism

➤ Relating to God

➤ Love makes saints

➤ The holy name

➤ Religious ecstasy

What's the most intoxicating liquor of all? Southern Comfort? Sake? According to the Hindu sages, it's love for God. Devotion is the divine nectar that makes even the most bitter life sweet.

Throughout the millennia, in the same way other countries have been rocked by earthquakes, India has been rocked with convulsions of religious ecstasy. Waves of *bhakti*, massive movements of devotion for God or Goddess, have swept through the subcontinent like shockwaves. Hinduism is a religion of *bhaktas*, of devotees who deeply and truly love their maker.

Bhakti Yoga is the path of the heart. Hindu sages claim it's the quickest way to the Lord of Light whose infinite love embraces all the beings in all the galaxies in all dimensions of time and space.

The Heart and the Head

Recently a student asked Ammachi (the South Indian saint you met in Chapter 20, "The Path of Action") what is the most dangerous spiritual path. He was expecting her to say Tantra and to warn him away from the alleged sensual pitfalls of "the left-hand path." Instead she instantly answered, "The path of the intellect."

The student was astonished. Many Hindu spiritual masters have been intellectuals of the highest caliber. "Reasoning is necessary, but we should not allow the intellect to eat up our heart," Ammachi went on to explain. "Too much intellectual knowledge too often leads to a big ego. The ego is a burden, and a big ego is a big burden."

"Devotion without spiritual knowledge cannot free us," Ammachi continued. "But knowledge without devotion is like eating stones." She pointed to a nearby jackfruit tree. This tree produces fruit near the bottom of the trunk, where you can reach it effortlessly. Her point was that on other paths to God you do a lot of spiritual work first before you begin to experience the divine presence. Rather like having to climb a coconut tree to reach the coconut.

New Word Alert!

Bhakti is love for God or Goddess. Spiritual devotion.

A **bhakta** is a person filled with love for the divine.

"On the path of devotion we can enjoy the fruit from the very beginning," Ammachi concluded. The Goddess's loving presence suffuses our lives the moment we open our heart. Instantly she takes us into her lap, and we feel at home in the very heart of the universe. This is Bhakti Yoga—reaching straight for the cup of joy.

Intellectuals spend a lot of time discussing the nature of Divine Being. Is it conscious or unconscious? Is it one unitary reality or is matter something different from spirit? How does the One split into the manifold universe we see in front of us? Bhaktas aren't overly concerned with these nit-picking details. They just want to hang out with God!

The Divine Relationship

You can't really hang out with an abstraction. At least most people can't. But you can easily relate to another person. So most bhaktas imagine the Divine Being as a sort of Super Person. In the Judeo-Christian-Islamic tradition, there's basically one type of relationship you can have with God. He's the father, you're his child. Hinduism, however, includes a lot of different ways we can relate to the Supreme. For example, we may picture the Divine Being as our:

➤ Father

➤ Mother

➤ Master

➤ Friend

➤ Lover

➤ Child

➤ Enemy

Consider the many different ways people looked at Lord Krishna during his lifetime. To Yasoda, who raised Krishna in the tiny village of Vrindavan, the Lord was her little baby. To Radha and the other milkmaids in Vrindavan, Krishna was their lover. To Arjuna, Krishna was his closest friend.

Hindus still relate to Krishna in these ways. Some Hindu women keep a statue of Krishna as a small child in their homes. They tend to it as if it's their baby! Others look on their own children as baby Krishnas. Still other Hindus carry on a continual internal dialogue with Krishna as if he is their best friend. They feel he is actually present, listening to their problems and providing guidance as he did for Arjuna.

To the Bengali saint Ramprasad Sen (the failed accountant you may remember from Chapter 15, "The Main Denominations"), Divine Being was Mom. He would plead with her and argue with her as if she were his real life mother! Some Hindu saints look at Vishnu or Shiva as their divine father, much as Christians and Jews do.

Sages Say

"Five minutes of sincerely crying to God is worth more than hours of unfocused meditation."

—Amritanandamayi Ma

Many Hindus think of themselves as the servants— even the slaves—of God. Their lives are totally in his hands, and they live only to do his will. Hindu names like Ram Das or Bhagavan Das literally mean "servant of God."

Hating God

You may be surprised to hear that Hindus consider people who hate God to be in better shape spiritually than those who never think about God at all. This is because at least those who see God as their enemy think about him continually. That's all the hold God needs in order to begin doing his transformative work in their lives. He just needs their attention! Remember, Valmiki chanted "Mara, mara" ("Evil, evil") and became a saint because unwittingly he was chanting God's name ("Rama, Rama").

Hindus even believe that being killed by God is the greatest possible blessing! For example, remember that Rama, who was God in human form, killed the cruel king Ravana. At that moment—Ravana went straight to the highest heaven! That's because he'd been obsessing about Rama constantly. Even though his mind was filled with hatred, Ravana was totally focused on Rama at the moment of his death. So God was able to reach into his soul and liberate him instantly. God's grace really is amazing!

The Divine Lover

For Hindus, one of the favorite ways to picture God is as the divine lover. Krishna and Shiva particularly lend themselves to this role—Krishna because he had so many girlfriends and Shiva because he is Kameshvara, the Lord of Desire. When Shiva makes love to his wife, Parvati, he has such perfect yogic control that he never ejaculates. So according to the holy texts, when Shiva and Parvati start getting it on, the action continues for years!

Shaivite saints, like Lalla and Antal, pined for the love of Shiva. The Vaishnava saint Mira Bai literally considered herself married to Krishna—a fact her real-life in-laws didn't appreciate. Some male saints, like Chaitanya, would think of themselves as spiritually female in order to imagine being brides of Krishna.

In the Shakta tradition some images of the Goddess, such as Lalita, are breathtakingly voluptuous. If you're filled with erotic energy, why not redirect that drive toward the divine? Then instead of dragging you off into steamy fantasies, your romantic desires actually help increase your sense of intimacy with the Supreme Being.

God in the Guru

As I mentioned in Chapter 11, "'Can You Show Me God?'" for many Hindus, the guru is the physical embodiment of Divine Being. "The water in which the guru's feet are bathed is the holiest water in the world," says the *Guru Gita*. "This water can wash away your sins, ignite the fire of Self-realization, and carry you to safety across the stormy ocean of this world."

Devotion to the guru is another popular form of Bhakti Yoga. It doesn't require you to be so lucky that you happen to be living at a time and place when an avatar like Rama or Krishna are physically present. The guru is for all practical purposes your equivalent of Rama. And you don't have to use your imagination to visualize a relationship with God. If you honor your guru as a divine embodiment, then God or the Goddess is standing in front of you in the flesh, walking with you and giving personal guidance.

Obviously, care must be taken to ensure the guru truly is Self-realized and is able to actually handle such powerful projections. My personal observation is that the occasional guru lets the adulation go to his or her

Guidepost

Guru gone bad? Occasionally a Hindu teacher begins abusing his or her power. Out of respect for the teacher's spiritual lineage, Hindus rarely publish embarrassing exposes. Instead they quietly withdraw their support. And go find another guru!

head. But most of them take the job of spiritual mentorship very seriously. They are ultimately servants of the Supreme Guru whose wisdom manifests through them when they align themselves with their Highest Self. Being someone's guru is a huge responsibility with major karmic implications.

The vital importance of the guru lineage is another safety valve built into the Hindu system. If you're a guru, you have your own guru and the other masters of your lineage to answer to if you mess up. The disciple answers to the guru, but the guru answers to the lineage.

The Saint Factory

The Hindu tradition is a virtual saint factory, having produced more holy women and men than any other religion. In fact, at any one moment, there are far more fully acknowledged Hindu saints than Catholicism has recognized in its entire 2,000-year history!

What transforms an ordinary person into a saint? Does it happen spontaneously or can you actually go into training to become a saint? Some people are born saints. The Hindu sages explain that this is either because these people have tons of great karma from previous incarnations and spent lifetimes purifying themselves and serving others, or it's because they're visitors dropping in from higher planes of reality.

And other times, well, it just kind of seems like the Goddess picks someone out of the crowd and zaps them!

Spontaneous Combustion

Let's talk about the divine zap. In all cultures, in all times, certain people—with or without any previous interest in spirituality—spontaneously have extremely powerful mystical experiences. There can be incredible feelings of self-transcendence, a tremendous sense of unity with all things, and the feeling of melting into all-pervading awareness. These experiences seem to come out of the blue, but they're so vivid and powerful they shake an individual to the core.

In some cases, the experience is drug induced. In other cases, it's triggered by an accident, a major shock, or even by seeing or hearing something mind-blowingly beautiful. There have been numbers of reports in recent years of people having extraordinary mystical sensations during a near-death experience. In other cases, there doesn't seem to be

It's News to Me!

Hindu psychology focuses mostly on higher states of consciousness. Western psychology focuses mostly on dysfunctional states. Only a few Western psychologists, like Abraham Maslow, have emphasized the value of "peak states" or mystical experiences.

any trigger at all. You're just walking across the room when—*zap!*—your awareness explodes out of your body and you experience yourself merging into the universe.

Yogis attribute these events to the sudden temporary triggering of kundalini, the energy underlying consciousness, which causes an abrupt awakening to mystical awareness. It could be a fluke and never occur again. Or it may be that the person did lots of meditating in a previous incarnation and is just now reawakening to inner life. Then again, it may just be the whim of God. "He chooses whom He chooses," the *Upanishads* say rather wistfully.

But for the vast majority of people, mystical awareness is something you have to work at developing, like any other skill. What turns average people on to God as opposed to soccer or real estate development?

Four Motives for Devotion

In the *Bhagavad Gita,* Krishna says there are four conditions under which people turn to God.

First there are those who are in big trouble. There is nothing like a life crisis to turn the mind to religion! Someone's sick or dying, his house is about to be swept away in a flood, or he's going to lose his job. Suddenly the devotee is on his knees pleading to Krishna to save him from calamity.

Then there's the person who wants something really, really badly but can't get it on her own. It could be a great job for which she's less qualified than other applicants, a potential boyfriend who doesn't seem attracted to her, or a new house that's out of her price range. She's on her knees begging the Lord for the blessing she desires so desperately.

Next there's the type who just wants to understand. Who is God really? How does karma operate? What are worlds in other dimensions like? The quest for knowledge is their burning motivation. They're so boggled by the beauty and complexity of the universe that they spontaneously turn to its living source in worship and wonder.

The final type is the one who loves God for God's sake alone. God is just so lovable! There's no ulterior motive. There's just love. Krishna says he's delighted to accept the prayers of each kind of devotee. But the soul who delights him most is the one who comes to him out of pure, unselfish devotion.

Sages Say

"If I say God is within me, it sounds like blasphemy. If I say He's not in me, it's a lie. In God the inner and outer worlds are one world. He rests His feet on both."

—Kabir

Deepening Devotion

Once an interest in spiritual life is aroused, how do you increase your enthusiasm? The pressing affairs of our mundane life intrude from all sides. Diverting our attention to a nonphysical entity like God comes naturally to a handful of innately mystically inclined individuals, but for most of us it takes some effort. Here are some of the tried-and-true methods bhaktas use to deepen their connection with the divine.

Satsang: Spiritual Fellowship

Satsang means keeping company with fellow devotees. The mutual support of others with similar interests, especially those further along the path, can be a continual source of inspiration. Seeking out the company of a God-intoxicated mystic is the best form of satsang short of the ecstatic experience of God's presence itself. Reading books about gods and saints and keeping their pictures around is a second-tier form of satsang.

Kirtan: Making a Joyful Noise

Kirtan means singing about God or the Goddess. Frequently bhaktas get together to chant the glories of the Divine and sing the beautiful hymns of longing and love composed by the saints. Devotional music is a particularly soul-stirring form of worship. "Kirtan is the calling, the crying, the reaching across infinite space—digging into the heart's deepest well to touch and be touched by the Divine Presence," says singer Jai Uttal.

Smarana: Divine Obsession

Smarana means remembering God throughout the day. You constantly think about the superlative attributes of the divine: his strength, nobility, purity. Her power, love, grace. Reading the inspiring stories in Hinduism's holy scriptures helps. So does chanting your mantra. Eventually even your dreams are imbued with divine remembrance.

Archana: Ritual Practice

Archana is ritual worship. Several times a day you sit down before your home altar to make a living connection with the Supreme by enacting a short ceremony of worship and prayer. It's like making a telephone call to God, keeping in regular contact. Going through the physical motions of a ritual is especially helpful for people who need something external to focus on in order to keep their minds concentrated.

Guidepost

Don't waste time sleeping! Yogis worship and meditate even in the dream state. In laboratory experiments, advanced yogis, hooked up to EEG equipment, have proven they can remain fully conscious while their brains are sleeping.

Atma Nivedana: **Surrendering Your Attention**

Atma Nivedana means offering your innermost being to God. This is total self-surrender, offering not just your stream of thoughts but your continual awareness back to its source in Divine Being. Staying in a state of spiritual balance like this isn't easy at first. It's like learning to ride a bicycle. Once you get the hang of it, you're just naturally in balance.

Good Company

I mentioned satsang, spiritual fellowship. It's the root practice of Bhakti Yoga. As anyone who's tried to start a fire by rubbing two sticks together knows, fires don't start easily! But if someone brings you a burning stick from the campfire they've already got going, you can ignite your pile of twigs and dried leaves effortlessly.

The guru, and other devotees farther along the path, have already got their fires roaring. When you spend time with them, you see love for God actually happening. You see spirit being lived. For many the effect is galvanizing. Saints who're enlivened with shakti, with divine energy, transmit it to others as if they're spiritual tuning forks.

Some people's spiritual batteries have run down so low that they have to be repeatedly jump-started before they're able to keep their inner light glowing. Once your own light starts burning night and day, whether anyone's there to pump you up or not, you are now a bhakta, a genuine devotee.

Sages Say

"Kirtan is singing over and over the many names of God and the Goddess, the multicolored manifestations of the One. It is said that there is no difference between the name and that which is being named, and as the words roll off our lips in song, the infinite is invoked, invited, made manifest in our hearts."

—Jai Uttal

What's in a Name?

Who's your God? The form of God or Goddess you relate to most naturally, the face of the divine you love most dearly, is your *Ishta Devata.* This is your beloved deity, your personal divine contact. Hindus relate to their Ishta Devata somewhat as Christians think of their guardian angels. The personal deity shields you from harm and guides you through life by supplying just the right information or just the right experiences at just the right time. In another sense, the Ishta Devata is your own Higher Self.

An important technique many Hindus use to cement their relationship with the deity is to chant the God or Goddess's name constantly. *Nama Japa* or "chanting the name" purifies the mind, opens the heart, makes the subtle body vibrant and the physical body healthy, and surrounds the devotee with a vibratory aura of protection and blessing.

For Hindus the name of God *is* God. To name him or her is to invoke the Divine's living presence. It's said that in the beginning you chant the name. Then the name chants you. You no longer have to make a conscious effort to repeat it. It repeats itself in the echo chambers of your mind. This doesn't mean you're continually distracted by the syllables humming in your head! When you have to focus your attention on the job in front of you, the divine name shifts into the background of your awareness. You no longer hear the sound, but the *feeling* doesn't stop resonating in your heart.

A teacher of mine told me about an elderly Hindu woman who locked herself in her room to spend the last few years of her life doing Nama Japa, chanting the name of her Ishta Devata. Her devotion was extraordinarily intense. After her death, people claimed they could still hear the mantra sounding in her room. My teacher thought they were exaggerating. But when he stopped by her room and pressed his ear to the wall, he swears he could actually hear God's name sounding over and over again!

New Word Alert!

Your **Ishta Devata** is your personal deity, the God or Goddess you're closest to.

Nama Japa is constant repetition of God's or the Goddess's name.

All Blissed Out

In Hinduism, there are manuals for everything, even for love. Two of the famous manuals for lovers of God are the *Narada Bhakti Sutras* and the *Shandilya Bhakti Sutras*. Bhakta literature lists certain signs that a person is entering higher and higher grades of spiritual ecstasy. Some of these signs are:

➤ The bhakta spontaneously weeps with love.

➤ The hair stands on end. (With joy, not horror!)

➤ The bhakta collapses or rolls on the ground in ecstasy.

➤ The devotee sings or dances in total self-abandonment.

➤ The devotee slips into ecstatic trance.

➤ The devotee is always radiant.

➤ Miracles occur in the bhakta's presence.

It's important to note that there's a distinction between genuine states of spiritual ecstasy and mental illness or epilepsy! Unbalanced or physically sick people often emerge from similar sorts of "fits" frightened and unable to cope. Bhaktas experience "fits" of divine love and come out refreshed, joyful, and transformed in the most positive ways.

Advice from the Source

In the *Bhagavad Gita,* Krishna distinguishes between three levels of devotees. The purest, he says, worship the one God in any of his manifold forms out of sheer love. The middle group is really only "using" God, hoping he'll help them in their quest for wealth and power. The lowest type worships ghosts and evil spirits. Lower types may also practice asceticism to such an extreme that they practically destroy their bodies, a practice of which Krishna strongly disapproved. He taught that the body was the temple of spirit and must be kept in good health.

The appropriate practice for bhaktas, Krishna said, is "respect for the gods and goddesses, the forces of nature, the saints, sages and gurus. You should be guileless, honest, clean, and have your sex drive firmly under your control. Speak the truth but without causing pain to others. Study the holy books every day. And don't talk too much!"

"Remain calm and tranquil," Krishna continued. "Be kind to others. Always act with the highest integrity. And for some time every day pull your awareness away from the outer world. Pull it even out of your body, and focus on your Inner Self. When you act in the world, dedicate all your actions to the Supreme Being. In this manner you will come to Me."

Quick Quiz

1. When your kundalini is suddenly activated you may …

    a. Spontaneously experience the unity of all being.

    b. Be able to receive broadcast TV programs in your mind.

    c. Be eligible for disability benefits.

2. According to Hinduism, hating God …

    a. Leads straight to the lowest pit of hell.

    b. Is a legitimate form of relationship with the divine.

    c. Can be perfected through Hatha Yoga and vegetarianism.

3. One sign that a bhakta is entering higher states is she …

    a. Locks herself in her room and cries all the time.

    b. Is radiant with love.

    c. Starts running full-color ads advertising her seminars.

4. Ishta Devata means …

    a. Rolling on the ground in ecstasy.

    b. Torturing your body in order to experience your Inner Self.

    c. The God or Goddess you're mostly closely linked to.

Answers: 1 (a). 2 (b). 3 (b). 4 (c).

The Easiest Path—Or the Hardest?

Hindu saints frequently recommend Bhakta Yoga as the easiest and most enjoyable path into the Divine presence. Some strict Hindu practitioners avoid rich foods as a form of self-denial. Yet often when you attend bhakta gatherings you'll find all kinds of sweets laid out on the table. They're a reminder that God's love is sweet and that walking the path of devotion is life's greatest pleasure.

But when you read the requirements for Bhakta Yoga Krishna spells out in the *Gita,* you begin to suspect the path of devotion isn't all singing, dancing, and dessert! "Don't hate or harm any creature. If you truly love Me, you'll love everyone," Krishna says. Easier said than done! "Don't kid yourself that anything belongs to you. Everything in this universe is Mine alone." He continues:

> A real bhakta is serene, forgiving, content, and self-controlled. My devotee is constantly engaged in meditation. Nothing disturbs the one who trusts in Me. My bhakta is unswayed by fear or jealousy, and doesn't desire anything in this world but Me. Whatever occurs in life, he remains relaxed. He doesn't dread the difficulties of life, or waste time grieving over what he's lost.

> Friend and enemy—My bhakta honors them both. Praise and blame—they're both the same to him. His thoughts are always running toward Me, and his heart is always brimming with love.

True bhakti is a tall order. God is present in everyone and everything. If you *really* love God, you love the Divine everywhere it appears. Even in your worst enemy. Even in your worst nightmare. The lightness of heart that comes from such total surrender is moksha: freedom and enlightenment.

Pitfalls on the Path

Could a path that's all about love possibly have any pitfalls? There are plenty, actually. Unfortunately there *is* an all too common shadow side to bhakti.

Some of the serious problems people on the path of devotion need to watch out for are ...

➤ Imagining your surging emotions are the highest possible state of spirituality.

➤ Mistaking your own opinions for the will of God.

➤ Fanatic devotion to your ideal that begins excluding and condemning others.

➤ Developing a fortress mentality. "Anyone who isn't with us is against us."

The *Yoga Vasishtha* explains that devotion to the Divine and selfless, ethical actions—Bhakta Yoga and Karma Yoga—are the two wings of the bird of authentic spiritual life. Without both wings, the bird can't fly. But the tail feathers, the "rudder" the bird uses to navigate, is reason and common sense. Without the guidance of the intellect, religious emotionalism can spill over into blind and destructive fanaticism.

The Least You Need to Know

➤ Bhakti Yoga is the spiritual path of devotion.

➤ Some people have spontaneous flashes of cosmic consciousness due to the abrupt activation of kundalini. Others turn to God out of fear, desire, wonder, or love.

➤ Bhakti Yoga offers methods to help deepen your relationship with the Divine.

➤ Emotionalism that abandons rationality completely can lead to trouble.

Chapter 22

The Razor in the Mind

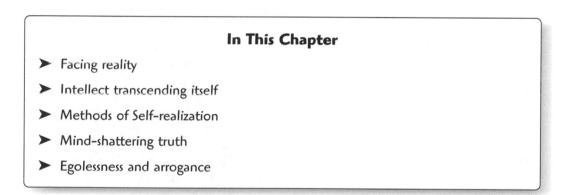

In This Chapter

➤ Facing reality

➤ Intellect transcending itself

➤ Methods of Self-realization

➤ Mind-shattering truth

➤ Egolessness and arrogance

Imagine a tornado. It sweeps through a neighborhood with devastating force. But what is this monster, really? It's just air—like the air inside it and the air outside it. Looking at it you'd think the funnel had some kind of independent reality. Yet as the currents feeding it simmer down, the killer storm dissolves back into its source—thin air.

Part of the magic of a tornado is its eye. If you could sit in the center of the swirling storm, you'd find that the air is absolutely motionless. It's calm, peaceful and perfectly safe! And when the tornado dies, that tranquil eye merges seamlessly into the atmosphere around it. Which it really was part of the whole time.

Jnana Yoga, the path of Self-awareness, is the mind's attempt to understand the storm of life and the calm eye of the Inner Self. When intellectual understanding matures into experiential realization, the tornado ends. The Inner Self merges back into the all-pervading consciousness from which it was never really separated in the first place.

Lead Me from the Unreal

At the ashram where I lived, several times a day we'd chant one of the oldest prayers in the world. It comes from the *Rig Veda* and in English it goes, "Lead me from unreality to truth. Lead me from darkness to light. Lead me from death to immortality."

Jnana Yoga leads from ignorance to Self-knowledge. The metaphor usually used to explain this transition involves a snake that's not a snake. You're walking through the forest on your way back to your village on a moonless night. Suddenly you see a cobra coiled in the path before you. You freeze. One false move and it could strike. And that would be the end of you!

Sages Say

"There's no difference between the air in a jar and air everywhere else. Nor is there any difference between the consciousness within you and the consciousness that pervades the universe. Stop imagining that you're separate from the Supreme Consciousness! Enter the inner stillness where truth resides!"

—Viveka Chudamani

You stand there for minutes that seem like hours, paralyzed with fear. Eventually you notice that the snake hasn't moved. I mean, it hasn't moved *at all*. You build up your courage, take a tentative step forward, and look more closely. Turns out it's not a snake at all, just a piece of coiled rope someone had left on the path.

You're giddy with relief. You also feel a little foolish. You had reacted as if your life was in jeopardy when in fact there was no danger at all. The master jnana yogi Shankaracharya says that's what enlightenment is like. At first you think this world is a big, scary place that sooner or later is going to kill you. Then you finally realize that it's all God. It's absolutely nothing but Divine Consciousness. When you *really* see that, when you know it in your gut, fear vanishes forever. Now you're a jivanmukta, a liberated sage.

Confronting the Snake

Here's another way to look at it. You're walking through the forest on a moonless night. Apparently someone's dropped a coiled rope in the path. You stop to kick it out of the way. Instantly the snake you mistook for a rope sinks its venomous fangs into your leg. And that's the end of you!

You can't be too careful because ignorance is a dangerous thing. Ignorance, called avidya or "lack of knowledge" in Sanskrit, leads from death to death. "Everything you see here is that one Supreme Reality. That one Being is everything everywhere. He travels from death to death who imagines there is any difference," warns the *Katha Upanishad*.

Most of us are caught up in maya, the illusion that the snake is a rope or the rope is a snake. But the illusion itself is an illusion! Because never at any point in the process were the snake or the rope anything other than themselves. The entire cosmos is not and never has been anything other than Divine Being. We need to get this straight. And straightening out our misperception is what Jnana Yoga is all about. It helps us see the universe *as it really is*. As God sees it, you might say.

Got What It Takes?

Jnana Yoga is a tough path. It ain't for everyone. The path is straight, but it's awfully steep. Centuries ago, the great philosopher-yogi Shankaracharya traveled around India setting up monasteries where monks could devote themselves to this form of spiritual practice. But the entrance exam was rough.

As Shankaracharya explained, there are four requirements you have to meet before you can think seriously of getting on this path.

First, you need to be able to discriminate between the eternal and the noneternal. Okay, what's that mean? It means you have to recognize that everything in this world, including your life, is fleeting. But that behind this world there's an abiding Reality that endures forever. If this isn't 100 percent clear to you, another path like Bhakti Yoga or Karma Yoga might be more appropriate for you.

Second, you must have Karma Yoga under your belt already. If you're still craving fame or success, sex, drugs or rock 'n' roll, forget it! Jnana Yoga requires intense concentration. Desires will distract your mind. This intensely mental path demands freedom from distraction. All your actions and all your desires must be fully surrendered to the divine so that you can focus not on the noneternal, like just about everyone else, but on the eternal, like the great masters and mystics.

Third, you've got to have your psychological and ethical act together. In other words, virtue must be your second nature. You're already tranquil, even-minded, honest, and self-controlled. If you're not, the power that comes with the superior will power and laser-like mental focus developed on this path could be misused. This is the sort of thing that happened to Rama's arch-enemy Ravana. He started out as a yogi focused on Lord Shiva. But he wound up misapplying the tremendous mental power he developed and started exploiting others.

Fourth, your desire for liberation must be real. If it's not incredibly strong, there's no way you'll reach the goal on this difficult path. Jnana Yoga is not for dabblers. Nor is it for intellectuals who

Guidepost

Think you're smart? Surprisingly, Hindu gurus often advise bright people to take up the path of devotion, not Jnana Yoga. That's because very intelligent people often benefit more by learning to open their hearts. Jnana Yoga is not so much for intellectuals as for people with a strongly developed mystical sense and a burning desire for the actual experience of God-realization.

want to read all about spirit but aren't prepared to make the sacrifices necessary to actually experience the Divine Reality. Anyone with reasonable intelligence can become a pandit. But very few have what it takes to become a Self-realized sage.

Study, Think, Act!

Once you and your guru have decided Jnana Yoga is the right path for you, you don't have far to go. According to Shankaracharya, there are only three steps on the path to spiritual illumination.

Step 1 is *shravana,* intensive study. It begins with listening to the words of the guru and reading the scriptures carefully. But the point is to develop the intellect as a tool for Self-realization, not just for shooting the breeze with fellow eggheads. If you can, proceed to Step 2.

Step 2 is *manana.* This means contemplating what you've learned intellectually till it actually becomes your own. Till you really, deeply understand it and live it. You can't just sit around memorizing scriptures. You've got to assimilate what they say. It's easy enough to parrot, "My Inner Self is one with the eternal Reality." But do you really grasp what that means? Do you sense its actual truth? When you start to get it, really get it, then proceed to Step 3.

New Word Alert!

Shravana is listening to the words of the guru and carefully studying the scriptures.

Manana means deeply contemplating the spiritual truth you've been taught.

Nididhyasana means deeply contemplating your own Inner Self.

Step 3 is *nididhyasana.* This is your practicum. Stop worrying about what your guru says. Stop memorizing the holy texts. No more focus on anything outside yourself. You've got to stop and actually get to know that Divine Reality the teachers and the texts are talking about. This means diving deep into your own spirit. Paying attention to your inner states. Going beyond the thoughts and images in your mind to the pure awareness behind them. And finally going beyond your own consciousness into cosmic consciousness, the divine light that holds you and every other thing in its illumined awareness. This inner act turns the truths voiced in the *Upanishads* into your actual living experience.

Truths to Chew On

The sages pulled four great sayings from the scriptures, one from each of the four Vedas, for jnana yogis to chew on. These are …

➤ *Prajnanam Brahma*—The Supreme Reality is illumined awareness.

➤ *Aham Brahmasmi*—I am the Supreme Reality.

➤ *Tat Tvam Asi*—You are that Divine Being.

➤ *Ayam Atma Brahma*—The Inner Self is the Supreme Consciousness.

Some Buddhist monks contemplate koans, perplexing statements designed to shatter the rational mind and carry human consciousness to a higher level of clarity. These four statements are the koans of the Vedic tradition, except that they're not perplexing at all. In fact, they're the simplest statement of the ultimate truth, "I and the Supreme are One."

Jnana yogis contemplate these truths until their living reality unfolds itself in their experience. They shut everything out of their awareness except awareness itself and ride it to its source. By stabilizing their attention in the unchanging eternal reality of Divine Consciousness, they transcend birth and death and achieve true immortality. The drop is assimilated back into the ocean. The spark falls back into the fire. The racing wind of the tornado dissolves back into still air.

Sages Say

"The divine fragrance of the Inner Self is overwhelmed by the awful stench of our petty thoughts and desires. But foul odors disappear when you rub a stick of sandalwood, which fills the air with its own sweet smell. Rub your mind with the thought, 'I am Brahman. I am the Supreme Reality,' and your mind will be become pure and fragrant."

—Shankaracharya

Living Like a Tortoise

In the *Bhagavad Gita*, Krishna spells out the essentials of Jnana Yoga. "That which truly exists will never stop existing. The Supreme Reality which pervades the universe has always existed and always will. You are that Reality. Bodies die but the awareness which inhabits the body lives on. It is impossible to kill it." Krishna continues:

> The Inner Self was never born. It will never die or ever change. You, the Inner Self, drop one body and put on another like a change of clothes. This Inner Self is not harmed by weapons or affected by the elements. That which is born must die. That which dies must be reborn. But the One who dwells within is never born and never dies.

> Like a tortoise drawing its legs back into its shell, draw your attention out of your body into your innermost spirit. He who controls his senses and withdraws his mind into the undying spirit, lives beyond birth and death. I call him enlightened.

Krishna tells Arjuna to dive into the changeless heart of Reality and experience deathless awareness. At the same time, he had to keep his day job. Enlightenment doesn't just mean sitting around like a vegetable merged in cosmic consciousness (although that option may be available). For Krishna, it means living an active life, fulfilling your duties and responsibilities, while merged in cosmic consciousness. Now that's real mastery!

It's News to Me!

Jnana Yoga is an extremely ancient path going back to the time of the *Upanishads* at the very least. But the form in which it's best known to Hindus today was popularized more than 12 centuries ago by Shankaracharya and his main disciples, Mandana Mishra, Sureshvara, Padmapada, and the rather dull Totaka, who in the end turned out to be the brightest student of them all.

Knowing the Unknowable

Jnana Yoga is a mental path, yet the mind can never know the truth. The truth is too big. The mind is too small. When the *Apollo* spacecraft bound for the Moon blasted off, the bottom stage of the rocket—filled with the fuel needed to blow the space vehicle off the earth's surface—was ejected and fell back to Earth. Think of intellect as the booster rocket for soul. Intellect helps propel inner awareness into the vast, still cosmos of consciousness. Intellect can't go there itself, but it can point you in the right direction and give you a lift upward.

Reality is mind blowing. God/Goddess is utterly beyond human comprehension. But because the innermost core of human awareness comes straight from the heart of divine awareness, all it needs to do is lapse back into its true nature and it abides in the divine. The mind shatters itself to free the inner spirit.

Junior Level Masters

Does spiritual illumination happen all at once or in stages? Some yogis say the moment of liberation is like flipping on a light switch. The light doesn't come on gradually. The room fills with illumination instantaneously. There is no darkness left anywhere.

Other sages frankly discuss different levels of mastery. Depending on the intensity of your level of practice, and how much spiritual work you've already done in previous lives, enlightenment may come quickly or slowly. And, disconcertingly, it may not stay! The *Tripura Rahasya* describes three levels of *jnanis,* of "knowers" or Self-realized sages. Which level you're at depends on how fully you've established yourself in the field of enlightenment.

Level One: Remembering and Forgetting

Level-one *Manda* yogis have experienced spiritual illumination, but they're not yet able to remain fully focused in that state. It's like going to see a movie. If it's a good film, most of us completely forget ourselves and become wrapped up in the characters and plot. This is exactly analogous to the way the mind forgets its true nature, Divine Consciousness, and gets caught up in the drama playing in the external world. Level-one yogis sit in the theater remembering who they really are, experiencing their inherent divine nature. And then the movie gets so exciting they forget their real nature and are caught up in the maya again.

These beginning-level jnanis remember and forget. Sometimes you sit with them and you're convinced they're fully realized masters. The next time you see them they seem just like average people. Their attention fluctuates between the inner and outer worlds. Treading the path of Jnana Yoga is like walking on a razor's edge, the *Upanishads* say, because the mind can slip so quickly from its focus on the inner reality.

New Word Alert!

Jnani literally means "knower." A Self-realized sage. This is someone who knows the truth from direct experience, not just a person who knows *about* it. (Think of the related English word "gnostic.")

Manda yogis have experienced enlightenment but can't hold their attention there indefinitely—they slip back out into ordinary awareness.

Madhyama yogis are continually absorbed in deep mystical states and are barely able to function in the external world.

Uttama yogis are permanently established in enlightened awareness and fully functional in the physical world at the same time.

Level Two: Mad Mystics

Eventually the jnani reaches a stage where she becomes almost totally engrossed in the Inner Self. At this point, it becomes as difficult for her to bring her attention back to the external world as it is for most of us to center our awareness in the inner world. These saints, called *madhyama* yogis, may seem crazy or dysfunctional. They may sit without moving for hours on end or lose the ability to speak comprehensibly.

Sometimes jnanis at this stage have to be taken care of like small children. Ramakrishna and Anandamayi Ma both temporarily lost the ability to feed themselves and had to be force fed by disciples. Neem Karoli Baba had to be reminded to go to the bathroom or he would forget about his bodily functions altogether!

Level Three: Full Mastery

In the highest state of realization, a person can attain while still in a physical body, he or she gains full mastery of both the inner and outer worlds. "He remains in the world, but above it," as my teacher Swami Rama would say. His awareness never leaves the Supreme, yet he's able to function quite normally in the world. This adept, called an *uttama* yogi, becomes a fountain of blessings as the Higher Self pours its grace through him in the form of inspiration, healing and blessings that engulf those fortunate enough to enjoy his company.

Finding What You Never Lost

Karma yogis want to live in the world without anxiety, and at the end of life, to be free from the bondage of karma that keeps drawing us back to death after death. Bhakti yogis want God or the Goddess's company. Love is its own reward and there is no greater love than the Divine.

Sages Say

"Rama didn't remember that he was an incarnation of God till the sages helped reawaken him to his true identity by praising him as Lord Vishnu. We also are identical to the Highest Being. We also have to be reminded who we really are."

—Totaka, disciple of Shankaracharya

Jnana yogis want to actually *be* God. This doesn't mean they think they'll now be lord of the universe and everyone else will worship them. It means they recognize their innermost nature is identical in essence with God's, just as the air in a jar (signifying the body) is the same as the air outside a jar. To attain Self-realization is not to obtain anything new. It's simply to consciously recognize what has always been true anyway: that you and the Supreme Being are, always have been, and always will be one in essence.

Some Western psychologists mock this goal as a desire to "return to the womb." Which only shows that they miss the point completely. Jnanis aren't negating themselves in a retreat from life but expanding their awareness to the ultimate extent possible. They seek to literally embrace the living cosmos permeated with Divine Consciousness. They're not running away from reality but running toward its fullest possible expression.

Center of Joy

There's the famous Hindu tale of the musk ox that searches everywhere for the heavenly fragrance it smells all around itself. It doesn't realize the fragrance comes from its own body. Just so, jnanis say, most people search everywhere for happiness, everywhere but where happiness really lies. Which is in one's own Self.

Hindu texts like the *Vijnana Bhairava* point out that in moments of rapt ecstasy like during sexual climax or while eating really excellent premium ice cream, your mind isn't running to the future or the past. It's totally focused and it's totally present. At that moment the nature of the Self manifests and you experience rapture.

The Inner Self and the Supreme Reality, to the extent that they can be characterized at all, have three qualities according to Shankaracharya: being, awareness, and bliss. We imagine that objects outside ourselves make us happy. But really they're just serving as focal points to put us in touch with the rapture that's always inside us. Though we're usually not focused enough to feel it!

The jnani aims for the highest possible goal, the absolute bliss at the center of the universe. The absolute bliss at the center of one's Self. That is the highest state of consciousness. That is the underlying reality from which this universe appears to arise, like the snake that temporarily appears in the harmless piece of rope. And it's found at the center of one's Self.

From the point of view of duality, Shankaracharya admitted, universes appear to come and go. Our minds superimpose them on Divine Being the same way the fellow in the forest superimposed a snake on the rope. But what exists forever, the realization of which the *Upanishads* assure us leads to immortality, is absolute being, awareness, and bliss.

It's News to Me!

Gold rings, gold necklaces, gold bracelets. See all the beautiful golden objects? A jnani sees only gold. The shapes come and go. It's the gold itself that's real and valuable. Jnanis shift their attention from the forms consciousness takes, like you and me and the galaxy, to consciousness itself, the everlasting reality.

The Most Dangerous Path

The *Upanishads* say that to walk the path of Jnana Yoga is to tread the razor's edge. The intellect can lead you toward the Supreme, or it can lead you astray. Avidya, self-delusion, is an ever-present danger.

The Hindu tradition is full of tales of warning. There was the pandit with a huge following who continually repeated, "Everything is One. I am that one Supreme Reality. You are that one Supreme Reality." Then one day his wife forgot to add salt to his dish of stewed beans and vegetables. The pandit was furious. "If everything is consciousness and there's no distinction between anything, how can you even tell there's no salt in the beans?" his wife taunted.

Even Shankaracharya himself slipped up from time to time. In one very famous episode, he was about to enter a Shiva temple but discovered a dead body on the steps. The dead man's widow was wailing with grief. For Hindus, corpses are psychically polluting, so Shankaracharya gruffly told the low-caste woman to get her husband out of the way so people could enter the temple without contaminating themselves.

"Aren't you the teacher who says there's nothing but Divine Consciousness any-where?" the woman cried. "What is it you see in my husband's dead body that isn't divine?" Shankaracharya was a great enough soul to recognize words of truth when he heard them. He prostrated before the widow and thanked her for the lesson.

Confronting the Elephant

Then there was the disciple who took the teachings so seriously that when he saw a charging elephant, he stepped out into the street anyway thinking, "I am the Reality. The elephant is the Reality. It's all Divine Awareness." The elephant's owner screamed at him, "Get out of the way!" But the disciple remembered his guru's instructions about maintaining perfect fearlessness and walked straight in front of the elephant.

Needless to say, the disciple spent months flat on his back recovering from his in-juries. "This is what I get for believing your teaching!" he yelled at his guru. "I should never have listened to you!"

"What you should have done, you idiot," his guru answered, "was listen to the man who owned the elephant and get out of the way. He was the Supreme Reality, too!"

Quick Quiz

1. Jnana Yoga leads to …

    a. Intellectual brilliance.

    b. The living experience of Self-realization.

    c. Getting bitten by a snake.

2. Jnana Yoga consists of …

    a. Studying, contemplating, and meditating on the Self.

    b. Making other people feel dumb.

    c. Uncoiling a rope.

3. If an elephant charges, a jnani should …

    a. Merge into the elephant's consciousness.

    b. Call the local zoo.

    c. Get out of the way.

4. The Inner Self is like …

    a. The eye of a tornado.

    b. The eye of a needle.

    c. The eye of a potato.

Answers: 1 (b). 2 (a). 3 (c). 4 (a).

Practical Transcendence

There are two common problems that arise on the path of Jnana Yoga.

The first is gaining some intellectual knowledge and then thinking that you know something. Immature jnanis are frequently criticized for their arrogance. Jnana is not knowledge about Reality. It is the living experience of the Reality. People with a lot of facts in their heads can be quite vain about it. But real jnanis, those who actually live in Divine Being, are impressive for their deep humility.

Fully realized masters don't just see the divine in themselves. They see it in everyone. This is not an ego-inflating experience. On the contrary, it opens the heart to all living things. This is why universal love is a quality Krishna and the other sages so often associate with real jnanis.

The second problem half-baked jnanis may run into is lack of practicality. From time to time, the Jnana tradition has come under criticism for contributing to a sense of otherworldliness and a lack of concern for the horrible suffering and injustice in the material world.

Different saints have different missions. It may not be the purpose of all sages to solve our social problems. But it's clear from the *Bhagavad Gita* that Krishna himself saw Jnana Yoga as an adjunct to effective and successful life in the world, not as a retreat from it. One of the most famous jnanis of all time, King Janaka of Videha, remained in a state of God-realization while ruling a kingdom. Spiritual illumination ultimately increases a soul's ability to bless and serve the world.

The Least You Need to Know

➤ Jnana Yoga is a mental path leading to the actual experience of Self-realization.

➤ The path of knowledge has three steps: intensive study, contemplation of the truths you've studied, and meditation.

➤ A jnani may go through several stages before stabilizing in fully enlightened awareness.

➤ Jnana Yoga simply makes us aware of who we really are and always have been.

➤ Jnani yogis have to be careful not to confuse intellectual understanding with genuine Self-realization.

Chapter 23

The Royal Road

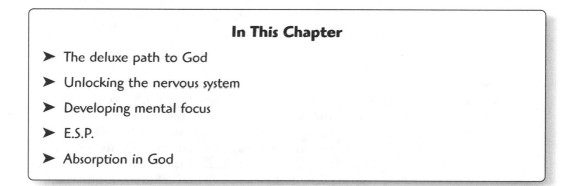

In This Chapter

➤ The deluxe path to God

➤ Unlocking the nervous system

➤ Developing mental focus

➤ E.S.P.

➤ Absorption in God

Around the beginning of the twentieth century, Swami Vivekananda wrote a series of highly influential books called *Karma Yoga, Bhakti Yoga, Jnana Yoga,* and *Raja Yoga.* These popular little volumes first introduced the West to Hinduism's time-tested methods of God-realization.

Raja Yoga, the "royal path to realization" (*raja* means "king"), is traditionally known as Ashtanga Yoga in Hinduism. (*Ashtanga* means "eight limbs.") Just as the Hindu deities have many arms so does this path of yoga. It doesn't have rungs that you climb up one at a time like a ladder, but eight separate components that all work together to get you to God.

The Eight Limbs of Yoga

The eight components of this form of spiritual practice are …

1. *Yama*—Morality.

2. *Niyama*—Ethics.

3. *Asana*—Posture.

4. *Pranayama*—Control of the Breath.

5. *Pratyahara*—Control of the Senses.

6. *Dharana*—Concentration.

7. *Dhyana*—Meditation.

8. *Samadhi*—One-Pointed Absorption.

You already met the first two, yama and niyama, in Chapter 17, "The Ten Commitments." These are the elements of a decent and humane life—not injuring others, being honest, not stealing, keeping a lid on your sensual desires, not being greedy, practicing inner and outer purity, being content, disciplining yourself, learning about God/Goddess, and surrendering to the Divine.

Sitting Still

It makes sense that ethical behavior is the very root of spiritual practice. But what does posture have to do with spirituality? Plenty, it turns out. All the rest of the components of Raja Yoga involve controlling the mind so you can begin your inward journey toward Self-realization. This is extremely difficult if the body is out of order. If you're sick or physically restless, it's tough to concentrate. The key to successful meditation, and to some extent to health itself, lies in how you hold your body.

New Word Alert!

Raja means "king." Raja Yoga is therefore, the "royal" yoga.

Ashtanga means "eight limbs." Ashtanga Yoga is the yoga with eight equally important components.

The optimal condition for intense concentration is to sit upright with your head, neck, and trunk straight. You should not be bolt upright in a strained position, but sitting straight yet relaxed. Try this next time you have to study for an exam or listen to a lecture. You'll be amazed at how much clearer your awareness is. This is because the nerves running between your spine and brain aren't being obstructed or constricted.

The classical meditation postures involve sitting cross-legged on the floor. But a whole system of more varied postures, called Hatha Yoga, eventually developed to help keep the body healthy and supple, in perfect shape for meditation. These involve exercises ranging from the head stand and shoulder stand to twists, stretches, and balancing poses. Unlike aerobic workouts, which exercise the cardiovascular system, Hatha postures work more with the endocrine system (the endocrine glands are associated with the chakras in the subtle body) and tone the internal organs. There's a lot of emphasis on keeping the spine limber.

People who've been practicing Hatha conscientiously for some time can often sit comfortably in a meditation posture for hours on end. The original purpose of Hatha postures was not to promote beauty and a youthful appearance, but to promote meditation!

When you say the word "yoga" to a Hindu, he or she will automatically think of meditation. Yoga literally means "union with Divine Consciousness," which typically happens in deep states of meditation. In the West, though, most people think of Hatha exercises when you say "yoga."

Hold Your Breath!

"Breath is the flywheel of life," my teacher Swami Rama would insist. The yoga masters have an amazingly advanced understanding of how the body operates. It wasn't until yogis like Swami Rama began coming to the West in the early 1970s and allowing scientists to experiment on them that our physiologists even began to suspect how profound the link between the breath and the nervous system is.

Swami Rama called breathing a flywheel because it's one physical function that's both voluntary and involuntary, and it affects every other system in the body. That means although the breath runs by itself, we can override its automatic function with a little bit of mental effect. We can breathe faster, slower, or even stop our breath temporarily just by willing to do so.

The yogis noticed that how we breathe has an enormous impact on our emotional state and also affects our heart rate, blood pressure, and other bodily functions. If you make yourself take rapid, jagged breaths, you'll start feeling anxious, for example. If you breathe slowly, evenly and smoothly,

Sages Say

"Hatha Yoga without meditation is blind, and meditation without Hatha Yoga is lame. The combination of the two is called Raja Yoga—the balanced path."

—Swami Rama Bharati

Guidepost

Please don't experiment with yogic breathing exercises without the close supervision of an experienced teacher. People have done serious damage to their heart and nervous system by practicing some of the more advanced techniques prematurely.

you'll relax. If you hold your breath, you'll be awfully uncomfortable, but your mind will become incredibly focused.

The great Hindu masters studied the breath so intensively they created a whole science of breathing called *Svarodaya*. By applying its principles, they could manipulate functions in their bodies that otherwise wouldn't be possible to control through the power of thought, such as the heart rate and involuntary nervous system. This led to control over brain states, which led to the attainment of focused states of awareness beyond the imagination of nonyogis.

Western linguists have asked how it could be possible that Panini achieved an understanding of the mechanics of grammar that modern researchers couldn't duplicate even with advanced computers. To Hindus the answer is obvious. It's because Panini was a yogi. States of awareness that seem like genius to the rest of us are available to yogis who master the science of breath, which gives them amazing control over their brain and tremendous powers of concentration.

Diving Deeper: Controlling the Senses

By clearing the conscience through ethical behavior, stabilizing the body through correct meditative posture, and controlling the breath in order to calm and steady the nervous system, the yogi is getting ready to meet God. Not the deity in the temple, but the deity in the body, shining splendidly from behind the physical, astral, and causal bodies. That deity the *Tripura Rahasya* calls "Her Majesty, the Supreme Sovereign Empress, Pure Consciousness Herself." In Raja Yoga the Divine One is called Purusha, the Higher Self.

Through breath control, the body and mind become quite still. Now we move on to pratyahara or sense withdrawal. This means drawing the attention away from the body, away from the breath, and focusing it entirely in the nonmaterial realm of pure mental awareness. In Hinduism, there are a number of different ways this is accomplished. One is to move the awareness up through the spine, severing your connection with the elements earth, water, fire, air, and ether as you move upwards toward pure awareness. The steps of the inward journey are detailed in the sage Patanjali's notes on Raja Yoga, called the *Yoga Sutras*.

It's News to Me!

There's an entire class of Hindu scriptures whose characteristic feature is that nobody can understand them! Sutras are the guru's lecture notes, a list of often meaningless words and phrases that the guru "unpacks" for the students during class. Disciples began memorizing sutras as a way to keep the course material organized in their minds.

The Flight to God

You're heading from New York to New Delhi. Your jet starts slowly taxiing down the runway at LaGuardia. It goes faster and faster and suddenly you're in the air. As you move higher, you encounter some unsettling turbulence but the jet keeps chugging. You race into the clouds, through the clouds, and suddenly—*poof!*—you're above the clouds. Now you're at 35,000 feet and the rest of the flight is smooth sailing.

The last three components of Raja Yoga are exactly like that. You take off slowly as you begin to concentrate. You move higher into the state of meditation, quickly passing through the mental turbulence of thoughts and emotions on the way to a state of tranquil clarity. Finally you enter a realm above space and time where you float unperturbed in the horizonless atmosphere of consciousness. This process of moving from concentration to meditation to total absorption, soaring from 0 to 600 m.p.h. in your mind, is called *samyama* in Sanskrit. It's the door to higher worlds.

Degrees of Attention

What's the difference between concentration, meditation, and absorption? When you concentrate, you think about one subject. There may be numerous thoughts in your mind, but they're all about the same topic. "Krishna is so handsome. He's so compassionate. He's incredibly wise."

In meditation, there is only one thought in your mind. You're not thinking *about* Krishna, you're thinking only Krishna. His form (his smiling face or his holy feet for example) or one of his qualities (such as radiant divine love) is the only image or feeling in your awareness. Hindu sages compare this state to pouring oil into a bowl. The flow of your attention toward God, or whatever object you're meditating on, is as unwavering and unbroken as the stream of oil.

Samadhi—total meditative absorption—takes your mental focus to the highest level. When you're in samadhi, you erase yourself. You're no longer present. The only thing present is Krishna, or whatever the object of your meditation is. Your focus is so total that you, the process of meditation, and the thing you're meditating on fuse into one experiential reality. Krishna totally dominates your field of awareness, not you. In a sense, you have become Krishna.

New Word Alert!

Svarodaya is the yogic science of breath.

Samyama is the movement of attention from concentration through meditation into total mental absorption.

Guidepost

Worried that meditation masters take over their disciples' minds? It's mistaken to confuse deep stages of meditation with hypnotic states. Hypnosis and trance are passive conditions. The meditator is fully lucid and alert. She is directing her own experience, not being "taken over" by any entity outside herself.

Merging with the Divine

If you can catch hold of Divine Being in meditation, then through samadhi you can actually merge into it. Your own being fuses with the Divine. This is what yoga technically means. Your awareness becomes "yoked" or united with its object. If that object is the Supreme Being, you are now in a very, very high place in consciousness.

Psychic Powers

Not everyone meditates on God. People have very different interests. Where I live in Northern California just about everyone experiences "computer samadhi." They sit in front of their computer screens in a state of full mental absorption. One of my mentors, Shree Maa of Kamakya—a saint who's capable of shifting virtually effortlessly into the highest states of consciousness—recently commented that computers are actually good because they teach people to concentrate. That's the first step on the road to Self-realization!

But what to concentrate on? Some people focus intently on sex. This leads them to a state of bliss. Others focus intently on art or music or poetry. This leads them to another kind of blissful experience. In the *Yoga Sutras,* Patanjali admits that many inner explorers focus on developing psychic powers. The sutras list some of the supernatural abilities you can develop through intense mental control.

Through intense inner focus on various internal or external objects that Patanjali carefully describes, you can, for example …

Sages Say

"If you practice regular meditation, you are bound to get some psychic powers. You should not use these powers for base and selfish purposes. I again and again seriously warn you! Desire for psychic powers will act like puffs of air which may blow out the lamp of Yoga."

—Swami Sivananda

➤ Remember your past lives.

➤ Gain knowledge of past or future events.

➤ Read other peoples' minds.

➤ Become invisible.

➤ Gain the strength, swiftness, or skills of certain animals.

➤ Gain full knowledge of cosmology—no telescope required!

➤ Communicate with higher beings in the subtle worlds.

➤ Enter someone else's body after that soul has vacated it.

➤ Travel without dragging your physical body along.

➤ Pull any information out of the universe that you may have use for!

Psychic Science

Spiritual healing, talking with beings in parallel universes, materializing objects, teleporting from one place to another, astral travel, sending messages telepathically—these things are viewed as spiritual realities, not superstition, in Hinduism. Even average people experience extrasensory perception from time to time. In India, saints, sages, and yogis demonstrate so-called miraculous powers routinely. After all, becoming a sage means your normally limited human consciousness is expanding to superhuman proportions. So of course you develop extraordinary mental powers!

Late one night the great Bengali saint Anandamayi Ma abruptly announced to her astonished devotees that she was leaving for Sarnath. Her disciples trotted after her as she boarded a train that was not scheduled to stop at Sarnath. At Sarnath, however, the train pulled to a halt. Anandamayi Ma jumped off, trailed by her disciples, and started walking through town obviously looking for something.

When they arrived at the Birla Hotel, Anandamayi Ma walked in without bothering to stop by the reception desk. She burst into a guest room and there sat her devotee Maharattan, who was stranded in town and had been crying to Anandamayi Ma for the past several hours. "It's all right!" Ma said. "I'm here!"

This was back in the 1930s—there were no phones in Sarnath at the time. How did Anandamayi Ma know Maharattan was in trouble? And how could she have known where to find her? "There is only one all-pervading consciousness everywhere," Ma explained. "In reality, appearance, continuance, and disappearance occur simultaneously in one place." Anandamayi Ma was constantly in the highest state of samadhi whether she was sitting in meditation or interacting with others in the physical world. She experienced her unity with all being so completely that, like other advanced meditation masters, she seemed to know everything that was going on everywhere all at once!

Sages Say

"The kingdom of consciousness is a unity, and until you experience it in its totality, you will never be content. You, a child of immortality, can never feel at home in the realm of death. Man's true nature—call it what you will—is the Supreme Self of all."

—Anandamayi Ma

New Word Alert!

Siddhis are supernatural powers.
Siddhas are advanced spiritual adepts.

Setting Priorities

In the West, we make a distinction between the natural and the supernatural. In Hinduism, this distinction doesn't exist. The so-called supernatural is just a higher octave of the scale of consciousness. As we continue to grow spiritually, we also experience these *siddhis* or psychic powers.

To cavalierly show off one's siddhis is considered a sign of spiritual immaturity in Hinduism. Which is not to say Hindus don't get as much of a thrill out of watching *siddhas,* spiritual adepts, display their special powers as we do in the West!

Yet in the *Yoga Sutras* Patanjali carefully distinguishes between psychic powers that can enhance spiritual development and those that may actually sabotage it. The appropriate use of intense states of concentration, he says, is to learn to distinguish between the eternal Purusha—the Self within—and the transient things of the world. He discourages disciples from pausing on the path to play with psychic powers. Patanjali encourages them instead not to stop till they reach the final goal: spiritual liberation.

Spiritual Power

You can't force yourself to relax. You can't make yourself sleep. You "slip" into relaxation. You "fall" asleep. Just so, you "fall" into meditation. When you're really meditating, it's effortless. When you rise from meditation, you're as refreshed and invigorated as if you've had a good sleep. But you're not any wiser when you climb out of bed in the morning. Yet if you've truly made contact with your Higher Self in meditation, you get up from your meditation cushion brimming with intuitive insight, creative energy, and healing power.

"The Self, like the sun, is reflected in all," wrote Swami Vishnu Devananda. "The quality of the reflection depends on the purity of the reflecting surface. A person whose reflection is obscured by ignorance might be called a sinner, and one whose reflection is bright could be called a saint." The Self-awareness in the worst person and the best is the same transcendent consciousness. The one person is more full of the distorting desires of the world. The other is more full of the light of the Supreme.

Linking Minds

As your consciousness begins to expand through the practice of Raja Yoga, you begin to link with other entities everywhere. Swami Rama Bharati explained that each of us is like a light bulb while the cosmic mind is like the electric current that sets all the individual bulbs glowing. "The cosmic mind is very subtle, and it is in close contact with other minds," he said. "As one's mind evolves one enters into a conscious relationship with other minds. Numerous minds are linked in this way, and this network forms part of mahat, the cosmic mind."

For Christians, mature faith is the key to salvation. For Hindus, actual *experience* of higher realities is what spirituality is all about. When Jesus said he was the bough and everyone else was his branches, Christians take it as an abstract statement about members of their church. When Hindu saints make similar statements, Hindus take it as literally true. We really are linked in divine consciousness. Through advancing in meditation we can personally experience this truth as a living reality.

Quick Quiz

1. Raja Yoga begins with ...

    a. Moving to the Himalayas.

    b. Moral and ethical principles.

    c. Standing on your head so you get a fresh perspective on life.

2. Raja yogis control their breathing in order to ...

    a. Turn their faces a dark shade of blue.

    b. Diminish the symptoms of allergies and asthma.

    c. Calm and steady their nervous system and mind.

3. Developing psychic powers ...

    a. Is the whole reason for practicing Raja Yoga.

    b. Allows yogis to mentally bend forks and spoons so they don't have to eat with their fingers.

    c. Can be a distraction on the spiritual path.

4. Hatha Yoga postures were originally designed to ...

    a. Help you sit in meditation comfortably for hours.

    b. Make the social elite look and feel great!

    c. Torture prisoners in Soviet gulags.

Answers: 1 (b). 2 (c). 3 (c). 4 (a).

Inner Enemies

Raja yogis hate and harm no one. But they are not without enemies. And real power, as any politician knows, comes from conquering your enemies. The five enemies of the Raja yogi are ...

1. *Avidya*—Spiritual ignorance.

2. *Asmita*—Self-centeredness.

3. *Raga*—Attachment.

4. *Dvesha*—Aversion.

5. *Abhinivesha*—Fear of death.

Avidya or ignorance of one's true nature is the root cause of all suffering. No one would harm anyone else if they saw into the heart of reality. In the experience of cosmic consciousness, you literally experience every living being as yourself. Avidya leads to asmita or the sense that you exist apart from others. You might begin perceiving them as a threat or as competitors. This is to fundamentally misunderstand the unified nature of all things.

Attachment and aversion, desire and repulsion, are offshoots of avidya. So is clinging to life, mistaking your physical body for yourself.

These enemies are really, really tough to conquer. But by expanding our consciousness through deeper and deeper states of meditation, we pass the knot in consciousness we call "me" and move into a wider experience of reality.

Patanjali says that in the light of pure knowledge experienced in samadhi, the very highest state of meditative absorption, we become free from karma. Our past karmas are roasted like seeds fried in a pan. They can never germinate again. What this means in our practical experience is that we're no longer governed by our habit patterns, cravings, and fears. Instead we now live in the pure wisdom of the Higher Self.

Divine Isolation

Patanjali, author of the *Yoga Sutras*, was a great yoga master. He was an ascetic type who didn't believe life in this world had much to recommend about itself. Most people might be prepared to put up with disease, suffering, and death but he wanted out. He belonged to the Sankhya school of thought (like other world-negative sages, such as the Buddha).

For Patanjali, the ultimate aim of Raja Yoga was retreat from the outer world into the undying reality of the Inner Self. In the highest state of consciousness, he wrote, your consciousness subsides into itself. It locks itself away from the surging and heaving of matter and energy and from the fluctuations of thought. It rests instead in its own nature, pure consciousness alone, remaining aware of nothing but itself.

There is another, very large group within Hinduism that sees life differently. Life—including suffering and death—is the play of consciousness and therefore is sacred and deserves our respect, not our contempt. For these people, called tantrics, Patanjali's highest state—consciousness resting in itself—was not the end point of spirituality, but the beginning of an even more extraordinary journey into mystical awareness.

Sages Say

"Yoga means control of the contents of your mind. When your thoughts are stilled, your consciousness experiences only itself. But when thoughts begin to flow, you get caught up in them and the images they place before you."

—*Yoga Sutras* 1:2–4

The Least You Need to Know

➤ Raja Yoga is a systematic meditative path to Self-realization.

➤ Breath control is an important tool for mastering the body and mind.

➤ The deepest states of mental absorption lead to merging in the object being contemplated.

➤ Psychic powers are a natural but potentially distracting result of developing intense inward concentration.

➤ The goal of Raja Yoga is to establish yourself in your true nature—Pure Consciousness.

Chapter 24

Tantra: Making Love to God

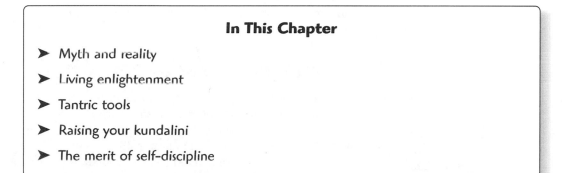

In This Chapter

➤ Myth and reality

➤ Living enlightenment

➤ Tantric tools

➤ Raising your kundalini

➤ The merit of self-discipline

Wine, women, and song? Sex orgies in God's name? Western ideas about Tantra are so outrageous Hindus hardly know whether to laugh or cry. The myth that Tantra is "the yoga of sex" says more about the projections of the repressed Victorian Europeans who took over India a few centuries ago and first started circulating these stories than it does about Hinduism!

Today there is a whole industry built around "tantric sex," complete with numerous provocatively illustrated paperbacks and "spiritual sex" seminars in Hawaii. A few Hindu businesspeople, who know how to make a buck as well as the next person, have gotten in on the act. There are now professional artists in India who produce paintings of couples having "tantric sex" to sell to the naive Westerners who actually believe this is a common Hindu practice!

Tantra in Real Life

Most of the Hindu teachers I've studied with over the decades have been practicing tantrics. People who believe the sensationalized stories would be disappointed to meet them. Rather than being masters of exotic sexual postures, most of them live lives of extraordinary austerity. Some have engaged in disciplines the Western mind can hardly imagine—such as meditating in a cramped Himalayan cave without any light for eleven months straight or surviving in the jungles of Assam for months on end with little or no food.

In fact, there are still tantrics today who live without food at all. In addition to an occasional sip of water, all they eat is sunlight. They assimilate prana, or vital energy, directly out of the atmosphere. Others sit for hours without breathing (do *not* try this at home!), their bodies in a state much like hibernation while their minds remain absorbed in meditation.

Stories about tantric adepts sound like fantasies out of a *Harry Potter* novel. But those of us who've spent time in areas of India where these ancient techniques are still practiced can verify that we've seen these things with our own eyes. In some ways, the *true* story of Tantra is far more fantastic than the garbled tales of spiritual eroticism you hear in the West.

Sages Say

"After Self-realization you become absolutely fearless. You can only be afraid if you think there's something apart *from* you that threatens you. When you become Self-realized you see that everything is a part *of* you. There can't be fear in that state anymore than there can be darkness after sunrise."

—*Tripura Rahasya* 20:63–65

Enlightenment or Liberation?

The vast majority of people practicing Tantra are not miracle-working adepts, but ordinary Hindus with an extraordinary goal: enlightenment in this lifetime. You'll remember from Chapter 23, "The Royal Road," that Patanjali considered the highest state to be liberation *from* this world. Tantrics believe the highest state is enlightenment *in* this world. Their goal is *sahaja* samadhi. This means to remain in the highest state of consciousness not just while withdrawn from the world in meditation, but while active in the world, fulfilling one's duties, supporting one's family, and enjoying life.

In the *Tripura Rahasya,* the prince Hemachuda achieves samadhi, a blissful state of mental absorption, while on a meditation retreat. "Don't bother me," he tells his wife, Hemalekha, when she comes to pick him up. "I'm experiencing the greatest possible joy."

Hemalekha, who's a tantric master, not a beginner like her husband, teases him. "What kind of supreme state is this that vanishes when you open your eyes? You're still as far from the supreme state as the stars are from their reflection in a pond. When you're permanently in samadhi, you'll enjoy that same bliss whether you're sitting meditating in a cave or sitting on your throne ruling the kingdom."

Ladder to Unity

To give you a clearer idea of what Tantra is about, I'm going to ask you to cast your mind back to Chapter 9, "Truth Is a Multi-Layer Cake." That's where I was talking about Sankhya, the perspective on reality the yoga tradition is based on. I mentioned that Sankhya breaks the world down into the five physical elements, plus the senses and powers in the subtle body, plus the three parts of the mind, and finally the matrix of energy from which the universe and our bodies and mind evolve. At the top of the heap and totally separate from the rest of them was purusha, the Higher Self. In the *Yoga Sutras,* Patanjali takes you to the Higher Self. You experience your own undying spirit apart from your physical and subtle bodies and apart from your thoughts.

In very advanced states of meditation, the tantrics found that the Higher Self is not the ultimate reality. Your individual soul is a stop on the way to your final goal, but it's not the destination itself. The ultimate reality is Shiva/Shakti, the sublime unity of God/Goddess, the Supreme Consciousness and its limitless omniscience and omnipotence.

Here's how the tantrics explain the nondistinction between your innermost Self and God. Beyond the Higher Self lies maya, the force that leads the Inner Self to mistakenly feel that it exists in itself, apart from God's all-pervading divine consciousness. Maya operates through five restraining factors:

New Word Alert!

Sahaja means the natural state. Sahaja samadhi therefore is to be in the highest state of consciousness continuously, both in meditation and out of it. Enlightenment has become your natural condition.

1. *Niyati* limits omnipresence, creating the illusion that you exist in one particular place in space.

2. *Kala* limits time, creating the illusion that you exist in the here and now rather than in eternity.

3. *Raga* limits your sense of universal ownership, creating the impression that there's something outside yourself that don't belong to you.

4. *Vidya* limits omniscience, creating the illusion that you don't know everything!

5. *Kala* (pronounced with a long "a" at the end, unlike the first kala in this list) limits omnipotence, creating the illusion that you can't effortlessly will things into existence.

Beyond these five faces of maya lies your true identity. Not jiva, the individual soul, but Shiva, the universal soul.

Guidepost

So you think you're God? Hinduism claims that each of us is an actual part of God, just as a spark is part of a fire. But it never confuses God-realization with megalomania. Megalomaniacs see God only in themselves. Genuine saints see God in everyone. That's why so many saints are the humblest people you'll ever meet!

It's News to Me!

Ancient Hindu sages divided the celestial ecliptic into 27 sectors called *nakshatras* or lunar mansions. Each of these in turn was divided into four equal quarters, 108 in all. Each is governed by a different Vedic deity. When you chant the 108 beads on your Hindu rosary you're invoking the blessings of all the gods in heaven.

Divine Identity

For tantrics, the universe is not a vale of suffering, as it appeared to ascetic yogis like Patanjali. It's not a place you escape from. Rather, tantrics see it as the play of consciousness, a divine realm projected by the Supreme Being in which we all exist together as seemingly separate entities—when in fact we are one unified whole.

Most Hindus share the tantric perspective that all of nature is holy. It all deserves our reverence. And by learning to control the shaktis or energies inherent in the cosmos, we can live in the universe like mini divine beings or angels rather than like victims crushed beneath the wheel of death and rebirth. We become companions of the Divine, exercising the compassion, intelligence, and creative power that is our birthright as divine beings.

Mantra, Yantra, Tantra

The tool kit Hindu tantrics use to expand their consciousness and navigate the sea of energy we misperceive as a physical world is extremely extensive. All the methods and techniques of Karma, Bhakti, Jnana, and Raja Yoga are called into service. But two of the most important practices used in Tantra are mantra and yantra.

Chant Your Mantra!

Tantrics use mantras to create a link between our human awareness and the cosmic awareness we carry deep inside ourselves. According to the yoga tradition, the sacred syllables of a mantra create a vortex, like a wormhole between worlds that links the subconscious, conscious, and superconscious minds. We can use this vibratory gateway to bring through guidance and healing power from the depths of our being. Tantrics also use it to move consciously into their subconscious mind, and operate on the unhealthy aspects of themselves, their complexes and neuroses. They literally replace "bad vibrations" with "good vibrations"!

You will often see Hindus using a *mala* or rosary to keep track of the number of times they've repeated their mantra. Every mala has 108 beads, which may be made of sandalwood, crystal, lotus seeds, or the rudraksha seeds sacred to Shiva and Shakti. You chant a mala of mantras and give yourself credit for 100 repetitions. The extra eight cover the moments when your mind strayed from the mantra. If you were completely focused while chanting, then the extra eight mantras are donated to the universe for the welfare of all beings.

It's not unusual for pious Hindus to commit to repeating a sacred mantra hundreds of thousands or even millions of times! These practices can take *years* to complete.

Draw Your Yantra!

A yantra is an abstract geometric diagram that represents the structure of the universe. It starts from the center point of consciousness and radiates out through all the shaktis or universal energies into every plane of manifestation. Yantras may be drawn on paper or fabric, carved in wood or inscribed on metal.

Various yantric designs represent different cosmic energies or deities. Tantrics empower yantras with sacred mantras and enliven them by transferring the center point of their own awareness into the yantra for worship. Yantras can transmit strong blessings and healing vibrations when they're properly "turned on."

Yantra literally means "machine." These are machines for consciousness, with each square and triangle, petal and circle, representing not only a cosmic force but an energy in the tantric's own body and mind. By aligning physical, mental, and cosmic circuits, tantrics hope to achieve specific effects, such as enhancing their awareness, creating a protective aura, attracting prosperity, and so on.

The most powerful yantras are those tantrics draw in the subtle matter of their own minds. These become internal maps tantrics follow to the center of

New Word Alert!

A **mala** is a Hindu rosary. It usually has 108 beads.

A **nakshatra** is a Moon sign or a 13°20' sector of the Hindu zodiac.

It's News to Me!

Mantras were used by the ancient Greeks and Egyptians, too. In the fourth century C.E., the Neoplatonic master Iamblicus complained that Greek mantras didn't work nearly as well as Egyptian ones—because the Greeks would make up mantras off the cuff. Egyptian mantras, on the other hand, had been empowered by thousands of years of repetition and had immensely powerful effects.

311

the inner universe. That innermost point is the source of the worlds—of all manifestation, in fact. It's also the point you travel through on your way out of these worlds into a place beyond space and a moment beyond time.

Sri Yantra, a geometric design representing the powers of the Goddess.

Kundalini Rising

Interested in "raising your kundalini"? A book called *The Serpent Power* first introduced the subject of kundalini to a non-Hindu audience. It was written by Sir John Woodroffe in the early twentieth century. Sir John was Chief Justice on the Calcutta High Court at the time. During his tenure in India, he happened to see a tantric drop his own aged body and take over the body of a younger man whose corpse was being prepared for cremation!

The experience shook Woodroffe up so badly he devoted the rest of his life to studying the tantric tradition. He went so far as to get initiated in the Hindu tradition of the Great Goddess. Woodroffe was one of the very few Europeans of his era to treat Hinduism respectfully. His scholarly books remain among the finest and most accurate works on Hindu Tantra in English to this day.

"Kundalini is the Divine Cosmic Energy in bodies. Kunda means coiled. The Goddess Kundalini," wrote Woodroffe, "is that which is coiled; for Her form is that of a coiled and sleeping serpent in the lowest bodily center, at the base of the spinal column." He explained that tantrics lead the serpent power up the spine into the brain, where it produces an intensely blissful experience. Woodroffe also said that myths about yogis' adventures throughout the "seven worlds" actually refer to this inner journey through the different states of awareness represented at each *chakra* or center of consciousness in the body.

The Inner Pilgrimage

The inner journey proceeds from the bottom of the spine upward through six more pilgrimage sites:

1. *Muladhara Chakra*—base of the spine
2. *Svadhishthana Chakra*—near the genital organs
3. *Manipura Chakra*—behind the navel
4. *Anahata Chakra*—at the heart
5. *Vishuddha Chakra*—at the throat
6. *Ajna Chakra*—behind the point between the eyebrows
7. *Sahasrara Chakra*—corresponds to the cerebral cortex

There are hundreds of other smaller chakras, such as the vortices of spiritual energy in the hands and feet through which saints can direct blessing energy.

Jokes about yogis "contemplating their navels" actually refer to meditation on the manipura chakra. According to Patanjali, with the blessings of a guru, intensely focused concentration here can lead to extraordinary insights and powers.

Each center, in fact, is associated with a different set of psychic powers and spiritual experiences. Mastering the anahata chakra, for example, brings the experience of universal love. Controlling the vishuddha chakra in the throat bestows the powers of telepathy and prophecy. Opening the ajna chakra brings universal knowledge. When the "lotus" of the sahasrara chakra blooms, the tantric merges in Shiva, divine consciousness.

Specific colors and sounds are associated with the different chakras and are used to activate them. Spending too much time at any of the lower chakras is not advised in Tantra, as it can lead to getting lost in the astral worlds, rather than transcending them and achieving full-blown spiritual awareness.

Sages Say

"That which is the general characteristic of the Indian systems, and that which constitutes their real profundity, is the paramount importance attached to Consciousness and its states ... And whatever be the means employed, it is the transformation of the 'lower' into 'higher' states of consciousness which is the process and fruit of Yoga."

—Sir John Woodroffe

The Mushroom in the Brain

The Vedas are full of references to *soma,* a drink brahmin priests offer into the ritual fire. Indra, king of the gods, is said to become exhilarated when he takes this beverage. Western scholars have long assumed soma is some kind of intoxicant or hallucinogen. Yet brahmins still drink soma during some of their rituals, and it has no intoxicating effects at all.

Scholars today speculate that the original soma may have been a hallucinogenic mushroom called *amanita muscaria.* Others think it may have been the drug harmaline. Identifying it is difficult because although it is mentioned frequently in Vedic literature, explanations of what it looked like and how it was prepared are confusing and obscure.

When I mentioned the suggestions Western ethnobiologists have offered for soma's true identity to a yogi from Rishikesh, he howled with laughter. "Your scientists know nothing! They think soma is something you find outside yourself!"

In the esoteric Hindu tradition, soma is understood as a type of energy-fluid produced in the soma chakra, an important center of awareness between the ajna chakra behind the forehead and the sahasrara chakra at the top of the brain. The psychoactively harmless soma prepared by brahmins for their rituals is just a symbol of this inner nectar tasted by yogis in high states of meditation.

New Word Alert!

A **chakra** is a center of consciousness and energy in the subtle body.

Soma is the divine ambrosia drunk by gods and yogis.

Getting High Without Drugs

While some Hindu yogis use hashish, most avoid hard drugs and mind-altering substances. Swami Rama Bharati told me hallucinogens like LSD can do irreparable harm to the impressionable energies of the subtle body.

In the Hindu mystical tradition, aspirants are advised to avoid mental crutches like drugs. Instead they need to develop mental clarity and strength—something drugs can't give. Yogis alter their consciousness by manipulating the internal energies of the subtle body and get "high" on consciousness itself. Yogis think ahead, considering not just this life but existences to come. They note that once you're dead no physical drug can help you! Self-control and mastery of the

Guidepost

Want to expand your consciousness? Try meditation—not drugs. Yogis say that drugs weaken the will, damage the subtle body, and stupefy consciousness. One yogi told me he'd seen heavy-duty drug users so internally damaged they would need *lifetimes* to detoxify their subtle body.

processes of the subtle body will serve you well in the after-death state. Hashish and other mind-altering drugs are worthless to disembodied spirits!

Spiritual Self-Discipline

The amount of effort and self-discipline it requires to become a tantric adept is the equivalent of what an athlete needs to win an Olympic medal. I myself have watched tantrics sit for a half hour or more without breathing as they shifted their awareness into the increasingly high states that breath retention makes accessible. If you've tried holding your breath for even 30 seconds, you can well imagine how difficult these practices are to master.

I've also spent winters in the north of India, wrapped in my parka and covered with my arctic-certified sleeping bag, and still freezing, while naked tantrics sat outside meditating as if they were on a beach in Hawaii! In the Hindu tradition, tantrics like these who live outdoors in winter have mastered the yogic science of generating internal heat from the energy center in the solar plexus.

No one who's spent time with the tantric masters would claim that tantric science isn't for real. Most of the tantric techniques remain unknown to Western science. The number of Hindus who actually master them is small because the amount of self-discipline these techniques require is so rigorous. It's ironic then that Westerners tend to think of tantrics as libertines!

Want to Practice Tantra?

Most of the more esoteric aspects of the Hindu tradition are carefully guarded secrets. Qualifying to participate in certain rites is difficult and in some cases impossible, particularly if you're female or from a low caste. If you were a brahmin male—whether you were a spiritually oriented person or not—you qualified to receive the holy Gayatri mantra in the orthodox Vedic tradition. If you were a woman or outcaste, it didn't matter if you were the greatest saint in India, you still didn't get the Gayatri.

Many tantrics had a far more liberal policy. As long as you qualified through your sincerity and determination to work hard toward your spiritual goal, you might be accepted into a tantric circle regardless of your gender or social rank. In other ways, qualifying to practice Tantra was even more difficult, however. Would-be disciples were often severely tested for their level of motivation, intelligence, ethics, and spiritual aptitude.

A Hindu friend of mine described his own qualifying exam to join a tantric circle. First he had to be recommended by other spiritual adepts who knew him well. Then he had to fast for a week and repeat a particular lengthy mantra *millions* of times within seven days! To recite so many mantras so fast meant there was no time for visits to the bathroom, much less sleep!

A Tantric Orgy

At the end of the week, my friend was in an intensely "high" state due to the force of concentration needed to say so many mantras so fast—and due to the spaciness from not having eaten for a week! Then he was invited into a tantric circle in which participants ate small amounts of meat. Meat eating is extremely disgusting to many conservative Hindus. Tantrics take meat to help them overcome this sense of revulsion. The point is to realize experientially that *everything* is divine. No object is inherently repugnant, not even decaying flesh.

Then liquor was taken. The least sign of drunkenness disqualified you from the circle immediately. The point of taking the intoxicant was to practice remaining completely clear and lucid under any conditions. Then red and white powders were smeared together to represent the union of male and female energies.

Sages Say

"The Moon has a blemish on his face he can't get rid of. I can't get rid of my attachment to the things I own. I throw myself at Your feet, O Lord. They're the only force strong enough to help me overcome my weakness!"

—Tulsi Das

Rumors of men and women "mixing their energies" while consuming intoxicants led Europeans to believe tantrics engaged in wholesale orgies, just as stories of Christians eating "the body and blood of Christ" during Communion led to charges that the Christians were cannibals!

What was really happening was that in the sacred tantric circle, participants raised their awareness together through extraordinarily demanding concentration exercises. Elevating consciousness—raising the kundalini to the top of the head—is a major focus of the practice. This is so that at the time of death, tantrics can consciously exit the body through the top of the skull. A conscious yogic exit leads to a conscious after-death experience. And also, if the tantric wants, to a choice of which world he or she wants to explore next! Tantric adepts are no longer driven willy-nilly by the force of their karma but consciously direct the course of their spiritual evolution.

Tantrics on the Loose

The greatest Hindu tantric masters have usually been treated with tremendous respect. But there's no doubt that a minority of practitioners misuse the tantric techniques for entirely selfish purposes. And while Tantra gives the power to bless, it also gives the power to curse. In some Hindu communities therefore, tantrics are greatly feared.

Tantra is about power. The power of consciousness. The power of will. The power to direct your own destiny. The power to enter the limitless expanse of divine awareness. With power inevitably comes the potential for misuse. For this reason, gurus screen potential disciples carefully and keep close tabs on their students' progress.

Quick Quiz

1. Tantra is a path to higher consciousness involving ...
   a. Complicated sex postures.
   b. Mantras and yantras.
   c. Expensive seminars in Hawaii.

2. Chakras are ...
   a. Centers of consciousness and energy in the subtle body.
   b. Colors and patterns you see when you close your eyes.
   c. Geometric diagrams representing cosmic energies.

3. The purpose of Tantra is ...
   a. Great sex.
   b. Liberation from the world.
   c. Enlightenment in the world.

4. Drug use is ...
   a. Highly recommended by tantric yogis.
   b. Generally not advisable according to tantrics.
   c. Okay with a doctor's prescription.

Answers: 1 (b). 2 (a). 3 (c). 4 (b).

The Least You Need to Know

➤ Tantrics seek spiritual mastery in the midst of worldly life.

➤ Mantras and yantras are used to master cosmic energies, both within the mind and outside it.

➤ Kundalini is the illuminating power of consciousness as it manifests in the body.

➤ The chakras represent increasingly higher levels of awareness within the subtle body.

➤ Mastering advanced tantric techniques gives extraordinary powers and requires a commitment to ethical behavior.

Part 6
A Timeless Tradition

At the same time that Hindu India faces nearly insurmountable challenges in its homeland and with its Communist and Muslim neighbors, Hinduism abroad is meeting with increasing success. Basic Hindu tenets, such as reincarnation and karma, as well as Hindu practices, such as vegetarianism and yoga, are being enthusiastically embraced in the West. The value of Hindu techniques such as meditation and hatha postures, as well as some aspects of ancient Hindu history and cosmology, have been validated by Western scientists.

In many North American bookstores, books on Hinduism are found on the "New Age" shelves. The most ancient religion in the world is still as "new" and exciting as it was in the days when the Vedic seers first chanted the exquisite hymns of the Rig Veda to the divine forces around us and within us.

Chapter 25

Timeless Tales

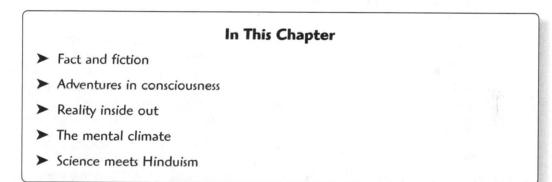

In This Chapter

➤ Fact and fiction

➤ Adventures in consciousness

➤ Reality inside out

➤ The mental climate

➤ Science meets Hinduism

When I first started spending time with Hindus, I was amazed at how naive they seemed to be. Stories that were obviously fairy tales were taken completely seriously even by educated Hindus.

Yet over the years I gradually began to doubt that my Western understanding of reality was more valid than theirs. Their legends, for example, tell of other races of humanity who lived on the Earth in remote times. Is that any different from our fossil evidence of Neanderthals and Cro-Magnons?

Hindu texts two thousand years old spoke of great adepts who lived on the opposite side of the Earth, where the sun sets while it rises in India. Can we really be certain they're not talking about the advanced cultures of Central America, supposedly unknown in the Old World at that time? And most of us in the West didn't believe tales of Hindu mystics' fantastic powers—till yogis began visiting our scientific laboratories and proved they could actually do what Hindus always said they could. I started to suspect there was a great deal to learn from the "unbelievable" stories Hindus have passed on for countless generations.

Tales from Outside Time

One of my favorite sources of Hindu lore is the *Yoga Vasishtha,* a mind-boggling book written sometime before the twelfth century. It describes the universe from the yogi Vasishtha's point of view. To the Hindu adept the cosmos is not actually solid but is composed of layers upon layers of dimensions in consciousness that only appear solid to their inhabitants. In reality, these worlds are composed of Shakti, Divine Energy. Shakti is inherently intelligent, reflecting the supreme intelligence of Divine Being with whom she is, in essence, identical.

Vasishtha, the sage who narrates the many stories in the book, describes how from one perspective vast intelligences like Brahma the Creator shape fields of energy into living worlds, and yet, from another perspective, the consciousness/energy underlying the cosmos is never really anything other than itself. So even Brahma himself is in some sense an illusion!

It's News to Me!

Hindu scriptures say the Earth goes through cycles where it flourishes and other periods where it's virtually uninhabitable. Sometimes things get so intolerable the souls who live here flee to other world systems entirely. But don't start packing yet! The texts say these cycles occur over many tens of thousands of years.

Other great intelligences are emanated from the Supreme Being. They direct the flow of evolution on planets like the Earth. The *Puranas* describe how once, when evolution got stuck, Lord Shiva devised a new strategy called sexual reproduction that allowed for a wider variety of characteristics in each new generation!

Through cycles of creation and destruction, whole new sets of creatures and humanities are abruptly placed on Earth, then removed. It's rather eerie how closely this scenario matches the punctuated equilibrium theory set forth by our paleontologists today. They note that at the end of each biological epoch, vast numbers of species (like the dinosaurs) suddenly disappear, and completely new creatures show up practically overnight!

The major difference between the Western and Indian concepts of evolution is that Western scientists assume the process is purely random. Hindu spiritual texts claim it's guided by intelligences from higher planes of understanding.

Are You Sure You're Alive?

My favorite tale in the *Yoga Vasishtha* is the story of Queen Lila. When her husband dies, Lila appeals to Sarasvati, goddess of wisdom, to reveal the secrets of life after death. She wants to know where her husband is and understand what he's experiencing in his disembodied state.

Sarasvati, who has quite a few amazing powers, transports Lila into her husband's consciousness. It turns out the king doesn't even realize he's dead! In the after-death state his mind has projected a whole new kingdom, an exact replica of the physical realm he just died out of. In that world made of the subtle matter of his thoughts, he's still ruling his kingdom, and Lila is still at his side!

Sarasvati shows Queen Lila how we unconsciously create our own after-death state based on our expectations and desires during life. The Goddess explains that people find themselves in the heaven or hell realms they created in their own consciousness. In the dream-like disembodied state, their unconscious tendencies, called *vasanas* in Sanskrit, are projected onto the screen of their consciousness and become their reality. (In the waking state, vasanas determine how we interpret and respond to external reality.)

When people who're absolutely convinced there's no life after death actually do die, they go into a deep sleep-like state that can last for years, the Goddess says, because they're unwilling to allow themselves to come back to consciousness and have to admit they were wrong!

Traveling Without Your Body

When Lila cries that she wants to rejoin her husband, Sarasvati coyly asks, "Which one?" The Goddess points out that Lila has had many lifetimes and numerous husbands! She teaches Lila the technique for detaching herself from her physical body so that she can travel astrally into the past and future, where she witnesses her next and her last lifetimes. This also helps Lila understand how our thoughts, actions, and desires shape our future lives.

Lila sees how her selfish and aggressive acts in past births led to miserable nonhuman lives. And how spiritual practice and kind acts eventually led her to her present life of prestige, luxury, and a fulfilling marriage. It also becomes clear how attachment to particular other souls (whether the attachment is in the form of love or of hate) leads to reincarnating with those same souls over and over again.

Next Sarasvati takes Lila on a tour of the universe. They leave the glittering globe of the Earth behind, pass the planets, and sail through the black void of space to other world systems where whole other types of creatures are living. Some of the life forms in outer space are so peculiar, the text says, "that even the yogis don't understand what they are!"

Sages Say

"Nothing exists apart from Divine Being, which is an undivided whole without parts, existing now and always. There is no more difference between the Supreme Being and the world than there is between you and a city you see in your dream."

—*Yoga Vasishtha*

Facing Reality

The most dramatic moment in Lila's journeys through time and space occurs when Sarasvati takes her to see her next incarnation. Due to her immense attachment to her husband, Lila will find and marry him again in her next life—only to see him butchered on the battlefield!

The *Yoga Vasishtha* describes the scene vividly. An invading army is slaughtering the population. Families are being burnt to death in their houses, women are being raped, little children are being hacked to pieces. Lila recoils in horror. Then Sarasvati turns to her and says, very seriously, "Lila, can you see that this is also the play of Divine Consciousness?"

New Word Alert!

Vasanas are unconscious habits and tendencies.

In the most dramatic terms possible, the *Yoga Vasishtha* shows how karma plays out in our world. The horrific killing is the result of the group karma of warriors who love and crave war. Innocent victims, whose wills are far weaker, are sucked into the vortex of the warriors' psychopathic but strong-willed desires. And yet, at a deeper level, it is all merely the play of energy in Divine Consciousness.

The sage Vasishtha is telling young Prince Rama the story of Lila and Sarasvati. "Rama," he pauses to explain, "you must understand that at one level nothing in this world or any other has any inherent reality. It's all just God's dream. But never forget that each of us has a role to play within this dream. When you grow up to be king, it will be your job to stop this kind of injustice and protect the innocent."

"While you are in this plane of reality," Vasishtha continues, "you must help and serve others to the full extent of your capacity. But never lose sight of the final truth. That behind all the ugliness and evil men create for themselves, lies the beauty and wonder of the Supreme Being. Whenever you feel discouraged, sit down and meditate. Feel the inner truth hidden in your heart and you'll regain your strength and composure."

Tales from Inner Space

In this book, I've already mentioned Shankaracharya a couple of times. He was a great saint and yogi who had a massive influence on Hinduism. According to the Hindu tradition, he lived about five centuries B.C.E. According to Western scholars, he lived somewhere between 600–800 C.E. (Remember there's massive disagreement about dates in Hindu history before about 1000 C.E.) There are lots of stories about Shankaracharya's incredible yogic prowess, all considered true episodes from his biography.

Once Shankaracharya was having a debate with Mandana Mishra, who belonged to the Mimamsa school of thought. (They're the guys who believe in performing religious rituals within the context of family life and the prime desirability of attaining heavenly states after death.) In those days, public debates were serious business because if you lost, you had to renounce your own views and become a disciple of the person you lost to.

Shankaracharya defeated Mandana, which meant Mandana would have to renounce the world and become a wandering monk like Shankaracharya. Needless to say, Mandana's wife, Bharati, wasn't particularly thrilled. So she went to Shankaracharya and demanded, "The Vedic tradition says husband and wife are one being, doesn't it?" Shankaracharya admitted it did. "Then you haven't won the debate till you've conquered me, too!" she said.

Shankaracharya and Bharati started debating. Well, the lady gave him serious trouble. Shankaracharya admitted he didn't know the answers to some of her challenges about the value of married life since he'd been a renunciate since the age of eight. Embarrassed, he asked if he could have six months to ponder her argument. Knowing that Shankaracharya would never break his vows of celibacy and that he therefore would never be able to adequately respond to her statements about married life, Bharati granted his request.

Guidepost

If you're a fan of fun short stories, check out a Hindu classic called the *Pancha Tantra* at your library. It's a collection of tales about talking animals and the practical life lessons they learn the hard way. You may know this book better as *Aesop's Fables*, as the *Pancha Tantra* came to be called when it first arrived in the West.

Borrowing a Body

Fortunately for Shankaracharya, right at that time a local maharajah passed away. Shankaracharya asked his disciples to keep an eye on his physical body, then flew off in his subtle body to borrow the king's corpse. Just before his family was about to cremate him, the king suddenly sat up on his pyre and demanded to go home!

Now maybe you think borrowing a used body is an easy thing. (Or maybe you don't!) But even for advanced yogis like Shankaracharya there *are* complications. One is that a cast-off body is still basically hard-wired for its previous occupant. So the yogi winds up struggling with a nervous system programmed with the ex-owner's habits and desires. Shankaracharya started living in the maharajah's body in the maharajah's lavish home, with his numerous gorgeous courtesans and every other luxury and convenience a man of that era could desire. I'll leave the consequences to your imagination.

Back at their campsite, Shankaracharya's students began wondering why the master was taking so long to complete his research project and return to his own body.

Asking around, they heard that a raja from a nearby kingdom had died a few months ago, then suddenly revived during his funeral. The disciples thought "That's our guy!" and rushed off to see what was wrong.

Rescuing the Guru

At the maharajah's palace the disciples were shocked to see the "king" having an absolutely wonderful time partying with his girlfriends and enjoying the good life. This wasn't like the sternly ascetic teacher they'd once known! These disciples were sneaky guys though. They innocently sat down near the king and began to sing one of the songs Shankaracharya himself had composed about the ultimate emptiness of sensual indulgence and the everlasting glories of spiritual life.

Sages Say

"Souls are in bondage because they mistake their body for themselves! They take good care of the body, believing that's who they are. They become enmeshed in it like a caterpillar in its cocoon. And so they are swept here and there, rising and sinking in the ocean of death and rebirth. In reality, only the body dies. The Inner Being is forever."

—Shankaracharya

A stricken look appeared on the raja's face. Suddenly, to his family's horror, the king once again dropped dead. The disciples raced back to their campsite where, sure enough, Shankaracharya had already picked up his physical body and gone back to finish his debate with Bharati Mishra. Shankaracharya won the debate, and the Mishras were forced to become his students.

In the end, Mandana Mishra was so blown away by Shankaracharya's wisdom and yogic power that he became his leading disciple. As for Bharati Mishra, Shankaracharya had so much respect for her that he named one of his monastic orders after her.

Stories about advanced yogis temporarily abandoning their bodies to travel abroad are quite common in the Hindu tradition. In one famous incident some years ago, a yogi—a disciple of the legendary adept Bengali Baba—left his body in a locked room in a hospital in India. The doctor who had promised to look after it was called away on an emergency. Hospital staff found the "dead" body and carted it away. The yogi was startled to wake up several hours later in the morgue. But not as startled as the staff in the morgue when he got up and walked away!

Tales from Today

Last year my husband and I were fortunate enough to spend Guru Purnima, the holiday in which Hindus honor their spiritual teachers, with Shree Maa of Kamakhya. She's one of the greatest saints of northeastern India. She'd just returned to her ashram following an extensive tour and was disappointed to find that in her absence the ground had baked dry and her garden had withered away. No rain was due for several months until the rainy season began.

Shree Maa of Kamakhya.

© Photo courtesy of Devi Mandir, Napa, California.

Shree Maa told Parvati, one of her disciples, to go into the temple and recite mantras to Lord Indra, god of thunder and rain. Unfortunately Parvati obeyed her immediately, rather than waiting till after lunch. Many of us devotees were enjoying a picnic on the ashram grounds when abruptly the temperature plummeted ten degrees, dark clouds gathered, and suddenly we found ourselves and our plates of curry and chapattis getting soaked!

Later I asked Parvati about the unseasonal shower. "It wasn't me!" she protested. "It was Shree Maa. She just wills it and it manifests." Welcome to the magic of Hinduism, to the sympathetic connection between us and the universe. In the Hindu worldview, all nature is alive and is literally "all one." If Shree Maa needs her garden watered, she simply goes into that part of her consciousness that's one with the atmosphere. And turns on the rain!

Bringing Back the Dead

There are zillions of stories I could tell you but let me throw this one into the mix because it's so well documented in India. While these events were going on in the mid-twentieth century, they were headline news in Indian newspapers. Several movies have been made about it. The story is about the late Bengali Baba, one of the legendary holy men of the Himalayas, who left his last known physical body in 1982.

The prince of Bhawal had just died and was taken to the riverbank to be cremated. As his pyre started burning, monsoon rains struck so fiercely they put out the fire and swept the body into the river. It washed up on shore miles downriver where Bengali Baba and a group of his disciples were staying. Bengali Baba asked his students to free the body, which was tightly wrapped in linen sheets. Then he asked the recently deceased prince to get up—and he did!

The prince of Bhawal spent some time studying with the yoga master. The baba advised him to forget his worldly life and devote the rest of this incarnation to spiritual growth. But the call of worldly pleasure was too strong. The prince headed home.

Reclaiming Your Identity

The prince was anything but welcome when he got there. He'd been filthy rich and his money had already been distributed to his relatives. His wife had also taken up with a new lover. And besides, they just couldn't believe it was him. He was supposed to be dead!

The prince had to go to court to prove he was himself and get his land holdings back. It was one of the most publicized cases in Indian judiciary history. His relatives did everything in their power to prove the old prince had really died—including providing the testimony of the physician who had pronounced him dead! The prince, on the other hand, did everything in his power to prove he was still the same man he'd been before he "died."

This was Hindu India where, you will recall, all kinds of different versions of the truth can be true at once. The jury decided the prince had in fact died. But since Bengali Baba was a respected spiritual master, it didn't seem unlikely to them that he could recall the prince's soul to his body. The yogic practice of transferring someone's consciousness into a particular body is called *parakaya pravesha* in Sanskrit. So the jury pronounced in the prince's favor, and he got his property back! The case made Bengali Baba so famous that he disappeared into the mountains to avoid the crowds that flocked to see him.

It's News to Me!

Hindus believe the climate in the world is affected by the climate in our minds. Droughts, cyclones, floods, and other natural phenomena may be caused by our collective karma. If a change in weather is needed, ritual specialists can be hired to make offerings to the subtle intelligences who control the atmosphere. These priests work to improve the community's relations with the gods and request them to send better weather.

New Word Alert!

Parakaya Pravesha is the yogic practice of transferring your consciousness into someone else's body or restoring a dead person's life. Based on stories in the New Testament, some Hindus believe Jesus Christ mastered this yogic science while studying in India.

There's more than a little irony in the story. If the prince had stayed with Bengali Baba, he would also have had the opportunity to reclaim his identity. But it would have been his inner identity as an immortal being of chit and ananda, consciousness and bliss. Not as a prince in this world of funeral pyres.

Emergency Medicine

Recently K. N. Rao, a prominent Vedic astrologer in India, was glancing over a friend's horoscope when he noticed that the man was about to enter an extremely dangerous planetary cycle. Death was imminent. Rao didn't mention what he'd seen but strongly advised his companion to chant the Maha Mrityunjaya mantra faithfully every day. His friend wasn't an idiot. Knowing that an expert Vedic astrologer wouldn't recommend this particular mantra unless there was a darn good reason, he immediately began to chant it.

The Maha Mrityunjaya mantra is the great Vedic mantra for staving off death. Translated into English it goes something like, "I honor the All-Seeing One, Whose grace is all-pervading like the fragrance of a flower. May He release me from the grip of death as easily as a ripe fruit is released from a vine!"

A few weeks later this gentleman was conducting an inspection in a warehouse. A girder suddenly gave way and several tons of cement bags came tumbling down over his head!

Workers rushed to drag the heavy bags off him. But they were certain he'd been killed. If he hadn't died instantly from a blow to the head or been crushed, he should have suffocated in the time it took them to free him. It turned out that although Rao's friend had been knocked unconscious, once he came to he was no worse for the wear. He had a hairline fracture to a leg bone but was otherwise A-OK!

I guess most of us in the West would think this was just dumb luck. But Hindus take this kind of story as evidence for the protective power of mantras—and as proof that we can change our destiny with maybe a little boost from God's grace.

Sages Say

"Do not be frightened by God's cinema. Movies, whether enjoyable or disturbing, are merely movies. Is it not wiser to place our attention on that Power which is indestructible and unchanging? Make God the polestar of your life."

—Paramahansa Yogananda

Tales from the Lab

Christianity has always had an uneasy relationship with science. Some of the medieval Christians' fundamental beliefs, such as that the universe is about 6,000 years old or that the Sun circles the Earth, have taken a beating at the hands of scientists.

Although the Church is no longer allowed to burn scientists at the stake, the relationship between science and religion in the West remains embittered. In fact, scientists continue to wash their hands of so-called "supernatural" phenomena, which they refuse to research at all. And Christian fundamentalists still seek to keep some aspects of science, such as the theory of evolution or the explanation of human reproduction, out of public school education.

The relation between modern science and Hindu spirituality has started going much more smoothly. Although Western researchers were initially even more hostile toward Hindu teachings than Christian ones, many Hindu beliefs have stood the test of laboratory research and demonstrated their real value.

"We're Not in Kansas Anymore!"

The fireworks started in 1970 when Swami Rama of the Himalayas, who had been a high-ranking monk in the Hindu tradition, showed up at the Menninger Foundation, a leading research institute in Topeka, Kansas. He'd been recruited to serve as a human guinea pig in the Foundation's experiments on voluntary control of internal states.

Carefully monitored on some of the most advanced scientific equipment available at the time, Swami Rama quickly showed that he could control his heart rate, brain waves, and body temperature to an extent that up till that day had been considered humanly impossible by Western physiologists. He could effortlessly mimic brain death, for example, as well as alter his heart and breathing rates to barely perceptible levels. These were skills any yogi who had mastered the state of samadhi, deep meditative absorption, could demonstrate, Swami Rama explained.

It's News to Me!

Many Hindu mystics consider yoga to be spiritual science. In recent years, a spate of bestsellers by popular authors like Fred Alan Wolf and Gary Zukav have explored the astonishing similarities between the most advanced thinking in Western physics and the ancient tenets of Hindu spiritual science.

The results of these amazing experiments were written up in science journals and encyclopedias. But there was one experiment the researchers didn't report for years. The results were so unbelievable they feared that telling anyone about it would destroy their careers.

In that painstakingly controlled experiment, Swami Rama moved a metal spindle *just by looking at it.* Of course telekinesis—and even teleportation—are just two of the many abilities ascribed to advanced masters in the Hindu mystical tradition. But no one in Kansas, or just about anywhere else in the West, was ready to hear about that yet!

Researching the Impossible

I actually got to know Swami Rama fairly well over the years. He often complained how frustrating it was to work with Western scientists. They were only interested in what Swami Rama considered the most superficial aspects of yoga, the physical stuff. The real juice, he claimed, lay in what yogis could do *in consciousness*. But Western scientists refused to go anywhere near the fabled nonphysical skills of the yogis—even with a 10-foot pole!

Quick Quiz

1. The sage Vasishtha advised Prince Rama to ...

   a. Serve humanity and protect the innocent.

   b. Renounce the world and live in a cave.

   c. Shake—not stir—his coconut milk.

2. The goddess Sarasvati taught Queen Lila ...

   a. The secrets of life here and hereafter.

   b. The arts of cooking and sewing.

   c. How to operate a DVD player.

3. Hindus believe you can generate rain by ...

   a. Washing your car.

   b. Seeding clouds with ice crystals.

   c. Propitiating the deities who control the weather.

4. In science labs, the claims of yogis have ...

   a. Held up remarkably well.

   b. Been utterly disproven.

   c. Led to lawsuits over patents.

Answers: 1 (a). 2 (a). 3 (c). 4 (a).

Nevertheless, over the years Hindu mystical techniques scored again and again in the laboratory. Yes, meditation delivered as promised in terms of enhancing physical and mental well-being. So did Hatha Yoga postures. So did a balanced vegetarian diet.

Only a handful of Western scientists, such as Dr. Ian Stevenson of the University of Virginia Medical School, dared to venture into the realms of consciousness that Hindu mystics explored. Dr. Stevenson produced a large number of thoroughly researched case studies suggesting that reincarnation might possibly be a reality.

So the stories continue even into our own time. And still most folks in the West refuse to believe them!

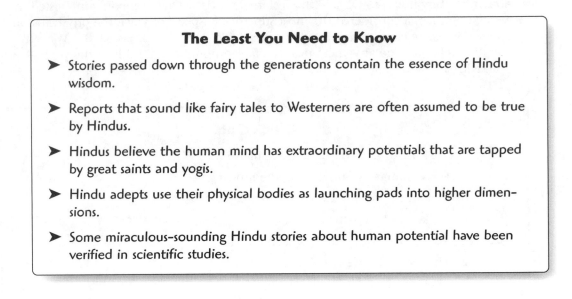

The Least You Need to Know

➤ Stories passed down through the generations contain the essence of Hindu wisdom.

➤ Reports that sound like fairy tales to Westerners are often assumed to be true by Hindus.

➤ Hindus believe the human mind has extraordinary potentials that are tapped by great saints and yogis.

➤ Hindu adepts use their physical bodies as launching pads into higher dimensions.

➤ Some miraculous-sounding Hindu stories about human potential have been verified in scientific studies.

Ranadasa

Living the Light

Saints come from all strata of Hindu society. Some have massive humanitarian missions with the goal of serving and illuminating the entire society. Others work in small groups for the purpose of achieving personal enlightenment. Many are totally unknown outside their own neighborhoods or the caves or huts where they quietly live.

There's not room enough in this book to tell you about the countless great souls of the Hindu tradition. Still, let me introduce you to at least a handful of the holy men and women of India. These are the people who continually recharge the Eternal Religion with the electricity of their devotion and illumined awareness.

Saints and Sages

Traveling through India now or in any other century you find a country of saints, sages, and yogis. The saints are known for the purity of their lives and for their love for God or Goddess. The sages are honored for their knowledge and wisdom. The yogis have mastered higher states of consciousness through intensive inner contemplation.

Some of the great souls marry and live among the rest of us. Others retreat from society to focus exclusively on the inner world. Both inner and outer paths are respected in the Hindu tradition. Some saints teach, others don't. Some, like Nammalvar, live in the world of silence from which all knowledge echoes.

The Silent Sage

Nammalvar's story is so incredible that if it hadn't happened in India, it wouldn't be believable. Some think this great master was born around the ninth century C.E. (Dating of events in Hindu history remains controversial.) He immediately caused his parents quite an upset. The baby didn't cry, didn't suckle—in fact he hardly moved! The bewildered parents eventually abandoned hope for his life and left him under a tamarind tree at their local Vishnu shrine.

The boy grew up under that tree in Kurukur, South India. He never uttered a word. One day a saint named Madhura Kavi happened to pass through town. He immediately noticed a 16-year-old sitting under a tree radiating the light of Self-knowledge. The saint sat down next to him and asked, "When we find the everlasting light within us, how do we nurture it?"

It's News to Me!

In Hinduism, there is a popular convention among male saints to imagine themselves as female in relation to God. Many Westerners are uncomfortable with men identifying with the female role. Hindus don't have this hang-up. They recognize that the depth and beauty of a woman's feelings are something men can benefit from imitating!

For the first time anyone knew of, the boy actually spoke. He said, "Immortality feeds off mortality and then rests above it." Did you understand that? Well, Madhura Kavi did. He realized he was in the presence of a truly great sage.

Remember in Chapter 7, "Born Again!" when I told you about vaishnava shakti, the force that takes effect at the moment of our birth, making us forget our previous lives? Devotees would later explain that vaishnava shakti failed to act in Nammalvar's case because of the high stage of consciousness he had attained in his last life. His parents had thought there was something wrong but in fact their baby was in a state of samadhi, deep meditative absorption. That was why he struck them as so unresponsive.

Love and Knowledge

Having finally broken his silence, Nammalvar went on to become one of the best-loved teachers of his era. He also composed a famous collection of poems to Lord

Vishnu called the "Tiruvaymozhi." Some are beautiful poems, told from a woman's perspective, of her passionate yearning for God. Nammalvar deeply identified with the feminine approach to the Divine.

Others of Nammalvar's poems are less devotional, more educational. For example, he writes:

> Each person, every person,
> all of them in their own manner
> honor their own gods.
> Each person, every person
> all of them sincere,
> will be embraced by God.

There is only one God, Nammalvar insisted, by whatever name or image you worship him. He advocated *prapatti,* total surrender to God, as the ideal spiritual path. This involves complete submission to God's will and total trust in his grace. God's ceaseless loving compassion was the inspiration of Nammalvar's life. Hindus consider him one of the two greatest South Indian saints of the Vaishnava tradition.

The Bride of God

The other greatest saint of the southern Vaishnavas is Andal, who may have lived in the ninth century. In the 16 years of her far too short life, she earned a place in Hindu hearts forever.

Like Nammalvar, Andal was abandoned as a baby. She was taken in by the famous saint Periyalvar, whose deep love for Vishnu influenced her profoundly. Periyalvar's devotional practice, incidentally, was to relate to God as a mother adores and cares for her child. Another instance of a male saint adopting a feminine approach to God!

As for Andal, from earliest childhood she could imagine no other husband than Lord Vishnu himself! When her foster father would prepare garlands to offer to the statue of Vishnu in the local temple, Andal would sneak in, put them on herself, and pretend she was a beautiful bride going to meet her divine groom. This was not cool. Hindus are not supposed to even *smell* a flower garland, much less put it on, until the image of God they're offering it to has had the first whiff.

Sages Say

"I consecrate my swelling breasts to Lord Vishnu, holder of the conch. If anyone even thinks of offering me to a mortal man, I couldn't bear to live! God of Love, would you allow a jackal to devour the food offered to the gods?"

—Andal

When Periyalvar discovered what his daughter had done, he left the spoiled garland at home. That night Lord Vishnu appeared to him in a vision. "Why didn't you bring your garland?" he complained. "The flowers Andal puts around her neck in such innocent devotion are my favorites!" After that Periyalvar let Andal play with the garlands as much as she wanted.

Eventually, however, Periyalvar became concerned that his daughter was taking bridal mysticism a little too seriously. She didn't seem to realize it was supposed to be a metaphor. You can't *really* marry God! He tried to arrange a marriage for her with a nice local boy but Andal wouldn't have it. "I won't marry a mortal!" she pouted. "I want God!"

The Passionate Poetess

Andal wrote two passionate poems for which she'll be remembered forever. The first is called the "Tiruppavai." In it Andal imagines she's a milkmaid in Vrindavan in the days when Lord Krishna lived there as a boy tending cows. She jumps out of bed in the morning and runs to collect the other milkmaids, so they can slip over to Krishna's house and catch a glimpse of his breath-takingly handsome face. She moans her jealousy of Krishna's conch because it enjoys the touch of his beautiful lips. In delightfully vivid imagery, she goes on to describe Krishna's mischievous escapades.

The "Tiruppavai" is so popular in Tamil Nadu that for the entire month of Margali (December–January) each year it's sung every day, especially by young girls on the lookout for husbands! Sections of Andal's other famous poem, the "Nachiyar Tirumozhi," which is explicitly erotic, are traditionally sung at every wedding in Tamil Nadu.

New Word Alert!

Prapatti means total surrender to God and complete faith in his loving care.

Andal got the wedding of her choice at the age of 16. It was a doozy! In a vision, Vishnu visited a priest at his temple at Srirangam and commanded him to bring his bride Andal to him. Andal's father Periyalvar had the same vision! Priest and foster father decked the teenager out as a bride. They then brought her to the temple where she joyfully approached the statue of her beloved Vishnu. She embraced the Lord—and vanished into thin air!

I don't know what to make of stories like these. Several other ecstatic devotees were similarly seen to simply disappear when they touched a statue of Vishnu, as if the Lord had simply whisked them away to heaven!

In following centuries, Andal became so popular that even Indian emperors considered themselves her devotees.

Manifesting Mangos

Ammaiyar is another extremely famous saint, who may have lived somewhere around the sixth century C.E. You'll see statues of her everywhere in South India. In fact, she's so well known you'll find images of her as far away as temples in Cambodia. Yet she and Andal were different as night and day.

Ammaiyar made her husband extremely uncomfortable. It started the day she began materializing mangos. He had brought home two mangos and asked her to save them for his lunch. But while he was at work a holy man stopped by their door begging for food. She gave him one of the mangos. At dinner that day her husband feasted on his first mango, then asked for the second one. Ammaiyar didn't know what to do. So she reached out to Lord Shiva in prayer. Instantly another mango materialized in her hand.

Ammaiyar's husband couldn't believe how wonderful the second fruit tasted and suspected at once it wasn't the one he'd brought home earlier. When he demanded where it had come from Ammaiyar confessed. "Give me a break!" her husband shouted. "If you expect me to believe that, ask Shiva for another one!" She did—and a mango appeared in her hand. But it vanished into thin air the moment her husband tried to touch it.

Sages Say

"They call Him lord of heaven, king of the gods. Others say He is the ruler of the world. This is what I tell you: That all-knowing One is the Pure Being who dwells in my heart."

—Ammaiyar

Phenomena like these kept occurring until Ammaiyar's husband couldn't take it any more. It totally freaked him out! "You're not a woman, you're a goddess!" he said, and took off for ports unknown. Happy to be disencumbered of her tiresome husband, Ammaiyar determined to devote the rest of her life to her true love, Lord Shiva.

Dancing in the Ashes

The pretty divorcee was soon attracting unwanted attention from men about town. (Note: Divorce is extremely rare among Hindus.) Ammaiyar quickly had enough of their harassment. She prayed to Shiva, "Please make me ugly like the ghosts that serve you in the cremation grounds!" Instantly she was transformed into a grotesque, emaciated hag. Now the local men left her alone!

Ammaiyar spent the rest of her life traveling from one pilgrimage site to another, including Mount Kailas in Tibet where Lord Shiva and his wife, Parvati, have their main residence. Everywhere she went Ammaiyar sang of her passionate love for Shiva, but in terms the romantic teenager Andal might not have been able to relate to …

> Is that body really dead?
> Ghouls test it with their bony fingers.
> Jackals rip apart the flesh
> and owls feast on the eye sockets.
> In the midst of this dance hall,
> while vultures tear loose the bowels,
> our beautiful Lord Shiva dances!

To Ammaiyar, the world is a crematorium filled with death and decay. The only beauty here is Shiva, the Supreme Consciousness who animates the material world, bringing inert matter to life. I'm not sure a saint like Ammaiyar would win many devotees in the modern West. But quite a few Hindu Shaivites admired her whole-hearted, if somewhat macabre, devotion!

Himalayan Masters

When we in the West think of the great Hindu masters, a lot of us imagine yogis meditating in the caves of the Himalayas. A pandit explained to me that "Himalayan master" really mean the great meditation masters who don't necessarily live high in the mountains, but who do continually live in high states of awareness.

One of these great beings was Baba Lokenath. He was born recently enough that we can quote his dates with some degree of confidence. He was born in 1730 and left his last known body on June 19, 1890, in East Bengal (now called Bangladesh). Yep, that makes him 160 at the time of his death. That's somewhat young by the standards of the masters of the high Himalayas—some of whom, Hindus say, spend up to 400 years in the same body. Maybe you should sign up for that yoga class after all!

Guidepost

Want to live a long, healthy life? Studies have shown that the yogic lifestyle, including a light vegetarian diet, and lots of Hatha Yoga and meditation, can substantially increase longevity.

Training for Immortality

Lokenath began his yogic training at age 11. The training was rigorous. In fact, it may sound like child abuse to Westerners! His guru would have him fast for one day, then two, gradually working all the way up to 30-day fasts. He was expected to sit for days and nights on end without moving a muscle—not even getting up to answer the call of nature! His guru would sprinkle trains of sugar toward Lokenath's body so that ants would bite him. The point was to remain still, no matter what—to keep his attention trained within.

Lokenath and his fellow yoga students would sit completely naked in the high Himalayas through the winter. I know this sounds like a sadistic fantasy, but I've seen graduates of this type of education with my own eyes. Not only are they impervious to the freezing cold but, incredibly, they're healthy as horses!

Lokenath admitted later the training was really tough, but it did produce the desired result. Eventually he was able to sit in the highest states of samadhi, the deepest states of meditative absorption humanly possible, for weeks on end. And at the age of 90, he reached his goal, stabilizing his awareness in permanent cosmic consciousness.

What is this state like? Lokenath describes it this way. "Everything that exists within the cosmos I feel existing within myself. I am a limitlessly vast expanse of awareness existing throughout space and time. This state is impossible to put into words so most of the time I just keep quiet. Even when I'm sitting here talking to you, another part of me stays in that super-conscious state. The experience of my true identity as all pervading consciousness never leaves me for a moment."

Lokenath had achieved what Hindus consider true immortality. He had established his awareness in the part of himself—in the part of the universe in fact—that's undying.

Sages Say

"Everything is beautiful. I am in this world of yours but I lost the capacity to think the way you do the day I realized my true Self. That's why I can't find fault with anyone. Whatever I see, good or bad, it's all God."

—Baba Lokenath

Seeing the World

What do Hindu sages do with themselves after achieving enlightenment? Lokenath and his companions, apparently having nothing better to do, took off to see the world. Their first stop was Mecca. They walked the whole way and stayed for years to study the Koran with a Muslim saint. During his life, Lokenath would make the trip to Mecca three times in an effort to prove by his example that Hindus and Muslims can live together in mutual respect.

Back in India, Lokenath formed a gang of Self-realized yogis which included Trailinga Swami, another immensely famous long-lived saint who spent much of his life in Benares. They took off on a series of adventures, including walking naked all the way to Siberia! When the cold Russian winter became too much for them they would stop for a few months to acclimate to the temperature, then push on further north. Lokenath later described the sunless winter of the far north, mentioning how short the natives there were. Of course everyone was short to Baba Lokenath, who stood an incredible seven and a half feet tall!

Unblinking Vision

At the age of 134, Lokenath finally settled down and began his public service work. Devotees built an ashram for him in East Bengal. Immediately stories of extraordinary miracles began to circulate. Hindus and Muslims alike poured in a continual stream to the gates of his hermitage. Lokenath was a *kalpataru,* a wish-fulfilling tree, the pilgrims reported. All you had to do was sit in his shade. Infertile women became pregnant, the incurable were healed, the poverty stricken found aid.

New Word Alert!

A **kalpataru** is a "wish-fulfilling tree." This is a designation for those saints who are so gracious they'll grant you whatever you ask for. They've gained so much good karma through their saintly activity that they have plenty to share!

It's News to Me!

Today many brahmin boys are rejecting the priestly vocation of their fathers for secular careers. This has created a shortage of traditional Vedic priests, particularly in Hindu communities abroad. Now more women are being trained to assume the religious roles men are abandoning.

Lokenath would spend the entire day greeting the desperate souls who came seeking his blessings. Then he would lock himself away at night, leave his body, and head back to the Himalayas or into Tibet to teach the yogis in training there. The devotees who watched him closely over the 26 years of his public work reported that no one ever saw him blink! His eyes were *always* wide open. At night when he was locked away, his body would slump over without breath or pulse but his eyes would stay open! (Never shutting your eyes, even to blink, is part of an authentic tantric practice still taught by advanced adepts today.)

The master himself insisted he was not really performing the miracles. They were simply "happening," Lokenath said. When asked what was the root of his ceaseless compassion he answered, "I've traveled in the hills and mountains, the jungles and plains, all over the world, and I've never found anyone other than Myself. The One is everywhere. There is no other. When you truly understand this, you will know why I love you so much!"

A Wave of Women

While there have always been numerous women saints and spiritual teachers well known in their own communities, in the past most Hindu women have tended to avoid the national limelight. In the past century or so, however, there has been a movement on the part of a number of extremely prominent male saints to bring more women into roles of public prominence. Ramakrishna Paramahansa pushed his painfully shy wife, Sarada Devi, into becoming a world-renowned saint who initiated thousands into spiritual practice.

Early in the twentieth century, the famous tantric adept Upansani Baba formed a school to train women in the performance of Vedic rites. This upset many orthodox Hindus at the time, though the practice is gradually becoming more common. Upansani Baba's main disciple, Godavari Mataji, went on to become a famous saint in her own right.

One of the most respected Hindu sages of the twentieth century, Sri Aurobindo of Pondicherry, passed the leadership of his lineage to his female disciple Mira Alfassa. Swami Paramananda (the first yogi to move permanently to the United States) passed his lineage to Gayatri Devi. The list of recent leading saints and yogis putting women disciples in charge after their passing goes on and on: Swami Lakshmana of Ramana Maharishi's tradition, Dhyanyogi Madhusudandas, Swami Muktananda, Papa Ramdas, and Neem Karoli Baba, to name a few.

The male sages of Hinduism have given the signal: It's time for great women of spirit to come out from their hiding places and take their seat on the world stage!

Mother of Mysticism

Suppose you visit France. There you're amazed to find that all French people believe that Marquis de Lafayette is the father of American democracy. He conceived the idea of government for the people and by the people. He wrote the Declaration of Independence. He led the Americans in a victorious war against the British. You pick up a French textbook on American history, and it never mentions Thomas Jefferson, Benjamin Franklin, or John Adams. George Washington appears only as a blundering adjunct to the brilliant and inspired Lafayette. Would your mind boggle?

Okay, now imagine this. A Hindu visits North America or Europe. He arrives from India—the country with the most saints per capita per century of any culture in the world. A country where the ideal of selfless service has been the foundation of religious life since time immemorial.

Yet everywhere he travels in the West, the Hindu finds people who believe that a Yugoslavian Catholic nun named Mother Teresa was the preeminent saint of modern India. She alone served the teeming masses of Calcutta while Hindus leave their own people to die in the streets. Only white Christians, sacrificing their health and comfort, make any effort to help the poor and dispossessed in India. Can you imagine how the Hindu's mind would boggle?

Guidepost

When talking with Hindus, it's best not to run on and on about how wonderful Mother Teresa was. Most Hindus are shocked by the common Christian misconception that only Christians do humanitarian service in India.

Angels of Mercy

I myself lived in Calcutta (now called Kolkotta) for some time and can personally attest to the number of Hindu missions working to help the poor in that unfortunate city. It's really sad that they receive no coverage in the Western press. Western reporters focused exclusively on Mother Teresa's mission in Calcutta and never neglected to mention that across the street from the Catholic center is Kalighat Temple— where "superstitious" Hindus slaughter goats in sacrifice to the Goddess Kali. What they do neglect to mention is that the animals are killed humanely and the meat, along with other food, is distributed free to the needy.

For thousands of years, Hindu saints have been the counselors, healers, and reformers of India. The tradition continues to this day. Whenever an acknowledged saint arrives in town, Hindus flock to him or her to pour out their problems and describe their medical symptoms. Those who can't afford a doctor or professional advisor know they can count on the saints and their disciples to help them free of charge. And since saints are believed to have extraordinary powers due to their mastery of advanced meditative states, their blessings and advice are highly valued.

It's News to Me!

The Western media creates the impression that all Hindus live in desperate poverty and uses images from Calcutta to support this claim. In reality, much of the poverty in Calcutta is due to the continual deluge of refugees fleeing Bangladesh.

The Indian government is not wealthy, and unfortunately, it's usually not very efficient either. So when a community needs help, it often turns to Hindu religious leaders rather than federal officials for aid. For example, holy men and women like Swami Rama Bharati, Amritanandamayi Ma, Satya Sai Baba, and Karunamayi Ma have responded to people's health concerns by virtually single-handedly organizing huge medical facilities—in some cases, whole hospital cities! Saints have earned both the prestige and trust that inspires doctors, nurses, and wealthy donors to come forward to help build new hospitals, which serve the poor free of charge.

And during national crises, such as the 7.9 earthquake in Gujarat in January 2001, Hindu spiritual leaders were able to organize their own communities quickly to send food and medical relief volunteers.

Quick Quiz

1. The saint Nammalvar ...

   a. Merged into an image of God.

   b. Is the model for the fictional character Harry Potter.

   c. Remained completely silent till he was 16 years old.

2. The saint Ammaiyar ...

   a. Asked to be made beautiful for God.

   b. Asked to be made ugly for God.

   c. Couldn't make up her mind if she wanted to be beautiful or ugly.

3. The saint Lokenath ...

   a. Walked thousands of miles with his eyes closed.

   b. Was a wish-fulfilling tree to those who came to him for help.

   c. Reached a ripe old age by eating cultured yogurt.

Answers: 1 (c). 2 (b). 3 (b).

In the Light of Spirit

India is the mother of mysticism. While some Hindu saints are famous for their philanthropic efforts, Hindu sages are even better known for living the light. Religion is not an abstraction for most Hindus because saints still walk among them. They demonstrate through their own lives what it means to love God. They keep the link with the ancient Vedic masters strong by living the life of spirit just as the adepts of yesteryear prescribed. They prove that enlightenment is possible.

Hindu saints keep the roads open—even during the worst weather. Roads with names like Karma Yoga, Bhakti Yoga, Jnana Yoga, Raja Yoga, and Tantra. The roads to God.

The Least You Need to Know

➤ Contrary to Western belief, Mother Teresa was not the only saint in modern India.

➤ Some saints are particularly noted for their extraordinary devotion to God or the Goddess.

➤ Saints like Baba Lokenath are famous for their healing and blessing power.

➤ Increasingly, Hindu women are playing a prominent role in religious leadership.

Chapter 27

Ancient Religion in Modern Times

In This Chapter

➤ The best and the worst of ancient civilization

➤ Progressives in a conservative tradition

➤ The Hindu/Muslim conflict

➤ Hindu exodus

➤ Enlivening an ancient faith

Hinduism is by far the oldest of the world religions. No other faith even comes close. While other cultures around the world have aggressively stamped out their ancient traditions, Hindu civilization has preserved the wisdom of the ancients. When we listen to brahmin priests chanting the Veda today, we are hearing the echoes of the great spiritual masters who lived six thousand years ago. When we read the history and cosmology recorded in the *Puranas,* we may be catching a glimpse of legends that go back to the last Ice Age.

Archeologists have confirmed what Hindus themselves have always claimed: In thousands of years, their faith has changed little. The Hindu tradition is extremely conservative, having held its basic shape for millennia. This is a religion with a lot of baggage. Some of which, reformers claim, it's time to toss out.

Can such an old tradition meet the challenges of modern times? Can a religion so resistant to change accommodate the realities of technological progress and progressive social ideas? Will a faith so rooted in the past be able to flourish in the future?

From Bullock Cart to Computer

The Western world made the transition into the modern era relatively gradually, taking about two centuries to shift from a predominantly rural culture into an urban civilization. The Industrial Revolution heaved the West into a new technological era that ultimately catapulted astronauts to the Moon and put radios, then televisions, then microwaves, then computers in nearly everyone's home.

India is making the jump to light speed in an eyeblink. When I'd visit India in the early 1990s, Hindu children shared with me their dreams of one day moving to America. They hoped to find better paying jobs there than were available almost anywhere in India. By the early 2000s, migrating to the United States or United Kingdom had nearly dropped out of their dreams. The new buzz word was "I.T." (Information Technology). Bangalore is the new Silicon Valley. Plenty of good jobs in Bombay, too. Who needs the United States?

The Impact of the West

Against all odds, since expelling the British, India has been pulling itself up by the bootstraps and putting itself back on the map. In the early 1990s, finding a working telephone in India was always an interesting challenge. Less than 10 years later, almost everyone has access to a phone. Even many remote villages have electricity now and (I flinch to report this) satellite TV.

Sages Say

"Western culture gives freedom to the individual, regardless of the hurts he may cause to elders, spouse and children. Eastern culture gives freedom within the bounds of duty to elders, spouse, and children. The sense of duty is the foundation of Hindu culture, and in performing duty one finds freedom within oneself through the higher accomplishments of yoga."

—Sivaya Subramuniyaswami

There is no underestimating the impact that TV and cinema can have on a culture. Contentment and a lack of aggressive materialism have long been the bedrock of Hindu culture. These values could blow away like dust before the onslaught of Western TV programming, commercials, and pornography now being broadcast into Hindu villages.

Along with rampant consumerism, the media has brought a whole range of new ideas into Hindu communities. Imagine women actually getting university degrees, supporting themselves, and living on their own! Imagine the children of sweepers, even of butchers, growing up to take jobs that make them the virtual equals of priests and administrators. This is radical stuff for Hindus!

Most of the founders of modern India, men like Jawaharlal Nehru, were British educated. Their essentially Western worldviews inspired them to declare India a secular, democratic state. Western democratic ideals have not always sat well with Hindu orthodoxy and its entrenched belief in social hierarchy. (It may be useful to bear in mind that democracy was not exactly eagerly embraced by the upper classes in Europe either!)

Wisdom and Inertia

Hinduism has preserved both the best—and the worst—of ancient culture. Prejudices cherished for six thousand years are unlikely to change overnight—in fact, they're unlikely to be recognized as prejudices at all. And practices that have been in effect since before the dawn of history, such as dumping one's garbage in the river, are difficult to change now when there are a billion Indians throwing their refuse into the waterways. The practical consequence is that today even the holy Ganges itself is choking with pollution.

The rapid changes of modernization are forcing Hindus to begin looking at many issues that even the most prescient sages could hardly have foreseen. But as changes begin to occur, particularly among the younger generation which craves more of the material goods and freedoms of the West, there's the very real danger of throwing out the baby with the bath water. Down through the ages, Hinduism's most brilliant religious leaders have helped Hindus adjust to changing conditions that arose. But today's more material-minded Hindus may be less inclined to listen to their spiritual elders.

As Swami Vivekananda pointed out, rather astutely I think, "This is the only country where poverty is not a crime." In olden times, Hindus evaluated their quality of life based on the qualities they had in their hearts. Increasingly Hindus are joining the West in judging themselves and others by how much they own.

In the rush to change, ancient spiritual wisdom preserved in India—wisdom that once existed everywhere but has been forgotten in almost every other culture around the world—could be lost forever. What will happen when young boys like Lokenath (see Chapter 26, "Living the Light") no longer

Sages Say

"The tragedy of human history is decreasing happiness in the midst of increasing comforts."

—Swami Chinmayananda

Sages Say

"Shall India die? Then from the world all spirituality will be extinct; all moral perfection will be extinct; all sweet-souled sympathy for religion will be extinct; all ideality will be extinct; and in their place will reign the duality of lust and luxury as the male and female deities, with money as its priest; fraud, force, and competition its ceremonies; and the human soul its sacrifice."

—Swami Vivekananda

dream of becoming great yogis? Or when young girls like Andal (see Chapter 26) no longer fantasize about mystical union with God? Hindus may gain the material wealth they crave, but like much of the rest of the modern world, they could lose their soul in the process.

The Hindu Reformation

For all its strengths, Hinduism is burdened with all-too-evident weaknesses. For example, for all the lip service Hinduism pays to womanhood, the mistreatment of women is still far too common in Hindu communities. Most Hindu women leave home at marriage to move in with their in-laws. Parents know it is their sons, who remain in or near home, who will support them in their old age. (There is no Social Security system in India.) Therefore, a premium is placed on the birth of sons.

Overpopulation is perhaps the single most serious problem in India today. At a time when families should be cutting back on the number of children they produce in order to ensure that there are food, education, and jobs for all, parents instead still keep having more kids in the effort to produce more boys.

There's another serious problem. The Veda says that God divided himself into the four classes of society. Unskilled workers are his feet. Rather than recognizing that people need all their limbs to function optimally, some Hindus use this schema as an excuse to consider those in "lower" classes to be less worthy of respect than themselves. This caste consciousness has become endemic in much of Hindu culture—to the extent that even "low" caste people look down their noses at anyone unfortunate enough to be even lower!

Guidepost

How do you define happiness? I've often been impressed by Hindu villagers, who are dirt poor by American standards, but are healthy and cheerful. They haven't learned yet that they can't be happy because they don't drive a Lexus. Having enough food and shelter, combined with a rich culture, warm family relationships, and a satisfying spiritual life, is enough to make most traditional Hindus quite happy.

Caste and subcaste systems, originally designed to recognize the natural talents of individuals and to help organize society, are now too often used to demean and exploit people lower in the pecking order. That a religion whose central tenet is tolerance toward others should foster such intolerance toward its own members is a poor reflection on the equal vision of the Vedic seers.

Over the centuries, reform movements, such as that of the Vira Shaivites (who I introduced in Chapter 15, "The Main Denominations") and some tantric and bhakta groups, have had an impact on Hindu attitudes. Let's look at a few of the better-known recent reformers who have grappled with the painful issues of what they believe works, and what doesn't work, in Hinduism.

Making Room for Reform

Ram Mohan Roy (1772–1833) was the first major Hindu reformer of the modern era. Widow burning was not common but still did occur in India. A verse in the Veda calls on widows to step into their husband's funeral pyre. It then invites them to leave their husband (and their grief) and step back into the world of the living. A misreading of this verse was sometimes used to justify the immolation of widows. Some women would actually cremate themselves voluntarily, with the unshakable conviction that death would reunite them with a husband they loved very much.

Ram Mohan Roy pressured the British into passing laws against this practice. (Christians had pretty much stopped burning women alive by the end of the seventeenth century.)

In 1828, Roy formed a powerfully influential organization called the Brahmo Samaj with the idea of returning to the original Upanishadic vision of Hinduism. For him this meant throwing out ritual worship and using reason to uncover the Supreme Being who exists beyond all names and forms. The Brahmo Samaj founded schools to teach English and Western science so that Hindus could compete in the English-dominated world. Ethics and a rational approach to spirituality were emphasized.

Roy's successor was Debendranath Tagore (1817–1905). (If the name sounds vaguely familiar, you may be thinking of Debendranath's son Rabindranath Tagore, the Nobel prize–winning poet.) Tagore went so far as to suggest that the Veda wasn't infallible, though he still valued the *Upanishads*. But Keshab Chandra Sen (1838–1884) went even further—in fact, too far for even most liberal Hindus. He claimed that people of the lower castes were equal with the upper castes, and brahmins should stop wearing the sacred thread that symbolized their supposedly superior position in society. Since he wasn't a brahmin himself, this may have been a comparatively painless claim for him to make.

The Brahmo Samaj split in two, with Tagore at the head of the Adi Samaj and Sen heading the Brahmo Samaj of India. Keshab Chandra Sen would win a name for himself as a humanitarian, raising funds for disaster relief and schools, campaigning against child marriage, and campaigning for intercaste marriage and widow remarriage.

It's News to Me!

The Hindu reformer Ram Mohan Roy was deeply impressed by Jesus Christ. In fact, he translated the Bible into Bengali! However, he was not at all popular with Christian missionaries, whom he accused of distorting Jesus' words and not following his teachings.

Back to the Source

Swami Dayananda Sarasvati (1824–1883) ultimately had a more enduring impact than most of the other Hindu reformers of this era. He founded the Arya Samaj in

1875, launching an aggressive counteroffensive against Christian and Muslim missionaries. Unlike Tagore, he was very much pro-Veda. He advocated the return to the vision of the Vedic seers which, he said, did not include temple worship. Real Hindus, he felt, should take their guidance from the Veda itself. Not from supplementary and possibly misleading texts like the epics or the *Puranas*.

New Word Alert!

Shuddhi means purification. The shuddhi ceremony was used to restore Hindu status to former Hindus who had converted to Christianity or Islam.

Dayananda campaigned against the marriage of younger brides to older grooms. This practice inevitably led to an enormous population of widows. The Arya Samaj founded numerous schools where Sanskrit and the Vedas were taught. The Arya Samaj welcomed many Hindu converts to Christianity back into Hinduism through the rite of *shuddhi*. This was a purification ceremony through which even former outcastes could return to the Vedic fold with honor.

Many of the more militant Hindu organizations of today take their inspiration from the Arya Samaj and its no-holds-barred approach to reestablishing Vedic culture.

A Wider Agenda

Both the Brahmo Samaj and the Arya Samaj caused big stirs in their day. In fact, the Arya Samaj is still a force to be reckoned with. However, both organizations had difficulty connecting in a deep or lasting way with the masses. The main players in these organizations tended to be intellectuals to whom God was formless and transcendent. They didn't take into account the less intellectually sophisticated but perhaps more genuinely heartfelt devotion of the ordinary Hindu, who needed a picture of God or the Goddess to hold in mind while worshipping.

To most Hindus, temple worship, praying to gods and goddesses, and hearing about divine incarnations are deeply meaningful spiritual experiences. The nineteenth-century thinkers had been strongly influenced by Western values, for better or worse. They took too seriously the charge that Hindus were "idol worshippers" and missed the authentic spirituality of such ancient practices.

Saints, however, often have a very different approach to social reform than intellectuals. Most commonly, they focus on self-transformation as the key to improving social conditions. Unlike the nineteenth-century reformers, most Hindu saints sanction the expression of love for the Divine in temple worship and worship in the home shrine. They feel that to "reform" Hinduism of its loving connection with the many faces of the Supreme Being would be to purge it of its heart.

Amritanandamayi Ma is a remarkable example of an exceptionally successful contemporary reformer. She begins by calling for a reformation of the human heart. She calls on her hundreds of thousands of devotees to love all and serve the needy. By modeling a life of self-less service herself (just a few of her numerous service activities were described in Chapter 20, "The Path of Action"), Ammachi, as she is called, has connected with the masses in a way the leaders of the Brahmo Samaj were unable to. Saints walk their talk.

In the presence of Jesus, it's said the lion lies down with the lamb. In the presence of saints like Ammachi, the brahmin sits down with the shudra. And when a "supernova of spirituality" as *Hinduism Today* has called Ammachi calls for fair and respectful treatment of women or the lower castes, men are inspired to listen. It's hard to argue with the universal love and amazing wisdom of one of Hinduism's greatest saints.

Sages Say

"There's only one reason for human life. That's to help others through our actions, our possessions, our words and our thoughts."

—*Bhagavata Purana* 10:22.35.

Toe to Toe with Islam

Hinduism is facing a number of extremely difficult challenges today. First there is the overpopulation spurred in part by the Hindu concern for producing male heirs. Then there is treatment of women and people of the lower classes that fails to reflect the loftier vision of the more equal-minded Hindu sages. But today, Hindus face a problem with potentially cataclysmic results not only for themselves but for the world at large. If Hindus can't settle their difficulties with Muslims, a nuclear exchange is not outside the range of possibility.

The relationship between Hindus and Muslims has not always been a happy one. The passion of some Muslim commanders for converting the world to their religion had grim consequences for Hindus when Islamic warriors began pouring over India's northern borders around 1000 C.E.

Many Muslim rulers in India were relatively tolerant and a few, such as Akbar the Great (1556–1605), were practically half-Hindu. But other fanatic Islamic rulers laid waste to India in a deliberate attempt to eradicate Hinduism. At the beginning of the second millennium, Mahmud of Ghazni virtually annihilated whole cities, as did the Emperor Aurangzeb, who ruled from 1658 to 1680. Practically every major Hindu temple in North India was demolished. Tens of thousands of Hindus who refused to accept Islam were put to the sword. These activities did not do much to improve Hindu-Muslim relations.

A Clash of Cultures

Muslims say there is one God whose name is Allah, and Mohammed is his last authenticated prophet. Hindus say there is one God whose name is any name you want to give him or her, and prophets—even divine incarnations—appear on Earth all the time, including right now! Muslims say God is formless and should never be worshipped—or even imagined—in any form. Hindus say God is formless and can be worshipped in any form since he or she pervades them all.

Muslims teach the equality of men. This is an affront to Hindus, who tend to view all of nature, including humankind, against the hierarchy of caste and subcaste. Both Muslims and Hindus are patriarchal, but the Hindu view toward women tends to be somewhat more liberal. If you're a woman traveling alone in South Asia, in general you're safer in a Hindu country than a Muslim one. In India today, women are free to drive or attend college, though these things remain illegal for women in some Muslim nations.

Hindus have made room for outsiders who came to stay, often gradually absorbing invaders and immigrants into their culture. But Hindu and Muslim worldviews appear irreconcilable. Mohammed Ali Jinnah tried to solve the problem by calling for the splitting up of India when the British left in 1947. This led the Brits to partition India into two countries: India proper and East and West Pakistan. (East Pakistan is now independent Bangladesh.)

It's News to Me!

The Partition was one of the bloodiest events in human history. Some 600,000 people died in violent clashes as fourteen million Hindus and Muslims exchanged countries.

Jinnah's idea was that Muslims would live in the two Pakistans in the far north and Hindus in India. Mahatma Gandhi fought the Partition, as it came to be called, but his worst fears came to pass. The forced evacuation of millions of Hindus from the newly created Pakistans, and of millions of Muslims from India, led to some of the worst massacres in human history. Both sides participated in atrocities. The horrendous karma of the bloody Partition haunts India and Pakistan to this day.

Nuclear Tensions, High Stakes Hope

As the twenty-first century opens, the stakes have never been higher. India and Pakistan are fighting over Kashmir, the ancient stronghold of Shaivite religion. Both countries now have nuclear weapons. While both have promised to show restraint, emotions run extremely high.

In an effort to promote healing between the two belligerent religions, saints like Kabir, Lokenath, Ramakrishna, and Shirdi Sai Baba publicly acknowledged the value of both traditions. In some cases, even to the extent of adopting spiritual practices from both religions! The saints dramatized through their lives that Hindus and Muslims can set hostility aside, forgive the past, and meet in spiritual community.

Hindus Abroad

In the past two centuries, the population in India has increased by an incredible 500 percent. In 1800, 200,000,000 people lived on the Indian subcontinent. By 1900, the figure rose to nearly 300,000,000. But by the year 2000, with the world population hitting 6,200,000,000, India now held one fifth of the human beings on the planet: 1,200,000,000 souls.

It may be possible to churn out that many babies that fast, but feeding and creating jobs for that many new people is no hat trick. A massive exodus in the second half of the twentieth century saw Hindus heading for ports abroad. More than a million Hindus live in England now, working alongside the people who used to be their masters. Another 60 million Hindus are scattered across the globe.

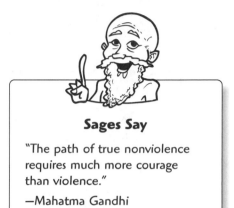

Sages Say

"The path of true nonviolence requires much more courage than violence."

—Mahatma Gandhi

Losing My Religion

A serious problem for Hindus abroad has been finding spiritual support. If there is no Hindu temple or cultural center nearby, children born in foreign countries can lose their sense of religious identity within a single generation. Kids want to fit in with their peers. For Hindu teenagers in North America that's often meant trying to seem a lot less "Hindu" in order to fit more smoothly into a predominantly Judeo-Christian culture.

I can't tell you how often I've heard Hindus in the United States bewailing the fact that their children don't know anything about their religious heritage. The problem is compounded by the fact that often the Hindus motivated to leave India in search of economic opportunities elsewhere are the very ones least educated in their own tradition—and therefore least qualified to pass it on to their kids.

It's News to Me!

Until recently, the word "religion," in Canada, applied only to Christianity and Judaism! When a Hindu couple tried to open a temple there, they ran into enormous legal obstacles because their religion wasn't recognized by the government. Because of their efforts, religions like Hinduism, Buddhism, and Islam finally achieved legal status in Canada in 1973.

A Spate of Temples

Is there a Hindu temple near you? If not, there may soon be. They're popping up all over! The million or so Hindus in North America have responded to their crisis in cultural identity by raising millions of dollars for temple construction—and thousands more to import brahmin priests from India. The priests conduct their age-old rituals for them and also, in some cases, teach their children classes on the *Bhagavad Gita* and other sacred texts and tales.

Quick Quiz

1. "I.T.", a booming industry in modern India, stands for ...

   a. International Terrorist.

   b. Information Technology.

   c. Inner Truth.

2. The Hindu saints Lokenath and Ramakrishna ...

   a. Taught that Hindus and Muslims can live together in mutual respect.

   b. Urged the Indian government to expel Muslims from India.

   c. Wore milk moustaches in a pro-dairy ad campaign.

3. The Partition ...

   a. Is the name of a popular television game show in India.

   b. Refers to the creation of India and East and West Pakistan.

   c. Divides the shower stall and toilet in an average Hindu home.

4. Brahmo Samaj ...

   a. Is a type of hump-backed Indian cow.

   b. Is the Hindu god of politics.

   c. Was an important Hindu reform movement starting in the 1800s.

Answers: 1 (b). 2 (a). 3 (b). 4 (c).

At my local Hindu temple in Napa, California, the major Hindu holidays are celebrated along with some Christian ones. On Christmas Eve, for example, we gather around the sacred fire to toss in our offerings of rice and barley grains while we chant Jesus' name in Sanskrit! Then Christmas gifts are distributed to all.

The walls of the temple are decorated with dozens of pictures of various deities and saints, including some from other religions. (Modern Hinduism is often truly universalistic in tone.) There are also statues of all the major Hindu deities and avatars. Since it's a Goddess temple, there are many images of the Divine Mother in her many guises. Some are benign, reminding us how much she loves us. Others are ferocious, reminding us both that she expects us to behave and that, when we have serious difficulties, all we have to do is think of her and she'll be here in an eyeblink to protect us.

About half the members of the temple are ethnically Indian. The others are blue-eyed Hindus like myself, non-Indians who have turned to this amazing ancient religion for the richness and beauty of its wisdom. I'll tell you more about us in the next chapter.

Guidepost

Do you know more about Hinduism than your Hindu neighbor? Some Hindu parents in America admit how embarrassing it is to run into non-Hindu co-workers who know more about Hinduism from taking a few yoga classes than their own children do.

The Least You Need to Know

➤ The rapid transition into a modern, democratic culture is challenging fundamental Hindu values.

➤ The Arya Samaj and Brahmo Samaj were influential Hindu reform movements rejecting ritual worship.

➤ Hindu-Muslim hostilities have a bloody thousand-year history with no resolution in sight.

➤ The population of India has soared from 200,000,000 to 1,200,000,000 in just 200 years.

➤ Hindus abroad are actively building more temples in order to preserve their heritage.

Hinduism in the New Age

"In the whole world there is no study so beneficial and so elevating as that of the *Upanishads*. It has been the solace of my life—it will be the solace of my death," wrote the early nineteenth-century German philosopher Arthur Schopenhauer.

Just about everywhere its teachings have been presented fairly, Hinduism has been a hit. Some of the important cultural components of Hinduism, such as the caste system, have failed to make a favorable impression in today's increasingly democratic world. But the mystical beliefs of the Vedic sages—from karma and reincarnation and the essential unity of all things to the mind-expanding powers of meditation—have been enthusiastically received wherever they've traveled.

As Hinduism leaves home and expands outward from India, it is winning increasing respect and support. Let's look at what's happening as Hindu teachers head West—and as more and more Westerners pack their bags for a pilgrimage to India.

Hindu Missionaries

It was 1893. The place was Chicago. Liberal religious thinkers like the Unitarian Universalists were sponsoring an event unprecedented in the West: a World Parliament of Religions. The concept was radical for the time. Representatives from all religions would be invited, and they all would be treated with equal respect. For the first time in the modern world, Christians and Jews would sit down at the table with Muslims, Buddhists, and Hindus and open-mindedly listen to what they had to say.

This extraordinary conference was widely reported in the world press. And by all accounts one man dominated the proceedings. Swami Vivekananda, the young man who demanded "Can you show me God?" (you met him in Chapter 11, "'Can You Show Me God?'"), blew away the attendees with his powerful presentation of Hindu wisdom.

"You are the children of God," Vivekananda thundered.

> The sharers of immortal bliss, holy and perfect beings. You divinities on earth, sinners? It is a sin to call a man so! It is a standing libel on human nature. Come up, live and shake off the delusion that you are sheep! You are souls immortal, spirits free and blessed and eternal. You are not matter, you are not bodies. Matter is your servant, not you the servant of matter!

Sages Say

"It would not be surprising to find Hinduism the dominant religion of the twenty-first century ... [I]t would offer something to everybody, it would delight by its richness and depth, it would address people at a level that has not been plumbed for a long time by other religions or prevailing ideologies."

—Professor Klaus Klostermaier

Vivekananda was deluged with requests to come teach throughout America and Europe. He would go on to found numerous Vedanta centers throughout the world—many of which are still in business today. Hinduism in the West was up and running!

Go West, Young Guru!

Vivekananda's spectacular success encouraged other Hindu teachers to set sail for foreign shores. Swami Rama Tirtha, a brilliant mathematician turned renunciate, headed for Japan and the U.S. in 1902. Besides fanning the flame of interest in Hindu thought, he was the first person known to have climbed to the summit of Mount Shasta in California! Rama Tirtha is still remembered in India with tremendous affection. His God-intoxicated poems and passionate essays on the spiritual rejuvenation of the world are prized treasures of the Hindu tradition.

Paramahansa Yogananda settled in the U.S. in 1920. Though he passed away in 1952, he continues to be one of the most influential Hindus of our era. I think it's fair to say his book, *Autobiography of a Yogi,* is one of the greatest spiritual classics of all time. It's still a top seller more than half a century after it first came out. Yogananda founded Self Realization Fellowship, a yoga society that remains popular in America today. Numerous other spiritual communities in the Western world base their doctrines on Yogananda's inspired teachings.

Meanwhile, Western pilgrims were beginning to head East in search of India's fabled spiritual wisdom. *A Search in Secret India,* Paul Brunton's 1935 account of his visits with Hindu masters like Ramana Maharshi, sold over a quarter million copies. Most people in the West were content with their own religion. But an increasing number looked to India for a spiritual tradition that satisfied their need for doctrines that made logical sense. And for time-tested avenues to mystical experience.

Advanced Spiritual Technology

American interest in the East simmered down during World War II and the conservative 1950s. But by the 1960s, India was once again attracting world attention as a homeland of spirituality. The Beatles' flirtation with Maharishi Mahesh Yogi, founder of the Transcendental Meditation movement, made headlines around the globe.

It's News to Me!

In the 1800s, Helena Blavatsky's Theosophical Society tilled the soil of Western interest in Eastern wisdom with its firsthand reports of the spiritual adepts of India. Blavatsky was continually attacked for insisting that Hindu sages were worth listening to. Yet it was her efforts to open Western minds that helped make triumphs like Vivekananda's possible. Her student Annie Besant was a major player in the bid for India's independence from Britain.

The late 1960s and early 1970s brought a massive wave of Hindu teachers to Western shores. Maharishi Mahesh Yogi was one of the most important. His widest impact came through his ability to inspire Western-trained scientists to actually test the claims of the meditation masters. Sure enough, one research study after another confirmed that yoga and meditation were valuable, health-promoting techniques.

I already mentioned Swami Rama Bharati (see Chapter 25, "Timeless Tales"), whose groundbreaking studies at the Menninger Foundation verified once and for all that yogis weren't just faking it. At least some of them truly had developed extraordinary, even superhuman-seeming, skills.

Yogis like these won legitimacy for the Hindu mystical tradition in the eyes of many previously skeptical Western critics. Clearly these yogis were custodians of an advanced spiritual technology the likes of which the West could hardly imagine. Members of some conservative church groups found this immensely threatening. I attended the first major yoga conference in America, held at the Palmer House in

Chicago in June 1976. Christian fundamentalists aggressively picketed the event. But the press was there to cover the strange and exciting spiritual ideas arriving from India.

The cat was out of the bag. A growing number of North Americans clamored to learn more about Eastern spirituality.

Hindu Ambassadors

One teacher after another arrived from India. Each offered a slightly different take on Hindu spirituality. Swami Muktananda offered shaktipat—the shot of enlightening energy that can be transmitted by some gurus—and encouraged his new disciples to honor the guru and chant "Om namah Shivaya!"

Bhaktivedanta Prabhupada was in his 70s when he showed up in New York City. He asked his devotees to give up drugs, alcohol, and free sex. Instead, he said, they should dance in the streets in honor of Krishna!

Satchidananda taught Raja Yoga, which he called Integral Yoga. His delightful sense of humor made him a favorite with the '60s generation. Anyone who attended the original Woodstock in 1969 will remember him opening the festival with his "wise cracks" and "Om!" chanting.

Sages Say

"To achieve realization a dying to the old self, the ego, is necessary. What has the old self given you that you should love it so? The divine self will give you all things and also give you bliss. Do not think in terms of 'giving up' anything. Think of 'growing.' Think of always growing stronger and more loving and more complete."

—Mother Meera

Then there was Sant Keshavadas, who settled in the San Francisco Bay area. Jyotirmayananda staked out Miami. Eknath Easwaran founded the Blue Mountain Community in California. Baba Hari Das set up the immensely popular Mount Madonna Community near Santa Cruz without so much as uttering a word. (He's been practicing silence for decades!) Vishnu Devananda, Hariharananda Giri, Amrit Desai, Yogi Hari—the list of Hindu teachers starting spiritual centers and even entire spiritual communities in the Western world runs on and on.

Neem Karoli Baba never visited America, yet he became one of the best-known gurus of all when an ex-Harvard professor named Richard Alpert changed his name to Ram Dass and wrote a massive best-seller called *Be Here Now* about the old saint. Satya Sai Baba, who never visited the West either, still managed to attract an enormous number of Western devotees with his message of universal love. His phenomenal psychic powers, such as his apparent ability to produce all kinds of objects seemingly out of thin air, attracted huge numbers of enthusiastic followers.

Women Gurus Win the West

Later in the twentieth century the ladies got their turn, too. Gurumayi Chidvilasan-anda took over the SYDA Yoga movement when Swami Muktananda left his body. Shree Maa of Kamakhya, Anandi Ma, Ma Yoga Shakti, and Karunamayi founded spiritual centers in America.

Some Hindu women saints were so popular they won large numbers of devotees without setting foot in America. Anandamayi Ma was so stunningly beautiful that many people fell in love with her just by seeing her photograph! This amazingly great sage left her body in 1982. Mother Meera offers her blessings from her adopted country of Germany. Devotees fly to Frankfurt from all over the world just to sit in the same room with her—even if she never says a word to them!

Amritanandamayi Ma (better known as Ammachi, which means "our dear mother") has attracted hundreds of thousands of devotees throughout Europe, Australia, and the Americas. She is recognized in India, and increasingly throughout the world, as one of the greatest saints of our time.

Hindu Culture vs. Hindu Spirituality

You may have noticed that my list of Hindu spiritual teachers who've had an impact in the West is composed entirely of yogis and saints. There's not a brahmin priest among them. And for the most part they function out of yoga and meditation centers, not Hindu temples. This is surprisingly different from Christianity, where it is primarily pastors and priests who spread the Gospel. They usually work out of churches and are financially supported by their denominations or diocese.

There are a couple of reasons for this difference. One is that until comparatively late in the twentieth century, U.S. and Canadian immigration laws kept a lid on South Asian immigrants. As a consequence, initially there were few Hindu temples in the Americas. The Indian population in North America was too small to support an influx of brahmin priests.

Secondly, the brahmins who run the Hindu temples in the West rarely see it as their job to go out and proselytize anyway. If sincere non-Hindus show up at their temple doors wanting to learn more, that's one thing. But the priests are not going to go out and try to steal people away from churches and synagogues they already belong to. Why should they? Hindus believe other religions lead people to God, too.

Western students attracted to Hinduism are often more drawn to yoga centers than Hindu temples

Guidepost

Where's the Hindu temple nearest you? Log on to the Hindu Universe Web site at www. Hindunet.org and find out!

anyway. The reason is that the temples represent both Hindu spirituality and Hindu culture. The majority of American and Canadian students are more or less comfortable with Western culture. It's the essence of Hindu mystical doctrine and practical forms of spiritual practice that the majority of Western students crave—not adopting the Hindu lifestyle complete with finding a place in the caste system and performing the traditional Hindu sacraments.

Most of the saints and yogis from India (with rare exceptions like Bhaktivedanta Prabhupada) didn't come to the West to impose Hindu culture on Americans. (This is the opposite of Christian missionaries, who often encourage their converts to adopt Western ways.) They don't even expect you to give up your birth religion. They're just here to offer tools and tenets from the Hindu tradition that will help you deepen and enliven your own spiritual practice, no matter what your culture or religion may be.

The Perennial Philosophy

One peaceful evening in 1876, a Canadian physician named Richard Bucke had a sudden, inexplicable mystical experience. He was relaxing quietly when, without warning, he felt an incredible sense of exultation and in "one momentary lightning-flash of Brahmic splendor" he actually experienced, to the core of his being, that "the Cosmos is not dead matter but a living Presence" and that "the foundation principle of the world is what we call love." The universe was actually consciousness itself! This was not a whim or an intellectual insight, but an actual explosion of awareness that knocked his socks off!

Sages Say

"[Cosmic] consciousness shows the cosmos to consist not of dead matter governed by unconscious, rigid, and unintending law; it shows it on the contrary as entirely immaterial, entirely spiritual and entirely alive; it shows that death is an absurdity; ... it shows that the universe is God and that God is the universe."

—Richard Bucke, M.D.

The experience lasted only a moment, but it radically transformed Bucke's life. What the heck happened? Bucke spent the rest of his life investigating the extraordinary phenomenon he called "cosmic consciousness." His book, *Cosmic Consciousness: A Study in the Evolution of the Human Mind,* came out at the beginning of the twentieth century. It catalogued descriptions of similar experiences recorded by historical figures, such as Jacob Boehme, Plotinus, Jesus, Mohammed, Swedenborg, Ramakrishna, and a friend of Bucke's, an American newspaper reporter named Walt Whitman.

At the time of his mystical experience, Bucke had known virtually nothing about Hinduism. Yet in one moment of illumination that quiet evening he rediscovered the central truths of Hinduism. This is the reason Hinduism can justifiably be called "the Eternal Religion." The experience of divine illumination on which Hinduism is based keeps reasserting itself. At any moment, at any place, someone somewhere spontaneously awakens. Hindus would call this the experience of *bodhi,* enlightened awareness. Dr. Bucke speculated that all humanity is evolving toward developing cosmic consciousness—a view many Hindu texts support.

In the early 1940s, Aldous Huxley explored similar themes in his classic anthology, *The Perennial Philosophy.* By this time, Hindu texts and teachers were better known to a wider Western audience. Huxley was able to quote at length from the *Upanishads* and the *Bhagavad Gita* as well as from Hindu sages like Shankaracharya. He pointed out the sometimes quite astonishing similarities between reports of mystical experiences in many different spiritual traditions.

Perhaps you noticed the title of Huxley's book is an alternate translation of the Hindus' name for their tradition, Sanatana Dharma, "the eternal religion."

Western Minds, Eastern Truths

From at least the time of the ancient Greek sage Pyrrho, who entered India in the entourage of Alexander the Great, some of the finest minds of the West have turned to Hinduism for inspiration. Many recognized in the Hindu tradition the clearest explanation of a perennial philosophy underlying the great mystical systems of the world. Some of the twentieth century's most progressive thinkers, such as Franklin Merrell-Wolff and Anthony Damiani, were avid students of Hindu philosophy.

J. Robert Oppenheimer is one of the fathers of the atomic bomb. What was he thinking when the first atom bomb was set off in the desert of New Mexico, reporters later asked. Oppenheimer admitted a verse from the *Bhagavad Gita* instantly flashed through his mind: "Death am I, cause of destruction of the worlds, matured and set out to gather in the worlds." It says something that a Western scientist working on the Manhattan Project should know the *Gita* by heart!

Numbers of leading American and European writers were deeply involved with Hinduism. William Butler Yeats helped translate several of the major *Upanishads,* the crown jewels of India's spiritual heritage. Christopher Isherwood helped translate

New Word Alert!

Bodhi is the experience of enlightenment. It's fully illumined awareness.

Sages Say

"[The Perennial Philosophy] is expressed most succinctly in the Sanskrit formula, *tat tvam asi* ('That art thou'); the Atman, or immanent eternal Self, is one with Brahman, the Absolute Principle of all existence; and the last end of every human being is to discover the fact for himself, to find out Who he really is."

—Aldous Huxley

the *Bhagavad Gita,* and wrote extensively on the Hindu saint Ramakrishna. Alan Watts's *The Book: On the Taboo Against Knowing Who You Are* was one of the best introductions to Hindu thought available in the 1960s.

Innocents in India

Mark Twain is perhaps the best-loved American writer of the nineteenth century. He's well known for books like *Tom Sawyer, Huck Finn,* and *Innocents Abroad.* Few of his American admirers know Twain traveled extensively in India. He called it the "cradle of the human race, birthplace of human speech, mother of history, grandmother of legend, great-grandmother of tradition."

Twain, usually quite a cynical fellow, was genuinely awed by the Hindu tradition. India, he said, was "the one land that all men desire to see, and having once seen, by even a glimpse, would not give that glimpse for all the shows of all the rest of the globe combined."

It's News to Me!

The nineteenth-century scientific genius inventor Nikola Tesla was an avid student of Hinduism. He and his friend Swami Vivekananda, the yogi who first taught Hinduism in America, liked to swap ideas about Western and Hindu sciences. Tesla borrowed Sanskrit terms like *prana* and *akasha* to describe the subtle forces at work in nature.

Joseph Campbell, the immensely popular American mythologist, traveled widely in India and was a good friend of the radical Hindu teacher J. Krishnamurti. He also assisted in the translation of one of the greatest spiritual classics of modern times, *The Gospel of Sri Ramakrishna.* At one point, he admitted that discovering the *Mandukya Upanishad* affected him more profoundly than the beginning of World War II!

Standing on Your Head

While Hinduism deeply affected some of the leading Western intellectuals, scientists, and artists, its most pervasive influence has been on Western popular culture. Today Hatha Yoga classes are taught at just about every physical fitness center throughout the world. Hatha was shaped into its present form over a thousand years ago by Hindu adepts in Bengal, such as Gorakh Nath and Matsyendra Nath. Its original purpose was to keep the physical body in optimal shape for advanced spiritual practices.

The "New Age" movement arose in the West in the latter half of the twentieth century. It grew out of an increasing disenchantment with the orthodox Western religions and a craving for a richer personal experience of spirituality. "New Agers" are sometimes satirized as superficial and superstitious. What their critics miss is the New Agers' open-mindedness, willingness to experiment, and heartfelt sincerity.

Hinduism, directly and indirectly, has contributed immensely to the New Age movement. The quest for understanding the Inner Self, meditation, visualization and stress-reduction techniques, vegetarianism, a fascination with "occult" powers, openness to the religious beliefs of indigenous peoples, some healing methodologies, recognition of past lives and the role of karma, and the search for the "spiritual master" were all adopted by New Agers from the Hindu tradition. In some respects, the New Age movement is virtually a beginning-level form of Hinduism.

Surveys show that over the past half-century, the number of Westerners who believe in "past lives" and who take the concept of karma seriously has skyrocketed. Most of these people would never identify themselves as Hindu. Yet their worldview has been profoundly altered by the great Hindu masters, whether they realize it or not.

Quick Quiz

1. At the 1893 World Parliament of Religions, Swami Vivekananda …
    a. Thundered that non-Hindus would go to hell.
    b. Caused an enthusiastic stir of interest in Hinduism.
    c. Sold hot dogs and cotton candy.

2. Maharishi Mahesh Yogi …
    a. Increased scientific interest in meditation.
    b. Encouraged youngsters to chant "Hare Krishna."
    c. Was the fifth Beatle.

3. The New Age movement was …
    a. Responsible for the recent decline in morals in the West.
    b. Started by a Mormon preacher named Joseph Smith.
    c. Deeply influenced by Hinduism.

4. Cosmic consciousness …
    a. Is the direct perception that everything that exists is consciousness.
    b. Is the basic experience out of which Hindu mysticism emerged.
    c. Has been independently rediscovered by individuals in many cultures.

Answers: 1 (b). 2 (a). 3 (c). 4 (a, b and c!).

Shaping a Hindu Future

From vast antiquity, Hinduism has been the mother of mysticism. It is the inspirational force behind some of the greatest saints and sages in the history of the world. It has spawned other major world religions like Buddhism and Sikhism. It has even served as foster mother of the modern New Age movement!

There are a billion Hindus in the world today, and hundreds of millions of non-Hindus deeply influenced by Hindu thought. As India matures into a First World superpower (it's already the biggest democracy in the world!), Hindus are poised to play an increasingly significant role on the world stage.

White Hindus

The twentieth century inaugurated a new phenomenon only rarely seen in the past: the white Hindu. At ashrams and temples throughout India, you'll see the white faces of pilgrims of European descent who have come to India in search of God and guru. (Asian pilgrims have been visiting India from time immemorial. Black visitors from Africa are no new phenomenon either. The Sidi people of Gujarat, for example, emigrated from Africa centuries ago.)

Today, tens of thousands of Americans sit down to meditate each day, repeating a mantra handed down through their guru lineage for centuries. At some of the Hindu temples in America, fully half the membership is white. You'll see young women of Dutch or Hungarian or Italian ancestry wearing saris, with a tilak on their foreheads. You'll see young men of Irish or French or Latvian ancestry playing traditional Hindu bhajans on their sitars—or their electric guitars!

Hinduism appeals on so many levels. There is the respect for nature and the communion with natural forces that was pervasive in ancient pagan religions but has been lost in the Judeo-Christian tradition. The Goddess, whose worship was stamped out throughout the Western world, is still a living force in Hinduism where the depth and inner mysticism of her tradition has been lovingly preserved from prehistory. There is the singing and dancing and worshipping before the images of the Divine where one's love for God and Goddess find full expression. There are the physical and mental exercises that expand one's capacity to directly experience spirit. And there is the guru. Having a realized guru is for Hindus like walking with Christ himself for Christians.

Whatever you call the Supreme Being, however you picture him or her, whatever name you give your faith, there is an inner core of genuine mystical experience that links your faith with every other one. Hinduism, the oldest world religion, has preserved the wisdom of the ancients and their techniques for transcendence. That's why Hinduism is still as vibrant and vital today as it was six thousand years ago.

A Beach Head for Hinduism

I'd like to close with a few words from my favorite American poet. In "Passage to India" Walt Whitman wrote:

> O Thou transcendent,
> Nameless, the fibre and the breath,
> Light of the light, shedding forth universes, thou centre of them...
> Athwart the shapeless vastnesses of space,
> How should I think, how breathe a single breath, how speak, if, out of myself,
> I could not launch, to those, superior universes?

Some white Hindus like me have made our hearts a beach head for Hinduism because we recognize in the Eternal Religion a launching pad for spirit. As the Goddess herself says in the *Tripura Rahasya*, between our own heart and the limitless being of infinity, there is no distance whatsoever. We have only to turn within to find the Divine One who exists everywhere. The Hindu sages show us how.

I hope this book has given you at least a little taste of one of the most delicious religions around. I offer my loving respect to the Divine One, to the saints and sages of all traditions, and to you!

The Least You Need to Know

➤ Swami Vivekananda's appearance at the World Parliament of Religions in 1893 led to widespread Western interest in Hinduism.

➤ Waves of yogis and saints have carried the essential teachings of the Hindu tradition to the West.

➤ Hindu spirituality, though not necessarily Hindu culture, has found enthusiastic adherents in the Western world.

➤ Notable American and European artists and intellectuals have helped transmit knowledge of Hinduism to the West.

➤ The experience of "cosmic consciousness" at the root of Hindu spirituality is increasingly recognized in the West.

Glossary

Here's some advice on Sanskrit pronunciation.

Hindus pronounce vowels something like Italians do. Depending on whether the vowel is short or long:

> a is pronounced like the u in "but" or the a in "father"
>
> e is pronounced like the a in "say"
>
> i is pronounced as in "it" or like the ea in "eat"
>
> o is pronounced as in "no"
>
> u is pronounced like the u in "push" or "brute"

There are a couple of vowels in Sanskrit that are almost impossible for Americans to pronounce, and for which we have no corresponding letter in the English alphabet. To save you trouble, I've transcribed them as "ri" and "lri," which is probably as close as we English speakers will get to pronouncing them anyway.

A few more tips:

> bh is pronounced like the bh between "club house"
>
> chh is pronounced like the chh between "church-hill"
>
> dh is pronounced like the dh in "adhesive"
>
> gh is pronounced like the gh between "dog house"
>
> kh is pronounced like the kh between "work house"
>
> ph is pronounced like the ph in "uphill"
>
> th is pronounced like the th in "anthill"

But:

> sh is pronounced as in "ship"

There are four different letters each corresponding to four different ways to pronounce the letters "d" and "t" in Sanskrit. Though Indians can easily hear the difference, we English speakers have a lot of trouble making them out. There are also two letters related to two ways to pronounce the sound "sh" as in shoe. These depend on exactly how you hold your tongue as you make the sound. Since most English speakers can't hear the difference, in this book I've transliterated them for you as just plain "d," "t," and "sh."

There is no "f" sound in Sanskrit, nor is there any "th" as in "that" or "thing."

For more information on Sanskrit, consult Judith M. Tyberg's wonderful *First Lessons in Sanskrit Grammar and Reading* (Los Angeles: East-West Cultural Center, 1964.)

Abhinavesha   Desire for life. Fear of death.

Adharma   Unethical behavior, unrighteousness.

Advaita   Nondual, one without a second.

Agama Karma   The karma generated by our plans for the future.

Agni   The god of fire. Fire itself. Matter in the process of combustion.

Ahankara   Self-identity. The sense of me and mine.

Ahimsa   Nonviolence. Nonharming.

Ajna Chakra   The center of awareness found several inches behind the point where the eyebrows meet.

Akasha   Extremely attenuated physical matter. The "stuff" of which "empty" space is made.

Akriti   Uncreated, eternal, from beyond time, space, and causation.

Allah   Muslim name for God.

Alvar   "One who dives deep." The 12 great South Indian Vaishnava saints of the eighth and ninth centuries.

Anahata Chakra   The chakra at the heart.

Ananda   Spiritual bliss.

Ananda Maya Kosha   The subtlemost body made of very rarified energy.

Anna   Food.

Anna Maya Kosha   The physical body.

Aparigraha   Nongrasping. Not being greedy.

Apas   Physical matter that's fluid (such as water).

Arati   Ritual waving of lights before a Hindu deity.

Archana   Ritual worship performed in one's home.

Artha   Wealth and material well being.

Ashram   A home where the central focus is spiritual practice.

Ashtanga   "Eight limbs." Another name for Raja Yoga, the form of yoga with eight components.

Asmita   Egotism and selfishness.

Asteya   Nonstealing.

Asura   A god. Or else a selfish, aggressive supernatural being.

Atma Nivedana   Surrender of the Inner Self to the Self of All.

Atman   The Inner Self. The immortal spirit.

Avatar   An incarnation of God or the Goddess.

Avidya   Ignorance, especially of our true spiritual nature.

Ayurveda   Indigenous Hindu medicine.

Baba   An affectionate term for a Hindu holy man.

Bhagavan   God.

Bhairavi   A female tantric practitioner.

Bhajan   A spiritual song, often extolling the divine qualities of God or the Goddess.

Bhakta   A person who's in love with the Divine.

Bhakti   Love for God or the Goddess. Spiritual devotion.

Bharat   The Indians' own name for India.

Bhava   Feeling of spiritual ecstacy.

Bhoga   Worldly enjoyment.

Bodhi   Enlightenment. Illumined awareness.

Bodhisattva   A Buddhist seeker who aspires to benefit all beings.

Brahmacharya   Celibacy. Avoiding unhealthy degrees of sensual indulgence.

Brahman   The Supreme Reality, the one all-pervading consciousness.

Brahmins   The caste of priests.

Buddhi   The mental capacity to make judgments. The higher intellect and conscience.

Dahl A dish of cooked beans.

Chai Indian tea, usually steeped in milk with spices.

Chakra A center of spiritual energy in the body.

Chakshu The sense of sight.

Chandas The sacred science of meter, used to help in pronunciation of sacred mantras.

Chappati A flat slice of fried, unleavened wheat bread.

Chit Consciousness.

Damodara Butter thief. This is an affectionate name for the mischievous child Krishna.

Darshana "Seeing." Any one of Hinduism's schools of theology, which are different ways of "seeing" God. Also, having the direct vision of the Supreme Being yourself, for example, when you see His or Her image in a temple.

Dasha Maha Vidyas The 10 great Goddesses of the Hindu mystical tradition.

Deva Literally, "a shining being." A divine being or deity.

Deva Loka The heaven world where exceptionally pure souls dwell.

Devi The Goddess.

Dhanur Veda The Hindu martial arts, particularly archery.

Dharma The best possible course, righteousness, the fulfillment of one's true purpose, virtue.

Dharma Megha The last hoop a yogi has to jump through before achieving enlightenment. When it is pierced by the kundalini, it releases a torrent of divine knowledge and bliss.

Dhruva The North Star.

Dosha Your constitutional type according to Ayurvedic medicine. There are three doshas: fiery, phlegmatic, and nervous.

Dvesha Hatred and aversion.

Gandha Matter that can be smelled.

Gandharva Veda The Hindu sacred arts of music and dance.

Garbha Womb, matrix, or the inner sanctum of a temple.

Ghee Clarified butter. An important ingredient in Hindu cooking and ritual offerings.

Ghrana The sense of smell.

Gita   A song or chant. Specifically, the *Bhagavad Gita.*

Gopi   Milkmaid. The gopis of Vrindavan are legendary as Krishna's most lovelorn devotees.

Guna   One of the three modes in which energy operates: rajas, sattva, or tamas.

Guru   Teacher. Specifically the spiritual preceptor.

Guru Shakti   Illuminating power, the energy of enlightenment.

Indriyas   The five senses.

Isha   An Indian pronunciation of the name Jesus.

Ishta Devata   Your personal deity. The god or goddess with whom you form an intimate relationship.

Ishvara   "Lord," a common name for God.

Ishvara Pranidhana   Remaining focused on God and surrendering to divine will.

Japa   The continual repetition of God's name or of a sacred mantra.

Jatkarman   The sacramental rite performed at the birth of a Hindu baby.

Jinva   The sense of taste.

Jiva   The individual soul.

Jivanmukta   A liberated soul who's still in a physical body.

Jnana   Knowledge, particularly experiential knowledge.

Jnani   A "knower." A Self-realized sage.

Jyotisha   The sacred science of Vedic astrology.

Kala   Time. Also the force that limits the soul's omnipotence.

Kalpa   Ritual science.

Kalpataru   A "wish fulfilling tree" or a saint who generously grants boons.

Kama   Sexual desire or desire in general. Pleasure.

Karana Sharira   The causal body or "seed" body. The body that reincarnates.

Karma   The law of action and reaction at work in the moral universe. "As you sow, so shall you reap."

Karmashaya   Karmic residue we carry from past lives, our old memories, habits, and desires, which are stored in our subtle body.

Kaya Kalpa   The technique for regenerating the physical body.

Kirtan   Devotional singing.

Kosha   A sheath or covering, such as one of the Inner Self's physical or subtle bodies.

Kripa   Divine grace.

Kriyaman Karma   The fresh karma we're producing in this lifetime.

Kshatriya   The warrior caste. Rulers, administrators, police, and military.

Kundalini   A subtle form of psychic energy, latent in most people, that lies at the bottom of the spine. When it is induced to rise through the spine into the brain, extraordinary states of mystical awareness are produced.

Linga   A conical or egg-shaped stone representing Shiva, Divine Consciousness beyond form.

Madhyama   Verbal thoughts heard with your inner ear.

Maha Deva   A "Great God" like Brahma, Vishnu, or Shiva, in charge of many minor Gods. This term is most often used for Shiva.

Mahat   The cosmic mind, the network of intelligence through which all living creatures are interlinked.

Mala   A Hindu rosary.

Manana   Deeply contemplating spiritual truth.

Manas   The part of the mind that processes sensory data and thinks.

Manipura Chakra   The chakra behind the navel.

Mano Maya Kosha   The mental body.

Mantra   A sacred sound, word, or phrase that leads the mind to a higher state of consciousness.

Manu   The forefather of the present race of humanity.

Mara   Evil, wrongdoing.

Maranatha   "Lord of Love."

Meru   The mountain at the center of the world. Astronomically it represents the north/south axis of the Earth. In yoga, it stands for the spinal column.

Mlecchas   Non-Hindu foreigners.

Moksha   Liberation from the bondage of karma and from the wheel of death and rebirth.

Mukti   Liberation. Another word for moksha.

Muladhara Chakra   The chakra at the base of the spine.

Murti   A statue of God or the Goddess, sometimes mistakenly called an "idol" by non-Hindus.

Nadi   A current of energy or "nerves" in the subtle body.

Nakshatra   A lunar mansion or a 13°20' sector of the Hindu zodiac.

Nama Japa   Continual repetition of the name of God or the Goddess.

Nayanar   The 63 great Tamil poet saints of the Shaivite tradition.

Nididhyasana   Deeply contemplating one's own Inner Self.

Nirguna   "Without qualities." Not having shape or form.

Nirguna Brahman   The transcendent God beyond the reach of thought.

Nirukta   The sacred science of etymology.

Niyama   A moral observance. Something you really ought to do.

Niyati   This force limits the soul's inherent omnipresence.

Pada   The ability to move around.

Panchama   Outcastes. People excommunicated from Hinduism.

Pani   The ability to handle objects.

Para Vak   Unmanifest meaning inherent in silence. The truth abiding in deep meditative states.

Parakaya Pravesha   The yogic practice of transferring someone's consciousness into a "dead" body.

Param Anu   An atom.

Pashupati   "Lord of tied-up animals." Shiva.

Pashyanti   Abstract concepts perceived in your higher mind.

Patala   Hell, a transient after-death state of mental terror and anguish.

Payu   Excreting.

Pitri Loka   The after-death realm of the ancestors where average-quality human souls dwell.

Prakriti   Primeval energy, the energy matrix from which matter emerges.

Prana   The breath or life energy, vital force, *chi.*

Prana Maya Kosha   The body made of life energy.

Prana Pratishtha   The process of infusing the image of a deity with life breath, so the image becomes alive. It is now a conduit for divine grace.

Prapatti   The devotional path of total surrender to God.

Prarabdha Karma   That portion of our karma destined to manifest in our present lifetime.

Prasad Food or some other offering you've brought to the image of a Hindu God or Goddess. It's returned to you with divine blessings.

Pratyabhijna Self-recognition. Recollecting the Divine Consciousness in oneself.

Prithivi Dense physical matter (like earth).

Puja A religious ritual, usually involving making offerings to an image of a deity.

Purana "Ancient chronicle" or "book of the ancient times." There are 19 major *Puranas* and an ever increasing number of minor ones.

Purushottama "The Supreme Person." God, Vishnu.

Raga Different styles of classical Indian music. Also, desire and attachment.

Raja King. Raja Yoga is therefore the "royal" yoga.

Rajas The guna of motion. It's active and energetic.

Rakhi A magical bracelet or "band of protection."

Rasa Matter that can be tasted.

Rasa Lila The dance of divine love.

Rasayana Ayurvedic rejuvenation. Hindu medical techniques for prolonging longevity.

Rishi Seer. The Vedic seers were saints and sages of the highest caliber. One Hindu tradition notes seven different levels of seers. Ranging from highest to least advanced they are the Deva rishis, Brahma rishis, Raja rishis, Maha rishis, Parama rishis, Shruta rishis, and Kanda rishis.

Rita The laws of nature, the natural flow of reality.

Rupa Matter that can be seen. Form.

Sadhu A man who has renounced the material world and wanders from place to place without any possessions, immersed in meditation and spiritual practice.

Sadhvi A woman renunciate.

Saguna "With qualities." Having shape and form.

Saguna Brahman The personal god who responds to our appeals.

Sahasrara Chakra The chakra at the top of the head.

Samadhi An intense state of concentration. Also, the burial shrine of a saint.

Samskara A tendency in the mind and personality. Also, sacrament.

Samyama The movement of attention from concentration through meditation into total mental absorption.

Sanatana Dharma   The Hindu's own word for their spiritual tradition. It means "the eternal religion."

Sanchita Karma   The karma we've accumulated in all our previous incarnations.

Sannyas   Renunciation.

Sannyasin   A Hindu renunciate.

Santosha   Contentment.

Sat   Pure beingness. Absolute truth.

Satsang   Keeping company with the guru or other devotees. Spiritual fellowship.

Sattva   The guna of harmony. Sattvic energy is light and clear.

Satya   Truth. Honesty.

Saucha   Inner purity and external cleanliness.

Seva   Selfless service.

Shabda   Matter that can be heard. Sound.

Shakta   A devotee of the Goddess.

Shakti   The Goddess. Shakti also means power, energy, or the illuminating power of consciousness.

Shaktipat   The transmission of spiritual knowledge and power. Usually the energy of enlightenment is channeled to an aspirant through the guru.

Shiksha   The sacred science of phonetics.

Shraddha   The sacraments performed for the dead.

Shravana   Listening to the guru's words and assimilating their truth.

Shruti   "That which is heard." It refers to divine revelation because it's what is heard directly from God. This would be the Veda, and its direct auxiliary texts like the *Upanishads.*

Shuddhi   Purification. The shuddi rite restored Hindu status to ex-Hindus who had converted to Christianity or Islam.

Shudra   The working class. Unskilled labor.

Siddha   An advanced spiritual adept.

Siddhi   Supernatural powers.

Smarana   Continuously remembering the Divine and its characteristics.

Smriti   "That which is memorized." Sacred scriptures authored by enlightened sages.

Soma   The divine elixir drunk by the Gods and yogis.

Sparsha   Matter that can be felt.

Sthapatya Veda   Hindu sacred architecture.

Stotra   A holy hymn or prayer. Also, the sense of hearing.

Sthula Sharira   The physical body and the vital force.

Sukshma Sharira   The astral body.

Sutradhara   A master architect who ensures that buildings are designed according to sacred principles.

Svadhishthana Chakra   The chakra near the genital organs.

Svadhyaya   Study and self-analysis.

Svarga   Heaven.

Svarodaya   The yogic science of breath.

Tamas   The guna of inertia. It's heavy, stupid, lethargic.

Tapas   Self-discipline. Austerity.

Tilak   The mark some Hindus wear on their forehead.

Trimurti   "The three forms of God." This refers to the three main gods of Hinduism: Brahma, Vishnu, and Shiva.

Tvak   The sense of touch.

Upa Veda   One of the four sacred sciences not directly related to scriptural study.

Upastha   The ability to procreate.

Vaikari   Physical sound you hear with your ears.

Vairagya   Dispassion, nonattachment.

Vaishnava Shakti   The force that stuns the soul at the time of rebirth, so it loses conscious memory of its past life.

Vaishya   The merchant caste. Business people, trades people, and farmers.

Vak   The ability to speak. The goddess of speech. The divine word.

Varna   The four basic castes of Hindu society.

Vasana   Unconscious thoughts and tendencies.

Vastu   The Hindu science of sacred space.

Vayu   Gaseous matter. Wind. The god of wind.

Veda   The Bible of Hinduism.

Vidya   Knowledge. Also, the force that limits omniscience, cutting universal knowledge down to human knowledge.

Vijnana Maya Kosha   The subtle body consisting of intelligence.

Vimana   A vehicle used in ancient times that was said to travel through the air.

Vira   Hero.

Vishuddha Chakra   The chakra at the throat.

Vyakarana   The sacred science of grammar.

Yama   A moral restraint. Something you shouldn't do.

Yantra   A geometric diagram in which the living presence of the Divine has been concentrated.

Yoga   Union with the Divine. Also, a path to that union.

Yoni   The base in which a linga rests. It represents the Goddess.

Yuga   A cosmic cycle. Yugas are of different lengths but all of them are quite long by human standards.

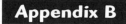

Who's Who in Hinduism

Listing all the major players in Hinduism's 6,000-year history would require an encyclopedia, not just a few pages here! Nevertheless, I've gone ahead and listed some of the most famous saints, sages, and religious leaders of Hinduism whose names are most likely to come up in conversation.

Please note that dates before about 1000 C.E. are speculative. They could be off by centuries or more. All dates are C.E. unless otherwise noted.

Agastya (prehistory)   Sage of the Vedic era. Carried Vedic religion to South India.

Ammachi (1953–present)   South India's most prominent modern saint and exemplar of unconditional love. Also known as Amritanandamayi Ma.

Ammaiyar (ninth century)   South Indian Shaivite saint who imagined herself as a servant of Shiva, the God dancing in the cremation grounds.

Anandamayi Ma (1896–1982)   One of the greatest saints of modern times. She is believed to have been fully enlightened from the moment of her birth in East Bengal.

Antal (eighth century)   The most famous female Vaishnava saint of South India. At age 16, she merged into the statue of Vishnu at the Srirangam temple.

Arjuna (sixteenth century B.C.E.)   Victorious warrior of the war at Kuruksheta. Hero of the *Mahabharata*.

Aurobindo Ghose (1872–1950)   Influential modern Hindu mystic and philosopher.

Basavanna (twelfth century)   Vira Shaivite teacher and Hindu social reformer.

Bengali Baba (1880?–1982)   Judge on the Indian Supreme Court who renounced his position and became a yogic adept.

Chaitanya (1486–1533)   Chaitanya walked through India chanting Krishna's name and triggered a massive devotional movement. The founder of the "Hare Krishnas."

Chinmayananda, Swami (1916–1993)   Founder of Chinmayananda Mission.

Chinmoy, Shri (1931–present)   International peace ambassador. Has often spoken at the United Nations.

Dayananda Sarasvati (1824–1883)   Founder of the Arya Samaj. Called for a return to Vedic values.

Gandhi, Mohandas (1869–1948)   Founder of the nonviolent movement to free India from British rule. Better known as Mahatma Gandhi.

Gautama Buddha (sixth century B.C.E.)   North Indian prince-turned-renunciate and propagator of Buddhism.

Guru Nanak (1440–1538)   Founder of Sikhism.

Gurumayi Chidvilasananda (1955–present)   Siddha Yoga guru based in Ganeshpuri, India, and South Fallsburg, Pennsylvania.

Jaimini (third century B.C.E.)   Author of the classic text on Mimamsa philosophy.

Jnanadeva (1275–1296)   Child-saint of Maharashtra. Author of the classic *Jnaneshvari,* a commentary on the *Bhagavad Gita.*

Kabir (1440–1518)   Popular, cantankerous cobbler-poet whose admirers include both Hindus and Muslims.

Kalki (Not due to be born for thousands of years)   Warrior who will lay waste the planet at the end of the present age of darkness and establish a new era of righteousness.

Kapila (prehistory)   Founder of Samkhya philosophy, one of the most influential mystical systems in the world.

Keshab Chandra Sen (1838–1884)   Radical leader of the Brahmo Samaj of India.

Krishna Vasudeva (sixteenth century B.C.E.)   Incarnation of Vishnu whose teachings in the *Bhagavad Gita* have inspired millions.

Krishnamurti, Jiddu (1895–1986)   Hindu philosopher who taught that "Truth is a pathless land."

Lalleshvari (fourteenth century)   Shaivite saint and poetess, famous for wandering the countryside nude like some Hindu and Jain male renunciates.

Lekhraj, Dada (1909–1969)   Founder of the Brahma Kumaris, a Shaivite reform organization emphasizing women's spiritual potential.

Lokenath (1730–1890)   Bengali yogi who walked to Mecca and Siberia.

Madhvacharya (1238–1317)   Devotee of Vishnu and founder of the Dvaita or dualistic school of Vedanta.

Mahavir (sixth century B.C.E.)   North Indian prince-turned-renunciate and propagator of Jainism.

Manu (remote prehistory)   Following a devastating world-wide flood, Manu became the father of the present race of humanity.

Manu (fifth century)   Author of *The Lawbook of Manu,* codifying Hindu legal conventions.

Mira Bai (1498–1546)   A Rajput princess whose ecstatic love for Krishna drove her in-laws crazy. Her songs are still sung throughout India.

Mother Meera (1960–present)   Contemporary saint based near Frankfurt, Germany.

Muktananda, Swami (1908–1982)   Kashmir Shaivite teacher who established the Siddha Yoga Dham. Famous for introducing "shaktipat" in the West.

Nammalvar (ninth century)   South Indian Vaishnava saint and teacher who didn't say a word until he was 16 years old.

Neem Karoli Baba (1900?–1973)   Hindu saint and devotee of Lord Rama popularized in Ram Dass's classic *Be Here Now.*

Panini (fourteenth century B.C.E.)   Genius grammarian and saint. (Western scholars assign a much later date.)

Parashu Rama (prehistory)   Hero of the Vedic era. A brahmin who battled the warrior caste and emigrated to South India.

Patanjali (third century B.C.E.)   Yogic adept and author of the *Yoga Sutras.*

Prabhupada, Swami Bhaktivedanta (1896–1977)   Hindu missionary and founder of the International Society for Krishna Consciousness.

Radha (sixteenth century B.C.E.)   Milkmaid and lover of Krishna during his frolics in the village of Vrindavan.

Radhakrishnan, Sarvepalli (1888–1975)   Hindu philosopher. First president of modern India.

Rama Chandra (twenty-first century B.C.E.)   Ruler of Ayodhya and hero of the *Ramayana.*

Rama, Swami (1925?–1996)   Yogi and philanthropist who demonstrated numerous advanced yogic skills to Western scientists.

Rama Tirtha (1873–1906)   Taught the principles of yoga and Hinduism in America and Japan.

Ramakrishna Paramahansa (1836–1886)   Priest of the goddess Kali. A religious universalist.

Ramana Maharshi (1879–1950)   South Indian meditation master who taught his students to inquire "Who am I?" in order to uncover their Inner Self.

Ramanuja (1017–1137)   Devotee of Vishnu and founder of Visishtadvaita philosophy, which teaches we are *almost* completely one with God.

Ramdas, Papa (1884–1963)   Saint known for his good humor and his devotion to Lord Rama.

Ramprasad (eighteenth century)   Devotee of the Goddess Kali. Became a poet-saint after failing as an accountant.

Ravana (twenty-first century B.C.E.)   King of Lanka who provoked—and lost—a war with the avatar Rama.

Roy, Ram Mohan (1772–1833)   Founder of the Adi Brahmo Samaj, a Hindu reform movement emphasizing a rational and humanistic approach to religion.

Sambhadar (seventh century)   South Indian Shaivite poet. Reconverted many Jains to Hinduism, sometimes forcibly.

Sarada Devi (1853–1920)   "The Mother of Bengal." Wife of Ramakrishna Paramahansa.

Satchidananda, Swami (1914–present)   Teacher of Integral Yoga whose "Oms" opened the Woodstock music festival in 1969.

Satya Sai Baba (1926–present)   Guru to millions, known for materializing sacred objects out of thin air.

Shandilya (second century)   Author of important texts on Vaishnava mysticism, including the famous devotional work, *Shandilya Sutras*.

Shankaracharya (eighth century)   Massively influential yogi who helped revitalize Hinduism in his era. Promulgator of Advaita Vedanta, which teaches that the only lasting reality is the Supreme Brahman (Divine Being-Consciousness-Bliss).

Shirdi Sai Baba (1850?–1918)   Beloved saint of Maharashtra claimed by both Hindus and Muslims.

Shivaji (1627–1680)   Founder of Maratha Empire. Warrior who reclaimed much of North India from the Muslims.

Shree Maa (1945?–present)   Deeply loved saint from Kamakhya in Assam. Believed by many Hindus to be the reincarnation of Sarada Devi.

Sita (twenty-first century B.C.E.)   Wife of the avatar Rama. The ideal Hindu wife who remained faithful to her husband even when abducted by Ravana, the evil king of Lanka.

Sivananda, Swami (1887–1963) Prolific author on Hinduism. Founder of the Divine Life Society. Numbers of his disciples, among them Swamis Satchidananda, Vishnu Devananda, Jyotirmayananda, and Sivananda Radha, became popular spiritual teachers in the West.

Subramuniyaswami, Sivaya (1927–present) Prolific Hindu writer and guru. Publisher of *Hinduism Today.*

Sundara (seventh century) South Indian saint who wrote over 100 famous hymns in praise of Shiva.

Tagore, Rabindranath (1861–1941) Hindu poet. Winner of the 1913 Nobel Prize for Literature.

Tirumular (third century B.C.E.) Author of *Tirumantiram,* a work summarizing Shaivite beliefs. Founder of Shaiva Siddhanta.

Tiruvalluvar (third century B.C.E.) Author of the Tamil classic *Tirukural* on politics and ethics.

Tukaram (1600–1650) One of Hinduism's best-loved poet-saints, born near Pune. He popularized the worship of Vithoba, a form of Vishnu.

Tulsi Das (1532–1623) Beloved poet whose Hindi language retelling of the *Ramayana,* called the *Rama Charita Manasa,* is now more popular than the original work.

Valmiki (tenth century B.C.E.) Author of the great Hindu epic, the *Ramayana.* Originally a bandit.

Vasishtha (prehistory) Sage of the Vedic era. Numerous sages till the present time have had the same name.

Vasugupta (ninth century) Revitalized Kashmir Shaivism, giving it the form in which it's known today.

Vivekananda, Swami (1863–1902) First brought the teachings of Hinduism and yoga to the West in 1893.

Vyasa (sixteenth century B.C.E.) Compiler of the four Vedas into their present form. The major *Puranas* and the *Mahabharata* are also attributed to him.

Yogananda, Paramahansa (1893–1952) Taught Hindu principles in America, where he wrote *Autobiography of a Yogi.* For many thousands of Westerners, this book was their first introduction to Eastern religion.

Zoroaster (prehistory) Broke with the Vedic tradition to found Zoroastrianism. Mentioned in the *Rig Veda.* His teachings about the resurrection of the dead and the return of a savior figure who'll inaugurate a new millennium are preserved in Christianity.

More to Read

I'm listing some of the top books on Hinduism for you in the happy event that you're inspired to learn more. I realize you don't have unlimited free time to sit around reading, so I'm also marking off, with an asterisk, the best of the best—the books I most strongly recommend for a newcomer to the subject. These are the books you might want to pick up first.

Histories and Surveys

Here are some fine general introductions to the Hindu tradition and issues related to Hindu history. Warning: Archeological finds in the late twentieth century have thrown the investigation of Hindu origins into an uproar. Be advised that many books written before 1995 contain badly outdated information about early Hindu history. Also be aware that any dates you find for events up to about 1000 C.E. may be wrong by centuries. Dates for events before 1000 B.C.E. may be off by more than a thousand years!

Basham, A.L. *The Wonder That Was India*. London: Sigwick & Jackson, 1985.

*Feuerstein, Georg, Subhash Kak and David Frawley. *In Search of the Cradle of Civilization*. Wheaton, IL: Quest Books, 1995.

Flood, Gavin. *An Introduction to Hinduism*. Cambridge, MA: Cambridge University Press, 1996.

Frawley, David. *Gods, Sages and Kings*. Salt Lake City: Passage Press, 1991.

Jagannathan, Shakunthala. *Hinduism: An Introduction*. Mumbai, India: Vakils, Feffer and Simons, Ltd., 1984.

Johnson, Gordon. *Cultural Atlas of India*. Oxfordshire, England: Andromeda Oxford Limited, 1996.

*Klostermaier, Klaus K. *Hinduism: A Short History*. Oxford: Oneworld Publications, 2000.

*——. *A Survey of Hinduism*. Albany, NY: State University of New York Press, 1989.

Lal, B.B. *The Earliest Civilization of South Asia*. New Delhi: Aryan Books International, 1997.

Rajaram, Navaratna S. *Aryan Invasion of India: The Myth and the Truth*. New Delhi: Voice of India, 1993.

Reddy, V. Madhusudan. *The Vedic Epiphany* (3 volumes). Twin Lakes, WI: Lotus Light Publications, 1990.

Talageri, Shrikant G. *The Aryan Invasion Theory: A Reappraisal*. New Delhi: Aditya Prakashan, 1993.

Hindu Saints

The Hindu tradition has more acknowledged saints per capita than any other religious tradition. The following books offer a tiny sampling of the remarkable lives of India's spiritual giants.

*Amritanandamayi, Mata. *Awaken Children!* (nine volumes). San Ramon, CA: Mata Amritanandamayi Center, 1988–1998.

Chetanananda, Swami. *They Lived with God: Life Stories of Some Devotees of Sri Ramakrishna*. St. Louis: Vedanta Society of St. Louis, 1989.

Dehejia, Vidya. *Slaves of the Lord: The Path of the Tamil Saints*. New Delhi: Munshiram Manoharlal Publishers, 1988.

Goswami, Satsvarupa Dasa. *Prabhupada: He Built a House in Which the Whole World Can Live*. Hong Kong: Bhaktivedanta Book Trust, 1983.

*Gupta, Mahendranath. *The Gospel of Sri Ramakrishna*. New York: Ramakrishna-Vivekananda Center, 1969.

Johnsen, Linda. *Daughters of the Goddess: The Women Saints of India*. St. Paul, MN: YES International Publishers, 1994.

Hallstrom, Lisa Lassell. *Mother of Bliss: Aanandamayi Ma*. New York: Oxford University Press, 1999.

Hawley, John Stratton and Mark Juergensmeyer. *Songs of the Saints of India*. New York: Oxford University Press, 1988.

Mahadevan, T. M. P. *Ten Saints of India*. Bombay: Bharatiya Vidya Bhavan, 1961.

Muktananda, Swami. *The Play of Consciousness*. San Francisco: Harper & Row, 1978.

Nikhilananda, Swami. *Vivekananda: A Biography*. New York: Ramakrishna-Vivekananda Center, 1989.

O'Brien, Justin. *Walking With a Himalayan Master*. St. Paul, MN: YES International Publishers, 1998.

*Rama, Swami. *Living with the Himalayan Masters*. Honesdale, PA: Himalayan Institute Press, 1999.

Ranade, R.D. *Mysticism in India: The Poet-Saints of Maharashtra*. Albany, NY: State University of New York Press, 1983.

Sarasvati, Swami Satyananda. *Shree Maa: The Life of a Saint*. Napa, CA: Devi Mandir Publications, 1997.

Shuddhananda, Swami. *Yogavatar Baba Lokenath*. Calcutta: Lokenath Divine Life Book Trust, 1986.

Venkataraman, Sri T. N. *Bhagavan Sri Ramana: A Pictorial Biography*. Tiruvannamalai, India: Sri Ramanasramam, 1981.

*Yogananda, Paramahansa. *Autobiography of a Yogi*. Los Angeles: Self Realization Fellowship, 1979.

The Living Tradition

These books transport you into the heart of the living tradition, explaining Hindu thought as it's actually understood and practiced by ordinary—and some quite extraordinary—people.

Dass, Ram. *Be Here Now*. Boulder, CO: Hanuman Foundation, 1978.

*Huyler, Stephen P. *Meeting God: Elements of Hindu Devotion*. New Haven, CT: Yale University Press, 1999.

Johnsen, Linda. *The Living Goddess: Reclaiming the Tradition of the Mother of the Universe*. St. Paul, MN: YES International Publishers, 1999.

Lonnerstrand, Sture. *I Have Lived Before: The True Story of the Reincarnation of Shanti Devi*. Huntsville, AR: Ozark Mountain Publishers, 1998.

Subramuniyaswami, Satguru Sivaya. *Dancing with Siva: Hinduism's Contemporary Catechism*. Concord, CA: Himalayan Academy, 1993.

Svoboda, Robert E. *Aghora: At the Left Hand of God*. Albuquerque, NM: Brotherhood of Life, Inc., 1986.

Yoga and Hindu Mysticism

Here are some particularly readable introductions to various fascinating aspects of the Hindu mystical tradition.

Feuerstein, Georg. *The Yoga Tradition: Its History, Literature, Philosophy and Practice*. Prescott, AZ: Hohm Press, 1998.

Rama, Swami. *The Royal Path: Practical Lessons on Yoga*. Honesdale, PA: Himalayan Institute Press, 1999.

*Tigunait, Pandit Rajmani. *From Death to Birth: Understanding Karma and Reincarnation*. Honesdale, PA: Himalayan Institute Press, 1997.

*———. *The Power of Mantra and the Mystery of Initiation*. Honesdale, PA: Himalayan Institute Press, 1996.

Hindu Scriptures

You would have to reincarnate many times if you hoped to read all the scriptures of Hinduism. Here are a few special gems from the enormous mass of spiritual literature.

Dimmitt, Cornelia and van Buitenen, J. A. B. *Classical Hindu Mythology: A Reader in the Sanskrit Puranas*. Philadelphia: Temple University Press, 1978.

Nikhilananda, Swami, trs. *The Upanishads*. New York: Bell Publishing Company, 1963.

Panikkar, Raimundo. *The Vedic Experience, Mantramanjari: An Anthology of the Vedas for Modern Man and Contemporary Celebration.* Pondicherry, India: All India Books, 1977.

*Prabhavananda, Swami and Isherwood, Christopher, trs. *The Song of God: Bhagavad-Gita.* New York: New American Library, 1951.

Prabhavananda, Swami, trs. *Srimad Bhagavatam: The Wisdom of God.* New York: Capricorn Books, 1968.

*Rajagopalachari, C. *Mahabharata.* Bombay: Bharatiya Vidya Bhavan, 1977.

*————. *Ramayana.* Bombay: Bharatiya Vidya Bhavan, 1976.

Saraswathi, Swami Sri Ramanananda, trs. *Tripura Rahasya or The Mystery Beyond the Trinity.* Tiruvannamalai, India: Sri Ramanasramam, 1980.

Shearer, Allistair, trs. *Effortless Being: The Yoga Sutras of Patanjali.* London: Unwin Paperbacks, 1989.

Tapasyananda, Swami, trs. *Sivananda Lahari or Inundation of Divine Bliss.* Madras, India: Sri Ramakrishna Math, 1985.

Venkatesananda, Swami. *The Concise Yoga Vasistha.* Albany, NY: State University of New York Press, 1984.

Hindu Philosophy

The Indian tradition is not only deeply devotional, it's also robustly intellectual. Hinduism boasts an extraordinary legacy of philosophical and theological thought going back to the dawn of human memory. If you're a pandit at heart, you'll enjoy these books.

Larson, Gerald J. *Classical Samkhya.* Delhi: Motilal Banarsidass, 1979.

Mishra, Kamalakar. *Kashmir Saivism: The Central Philosophy of Tantrism.* Cambridge: Rudra Press, 1993.

*Puligandla, P. *Fundamentals of Indian Philosophy.* New York: Abingdon Press, 1975.

Radhakrishnan. *Indian Philosophy* (two volumes). New York: Humanities Press, 1971.

Radhakrishnan, Sarvepalli and Moore, Charles A. *A Sourcebook in Indian Philosophy.* Princeton: Princeton University Press, 1973.

Woodroffe, Sir John. *Principles of Tantra* (two volumes). Madras, India: Ganesh & Company, 1991.

If you have trouble locating any of these books, remember that your local librarian would be delighted to help you track down a book through the Inter-Library Loan service. Or try contacting South Asia Books. You'll find their contact information in Appendix D, "Hindu Resource List."

Hindu Resource List

Want to learn more about Hinduism? Here's a few contacts that will put you well on your way to exploring any and every facet of the Eternal Religion.

Hindu Universe
Web Site: www.Hindunet.org

If you're online, have I got a Web site for you! *Hindu Universe* will help you find the Hindu temple nearest you, no matter where in the world you live. It also features more than 150,000 documents explaining the many fascinating components of Hinduism. It's got a special section addressing women's concerns and a section for kids. Plus it's got over 1,000 links to other Hindu-related sites.

Hinduism Today
107 Kaholalele Road
Kapaa, HI 96746
Phone: 1-800-890-1008
Web site: www.hinduismtoday.com

Hinduism Today is a superb, full-color bimonthly magazine covering current events in Hinduism. It features excellent interviews with leading Hindu spiritual teachers and engaging historical and educational articles on Hinduism. Informative, funny, inspiring. *Highly* recommended!

South Asia Books
P.O. Box 502
Columbia, MO 65205
Phone: 573-474-0116
E-mail: sabooks@juno.com

If South Asia Books can't track down a particular book on Hinduism for you, it probably doesn't exist. They can supply just about any English language book on Hinduism and stock the latest books from the major Indian publishers.

Organizations and Training Programs

The following are a few of the best contacts in North America for learning about Hinduism, yoga, and Ayurveda.

American Institute of Vedic Studies
P.O. Box 8357
Santa Fe, NM 87504
Phone: 505-983-9385
Web site: www.vedanet.com
E-mail: vedicinst@aol.com

Arsha Vidya Gurukulam
P.O. Box 1059
Saylorsburg, PA 18353
Phone: 570-992-2339
Web site: www.arshavidya.org
E-mail: avp@epix.net

The Ayurvedic Institute
11311 Menaul Blvd. N.E.
Albuquerque, NM 87112
Phone: 505-291-9698
Web site: www.ayurveda.com

Hindu University of America
8610 Vesta Terrace
Orlando, FL 32825
Phone: 407-277-5959
Web site: Hindu-University.Edu
E-mail: admin@hindu-university.edu

World Association for Vedic Studies
(WAVES)
7325 Palmetto Street
New Orleans, LA 70125
Phone: 504-483-7463
E-mail: bsharma@mail.xula.edu

Yoga Research Center
PO Box 1386
Lower Lake, CA 95457
Phone: 707-928-9898

Hindu Devotional Art

Hinduism is famous for its often charming and sometimes totally stunning devotional art. Here's the place to start if you're looking for beautiful images of Hindu deities and avatars.

Mandala Publishing Group
2240-B 4th Street
San Rafael, CA 94901
Phone: 415-460-6112
Web site: www.Mandala.org

Index

403

W–Z